Learning the Art of Medicine

A MEMOIR

Gordon Noel

Copyright © 2021 by Gordon Noel

All rights reserved including the right to reproduce this book or portions thereof in any form.

For information, please contact Quimby House Press:
info@quimbyhousepress.com

Published in the United States by Quimby House Press, Portland, Oregon, USA

Interior layout by The Book Makers
Cover design by The Book Makers

Library of Congress Cataloging-in-Publication Data
Names: Noel, Gordon, Author
Title: Learning the Art of Medicine—A Memoir/Gordon Noel
Description: First Edition. Portland Oregon 2021
ISBN Print Edition (paperback): 978-0-9992169-4-1
ISBN eBook Edition (ePub): 978-0-9992169-5-8

Learning the Art of Medicine—a Memoir is a work of non-fiction. The names of most patients have been changed and some of their descriptions and circumstances have been modified to protect their anonymity. In several instances, faculty members' names and some identifying characteristics have been changed.

For my wife Margaret and my daughters Katharine, Margaret Lea, and Jennifer Noel, without whom there would have been no stories to write.

In memory of Dr. Andrew Frantz, Dr. Hamilton Southworth, Dr. Thomas Jacobs, Dr. Arthur Wertheim, Dr. Earle Wheaton, and Dr. and Mrs. Robert Wilkins; and with great respect and gratitude for the Columbia University College of Physicians and Surgeons Class of 1967 and the Department of Medicine residents and faculty members who taught us, many of whom became my colleagues and make cameo appearances; and the University of Chicago Department of Medicine and especially Dr. Alvin Tarlov

Two roads diverged in a wood, and I—
I took the one less traveled by,
And that has made all the difference

—Robert Frost, *The Road Not Taken* 1915

Friendship is a relationship that has no formal shape, there are no rules or obligations or bonds as in marriage or the family, it is held together by neither law nor property nor blood, there is no glue in it but mutual liking. It is therefore rare...

—Wallace Stegner, *Crossing to Safety* 1987

Enduring satisfaction is most often a byproduct of participating in worthwhile activities that do not have happiness as their primary goal. Ultimate fulfillment comes from a sense of remaining true to core ideals and principles, and of using life for something of value that outlasts it.

—Deborah Rhode, *Ambition*, 2021

Medical School: Columbia University College of Physicians and Surgeons

1963 - 1967

CHAPTER 1

Prologue—Match Day, 1967

Columbia University's College of Physician and Surgeons and the Presbyterian Hospital run along 168th Street from Broadway to Fort Washington Avenue on Manhattan's Upper West Side. When I was a student, most of the floors of the austere medical school buildings were devoted to research space and faculty and administrative offices, but the medical school also housed a large library, student teaching laboratories, and several lecture halls. The ninth-floor amphitheater had been our class's staging area for every step of medical school. In 1963, after straggling into New York City from all over the United States and moving into our rooms in Bard Hall, 120 of us first met as a class there, seeing for the first time the 119 other students with whom we would be spending the next four years.

In March, 1967, forty-three months later, we assembled for Match Day in the amphitheater one last time to receive a white business envelope with our name typed on it, inside of which was a letter telling us where we would be going for residency after our graduation in early June.

The Match was like trying out for the Olympic Games—an opportunity to learn where we stood after years of training in comparison with classmates and 8000 other students across the country who had also been preparing for this moment, many of us hoping to have been selected by an exceptional residency program, others glad just to be learning where we would spend the next three or four years in training as residents. The previous autumn we had applied to five or ten or fifteen teaching hospitals asking to be considered for their residency programs in one of the medical disciplines—surgery, pediatrics, obstetrics and gynecology, internal medicine, ophthalmology, dermatology, anesthesiology, orthopedics, or psychiatry. In the late fall and winter we had travelled to those that offered us interviews. We ranked the programs in the order of our interest and sent off our list in February. We would go to the highest program on our list that had also ranked us highly.

On this grey, blustery spring morning the amphitheater was packed well beyond the number of seats. Many had brought parents or partners or younger brothers and sisters.

At 12 noon, the Dean of Students, Dr. Perera, walked in and began handing out the envelopes.

After opening and reading their letter, most students, smiling, quietly told those standing nearby where they would be going. Occasionally a student cried or left the room, distressed by what their four years of hard work had netted them.

When my name was called, I took my envelope and went off to a corner to open the letter, my hands shaking.

As I read the letter my anxiety turned into disappointment. I had matched into one of my lower choices.

My feelings oscillated: I was relieved that I had matched, but sad and embarrassed that I had been passed over by all four of the most renowned programs that had interviewed me.

Where I had matched was disappointing, but not surprising.

My mood was somber and resigned. What I didn't and couldn't have known then was that this was not the end of the race, but only the beginning. I had started medical school behind many of my classmates who had anticipated this moment more clearly and had been preparing for it for years.

Prologue—Match Day, 1967

But training in medicine and the practice of medicine are both long, long journeys, and in time I learned that matching where I did was one of the better days of my life, although no one would have been able to convince me at the time.

These are the stories of how my classmates and I learned the art of medicine at Columbia-Presbyterian Medical Center in 1960's and 1970's; about serving in the Army Medical Corps during the American War in Vietnam; and how, as my medical life expanded during my early years of teaching and practice, it consumed almost all of my time, and how that resolved.

CHAPTER 2

Wait Listed

My application to medical school was casual and sketchily planned compared to what medical school applicants go through now. Harvard did not offer a "pre-med" major. Harvard's philosophy was that we should study what interested us and if that happened not to be biology or chemistry, then all we needed to do was take the basic requirements of most medical schools: two years of chemistry, a year of physics, a year of biology, and a half year of math. Most premedical students took more chemistry and biology classes at their colleges, but in order to graduate with honors in English, I was required to spend half of my college time in literature, including a full year of graduate level reading in a foreign language. I studied Spanish literature and poetry for a year and a half, which turned out to be more useful than the German or Latin still encouraged by some medical schools.

Harvard had a minimal pre-medical advisory program. Each of the eight residential houses for upperclassmen had a tutor in residence who was a medical student or resident at Harvard Medical School. As a junior I had lunch with our Leverett House advisor, Paul Ehrlich. The sum of his advice was, "You're at Harvard. Apply to a few places and you'll get in." I never saw him again. Because I never knew another Harvard student who was planning to go to medical school, I was not exposed to anyone who was anxious or zealous about being admitted to medical school. That was probably a good thing, but I also missed out on any useful information a well-organized pre-medical student might have sought out about preparing for medical school.

I took the Medical College Aptitude Test (MCAT). I don't know whether anyone studied for it. I didn't— I had gotten A's in General Chemistry and Physics, and B+'s in the advanced biology courses and organic chemistry. I assumed that taking those courses was all I needed to do. I have no idea what my MCAT score was or what was considered a good score.

Because of the military draft, all male college students needed a plan for what they would do after graduation, or their draft board would give them their plan—two years in uniform. Among my friends, everyone expected to go to graduate school, but we never talked about their strategy or mine, or even what were the qualities we should be looking for in a graduate program. None of my classmates went into one of the services immediately after college; most went directly into graduate school, although the few headed for a stock brokerage or a business career or teaching had managed to get deferments.

I applied to four medical schools, chosen solely on the basis that they were "highly regarded"—the same method I had used to choose colleges to apply to. All offered me interviews.

My first interview was for Harvard Medical School. I met with a senior cardiologist at the Massachusetts General Hospital. He was friendly, courtly, and in no hurry. He wanted to know how a Montana high school student had chosen to come east to Harvard, what it was like to fight forest fires every summer, and why I had chosen English literature as my field of concentration.

I had not prepared for the interview, assuming that I would be able to handle whatever questions were asked. This turned out not to be true. When he asked me why I wanted to be a doctor, I gave what must have been the least persuasive answer he had ever heard: "I'm not sure I do want to be a doctor, but I thought I should go to medical school to find out."

He looked mildly surprised. He asked me what I knew about the life of a doctor and what it was like to be a medical student. My answers revealed that I knew very little about either. Finally, he asked again why I had chosen to focus on medicine, even if I wasn't sure I wanted to be a doctor. I told him that I wanted to take care of people, that though I had thought of becoming a professor of English literature or a minister, I felt that being a doctor would be a better fit.

A few weeks later I got a polite letter from him on embossed Harvard stationary:

"Dear Mr. Noel. I enjoyed talking with you about your life before and while at Harvard. Last week I presented your application to the Harvard Medical School Board of Admissions. The Board asked me to tell you that they would be very interested in meeting with you again should you decide that you definitely want to be a doctor. Best of luck. "

I later learned that he was quite famous.

After beginning medical school I was told by my more strategically gifted classmates that the answer they gave was that they had an unquenchable fascination with the human body and that they wanted to cure cancer. I could have said that, but it wouldn't have been true.

I don't remember much about my Johns Hopkins interview other than the long walk uphill from the train station to the medical school, passing through a run-down neighborhood, and being told that Hopkins was the toughest medical school on the planet; they took for granted that I already knew that it was also the best medical school on the planet. Like the MIT undergraduates I had met who lived and slept in sweatshirts with the logo "Tech is Hell," Hopkins medical students reveled in surviving the curriculum and earning the attitude.

At Cornell I was unable to perceive any interest in me whatsoever. The interviewers seemed snotty but I knew too little about Cornell to determine if they deserved to be.

Columbia was kind enough to overlook my many failings. My interviewer was Dr. Albert Lamb, an internist who also was the student health physician. He asked me what I had been thinking about on my train trip down from Boston.

"I noticed that the New Haven Railroad runs directly along the shore of the Atlantic Ocean in Connecticut," I said. "The tide was high this morning, barely a dozen feet from the rails, and I began to wonder why there are two tides. The first tide is easy to understand—its timing changed with the phase of the moon and could be explained by the gravitational pull of the moon, but at the same time, on the opposite side of the earth there is a second equally high tide. How can that be explained?

"What do you think?" Dr. Lamb asked.

"Well, I tried out a number of ideas. I thought about the axiom, "for every force there is an equal and opposite counter force. Or perhaps the tides should be regarded as a deformation of an elastic material. If you push down on a springy cylinder, it flattens on both the bottom and top and extends out equally on the two sides."

I asked him if he had an explanation. He didn't.

The interview lasted a half hour. It was a bit of a struggle. Dr. Lamb had lost an eye and his glass eye and his good eye did not both look at me at the same time: first one looked at me, and then the other did. At a distance of three or four feet, I kept trying to figure out which eye I should look at.

As I took the train back to Boston I was sure that the interview was a total failure. Dr. Lamb did not ask me any questions about why I wanted to be a doctor. Did he already know that I didn't have a clue? All we talked about were tides and my summer work fighting fires. I didn't ask him any informed questions about the Columbia curriculum that would imply that I actually knew what I was getting into. Beside that, as we talked I was also a little distracted, wondering how he lost an eye and how that had affected his life.

I was wait-listed at Columbia.

For two months I nervously checked my mailbox, looking for a letter from any of the schools. Cornell wrote to tell me that I was a very good candidate but, unfortunately, they had an unusually strong group of well-qualified applicants and they would not be able to offer me a place in the class of 1967.

By March I began to think I should apply to more schools. I arranged interviews at Boston University School of Medicine and the University of Rochester, but before those interviews a fat Columbia envelope appeared in my mailbox, offering me admission and a full tuition scholarship. I hopped, skipped, and jumped to find Margaret, the Radcliffe girl I had been dating for the past year and told her that I was going to be a doctor.

I always wondered if Margaret's father, who was the chairman of the Department of Medicine at Boston University and wanted me as far away from his daughter as possible, wrote the dean of admissions at Columbia urging him to admit me. If so, applying to BU was a brilliant strategic move on my part.

For weeks my feet never touched the ground. Apparently, I really did want to be a doctor, even though I had no idea what was in store for me.

A month after being accepted by Columbia, the Johns Hopkins School of Medicine also admitted me with the stipulation that I spend the summer improving my science knowledge by taking three chemistry courses— quantitative and qualitative analysis and physical chemistry. However, I needed the money from fighting fires during the summer, and I was glad to be going to medical school in New York City— I would be closer to Margaret and Columbia seemed to be a gentler place than Hopkins. I was grateful that Hopkins had given me a chance, but I turned them and the requisite 3 months of summer chemistry courses down.

CHAPTER 3

From a Forest Fire to New York City

After my Harvard graduation, I flew back to Montana from Boston and rejoined the U.S. Forest Service "hot shot" crew at Nine Mile Ranger Station where I had spent the previous two summers. My best friends from high school—Roland Trenouth, Ted Smith, and Bruce Sievers—were also spending this last summer fighting fires before going to graduate school in the fall. Fighting forest fires had paid enough to cover my college room and board every year because I earned a huge amount of overtime during bad fire seasons. That summer we got called out for a half-dozen big fires all over the west. When our hot shot crew wasn't on a fire I was foreman of the Nine Mile Ranger Station roofing crew, replacing the shingles on its historic buildings, where in the 1930's my uncle Lloyd Noel had created the first "remount stations" for supplying lookout towers and fire crews in the Rocky Mountain West with horse-led mule teams.

Near the end of the summer, a week before I was ticketed to fly back to the East Coast, our crew was dispatched to the biggest fire in Yellowstone Park in its history, with fire-fighting crews coming in from all over the country.

On a fire this big, there was no way our crew would be released for many weeks. The majority of crew members were ranch or farm kids who had graduated from high school and hoped to keep fighting fires late into the fall, but there were a few of us who would have to bail out early to go back to school.

We were flown from Missoula to a meadow landing field and then trucked to a base camp at the end of the National Park Service road nearest to the fire. From there it was a full day's hike from where the trucks dropped us. The thirty of us hiked on trails and then bushwhacked through the untracked mountainous wilderness to the base of the fire carrying our gear—a backpack with spare clothes and sleeping bag, shovel, and a combination axe and grub hoe called a Pulaski. A few of the crewmembers packed chain saws or a five-gallon gas cans. The first day we travelled, hiked, and built fire line for thirty-six hours straight. The next two days we worked sixteen hours, from six at night until midmorning, sleeping in the woods during the hottest part of the day when the fire was exploding up the mountains above us and too dangerous to tackle.

Once on the fire line there were only two ways to get out: one was to be carried out on a stretcher to a meadow for helicopter evacuation; the other was hiking back out to the base camp and flagging down a bus.

I wanted to stay as long as possible to get the overtime pay. On the fifth morning, after working all night, I said my farewells and took off alone. I made good time because I had left all my fire-fighting gear behind and I made it to the base camp in the late afternoon. A Park Service truck heading back to the local ranger station dropped me off on a state highway to wait for an Intermountain Express bus that came through around 6:30 every evening. Ranches were far from towns, and towns were often 50 or a hundred miles apart in eastern Montana, so someone needing to catch a bus just stood beside the road until it came along. After an hour of waiting I flagged the bus down and climbed aboard. My clothes were filthy, but no one much noticed. I changed buses in Bozeman for Missoula, and at 5 the next morning called Mom to pick me up at the Missoula bus depot.

She told me that I smelled like wood smoke. I wouldn't be fighting any more fires and we agreed that she could throw my clothes in the trash rather than fouling her washing machine.

My plane for the east left the next morning. I packed fast and scrubbed hard, but unsuccessfully, trying to get the dirt ground into my hands and under my nails cleaned out. That was my last summer "vacation", and the last time I lived in Missoula.

In the late afternoon, two days after I left Yellowstone Park, I landed at LaGuardia. The airport was crowded and hot and smelled of aircraft exhaust and fuel. The contrast with the cool, fresh morning air in Missoula twelve hours before was shocking.

My taxi driver was talkative and interrogated me all the way to Washington Heights: he wanted his son to become a doctor and he pumped me for information about what was required to get into Columbia, which annoyed me because I was excited to be moving to New York City's concentrated humanity and soaring skyline and wanted to savor the beginning moments of being there.

I checked into the medical student residence and was given a key to my street-side room on the second floor. I spent the rest of the afternoon unpacking my suitcases and then went out looking for a place to eat dinner a few blocks away on Broadway, with its endless ribbon of small shops and apartment buildings that ran for hundreds of blocks from the northern tip of Manhattan to its southern tip. I turned uptown and in a few blocks found Nelson's Delicatessen. It looked like it was in my price range: inexpensive. A stocky middle-aged woman wearing a grease-spotted brown apron over a faded cotton dress stood behind a refrigerated glass case full of unfamiliar cold-cuts and breads and salads, waiting without curiosity while I studied the menu on the wall.

"May I have a roast beef sandwich and a glass of milk, please?"

"We don't serve milk." She offered no alternatives.

"How about a milkshake?"

"No milkshakes."

I had never heard of a sandwich place that didn't have milk or a milkshake. The woman handed me a menu silently and pointed at a list of drinks, mostly bottled by Dr. Brown. I wondered if Dr. Brown was on the medical school faculty. I ordered a Dr. Brown Cel-Ray soda, which, not surprisingly, tasted like celery . . . unpleasantly like celery. I ate my sandwich in a dim, nearly deserted room furnished with unmatched Formica and chrome tables. Suddenly I seemed very far away from Montana and I realized that I didn't know a single person in New York City. I felt a twinge of sadness that my Montana life would now be only memories of open skies and empty valleys and nearly impenetrable forests—and restaurants that offered milkshakes with their sandwiches.

A few weeks later, Bob Grossman, who had grown up in New Jersey, explained to me that Nelson's was a Kosher Jewish delicatessen, that I could go either to a meat delicatessen, or a dairy delicatessen: no milk in one, no beef or chicken in the other. When I asked why, he gave me a look signifying that he was dealing with an unschooled gentile hick who had just crawled out from under a log. Given that I had been fighting forest fires two days before I stumbled upon Nelson's, with Rocky Mountain grit still ground into my calluses, he wasn't far off.

In college I had harbored the belief that I was sophisticated because I had crossed the great distance from a Montana childhood to a Harvard education. I had studied with great teachers and had listened to famous ones (although they often were not great teachers). I had gone to dozens of plays, watched Ingmar Bergman and French new wave films, read philosophy and theology and sociology. I had tasted French first growth Bordeaux and eaten in expensive restaurants. But believing that I was sophisticated was a delusion, one that took me a decade to shed.

Two days ago I had been in the vast wilderness of Yellowstone Park. The transition from the fire line to New York City and the world of medicine had been abrupt. I had little idea of what it would be like to live in New York City or study medicine. Until that day, medical school had been an abstraction about which I knew almost nothing and had not even tried to inform myself or imagine. I knew that it would be very different from being an undergraduate in Boston or a firefighter in the West, but now the first intimations of the enormity of the difference were beginning to appear.

CHAPTER 4

The Ninth Floor Amphitheater

The next day, our first medical school lecture was in the ninth floor P & S amphitheater, a steep-pitched, white-walled room that looked as though it had not been refurbished since it was built in the early 1920's. Beneath the seats the concrete floor had been polished by thousands of students' fidgeting feet. The tired-looking arm desks, for right-handed people only, were covered with countless layers of wrinkled varnish. Ten semicircular rows were divided into three sections by two steeply descending stairways—students could choose seats in the center or to the sides. The students entered from the ninth floor; the lecturers entered the pit from the eighth floor. Speaking without amplification, the lecturers turned back and forth from looking at us to writing on one of several blackboards.

I looked over the students who would be my classmates for the next four years. Of the 120 admitted, twelve were women, among the most of any medical school except the two women's medical colleges. Two of us were Asian and all the rest were Caucasian. There was not a single familiar face. We were wearing crisp short white coats that still showed the creases of being folded since their manufacture. The men wore ties and slacks; the women were wearing dresses. There was a quiet buzz as a few students chatted with each other or reached to shake the hand of a student taking a nearby seat. I looked at the front rows and wondered if today's seating predicted who would always take up those seats, as though proximity to the lecturer and the blackboard would enhance their learning—or telegraph their total commitment—or both.

There were no signs discouraging food or coffee—carryout coffee and carryout food had not yet arrived, and the question of eating in a lecture was never raised and never done.

I chose a seat high up on the left-hand aisle where I could see everyone in the room. This was where I sat for the next four years.

Eight or ten of my new classmates had been Columbia University premeds and already knew who was famous, whose English diction was difficult to understand, and whose lectures were incomprehensible because of their speed, poor organization or dense accent—or all three. They knew that four of the professors in the Department of Biochemistry—two of them war refugees from Germany and Austria—had won Nobel Prizes. And they knew that our first lecture would be given by the chairman of the Department of Biochemistry, David Rittenberg, who had won a Nobel Prize for first using a radioactive element in humans to track the survival time of red blood cells.

Dr. Rittenberg entered the room at exactly 1:05. He spoke a lightly accented English that I soon came to recognize as one of the several New York dialects. He looked faintly like Groucho Marx: wire rimmed spectacles, moustache, thick, twitchy eyebrows.

"Good morning ladies and gentlemen. It is my honor to give, as I have for the last eight years, your first medical school lecture."

He paused and stared expectantly at our eager faces. Eyebrows arched, he asked: "Are there any romance language majors? Economics majors? Anthropology majors? English majors? If there are, please raise your hands."

I raised my hand, not sure if being an English major was a good thing or a bad thing, but worried that this was a trap.

"Are there any philosophy majors?" A single hand went up hesitantly. "For god's sake, are there any art history majors?"

There were about twelve of us with raised hands. We were looking at him; our classmates were sizing us up as though we had suddenly turned into toads. I was hoping he was going to single us out for being broadly educated and was prepared to arrange my face into a modest smile.

"Those of you with raised hands may now leave. For the rest of you who are interested in learning science, I will begin my lecture."

The lectures in biochemistry were the most difficult I experienced at P & S, in part because of the massive amount of detail presented, and in part because the lectures were often quite confused. For every section—carbohydrate metabolism, proteins, nucleic acids, steroid hormones, fat metabolism, cellular function, hematologic function—a different faculty member lectured; each was expert in that area and likely to speed through the basics because he (there were no basic science lectures given by women) was accustomed to teaching graduate students who already knew the basics. We were expected to know the contents of the lectures as well as everything in the relevant pages of the biochemistry text. A few dozen students who had been pre-meds and were used to graduate level teaching organized a note club to help keep up: one student spent an entire day taking notes and then writing out the contents of the lectures. These were mimeographed and distributed to the members of the note group that evening. The professors used the chalkboards, speaking while they quickly drew molecules and cycles and pathways and even more quickly erased them. I didn't have the money to join the note group; I raced to keep complete notes, including the drawings, but it was impossible. At night I tried to understand what had been presented by reading the textbook, but the details there were even more overwhelming.

In Dr. Rittenberg's five lectures a lot of the terminology was unfamiliar to me—he continuously referred to "lesions" (by which he meant the failure of a sequence of chemical steps to occur because of a missing enzyme or other defect). I thought that he was saying "legions", which made no sense at all. What were Roman soldiers doing blocking the path between coprophyrinogen and protophyrinogen? and if they were, was that a good idea or a bad idea? And was there an "American Lesion," and a "Foreign Lesion?"

I am not kidding. For two days that is what I thought.

Then there were the terms bilirubin and biliverdin. I thought that Billy Rubin must be a New York City Jewish biochemist, and Billy Verdin an Italian biochemist. I looked them up. There were no listings of those names in the Manhattan telephone directory. In a few days I learned that bilirubin and biliverdin were products of the breakdown of hemoglobin.

I got a richly deserved C in Biochemistry.

Gross Anatomy and Biochemistry were our introductory courses. Biochemistry was clean and intellectual. Anatomy was "gross" in two senses: "coarse and disgusting"—corpses are greasy and we handled embalmed flesh, leaving our clothing and our hands smelling of formaldehyde. Most of us headed for a shower as soon as we left the anatomy lab.

Anatomy was also "gross" in the sense of "large". There were really two anatomy courses, the dissection course—gross anatomy—and microscopic anatomy, also called histology, in which we looked at hundreds of stained tissue samples with our microscopes to understand the cellular structures of the organs, tendons, nerves, and skin.

Gross anatomy is widely understood inside and outside of medical schools as a rite of passage for medical students. In no other profession does a student spend three months with a corpse, handling dead flesh, slowly deconstructing a body one blood vessel, one nerve, one eyeball, one lung at a time. In the sixteen- and seventeen-hundreds physicians who were striving to understand the body in health and disease had been social outcasts because they handled dead bodies and sometimes resorted to grave robbing to find a body to study, breaking civil and religious laws. By the Twentieth Century medical schools had arranged to have the unclaimed bodies of paupers or those who "gave their bodies for science" donated for student teaching, and the stigma of dissecting the dead had gone away. In 1963 anatomical dissections were considered fundamental in the training of physicians: an autopsy taught a physician whether he or she had made the correct diagnosis or had missed it. An autopsy could tell a surgeon why a patient died after surgery or inform a family about why their child or parent or partner had died and if there was any risk to other family members. Autopsies were considered so important for the education of physicians in training that the organizations that certified residency-training programs required that a high percentage of patients who died in a teaching hospital be autopsied so that doctors would know if their diagnosis and treatment were correct or incorrect.

The performance of a cadaver dissection was one of the first experiences that separated medical students from the rest of society; we all recognized that this was both an incredible privilege and a critical step in our education.

We were divided into teams of four by last name. Our table was ecumenical: Nagano, Noel, Novack, and Novalis. We worked quietly together, sharing the chores of carefully dissecting the arteries and veins, separating out each muscle and tendon and nerve from its supporting connective tissue, attempting to identify them from the illustrated anatomy manuals we each owned: "Is this the first or the second branch of the inferior mesenteric artery?" Twenty times during each of the two-hour anatomy labs someone would hold up a piece of tissue they couldn't identify to ask students at adjacent tables if they knew what it was—nerve, vein, artery, duct? Embalming had turned every tissue the same color: the arteries and veins were not red and blue as they were in the anatomy atlas's illustrations. There was no easy way to confirm our answers beyond asking for a consultation from other students who seemed more sure of themselves.

In late September I took a train to Boston to visit my girlfriend Margaret; I stayed in the off-campus rooms of my college roommates, Geoff and Ted, now a year behind me because they had travelled and studied in Germany after our junior year. Margaret and I walked through the upper-class houses to the Charles River from her dormitory on the

Radcliffe Campus. There was a sweet smell that I thought to be fall leaves burning. But it wasn't burning autumn leaves: one year too late for me, marijuana had boldly infiltrated undergraduate life at Harvard.

I took a medical book along but ended up reading a novel on the train and got little studying done that weekend. The next week we finished our dissection of the abdomen and had our first practical examination. Twenty of us at a time rotated around 20 tables; greasy baggage tags dangled from strings tied or pinned to various abdominal structures. We had to identify what the tag was marking. There was nothing easy—no pin stuck in the spleen or aorta. Everything was the color of boiled chicken skin. One long beige strand sagged down from the abdominal wall into the pelvis. Nerve or vein or artery? I guessed, and I guessed at a lot of other shreds of tissue.

I must have mostly guessed wrong. I got a D+.

That examination ended my trips to Cambridge. The only other time I had gotten a D since high school was on my first Harvard essay in the mandatory freshman writing tutorial, where it was considered an initiation ritual designed to dispel any misconception of competence. Both D's sobered me up.

There was one exception to the often indifferent and sometimes rude lecturers in biochemistry: Professor Erwin Chargaff was an Austrian-German scientist who left Germany for Paris in the 1930's, and then moved from Paris to the United States. Dr. Chargaff's lectures on DNA were delivered in a gentle discourse salted with dry, often sardonic humor that disparaged celebrity-seeking scientists who turned the painstaking process of research into a race to get credit for being first with a discovery, which often resulted in conclusions that were premature, incomplete, or wrong.

In the afternoon of 22 November, we were in our places in the amphitheater for his fourth lecture; no one cut lectures, there being no handouts or notes other than those we took. Just before Dr. Chargaff was expected, Barry Wenglin, our class president, rushed through the amphitheater's ninth-floor doors and—his face flushed—in a frantic, sobbing voice, announced, "President Kennedy has been shot in Texas." Late for class, he had heard one of the front door guards, hunched over a small radio, call out the news. We were stunned. No one carried portable radios; television sets had yet to appear in lecture rooms; we had no further details. In a few minutes Professor Chargaff, himself late, quietly walked into the pit from the 8th floor door, put his notes on the podium, and looked up at us.

"Ladies and gentlemen, you have, I see, already heard the terrible news. I have witnessed this kind of tragedy in Europe, but I never expected it to happen here." He paused, pacing back and forth in the pit, deep in thought, staring at the floor. He stopped pacing, and looked up at us again.

"I have decided to go on with my lecture, but today there will be no jokes."

He slowly began to lay out how he had discovered nucleotide base pairing, which led Watson and Crick to formulate the structure of DNA as a double helix, for which they won the Nobel Prize.

We bent over our notebooks, but few of us were writing. After four or five minutes Barry Wenglin stood up and quietly said, "Professor Chargaff, I don't think any of us can really concentrate on your lecture. We know that what you are lecturing about is important, but can we reschedule the lecture later in the week."

Professor Chargaff wordlessly nodded and swept his arm waving us to the exits. We silently filed out of the amphitheater and the medical school building and walked together to the large common room in Bard Hall, where a television set had already been hastily dragged into the front of the room. The rest of the afternoon the first- and second-year students sat watching the news unfold—first, that President Kennedy had been taken to a Dallas hospital to be operated on; then that he had been pronounced dead; and then that Lyndon Johnson had been sworn in as president and that a plane was bringing President Kennedy's body, Mrs. Kennedy, and the Johnsons back to Washington DC.

A few days later Professor Chargaff gave the postponed lecture and then his final two, but there were no more jokes. For weeks, in the amphitheater and at meals our conversations were subdued, as though a pall of mourning had been thrown over us all.

Until the Christmas holiday, we spent our mornings in anatomy and histology lectures and laboratories, and our afternoons in biochemistry lectures and the biochemistry laboratory. In the evenings we clarified our lecture notes from our textbooks and prepared for the next day's anatomy dissection laboratory.

We studied in our rooms or two blocks away in the dusty, cavernous medical school library. Most of us lived in Bard Hall except the few local or married students who had homes in the city. We each had individual rooms and shared communal showers and toilet rooms. The women lived on the fourth floor. At a time when college women usually lived in separate dormitories, I sensed that the fourth floor was a space in which men weren't welcome unless invited. I was invited only once. The rest of us were spread through the remaining seven floors in single rooms of graduated luxury. Mine on the lowest floor was the plainest and smallest and least expensive, looking out over Haven Avenue and the sooty grey apartment buildings across the street. Those who could spring for more had larger rooms higher up, the best overlooking the Henry Hudson Parkway, the Hudson River, and the graceful George Washington Bridge that connected Manhattan with northern New Jersey.

When the hours of studying became too tedious, we could swim or play basketball, squash, or handball in the basement gym. I had no regular habit of exercise since leaving Boston, where I had run a few miles along the Charles River before dinner almost every afternoon. Most of my trips to the basement were to join the queue of students washing and drying laundry.

There were no cooking facilities. In what was called the "ballroom", meals were served from a buffet line three times a day. The choices were limited. The portions of food were limited as well: if we wanted more than one slice of bacon and one slice of (cold) toast and one egg, we paid extra. In the expansive, drab room we sat at tables of six. We were usually rushing to get to the morning or afternoon lectures and conversation was superficial and subdued, often nothing more than "Good morning" and a head nod.

I was not used to being in lectures or laboratories or studying hours at a time. At Harvard I had spent a third of my waking hours reading the non-assigned books that I often found more interesting than what I was supposed to be reading in my English literature courses. I read all the plays of Eugene O'Neill and most of Shaw, Ibsen, and Strindberg. I trudged through Dostoyevsky and Tolstoy, the six volumes of Carl Sandberg's Lincoln, and much of Churchill on the Second World War. I read popular sociology and books about Zen Buddhism and the three-volume *Life and Works of Freud*. I saw movies frequently, mostly at the Brattle Theater—second runs of Bergman and Fellini and Antonioni, most of the French new wave directors, and a lot of Humphrey Bogart. Many of the drab books I was supposed to read—Milton, Spencer, Pope, Dryden, Tennyson—languished on my desk. I joylessly crammed in the assigned reading before exams or when a paper was due.

In medical school I struggled against my college habit of reading what interested me rather than the twenty or thirty pages of the basic science texts we were assigned each day. While studying I listened to classical music in my room, staying up late to hear "Listening with Watson" on WNCN, sponsored by American Airlines. Watson would come on at 11 and play recordings until 6 AM, sometimes turning the airline's ads into parodies. Watson played an incredible array of music I had never heard. He didn't interrupt full-length operas for commercials. Occasionally he would complete a performance of a symphony or opera and announce, "That was so good that we should listen to it again," and start over with side one. A few times I was awake listening until 2 or 3 AM and then would wake up from deep sleep at 8 to rush through showering, dressing, and breakfast before my 9 AM lecture.

I slogged through the masses of dull anatomy and biochemistry and microanatomy required reading, coping both with my procrastination and my shock at how much there was to learn and how much I didn't want to: I had come to medical school with no idea of what to expect, but I was not expecting to find that studying was drudgery. I rarely arrived in lecture with yesterday's information absorbed, let alone with preparatory reading for that day's lecture.

In medical school it was new to me that 120 of us were always doing the same thing in lockstep at every moment of the day. The whole class approached examinations en masse, and the anxiety and fatigue and grubbiness of each of us contributed to everyone else's. In college I rarely knew what was happening in the classes of my friends and roommates. Only during the end-of-semester reading periods before exams was there generalized tension, but even then, none of my friends were taking my courses: if I was slamming a month worth of Plato or Shakespeare into one week, they were cramming economics or social psychology or Boolean algebra. In the classes I was taking in preparation for applying to medical school—biology, physics, chemistry—not once did I know anyone else's exam score or how they had answered a difficult question; not once did I know anyone's final grades, or even who was planning on applying to medical school.

Even worse in medical school was the post-test group cross-examination: "what was the missing enzyme?" "Which cranial nerve moves the eyelid?" "Were those adrenal cortex cells the zona reticularis or zona fasciculata?" Whether they intended to be showing off or simply couldn't constrain themselves, the students who always got every answer right left me feeling increasingly inadequate. If there were others who were feeling the same, we never identified ourselves to each other.

Most of my Columbia classmates had been "pre-med" majors. Many had been focused on getting high grades in their undergraduate courses, keenly aware that they were competing nose-to-nose to get into good medical schools. In college they had traded anecdotes on which medical schools were best and what it took to get into them. The students from Columbia's undergraduate college told stories of students hiding books that had been reserved, tearing out pages with information on which they would be tested, and obtaining copies of the previous year's examination questions. Perhaps these stories were apocryphal—or real but rare—but they suggested to me a cutthroat aspect to education that I hadn't ever considered. I didn't know if I even had a GPA at Harvard, and I had no experience since high school of competing with other students.

My examination scores during the first year were consistently in the C+/B range. There were one hundred nineteen students from whom I might have gotten advice about how to study better. But I was too shy or too embarrassed to ask or to acknowledge that I wasn't performing at better than a mediocre level. I neither knew nor dared to ask what I needed from the basic science courses to be a good enough student during clinical rotations in the third and fourth year to be invited for interviews at the best residency programs.

At Harvard I had initially been awkward about coming from an unexceptional Montana family and having attended public schools, but gradually I became comfortable there. At Columbia I once again felt like an outsider. When I wasn't in class or studying I was usually alone. The students who grew up or went to college in New York and the nearby states came with friendships and family in place. Because I had a girlfriend in Boston, I was not dating. I was far from Boston and farther from Montana; none of my friends from those places were now in New York City. Washington Heights wasn't an area that lent itself to outdoor sports or exploring, so on most weekends I would go off on some kind of expedition in midtown Manhattan for at least a half day. When I left at 9 in the morning, I walked by Walt Berger's open door and saw him sitting at his desk, a goose-neck lamp aimed at a fat notebook in which he was rapidly writing; he would still be at his desk when I returned at dinner time. I started my studying at 7 pm, already torpid from a day of walking and fresh air and postprandial somnolence. I might have two or three hours of effective review, but Walt would have socked away fifteen.

The absence of any close friendships with other students contributed to my isolation. We knew each other superficially by the cultures in which we grew up and our behavior—brash New York City kid whose parents grew up on the Lower East Side or in Hell's Kitchen, small town New Englander with a down east accent, rich WASP Princeton snob, polite, quiet Asian from San Francisco. My category, "clueless, Montanan, English major", was a category of one and not in high demand. Had I attended the University of Montana rather than Harvard, no matter how good a student I had been, it was unlikely that I would have even been admitted to Columbia.

In Bard Hall, we were each sweating it out in our own monastic room. Everyone seemed too busy studying to visit or go out on weekends. For me there was no intimacy, no opening up about the past or present or future, and no way to explore how to study more effectively or be happier.

In the fall of 1963, we took our final exams in biochemistry, anatomy, and histology a few days before the December Christmas break. Margaret invited me to spend Christmas in Newburyport with her family. When I returned to Bard Hall in January the general atmosphere was noticeably different. While we continued to grub just as hard for the next eighteen months, we had survived the three most difficult courses, and those of us who had little preparation for graduate level science had figured out how to learn the material. Physiology and pharmacology, our second semester courses, seemed somewhat more like "medicine", and more of the faculty members had been trained as physicians and had a communication style that was less spiked with indignation that they were teaching medical students and not real scientists.

The winter of 1964 was a long, slow grind for us on the upper end of Manhattan. In the world beyond the walls of medical school tumultuous things were happening, but culture-shaking events went by me like meteors hidden behind clouds.

That year Lyndon Johnson enacted the first steps of the Great Society; he signed the Civil Rights Bill, effectively ending the Democratic Party's century-long domination of the southern states as senators and representatives switched to the Republican party; he expanded the

The Ninth Floor Amphitheater

American presence in Vietnam while hiding the real status of the war and falsifying excuses for bombing North Vietnam, Lao, and Cambodia; the Free Speech movement got underway; and Martin Luther King was awarded the Nobel Peace Prize. I didn't listen to news or watch it on television. What bits I read in one of the newspapers lying around in the common room might as well have been Dickens writing about 19th Century London. The stories didn't seem to have any immediate importance to me.

There was a single TV set in the Bard Hall lounge, but it was rarely watched—perhaps a few students would stop by for a few minutes to watch the Boston Celtics beat the San Francisco Warriors 4 games to 1 for the NBA championship, or to watch an early season baseball game. But I wasn't paying attention even to that.

We all did hear one piece of news— the Surgeon General's report that smoking was probably responsible for markedly increasing the likelihood of lung cancer, lung disease, stroke, and myocardial infarction. Many of the students smoked, and many of the faculty did as well, including lung and heart surgeons and cardiologists.

It took years for the news to sink in. Few of us quit right away, and some of the faculty never did. For another two years I bummed an occasional cigarette from smoking friends and off and on puffed on a pipe.

Social events were sparse. There was an occasional low-key reception in the Bard Hall lounge with beer and pretzels. Every few months the Columbia School of Nursing a few blocks away held a mixer but I wasn't good at striking up conversations with strangers, and, anyway, I wasn't dating.

While neither the Bard Hall beer nor the mixers were noteworthy, the invitations to faculty homes were. The school recognized that for first- and second-year students there were few activities to connect them to clinical faculty members until their third year, so they recruited faculty member to host groups of new students in their homes.

The first of these a few months into our first year was extraordinary: Sunday afternoon dinner at the rural New Jersey home of Professor J. Lawrence Pool, the chairman of the Department of Neurosurgery. Eight of us were invited and told to bring our swimming togs and tennis racquets. The home was an expansive rambling place with a swimming pool full of green algae that Dr. Pool said would be good for us. Several of the students were good tennis players. I sat on the sidelines and watched the match. I had never picked up a tennis racket—it wasn't part of my Montana childhood. We ate a dinner of rare roast beef and artichokes that I had to be taught to tear apart and dip in hollandaise sauce. Dr. Pool regaled us with stories for two hours, a smoking, aromatic pipe in his mouth much of the time. He and his brother had been the world pairs amateur squash champions; he had sailed across the Atlantic on a sailboat; he served in the 9th Evacuation Hospital in North Africa, Sicily, Southern France, and Germany during the Second World War. He had written thirteen books on subjects ranging from neurosurgical procedures to fighting warships and Valley Forge.

Dr. Pool went around the table and asked each of us to talk a little about ourselves. That was the first time in medical school I had heard much about who my classmates were before medical school. Two had gone to Princeton, another to Yale, one to Duke, East Coasters all, and apparently all well versed in the mysteries of the artichoke, which to me looked more like a reptile than a food.

Over many years I saw Dr Pool in the halls of the Medical Center, always with a pipe in his mouth, but of course he didn't recognize me.

In the depths of that winter I was one of a half dozen students invited to have dinner at the modest home of Professor Kent Ellis, a radiologist who a decade later became the department chair. Dr. Ellis was a leader in cardiovascular and chest imaging. After college he served in the north Atlantic and Pacific, earning eleven battle stars, and then went on to graduate from Yale Medical School and do a radiology residency at Columbia. That dinner was a much quieter affair. Dr. Ellis and his wife asked each of us polite questions about where we had grown up, what we had studied in college, and how we had chosen Columbia. Even as we answered we knew that they were being gracious and filling the silence. We asked nothing about them—it would have been impolite: fledgling medical students didn't ask a professor twenty years his senior how he met his wife, or what it is like to work at Columbia, and if we had asked and they had answered, we knew that we weren't going to hear any intimate details or grievances.

And yet we were grateful for the effort they were making to welcome us, as different as their lives were from ours. Unlike Dr. Pool, who seemed to occupy too lofty a perch astride American Medicine to aspire to, Dr. Ellis seemed more accessible. A few years later when we showed up in his radiology reading room, he seemed to glow as he unhurriedly went over films with us. He was perpetually fascinated by the cases we brought him, never dogmatic and always kind no matter how uninformed we were.

I didn't know the term "role model" then, but later I thought of him as the first physician after whose clinical acumen and supportive teaching style I tried to model myself.

CHAPTER 5

The Last Summer Break

When the first-year classes ended in May, we had the summer off. I had decided when I began medical school that I would not return to Montana to fight fires, although I could have used the money to pay the upcoming year's room and board and the personal expenses not covered by my scholarship. Instead, I planned to spend the summer doing research with Dr. Donald Dunton, an appealing professor who had given our introductory lectures in psychiatry once a week during the winter and spring. Columbia provided $400 stipends for summer research, enough to cover my board and room at Bard Hall for the summer, and I planned to take out a thousand-dollar loan—my first loan ever—to pay for the next year's board and room.

Sam Sobel, a junior student who was starting the demanding clinical rotations, asked if I wanted to take over his blood bank job at Delafield, the adjacent city cancer hospital. He told me that I would be paid five dollars a day plus meals all summer to be on call at night and on weekends in case emergency blood transfusions were needed. My job would be to type and crossmatch donated blood already in the blood bank to be sure that it was compatible with the recipient's blood.

He spent an hour showing me how to do the blood matching, and then showed me how to collect blood from a donor in the rare cases where more blood was needed than the blood bank had. I had never drawn blood from anything larger than an anesthetized rabbit.

Sam went through the drill once, showing me how to clean the skin overlying the vein from which I would drain the blood, how to attach plastic tubing to the needle and then to the vacuum collection bottle.

The collection bottles had a black rubber plug through which one pushed a pointed stout plastic tube with a sharp tip attached to a flexible plastic tube that attached to the collection needle that was inserted in the vein of the donor's forearm. Sam went over this once but I had no opportunity to practice.

Every week or two I would be called by Delafield and asked to type and crossmatch units of blood they already had collected. Most of the surgery done there was elective and the daytime professional staff prepared the blood for intraoperative and postoperative care the day before or during the day.

The Delafield cafeteria food was someplace between uninviting and disgusting, but it was free and the job wasn't hard.

On a steamy Sunday evening in late August I received a call from an extremely kind surgeon who had just removed part of a patient's colon because of bleeding.

"I am sorry to bother you, but we just finished operating on a patient and can't get his bleeding stopped. We have gone through all the blood we had ordered and the blood bank had told me when we started surgery that the patient had a rare blood type and neither they nor the New York Red Cross could supply us with any more. He has two family members who have the same blood type and they are heading for the hospital right now. Would you mind coming in and getting the blood and typing and crossmatching it? They should be here in about a half hour."

The worst had happened. I hadn't had to collect blood all summer, and only dimly remembered what Sam had told me.

I trotted down Ft. Washington Ave. By the time I reached the hospital I was soaking wet with sweat, and very anxious.

I unlocked the blood bank and was getting the equipment together when the front door guard brought the two family members into the room. They were both women with chubby arms and skimpy veins, but they were warm and friendly. I had the least chubby one lie down on the examination table used for collecting blood, found the easiest-looking vein, prepared her forearm with an iodine solution, and got the tubing and needle laid out beside her. In my nervousness, I mixed up the ends of the tubing, and began trying to insert the plastic needle intended to puncture the collection bottle's hard rubber stopper into her tiny forearm vein. She was writhing in pain and screaming, but I managed to get the needle—almost the diameter of a pencil—into her arm. I put the skinny needle end into the collection bottle. Blood was accumulating in the bottle very slowly when the woman said she was feeling faint and wanted to stop. I had about a half pint of blood.

The other woman had turned ashen watching her sister and wanted none of what she had just observed. She suggested that we wait to see if her brother really needed another unit of blood.

I was so nervous that I still hadn't figured out that the little needle went in the patient, and the big needle into the bottle.

By the time the half unit I had sent up had been transfused, the patient's bleeding had tapered off. The surgeon told me they could probably wait until tomorrow and see if the Red Cross could come up with another unit as a backup. If the two sisters talked with him about the nincompoop running wild in the blood bank, he didn't tell me.

A few days later I ran into Sam, who asked me how things were going in the blood bank. I described what happened. Sam was aghast and explained what I should have done. It says something about the state of healthcare in the New York City hospitals in 1964 that a barely-out-of-the first-year student with no experience was allowed to type and crossmatch blood, let alone do a collection for which he lacked both the skill and common sense.

I had only a loose plan for my summer research project. I had heard that there were summer research scholarships available from the school, and after one of Dr. Dunton's lectures in the spring, I asked him if he could take me on for a research project. He agreed and suggested that first I shadow him for a few weeks in his child psychiatry practice, sitting in with him during many of his clinic appointments and then making rounds on the child psychiatry inpatient unit. Seeing children with autism and schizophrenia and bipolar disease was interesting for a few weeks, but soon I found myself struggling to stay awake during the hour-long appointments. I practiced stifling yawns.

My research project was to record the voices of children with infantile autism. Dr. Dunton had noticed over his years in practice that autistic children had different speech patterns and he thought different voice pitches. He had arranged to collaborate with Dr. Larry Kersta, an electronics engineer at the Bell Laboratories, to make voiceprints of a half dozen children in Dr. Dunton's practice as well as children with typical development as controls. I sat with the children in a soundproof booth equipped with high quality microphones and tape recorders, talking with the children while I recorded their voices.

The autistic children were often hard to keep in the booth or coach to say specific phrases to compare with the control children. One was flirtatious; another would only say one phrase repetitively and it took multiple sessions to get decent samples. A few simply would not repeat the phrases that we were using.

Through the muggy Mid-Atlantic summer, I went on psychiatry rounds every day and attended the residents' conferences; in the afternoon I collected conversations. On the weekends I took long walks alone around Manhattan or caught foreign movies at the Paris or Thalia theaters. Perversely, I sometimes wished that I had returned to Montana to fight fires instead.

A few months later, after I had begun my second-year classes, a preliminary analysis of the voiceprints showed that there was no recognizable pattern that differentiated typically developed from autistic kids: voiceprinting failed to be a useful diagnostic test. Dr. Kersta went on to become famous in forensic science as his voiceprints began to be introduced in courts in the same way as fingerprints—showing whether a suspect was or was not the speaker in a wiretapped telephone call.

I had often been unhappy during the first year—primarily lonely, but also wondering if medical school and New York City were the right places for me. While spending the summer with the psychiatrists I learned that the psychiatry training program occasionally accepted students for free psychoanalysis by residents who were training to be analysts. I figured getting analyzed might help me figure out who I was and help me during my stumbling journey into adulthood. A Psychoanalytic Institute faculty member who had adopted Freud's beard, horned-rim glasses, and cigar habit invited me for an interview to explore my potential as a psychoanalytic patient. In a few weeks I received a short letter saying that he didn't think I would present a sufficient challenge for a trainee. I took that to mean that I wasn't crazy enough or screwed up enough or, worse, that as a Montanan, I was not even interesting enough to be worth untangling.

At the end of the summer I erased Psychiatry as a viable career option.

CHAPTER 6

Transition to Clinical Learning

The first year, we had been told, was learning normal human biology; in the second year we would be learning abnormal human biology. The courses were inviting: pathology, pharmacology, neuropathology, microbiology, parasitology, genetics and embryology. We were slowly working our way toward understanding the physiologic basis of diseases.

Our days continued to be divided among lectures and laboratories and studying. We still had minimal context for learning about how diseases were expressed because we had no exposure to patients. In pathology lectures we studied the body's organs one at a time—kidney, heart, lung, liver and on and on. First, we saw the whole organ as it appeared in health in photos and then by visits to the autopsy suite, where we could see fresh tissue that had not been preserved. Then we saw the organ as it appeared in disease—and then the organ sliced open to reveal the abnormalities apparent to the naked eye, and then microscopic slides of the particular disease. In our microscopic anatomy course during the first year we had learned the appearance of the normal kidney: we knew what the normal glomerulus and tubules looked like—the glomerulus is the part of the kidney where water and minerals are filtered out of the blood and the tubules are where the urine is concentrated and minerals either extracted from the urine to return to the blood or concentrated in the urine to be eliminated from the body. Now in our microscopy laboratories we examined how the normal structures were distorted or replaced by abnormal tissues in patients with diabetes, or inflammation of the kidneys, or infection of the urinary tract.

Similarly, we could see through our microscopes the appearance of a liver damaged by alcohol, but we did not yet know anything about alcoholism or cirrhosis of the liver. A slow crawl through ten pages of a textbook of medicine to learn the symptoms and natural history of those diseases was like reading the map of a huge country we didn't live in and had never visited. Some of my classmates found the time to read all those pages, but for some of us, much of what we learned for the tests had dissipated before we could put it to use a year later.

Still, we took notes and organized them, we poured over the slides, 120 of us sitting side by side in rows trying to compare what we saw to the atlases of pathology, hoping that we would know enough to pass the written and laboratory examinations, largely unaware of what would be useful and what we would never hear about again.

Microbiology was more accessible. Many of the bacteria and viruses and the diseases they caused were familiar to us—measles, smallpox, chickenpox, mononucleosis, strep throat, scarlet fever, polio, pneumonia, syphilis—all these we knew from literature or the newspapers or our own lives. Microbiology seemed like clinical medicine and practical, although the allied course—clinical pharmacology—was largely unfamiliar once we got by the few drugs we knew from our family medicine cabinets.

Still, by the spring I was not gasping to keep up; my skills at note taking had improved and I could read the science of medicine more easily because increasingly everything seemed relevant.

Our first contacts with patients also began in the late winter of the second year. We learned the art of physical examination from lectures given by Yale Kneeland, a charming retired physician who looked and sounded like a knighted English actor playing the role of raconteur and favorite uncle. When we learned about a Graham-Steele or Austin-Flint heart murmur, or Erb's point or the angle of Louis, we also learned about the physicians whose names were attached. We heard funny stories about earnest but inept students who couldn't hear or feel what their teachers were pointing out, or heard and felt things no one else could. He was broadly skeptical about physicians who never learned the ancient skills of physical examination and history taking, and subtly he inculcated in us a belief in the great honor of becoming physicians who cared enough about our patients to want to develop the highest level of the art.

For several hours each week he would lecture, and then we would wander around the hospital wards looking for patients who we had been told had a heart murmur or an enlarged spleen or abnormal fingernails. I felt sorry for the poor patients: four or five of us would arrive at the bedside at once, introducing ourselves like trick-or-treating kids on Halloween dressed up as medical students. We barely knew how to use our stethoscopes or ophthalmoscopes, but like the Lilliputians examining Gulliver, one of us tried to find the alleged heart murmur while several of us would inspect a toe or finger while another felt for the edge of the liver.

One spring afternoon we took the long subway trip from the upper West Side to Bellevue Hospital on the Lower East side, a museum of disappearing pathology, where the two Columbia wards were gymnasium-sized rooms with four rows of 12 beds, without curtains or screens for privacy. Our attempts at listening to the murmurs that the chief of service had found for us were thwarted by the thunder of pile drivers outside the ward window where the foundations of the third or fourth "New Bellevue" were being constructed. We couldn't hear a thing.

Our second-year science classes continued until the end of May. On May 28th, the last day of the term, those of us taking the National Board of Medical Examiners test were divided up between the 7th and 9th floor amphitheaters and were seated at our arm desks with enough spaces between us to make cheating difficult. With a break at noon, we worked on the examination until late afternoon. As far as I know, no one studied for it, nor were we encouraged to: we assumed that the curriculum we had been studying for the past two years was our preparation.

In 1965 the examination played no role in residency selection other than confirming that we had sufficient knowledge to merit a medical license, which was required to write prescriptions and sign orders when we started internships. All that was needed when we applied for residencies was to check a box that said NBME passed—yes/no. I don't remember my score, if one was given: the only thing I can remember is that I passed.

Some students didn't take the examination, since the states they expected to apply in—for example California or Florida—still required that doctors take their state's licensing exam, which candidates had to travel to the state to take.

And with that, the toil of the first two years was now done. A few days later, on the first of June, we began our clinical clerkships.

CHAPTER 7

Margaret

Margaret and I met at Harvard entirely by accident. As a sophomore, I had gotten an A in both physics and general chemistry; to meet the minimal qualifications for most medical schools I still needed a year of biology and organic chemistry. A legendary teacher and scientist, Louis Fieser, whose textbook was used by nearly every chemistry student in the United States, taught organic chemistry. This was a serious course, full of chemistry and biology majors and people like me heading for medical school. For an hour students bowed over their notebooks writing furiously, as Fieser lectured and drew formulas on the blackboard lightening quick. Even though there was a lot of pressure to do well, I enjoyed learning how synthetic rubber was made during World War II when the tropical plantations where rubber trees grew were fiercely contested by the Japanese navy, and I was fascinated by how cholesterol was transformed in the body to cortisone and testosterone and estrogen.

When I returned to Harvard after a summer of fighting fires I was fit and craved some kind of physical activity. On a couple of weekends our Forest Service hotshot crew had played six-man football against local high school teams and my love of tackling and blocking rekindled instantly, although at 135 pounds the physics were just as much against me then as they had been in high school. When I got back to Cambridge I signed up for the Leverett House tackle football team. About a month into the semester I was playing inside guard, pushing some palooka from another Harvard house to the left while our 210 pound fullback came around my right side through the hole I was supposed to have made. However, I was still pretty much in the same place as when the play started, with my right foot firmly planted in the hole. The fullback's boot caught my ankle, breaking both my tibia and fibula.

When I got back to my room from the student infirmary on crutches, I realized I was going to have to make some adjustments for my chemistry lecture and lab the next day—I would have to leave early to hobble to classes; and I would have to sit on the right side of the center seats in the lecture hall so that I had some place to put my casted leg and crutches.

The next day when I showed up for the laboratory, Skip, the very nice graduate student who was managing our laboratory section, took one look at me and told me I couldn't do the lab and would have to drop the course.

"Why," I asked.

"Well, as you already know, everyone has to hustle around the lab to pick up their glass ware from the storage cabinets, then get their reagents, and then stand throughout the experiment, and then run around to put everything back. How would you do that on crutches?"

"I think I can do that."

"How?"

I clearly couldn't use crutches, which tied up both hands. So, for three hours I hopped everywhere on one foot. It didn't hurt that I had been hauling heavy loads up and down the Rocky Mountains for three months: I had a really strong left leg, good balance, and a streak of stubbornness.

That night I fabricated a box from a Butler's tray I found at Good Will like the ones cigarette girls used at nightclubs in the 1940's. I fashioned a strap that would go around my neck; with the tray I could carry glassware and most chemicals while on crutches. For the next three months I bounced around the lab, still hopping when I was in a hurry and only had to grab one or two things. At the end of the semester I got an A from Skip, not because my experiments always worked out but because he had been absolutely sure that what I had done wasn't doable.

Meanwhile something was happening in the third row of the Mallinckrodt Lecture Hall. Because I didn't want to negotiate all the stairs to the higher back rows, I came early to sit in row three, my right leg angled out into the aisle, my crutches nested at my feet. It didn't take long to notice a Radcliffe girl who always sat in front of me with the same guy. She was pretty—he was geeky—they were clearly more than friends. Noting that she wore a different sweater for every lecture, the headings of my lecture notes for that semester were the date, the subject, and something like "bright red short sleeve sweater with matching cardigan".

Until then I hadn't had much experience with Radcliffe girls, who were, by reputation, smarter than we were, wore no makeup, had stringy unwashed hair, and were not likely to suffer fools gladly. I was too shy to talk with her, and as far as I could tell she never looked at me when she took her seat.

We had the Radcliffe freshman face books in our room, one for each of the last few classes. I went through the photos for the entering class of '63, but couldn't spot her. In the class of '64 book I went through page after page of the 300 girls and didn't find her until I got to the last page: "Margaret Dodge Wilkins, Biology."

With no particular strategy for meeting her, I hung out in front of the chemistry building before the 1:00 pm laboratory every afternoon and realized she didn't have her organic lab there. So I hung out at the Radcliffe science building a few afternoons and finally spotted her going into a lab there. I had no excuse for wandering into that building, and gave up. By Christmas break I had a notebook full of lecture notes and a log of her sweater collection, but I remained unknown to her.

After reading period and exams, organic chemistry continued and I began my first biology course. At the first lecture I spotted her without her chemistry beau. That improved my prospects. I had been too shy or too polite to hover over her seat on my crutches in organic chemistry to

Learning the Art of Medicine—a Memoir

introduce myself while her boyfriend looked on: best for him not to know I existed. That afternoon I showed up for my biology lab, but she wasn't there. Once again I stood outside the biology building every afternoon to see if she which day she was coming. Finally, on Friday, she came.

I immediately went inside the building and knocked on the door of the head section man.

I introduced myself, and said, "I'm in the Monday lab and it interferes with my job. I would like to switch into the Friday laboratory, please".

He looked at me kindly. "Can't do that. That's the biggest lab already. How about another day?" I hadn't expected that glitch. I put on my most stricken look. "I'm here on a scholarship and I have to work to pay the rest of my expenses. The only afternoon I can get out of is Friday. If I can't switch I'll have to drop out of Harvard." I hung my head in despair.

Now he looked stricken. His eyes were sad and worried. "Oh no no no no! Don't do that. We'll squeeze you in. It will be fine. I'll let the section man know. It'll be fine, don't worry."

I hadn't worked at Harvard since a horrid food service job my freshman year. I hadn't planned to lie. Not for the first time, making up something plausible, complete with emotionally appropriate intonation was as natural as scratching an itch.

The next Friday I showed up, and there she was.

I didn't find a way to talk with her immediately, but about the third week we were supposed to dissect a squid and study its anatomy. The section man said there were two buckets, one with female squid, one with male squid. "When you're done with the dissection find someone with a squid of the opposite sex and compare the sexual organs."

I watched where Margaret lined up and as she plunged her hand into the bucket of lady squid, I grabbed a gentleman squid.

I had never picked anyone up before, let alone picked up a total stranger while holding a squid, and I blurted out, "Wanna compare squid parts?"

She looked nonplussed, not expecting a total stranger to talk with her, especially on such a delicate subject. Nonetheless, she murmured something faintly positive and to be ready when she was, I dissected with a frenzy. I ended up waiting quite a while, and when she looked across the laboratory table to find me, she quickly checked the clock on the wall. Our first conversation was brief and she left the laboratory quickly. I assumed it had something to do with me.

But I had told her my name and now she had no excuse to totally ignore me.

The next week the assignment was to look at shellfish and plants under ultraviolet light. This required students to go into a small room where specimens were set up under UV lamps, some under magnifying lenses. When she got up to take her turn I dashed in behind her, although another guy got between us. When she was about to leave the room I abandoned my observations and scooted around him. I asked her how she was and she smiled a tiny bit and I asked her if she wanted to go out for coffee sometime. She hesitated, but said she would, and we set a date for the next Friday.

The next day, Saturday dawned sunny and warm, one of those rare March days when spring lurches six weeks ahead to May. I had only one class, the morning Bio 2 lecture. We sat in different parts of the room. When we left, I watched her route away from the building. She headed for a bike stand and unlocked a bike. I quickly walked diagonally between her and the street so that she would have to slow down or run me over to get by.

"Nice day."

"Yes."

"Where are you going?"

She smiled a bit. "I am going to the Connie Dee sandwich shop and then going down to the river to have a picnic."

Images of her meeting the boy who sat next to her in organic chemistry popped into my head. "Would you mind if I joined you?"

She didn't say no. She got off of her bike and we walked twenty minutes to the sandwich shop. She ordered cream cheese on date nut bread, entirely unknown to me and definitely not a Montanan's idea of a sandwich. I ordered one too. Then I suggested that we go to Brigham's on

Harvard Square, where we got a pint of mocha almond fudge ice cream and two spoons.

The banks of the Charles were populated by the pallid survivors of Boston's long, cloudy, icy winter. Many guys had taken their shirts off revealing an expanse of fish-belly white chests and tummies that made the green grass look more like a morgue than a vernal hotbed. In singles and pairs and clumps, students—more males than females—relaxed, read, dozed, tossed baseballs, and sat staring at the river with their arms wrapped around their knees, watching single and paired scullers sprinting downstream.

We had talked all the way to the sandwich shop, talked in the ice cream shop, and for two hours talked as we ate our sandwiches and then the ice cream. She learned that I grew up in Montana, that I spent my summers fighting forest fires, that I was an English major, that I was hoping to go to medical school. I found out that she had grown up not far away, on the northern Massachusetts coast in a town called Newburyport, where the first clipper ships had been built and where her mother's ancestors arrived even before Harvard was founded in 1636; that she had gone to school in Newburyport until she was sixteen and then transferred to Abbot Academy in Andover, Massachusetts; and that she was doing microbiology research with the president of Radcliffe, Mary Bunting.

A few weeks earlier Geoff, Ted, and I had decided to throw a party in our top-floor Leverett House rooms that overlooked the Charles. We had bought some cheap white curtains and I had promised that I would dye them red that afternoon. I asked Margaret if she would like to go see the rooms and, amazingly, she said she would. We walked the short distance from the Charles to Leverett House, parked her bike, signed her in, and climbed the stairs to the fourth floor. Jeff and Ted were there re-arranging furniture. They had known that I was trying to meet a girl in my biology and chemistry classes, but they were not expecting me to succeed. Knowing glances passed between them as I introduced everyone.

After we looked around our suite of three bedrooms, a living room, and a bathroom, I walked her back to Radcliffe. Jeff and Ted had both started seeing Radcliffe girls, who they had invited to the party. I expected to be turned down, but I asked Margaret if she would like to come too. Once again, I was surprised when she said she would. Having spent three hours with her would seem to have been enough, but I asked what she was doing that evening. She said that she was going to usher at a play. I asked if I could meet her afterwards and walk her back to her house, and she agreed.

In the week that followed we saw each other almost every day—I think eight times before the next Friday when we were originally going to have coffee.

Spring was heavy in the air in Cambridge. Only a few nights after we started going out, walking back to Radcliffe at the end of an evening together, I began to talk about what I thought I would be like as a husband, and what I thought would be important in a marriage. It was of course all theoretical, since I had never experienced a marriage after I turned six, let alone a great marriage. My model was derived from novels and movies and the weekly radio dramas like "Henry Aldrich" and the Nelson family on "Ozzie and Harriet." But full of my soaring romanticism I asked her if she would marry me. She was levelheaded enough to laugh and say no, but she was also by now fully aware that I was energetically impetuous; she found it more interesting than scary and she didn't run away.

Beyond her apparently unlimited wardrobe of sweaters, Margaret dressed simply, as did most of the Radcliffe girls. She usually wore blouses and skirts —I think never pants—and there was a freshness about her, a lack of pretension and an animated intelligence. She didn't wear makeup, and she didn't wear jewelry; her hair was shiny and clean and smelled good. She laughed at my weird jokes, enjoyed going on strange adventures and suggested her own, and she knew more about biology than I did or ever would.

At the end of our first week of dating about a dozen people showed up for the party in Leverett 41. I met Geoff's girlfriend, Molly Denman, born in Texas, planning to be a painter, and far from her conservative roots. Ted's girl, Ann Cool, was Molly's friend and politically and socially liberal. I thought we were dating the three prettiest girls at Radcliffe and was totally surprised, because up to a few months ago none of us were dating at all. Geoff, Ted, Molly, and Ann had rounded up dance records and we did the twist and the loco-motion, chanted along with Gene Chandler's "Duke of Earl", and close-danced Ray Charles' "I Can't Stop Loving You" and a bunch of hits by the Shirelles. We had beer and chips, and while we might have been a little high, I doubt that any one was even close to drunk.

A few days later Margaret told Dave Jackson, the boy she sat with in organic chemistry, that she was going out with me. And with New England candor that took some getting used to, she told me that the day I asked if we could compare squid parts, she found me annoying because she was trying to get out of the lab early to join her now ex-boyfriend at an event at Lowell House, where he lived.

Margaret went home to Newburyport for spring break, and, as happened every year, I stayed in Cambridge. None of us in Leverett 41 had the money to travel to Florida, or even to go to New York City. Margaret invited me to spend a day with her so that she could show me around her hometown. In the middle of the week I took a bus from Boston's North Station to State Street in Newburyport, and then, following her instructions, walked to her home on High Street. I had thought over my wardrobe choices carefully and decided that my usual charcoal grey herringbone tweed jacket over jeans with a blue button-down Oxford cloth shirt and a striped tie was a good compromise between Boston preppiness and a walking date in an old New England town.

The bus dropped me off in the downtown market square, a near-totally intact 19th Century business district of elegant but slightly rundown red brick buildings with lovely arched windows and granite lintels above doorways. The streets and the sidewalks were alternately paved with bricks or stones or newer asphalt, and nothing was level. The air drifting onshore from the Merrimack River smelled pleasantly of seawater, seaweed and rotting timbers. I was immediately captivated.

I walked briskly up State Street and, following Margaret's directions, turned right on High Street and walked along the edge of a large commons with a pond, and then passed dozens of beautiful colonial and pre-colonial houses, again well preserved and largely untouched by modern renovations, but here and there in need of repair. I passed the high school that I knew Margaret had attended for two years before transferring to Abbot Academy.

I spotted her house and as I jay walked across High street saw a faint fluttering as a parted white curtain dropped back in place. Margaret opened the door immediately upon my first knock. Her mother was a few feet behind her, her face fixed in a tight-lipped smile. Mrs. Wilkins was slender, wearing a dark grey dress set off by a string of pearls; her graying hair had an air of restrained dignity. I offered my hand and she took it with a small handshake.

Inside the house was overwhelmingly beautiful, with two front rooms, each like a model eighteenth Century sitting room in a museum, with portraits hung on the walls and over the fireplaces, large Persian carpets, and antique settees, wooden arm and side chairs, and wingback chairs. Mrs. Wilkins disappeared down a long hallway toward the back of the house, and Margaret took me into the more formal "company" sitting room, having me sit on the settee while she pulled up a wooden chair. She apologized for not offering me the wingback chair, which, she said, was her father's chair.

The comfort we had come to expect in our long conversations hour after hour for the past few weeks had entirely disappeared. Margaret explained that the furniture was originally her grandfather's collection, passed on to Margaret's mother and then expanded on as one of her father's hobbies. She identified several of the portraits of family members and told me about the early history of the house which extended back to the pre-colonial period. Her mother's Morrill ancestors had landed in close-by Newbury in 1635 and generations of them had been buried in the local cemeteries.

All of this—the house, the furniture, the family history, the entire town of two-hundred-year-old houses, some in genteel decline— felt like arriving in a hidden world that I had not known existed. Nothing I had heard from Margaret—not the way she dressed or spoke, not what interested her, not what she talked about—had prepared me for the vast cultural distance between her childhood home and family and mine.

While I wasn't speechless, all I could do was ask questions and express appreciation for the beauty of the rooms and furnishings. In this austere setting I felt like a child seated at a formal dinner party, wearing the wrong clothes, without anything to add to the conversation, wondering why I had been invited to a place I clearly didn't belong.

After about ten minutes her mother called her to the back of the house. I looked around the room, at her father's desk, at the magazines neatly stacked on several of the tables: *Antiques, Yankee, The New England Journal of Medicine*. I got up and began to study the portrait of a woman above the fireplace when Margaret walked back in and showed me to the dining room at the back of the house, across from the kitchen's closed door.

Her mother walked in just as I was holding a chair back for Margaret across from where she said I would sit. Mrs. Wilkins leaned over and placed a large platter on the table. I held the chair for her, which seemed to confuse her, and then I sat down. The long table that could seat about eight was covered with a white tablecloth, set with silver and china, with water in cut glass goblets. Mrs. Wilkins asked for my plate, and she placed a large portion of salad on it, then on Margaret's, then on her own. We passed around a dish with store-bought cloverleaf rolls. In silence we began to eat. The salad was very, very good.

"Mrs. Wilkins. This is delicious. I love crab."

She glanced at me briefly and then looking at her plate and continuing to eat responded, icily, "In New England, we think that lobster is better than crab."

My face burned. I was speechless. Margaret and her mother said very little. We finished the meal in silence. I offered to help carry the dishes into the kitchen but was refused.

Margaret wanted to show me around Newburyport. As I helped her put on her coat and held the door for her, her mother came back into the hall and watched. After the door was closed and we turned back down High

Margaret

Street I reached out for Margaret's hand and we walked back toward the high school with Margaret talking about where she had played as a child, where her friends lived, which houses belonged to her mother's relatives.

It was nearly five when I walked Margaret back to her house, thanked Mrs. Wilkins, and walked again downtown to State Street to catch the bus back to Boston.

I was a wreck. My only experience with parents of a girl I was dating was in high school with Layne Westrum, and although her parents seemed indifferent to me—neither warm and welcoming nor hostile—we were more or less cut from the same cloth and I didn't feel out of place in their home.

From the moment I confused Yankee lobster, which I had never eaten, with West Coast crab, and revealed my unfamiliarity with New England comportment it was as though I had vomited at a funeral directly on the dearly departed's corpse. As Margaret said goodbye, her mother's icy face and hasty closing of the front door signaled that I would not be welcome in that house again.

On Sunday a few days later Margaret returned from Newburyport. We spent the evening together and she was clearly upset. In what became a years-long stretch of conversations about her parent's reaction to my showing up in her life, she told me that her mother was outspokenly put off by me: when I had pulled up Margaret's chair I had revealed that I was treating Margaret as a date, not as an acquaintance who had invited me home for a visit. She thought that my holding her coat for her was more of the same, and that when I whisked a bit of breadcrumb from her lip as she buttoned her coat, that I was being too intimate.

Worse, when we left to tour downtown Newburyport her mom was watching as we walked away holding hands. Margaret was told that someone of her class would never hold hands in public (although we had been doing it constantly in Cambridge): the whole town probably saw her. And of course, it was my unarguable lack of class that was at fault in making Margaret look cheap.

For the next year and a half Margaret regularly reported her parents' opposition to our dating. They considered me to be fresh, presumptuous, and without "breeding." Because my dad left my mom, I was from a divorced family, and to them that meant that I was in some way damaged, or that Margaret would be.

By early April Margaret and I were seeing each other most days. We sat together in our biology lectures and labs and on many weekday evenings we met for dinner and studied. On weekends we explored the streets of Cambridge and often ate dinner in my room and then hung out until the 11 o'clock curfew, when I would walk her back to Radcliffe. Once, during a long spring evening, we walked along the Charles River, the air redolent of the tiny new maple flowers, lilacs, and freshly-mown grass. We passed by the Mount Auburn Cemetery. I led her in and we made out sitting on the lawn leaning against a tombstone. My guess is that wasn't the first time the cemetery had hosted visits of lovers.

Each of the Harvard Houses had a music and a theater committee that during the spring put on shows open to the whole campus. In May Quincy House put on a Shakespeare play—I have forgotten which, but perhaps something earnest like Macbeth or Richard III. The commons room where the play was put on was stuffy and Margaret squirmed a lot in her chair. At the first intermission she whispered that she was wearing a girdle under her tight dress and it was uncomfortable. She went off to the bathroom and when she returned, with an impish grin she said it was in her purse. After the play we walked toward the Charles River and I asked her why, slender as she was, she was wearing a girdle. Her answer was more or less that girdle wearing was customary for a proper girl. In my limited experience with several girls in Montana, it had not been customary there.

"Would you like to stop wearing them?" I asked.

"I would", she said.

"I have an idea. Let's walk out onto the bridge".

It was a moonlit night. We walked onto a footbridge that led from the Harvard College campus to the Harvard Business School campus. At the low brick wall at the edge of the bridge, looking east toward the Boston skyline, a great wrinkly patch of moon was reflected in the river. I suggested that she throw the girdle at the moon, and as it hit the water we sang the "Ode to Joy" in badly enunciated German as her last girdle ever floated away

In early June I left for Montana to fight forest fires. Margaret had arranged to spend the summer at an orphanage in St. John's, Newfoundland. I had been suggesting for weeks that she come to Montana before we returned to Harvard in the fall. I thought her parents would forbid this, but to my surprise she talked them into it, including, at my suggestion, that she take the Vista-Dome North Coast limited from Chicago so that she could see the prairies and badlands of North Dakota and Eastern Montana, and pass over the Rocky Mountain Continental Divide at Butte.

I met her at the Northern Pacific depot the evening of my last day with the Forest Service, still wearing my Forest Service work clothes. We spent the next week touring my childhood haunts in Missoula. After that we drove to Flathead Lake where we stayed in my dad's cabin one night and the next day stayed in the Woods Bay house in which I spent my childhood summers, where I introduced her to my grandmother. From there it was only a one-hour drive to West Glacier Park. We stopped at the Lake McDonald Lodge and then drove up the tortuous Going to the Sun Highway to Logan Pass and hiked into Hidden Lake and out along the Highline overlooking the valley of Lake McDonald 3500 feet below.

I had never introduced anyone to Montana—all of my adventures there had been with the friends with whom I had grown up. It was fun to be with someone seeing it all for the first time. My spirits couldn't have been higher—whatever Montana's differences were from New England's history and culture and landscape, I was suddenly aware of the great pride I felt for the amazing mountains and lakes and rivers that were our everyday playground growing up. Unlike meeting her mother and seeing her home and home town, which had added a discomforting dimension to my understanding of what Margaret might expect of me, I felt that her seeing me in my natural habitat was having a positive effect on Margaret: she seemed to instantly love Montana.

In my aging '55 Chevy I was reluctant to make the 500-mile trip through Montana, Idaho, and Washington and over two passes to visit my brother and the World Fair in Seattle. My father kindly loaned me his Volkswagen Beatle that he used to commute to the bank. We stayed with Sam and Pam and their newly born son and with their expert guidance visited the world fair and Ivar's, one of the famous seafood dives near the Pike Market.

On her last day, I drove Margaret 300 miles to Spokane, where she caught the first of several planes for her trip back to Boston.

Margaret and I continued to see each other almost every day during her junior and my senior year, and the Wilkins family continued to express their resistance. At Christmas I stayed in Cambridge to work on my senior thesis; she invited me to spend several days during the holiday in Newburyport. I was assigned a lovely small bedroom over the garage which would have required my passing by the doors of her parents and brother and sister to see her at night, a prospect so daunting that I never tried. Christmas day was awkward—I felt that it had been a mistake to intrude on what was clearly a beloved but private morning of opening presents and eating.

In the spring, on one warm Saturday evening we stopped off at Cahaly's Deli on Mt. Auburn Street to get something cold to drink. We each chose a carton of chocolate milk and from there walked up Quincy Street. Margaret had the carton tipped up as we stepped off the curb just as a car came racing around the corner. I was on the far side of the car, but it hit Margaret and threw her up on the hood and then to the pavement. There was a flurry of activity as the driver stopped, people gathered, an ambulance was called, and Margaret was taken to the Harvard Infirmary for observation because she had hit her head on the pavement.

Margaret

I of course was horrified and felt responsible. The next day I stopped at a store on Massachusetts Avenue that sold art reproductions and found a Picasso blue period print of a woman nursing a baby. I framed it between two pieces of glass and carried it to her room, where she propped it up on a chair.

That evening her parents came to visit and saw the print, which revealed the baby suckling at the woman's bared breast. They were mortified that Margaret had accepted and displayed the print. I dropped another notch in their estimation.

During my first year at P & S we saw each other either in New York or Cambridge every few months, and I was happy that she once again invited me to spend Christmas with her family. Still, I felt like I was sleeping with rattlesnakes, on my best manners but aware that many of their New England expectations were totally unapparent to me until Margaret pointed them out. I had assumed the uncomfortable task of making myself over under Margaret's tutelage in order to be suitable as her boyfriend. It was hard work.

After Christmas I returned to a dark, windy, cold New York City and resumed my first-year classes, and Margaret returned to finish her final semester at Harvard. Two months later, on 28 February at 8 PM the message buzzer in my room sounded. Some of the students had paid for their own telephones, but most of us used the hallway phone on each floor that connected to the Bard Hall front desk.

I walked down the hall and picked up the phone. The music student who was the evening desk clerk said that I had a call from a Margaret, did I want to talk with her.

I was surprised. Long distance calls were expensive and Margaret rarely called.

"Hello! Something up?"

"Well," she said, "I really wanted to make this call tomorrow, but I couldn't wait. So, you know, every fourth year, on the 29th of February,

Sadie Hawkins Day, it is acceptable for a girl to ask a boy to marry her. And I want to ask you to marry me."

Good god! I was deeply into sorting out the role of pancreatic enzymes in the digestion of protein in the foregut and marriage was the furthest thing from my mind.

"Umm. Wow! You're asking me to marry you. I'm stunned!"

"Yes, you've told me many times that you wanted us to get married and I never said yes. And now I'm asking you."

I couldn't muster more than a single syllable: "When?"

"Well, here's my plan. I want to teach high school science after we get married, so I have decided to go to Oberlin College after graduation to get a Master of Arts in Teaching degree. That will qualify me to teach in New York or New Jersey. I would be at Oberlin for a full year after college, your second year of medical school. Then we could get married that summer and I would move to New York City and be with you."

By now my mind had switched over to the tiny fraction of my life not devoted to being a medical student and I was becoming excited.

There was one thing she hadn't said, and so I asked, "Have you told your parents?"

There was a pause, and then she said, slowly, "N-o-o-o." Another pause: "But I plan to go home to Newburyport this weekend and talk with them about it."

"Um, they know nothing?"

"No, but this is what I want to do, and they can't really stop me, and, anyway, I don't think they will try to."

And so, without advanced warning, in a five-minute conversation a huge chunk of my future suddenly came into focus: at 7:59 PM I was struggling to sort out proteolysis, and at 8:04 I was more or less engaged to marry Margaret Dodge Wilkins in the summer of 1965 in her house on High Street, Newburyport (she had figured that out too), and move out of Bard Hall to live with her in a New York City apartment.

I still was laboring under the possibly mistaken notion that we were adults and therefore entitled to the rights, privileges, and responsibilities of adults. Her plan sounded pleasingly adult and perfectly natural. The magnitude of my cluelessness wasn't apparent for a few decades.

Margaret talked with her parents the next weekend. To describe their response to her plans for getting a teaching degree and marrying me as "unenthusiastic" would have been a full quantum of understatement. "Apoplectic" would have been more like it.

Undaunted, Margaret felt that I should meet with her father and, in the conventional way of doing things, ask for his permission to marry her. And so, on a Friday night in March, during Margaret's spring break, I again took the New Haven Line to Boston. Margaret picked me up at South Station and drove us to Newburyport. The next afternoon, while Margaret sat with her mother in the kitchen, I met with Dr. Wilkins in the more formal, "guest parlor." He sat in his patriarchal wingback upholstered chair in suit and tie, while I, also in suit and tie, was offered a less comfortable, armless wooden "side chair".

Dr. Wilkins had a pleasant, mild southern accent that he brought with him to Boston from his home in Greensboro, North Carolina. He was reserved, formal, and unaccustomed to talking with a 23-year-old boy in pursuit of his daughter.

He also had a significant psychological advantage beyond his age and fathership: he was a quite famous and powerful professor of medicine and department chairman who was instrumental in introducing new drugs into the treatment of hypertension that were more effective and had fewer side effects than the prevailing treatments, drugs like reserpine and thiazide diuretics. He was the president of the American Heart Association and author of a score of patents and book chapters; and he had won the Lasker Award for scientific contributions that improved the health of the public, joining a list of awardees that included a half dozen Nobel Prize winners.

I didn't feel nervous so much as out of place and outranked in his 200-year-old house furnished with antiques and historic paintings.

He asked how medical school was going and inquired about a few Columbia faculty members he knew who I had never laid eyes on as a preclinical student.

It was not appropriate for me to ask how his life was going, and I knew no faculty members he might know; I knew no human beings he might know, except his daughter, and that I knew Margaret was a source of deep regret to him.

"As you know, Margaret and I would like to get married. I would like to ask you for her hand in marriage."

Even at the time, that seemed both old-fashioned and bizarre: I didn't want her hand, I wanted her whole body. I was uncomfortable with the inference that she belonged to him, and that once her hand was turned over, she would belong to me. I had only been to one wedding and knew nothing about courtship. Worse, I had no preparation for marriage other than growing up in one that fell apart when I was six. But in this matter I was firmly of the opinion that Margaret belonged to herself and should be free to do what she wanted, which was also what I wanted.

"Yes," he said. "Margaret has explained to me a plan in which she would get a teaching degree and then the two of you would marry as you were beginning your third year of medical school."

He paused, grimacing slightly. I waited.

"I think you both are very young—too young for marriage and all that goes with it."

He looked me in the eye and I tried to hold his gaze.

"I am not sure Margaret ever should get married. Margaret isn't a doer. Margaret is a dreamer. She and Peggy are the same: they both can spend hours wrapped up in their thoughts. I have watched Margaret sit on the swing in the back yard hour after hour, with complex daydreams she has made up, her mind a thousand miles away. I have never seen a career in store for Margaret. Her sister Mary, now—Mary is an organizer and a planner and a take-charge kind of girl, not as smart as Margaret, but more practical."

He went on, "Margaret is like her mother, she needs someone who can manage everything and take care of her."

Peggy was Margaret's mother. Her sister Mary, younger by a year, was at that point a junior at Wheaton College nearby, studying art history.

Margaret

I told him that I saw Margaret differently, better at sticking to studying than I was, more responsible for performing as expected in her courses, and probably better in the courses we had taken together—advanced biology, genetics and a semester-long broad review of English literature.

His response to that was, "Oh, Margaret is smart, all right—very smart. She can do schoolwork like nobody else, no doubt about that. But she isn't practical."

Not having succeeded in persuading Margaret to drop me, Dr. Wilkins seemed to be trashing Margaret by pointing out what he saw as her failings, hoping to discourage me from thinking about marriage at this stage of my life. But while I listened to him politely, I didn't agree with his characterization of Margaret and dismissed it as a full-scale effort to get rid of me.

Dr. Wilkins was much older than I when he met and courted Margaret (Peggy) Morrill, who he had met at a wedding. He had already finished college, medical school, residency, several years of military service, and three years of research training in London and Germany before he began an academic career at the Thorndike Laboratory on the Harvard Service at Boston City Hospital. He felt that he couldn't marry until he was earning enough to support a family. Giving up the idea of any immediate marriage with Peggy, he moved to a position with a small salary at Johns Hopkins. After a year, Chester Keifer, who introduced penicillin into medical practice, said that he was organizing a new department of medicine at Boston University and offered Dr. Wilkins the lordly sum of $6000 a year to join him. Dr. Wilkins immediately drove to Newburyport and proposed to Peggy. She was not much older then than Margaret was now, but he was in his mid-thirties when they married.

I was a first-year medical student with no income and 23 years old. My only exposure to the world outside of Montana was four years at Harvard, which I imagined had validated my assumption that I was fit to marry his daughter. Until I met the Wilkins family I had not realized how little Harvard had made me like a New Englander from a proper family.

The Wilkins' children, he said, were slow to mature, and Margaret was simply still too young to make the decision to get married. He advised me to take some time away from Margaret and live a bit more, meet other people, and to not rush into marriage. He had already advised Margaret much the same way.

After Christmas I returned to medical school, not sure what would happen next. He had not given consent for me to marry his daughter. I thought of marriage as the necessary step for the two of us to live together for the rest of our lives, something that Margaret would not begin without being married. I had no sense that other people's desires needed to be considered if that is what the two of us wanted. But from his perspective I was asking to join his family and he had very little reason to be enthusiastic about that other than acceding to his daughter's whim. I didn't understand at the time what it might mean for the Wilkins family for a first child to move away, or for a stranger—particularly one they didn't like very much—to join the family.

By the time that Margaret graduated from Radcliffe a few months later, she had worn her family's opposition down and obtained the grudging consent of her parents.

And so, in August, at the end of the summer just before my second year, I drove with Margaret to Ohio in a car her family had bought so that she could commute into Cleveland for her student teaching experience, stuffed with clothing and furniture for her year at Oberlin.

We were not engaged: we were engaged to be engaged. Margaret's parents did not believe in long engagements. Perhaps they hoped that during a long period away from me Margaret would change her mind and rid herself of me.

It was Margaret's plan that we would get formally engaged in Newburyport during the Christmas break. I knew that this would be my last chance to spend Christmas with Mom. I told Margaret that I would fly to Montana, spend a few days there, and return to the East Coast the day after Christmas for an engagement party.

Northwest Airlines was the only airline flying into Montana from the East. Diner's Club and American Express had introduced credit cards during the 1950's, but most students didn't qualify for credit. To buy a plane ticket I had to go to the Fifth Avenue Northwest Airlines ticket office at Rockefeller Plaza a few weeks before Thanksgiving, stand in line, examine the paper schedule with the agent, and pay by check.

I flew from La Guardia to Minneapolis on the largest and last of its propeller-driven airplanes, the DC 7. From there I flew on the considerably smaller DC 6 into Great Falls, arriving in the late afternoon in a moderate snowstorm. That plane went on to stops in Spokane and Seattle, but to get to Missoula I boarded a third, even smaller plane that was scheduled to stop first in Butte, then Helena, and with any luck at all, in Missoula. Flying into the "mountain stations" was difficult in every season, especially in the winter.

We were rushed across the snowy tarmac onto the plane. The pilot announced that we were heading right into the teeth of a winter storm blowing in from Alaska. He would do his best to get us to Butte, and probably to Helena, but it was likely that he wouldn't have the visibility to take off for Missoula.

The snow was heavy in Butte, and heavier landing in Helena at about 9 PM. The pilot said that he couldn't get clearance for take off. Those who wanted to get to Missoula would be met by a limousine and driven there.

I called Mom from a pay phone and told her to go to bed.

It took an hour for the limousine to arrive at the airport. It was a down-at-the-heels vintage stretch Packard with worn upholstery, tires as bald as egg shells, and the stench of ten thousand cigarettes. The four of us going to Missoula climbed in, two men and a woman who were salespeople and I. They occupied the bench back seat and I sat on a jump seat facing the passenger side.

The driver fishtailed out of the parking lot and headed for the Continental Divide and McDonald Pass, 3000 feet of winding road above

Helena, the rear end of the Packard continually sliding back and forth on the sharp turns. The three salespeople began heckling the driver to stop at one of the roadside taverns so they could have a drink, and for an hour I sat grousing—and righteously drinkless— in the steamy bar while they sipped highballs and smoked and told jokes.

When we started our ascent again, the dim headlights only made about a hundred feet of road visible ahead of us; the driver began to complain that he shouldn't have been sent on this trip. At the top of the pass a highway patrol car was blocking the road, red light twirling, turning the snowflakes pink. The patrolman said the Packard couldn't go down the other side of the pass without chains.

I asked him whether the bus from Helena would also be told to turn around. He said that the buses had chains; he suspected it would be late, but would be coming. He shuffled through the snow in his heavy boots over to his patrol car and radioed the dispatch office in Helena to check if it had left the Helena bus station. The message crackled back, "You betcha."

The Packard turned around and headed back to a tavern a few miles down the pass, and I sat in the patrol car to wait for the bus. At midnight I flagged it down, crunching through the snow in my soggy oxford shoes, suit, and Harris Tweed overcoat.

Mom fetched me from the Missoula bus station at 7 AM. The streets of Missoula were snowy but plowed and no self-respecting Montanan would hesitate to drive on packed snow.

I only stayed with Mom for a few days, long enough to celebrate Christmas and spend an uncomfortable hour with Dad who, in that short period of time, managed to tell me that I would be a terrible doctor because I had "no bedside manner," which I received with indignation, but remained silent.

My flight to the east the day after Christmas was scheduled to leave Missoula at 10 AM. Two more days of drifting snow had made the Missoula streets more treacherous; Dad offered to drive Mom and me to the airport and in a rare truce she accepted.

The airport was empty except for a lone agent sitting behind the counter at a metal desk. I handed him my suitcase and he glanced at my ticket to determine my destination, saw that it was Boston, tagged my bag, went back to his desk.

It was awkward standing around with Mom and Dad, and I knew they weren't comfortable either. I suggested we say goodbye now and I could wait until the flight landed in about 15 minutes.

After they left I sat in the empty waiting room. It seemed strange that it was empty so close to the departure time, one day after Christmas. After 45 minutes with no arriving plane, I walked back to the counter and asked the agent about my flight to Great Falls, where I would connect with a flight to Minneapolis.

"You gotta long wait. That flight gets in around 2:45."

"No, my ticket says the flight leaves at 10, and it's 10:45 now."

He scowled and reached toward me. "Here, lemme look at that ticket again."

He looked it over, shook his head, and handed it back. "That flight was discontinued after Thanksgiving, a month ago."

I was incredulous. How could a Fifth Avenue Northwest Airlines ticket office book me on a non-existent flight?

"Can I get the next flight, the one at 2:45?"

He took my ticket and went back to his desk. There were no computers; he had to call Seattle to see if he could rebook me. After talking for a while, he looked over at me and said "we can get you to Great Falls, but the connecting flight to Minneapolis is full."

Without a moment of hesitation, I told him that I needed to get to Boston today, that I was getting married tomorrow and that Northwest Airlines had screwed up my flight.

He pursed his lips, nodded his head, didn't say anything, and walked back to his desk with my ticket. He pulled the microphone toward him:

"Northwest 372, this is MSO, have you left Spokane yet?"

The speaker crackled with static. And then a voice sounded, "Aaahh, yah, this is 372, we're just taxiing, should be taking off in a few minutes."

"You full?"

"No, whatcha got?"

"I gotta feller here that needs to get to his wedding. New York put him on 208, but that stopped flying last month. Can you pick him up?"

A pause, and then the speaker crackled as he came back on. "Aaahh, yah! We should be able to do that. I'll land and turn off the port engine, just have him walk out and we'll drop the stairs." Should be about 35 minutes. You gotta clear runway?"

"Yup, I do. This Bill?"

"Aaahh yah."

"Thanks, Bill. Hey, I found a new hole on Rock Creek that's too far back for lazy people to get to. Whatcha say we go fishing this summer. Let me know."

In a half hour I could hear an approaching airplane. It came straight in, emerging from the clouds a few thousand feet from the end of the runway. It taxied fast to the front of the airport building, blowing up a storm of snowflakes. The port propeller was slowing, and when it was barely moving the door opened and a stewardess dropped the stairs down to the tarmac. I climbed on, the door closed, and 4 or 5 minutes after he landed we were taxiing to the end of the runway to take off.

I managed to catch my original flights from Great Falls and from Minneapolis and arrived in Boston where Margaret met me, on time.

As Margaret was driving up to Newburyport, I told her the story with great pride, hoping that she would tell me how resourceful I was. I suspect she disapproved. She was incapable of lying and didn't tell me that I was amazing.

The next evening the Wilkins had invited family members and friends from Newburyport to a cocktail party in their High Street house to announce the engagement and to introduce me to Newburyport society, such as it was. I had bought a Brooks Brothers' navy blue three-piece suit and an assortment of new silk neckties for the party. The Wilkins had decided that the best way for me to meet people was to have me tend a bar

Margaret

set up in the formal parlor, while Margaret's brother Bobby tended bar in the family parlor across the hall.

The cocktails were appropriate for the genteel crowd of largely older men and women—gin and tonic, Tom Collins, Scotch and soda, rye and Coca Cola. There were no wine or beer and nothing as complex as a whiskey sour or Manhattan or martini. Although I barely drank, I figured I was up to the challenge. Gradually people drifted in. Margaret walked back and forth between the two parlors chatting with the entirely familiar company. I limited myself to shaking hands and cheerily handing out drinks.

Margaret went out of her way to introduce me to one of her favorite relatives, who had taken her side in the family debate on whether she should dump me or marry me. By now I had loosened up and Aunt Katharine and I talked while I filled her gin and tonic order. After that I didn't see her the rest of the night.

After the party Margaret's brother told me that she had gone to his bar in the other parlor immediately after leaving mine. "He gave me a tonic and tonic," she said. "I hope he does better as a doctor than he does as a bartender. Do you think you could mix a gin and tonic that includes the gin?"

The next day Margaret and I drove into Boston. Because both of us had been away all fall, there hadn't been time to choose and set a diamond before the engagement was announced. Margaret's standard was her mother's ring, a perfect diamond of just over a carat. Somehow I had managed to accumulate a thousand dollars for Margaret's ring, a stone just under a carat with a single tiny flaw not visible without a magnifying glass.

By hook or by crook, as my mother used to say, I had crossed the fortified border between Newburyport and the lesser world of my childhood on a trip that had included a hair-raising blizzard ride in an ancient Packard with three drunk traveling salespeople, a Shanghaied airplane ride, and a stint as an amateur not-very-good bartender.

It never occurred to me to tell Dr. and Mrs. Wilkins that the ways in which I fell short of their expectations weren't important to me—that I wasn't about to transform myself into whatever model they would have liked more. Actually, quite the opposite occurred: their expectations *were* important to me and I figured out what I needed to change in order for all of us to be more comfortable.

They clearly did the same. It was a mutual accommodation, and as time went on, they went out of their way to include me. A part of that was because I changed behaviors that made them uncomfortable, but mostly I think it was because of their love for Margaret, and their own decency.

Chapter 8

Neurology Clerkship

Our third year was divided into six-week blocks, an eighth of the students in each block. For my first block, from June to mid-July, I chose neurology.

The role of the clinical clerk varied from specialty to specialty. In neurology and internal medicine students actively participated in caring for hospitalized patients, at 7 AM visiting their bedsides, reviewing overnight events in the record, and reviewing results of tests. We presented the history of new patients and reported on the progress of continuing patients during bedside rounds at 10 AM. When new patients were admitted, we "worked them up" by taking a very complete history, examining them, and reviewing any records of earlier care at Columbia-Presbyterian. Our admission notes, written with fountain pens, were four or five pages long on closely lined paper.

For the first time in medical school I felt comfortable just being myself, at home talking with and examining patients, excited to be learning constantly during the day and looking up what I needed to know about my patients' diseases and tests and therapies in my room at night. There was just one other classmate there; we performed at about the same level of proficiency and I had no sense of being in a competition. It was as though I had been living underground rather unhappily for two years and suddenly had emerged into daylight and warmth. Finally, this is what I had expected medical school to be like.

The residents were supportive and welcoming. They enjoyed teaching, standing with us at the bedside as we performed the complicated but critical neurologic examination, and assisting us as we learned how to do spinal taps. They had all trained for two or three years in internal medicine before beginning their neurology residencies and were comfortable with caring for whatever medical issues the patients might have in addition to or as a cause of the neurological symptoms that had gotten them admitted. I began to sort out the various diseases of the peripheral nerves, the movement disorders like Parkinson's disease, the balance and tremor conditions that were a result of cerebellar disease, and the catastrophic wreckage of intracranial bleeding or stroke.

Each week the residents chose three or four patients to present to Professor Houston Merritt, Chairman of the Department of Neurology, the dean of the medical school, and the sole author of one of the two most famous American textbooks of neurology. The cases chosen to impress Dr. Merritt or to get his suggestions for diagnosis or treatment were either dramatic presentations of classic diseases, or diagnostic dilemmas.

In the fifth week my resident asked me to present a patient with a difficult-to-diagnose condition—tremors, slurred speech, difficulty walking because of poor balance, and lightheadedness when she stood up because of a drop in her blood pressure. I had spent hours with Miss Forest, admitting her, presenting the results of our latest tests every day, and talking with her about our plans and impressions. She was a young-looking forty-year-old woman with smooth brown skin and wavy black hair. She quickly grasped everything we told her and even after two weeks, with neither a diagnosis nor any treatment, she was still patient and gracious, as though she were taking care of us rather than we taking care of her.

We brought her in a wheelchair to the auditorium where Dr. Merritt sat at a small table, facing the room crowded with residents, nurses, students, and faculty. I stood off to the side facing both Dr. Merritt and the audience, with Miss Forest beside me.

It took four or five minutes for me to present her history, physical examination and data, all from memory, the expected standard at Columbia-Presbyterian.

Dr. Merritt looked bored throughout. When I finished, he asked, "What do you think is wrong with her?"

"She was initially thought to have Parkinson's disease, but we think she has Shy-Drager Syndrome, Dr. Merritt."

Houston Merritt was a man of many written but few spoken words. He got up from his chair and walked over to Miss Woods; bending over, he took off her slipper, watching to see if her toes spread when the back of the slipper stroked the bottom of her foot.

"She doesn't have Shy-Drager syndrome," he said, and sat down. "Keep working on it, Sonny."

The maneuver he had done was to evoke a Babinski reflex by stroking the bottom of the foot. If the toes fan out, which is abnormal, the test is positive. Hers didn't when he examined her, although I had evoked a positive response several times when I examined her. I didn't argue with him, although I thought he was wrong.

Apparently this was his usual style—he didn't teach, or really even demonstrate, he just made a judgment and it was up to us to figure out why. The residents made a game out of trying to prove him wrong. It was a lopsided game and he wasn't even working hard.

Because he often used the key to his Rolls-Royce automobile to stroke the foot, it was part of his mythology that he could evoke a Babinski when no one else could.

The six weeks went swiftly; I was enthralled with neurology. The residents were very positive and complimentary and I was sure that I was going to get an A. The day before the clerkship ended I asked if I could scrub in for a diagnostic operation on a patient I had admitted a few days before who had a brain mass with progressive loss of the use of her arm. The plan was to drill a hole in her skull and place a needle in the mass, sucking out some of its content to look for an infection or cancer.

In the operating room I could see nothing but the four heads of the neurosurgeons clustered around a small drill hole in the patient's skull. There were no effective imaging techniques to be sure that the needle was in the right place except operating room X-rays in three positions that had to be developed four floors below; each set of images took ten minutes while the whole surgical team stood at the table waiting for the radiologist's report.

An hour into the surgery they succeeded in getting a small amount of tissue and about two teaspoons of bloody liquid from the mass. The neurosurgery resident turned to me and handed me the stoppered test tube into which he had squirted the fluid, asking me to run it to the microbiology laboratory to have them do a quick stain and microscopic evaluation.

Thrilled, I grabbed the tube and instead of waiting for the agonizingly slow Neurological Institute elevators, I decided to take the stairs.

Rushing, at the third floor my heel caught on a stair and I fell headlong down the stairs, the tube smashing and its contents spreading on the stair's concrete.

My career as a medical student was certainly now ended. This was the worst possible thing I could have done, since a risky procedure and a patient's life were at stake and the effort was possibly worthless now that there was no sample.

I was in a panic. Four or five fake explanations immediately popped into my head, each more improbable than the previous one. I had to let them know while they were still working on her so that they could try for a second sample. I ran up the six flights of stairs and, breathless, rushed through the operating room doors. The circulating nurse threw her body in front of mine:

"You can't go in. You have to put on a gown and a mask first."

"Can I talk to them from the doorway, please."

"What is it?"

"I fell down the stairs and the test tube broke. Can they get another sample?"

Neurology Clerkship

I couldn't see anything of her face because of her mask, but her eyes widened. "I'll tell them."

And with that I was dismissed, probably mercifully.

The next day I finished the clerkship. I never heard about her diagnosis. Fortunately, the neurosurgeons hadn't bothered to learn my name and apparently didn't inquire. My grade in Neurology was an A.

CHAPTER 9

Married

Mom came to New York City for a few days before the wedding. It was her first visit to the East Coast. She appreciated everything she saw—responding at a high level of pleased amazement when we visited the Empire State Building, Rockefeller Center, the Fifth Avenue shops, and the Oyster Bar in Grand Central Station.

On the last evening we visited the World's Fair and then went to watch a baseball game at nearby Shea Stadium, where once again the hapless Mets were losing. She didn't care much about the game but was very interested in the size of the stadium and the number of people attending. When they announced the attendance shortly after the game started—about 34,000, not bad for a weeknight game—she was dazzled. "There are more people here than in any town in Montana!"

On Thursday evening we flew on the Eastern Airlines shuttle to Boston; Margaret met us at the airport and drove us north to Newburyport. For me introducing Mom to Dr. and Mrs. Wilkins was the most fraught event of the wedding. Mom also was nervous about meeting her future in-laws, whose background was vastly different than hers. When Margaret came to Montana to see me the summer after we met, she and Mom got along effortlessly. I had not told Mom anything about the Wilkins' opposition to our marriage but she knew that Margaret came from two families with ancient American roots and that the Wilkins were an affluent family with prominent friends. From a few fragmentary comments that she dropped, but avoided discussing, I knew that she was uncomfortable that she was divorced and that she worked as a relatively poorly paid administrator at the University of Montana. More openly she worried that she would not be able to keep up conversations with any of the people she would be meeting, including my medical school friends and college roommates.

Having given up their opposition, Margaret's parents had thrown themselves into wedding planning, as though Margaret were marrying the suitor of their dreams. They were warm and gracious with Mom, who quickly relaxed and enjoyed their house, learning about the beautiful antique furniture and the history of its original owners.

I followed behind her as they showed her to her room at the top of the stairs. In the hallway they had set up tables with wedding gifts. There were two large tables covered with linen cloths loaded with silver and china and crystal and elegant baking and cooking ware from the Wilkins's friends and family. There was a diminutive table with modest gifts from my friends and family—ice buckets, copper ashtrays, towels, hot plate holders, a set of carving knives from my dad, a cut-glass decanter from my brother Sam. In the middle were eight settings of Royal Dalton China tagged, "a gift from the groom's family." Margaret's mother thanked her and said that was exactly what Margaret had hoped for.

However, the China wasn't from Mom. I had secretly bought it and sent it in Mom's name without telling anyone, including Margaret. I was stunned and embarrassed: I had not realized that there would be a display of wedding gifts or that Mom would confront a gift attributed to her that she knew nothing about.

In a conversation about wedding planning a few months earlier, Dr. and Mrs. Wilkins suggested what they thought would be an "appropriate" gift from my family— that, since the Wilkins had given us substantial wedding gifts of silverware, it would be proper and traditional for my family to give us our China. I knew that paying for the flight to the east coast, her wedding clothes, and her hotel in New York City were straining Mom's budget; suggesting that she buy us English bone China was out of the question. So, I squeezed the money out of my shrunken checking account to buy the China, but hadn't told Mom, because I felt it would embarrass her to know that she had been expected to do something that was simply not possible.

Before dinner Mom and I took a walk in the garden and I mumbled an explanation. She looked uncomfortable, but as usual we didn't talk about feelings, hers or mine.

The style of marriage in Newburyport was beyond my experience and expectations in every way. I had been to exactly one wedding, my brother's, in Montana. The Wilkins began talking about Margaret's gift to me, and mine to her, as though they assumed that naturally we would give each other wedding presents. Buying her an engagement ring and a wedding band I had expected, but not a wedding gift.

I was trying to seem an appropriate son-in-law and during my spring break I set off on a search of Boston's antique jewelry stores to find a gift that seemed sufficiently generous. In a tiny shop on Beacon Street with dusty windows and the Dickensian name of Trefrey and Partridge I found a 19th Century gold and diamond brooch. I was wearing a suit and spoke in my most convincing Harvard/English accent, reserved for stuffy establishments where I felt outclassed. I wrote the check without blanching at the amount, $395, about what I paid for my Bard Hall room for a year.

The two rickety men who owned the shop invited me to come back. My guess is that they hadn't been able to find a buyer for the brooch for years.

Margaret and her parents found an early 19th Century banjo clock, circa 1840, made by Horace Tifts in Attleboro, Massachusetts as her gift to me.

I had three days off to get married—Friday and Saturday I would be in Newburyport, and Sunday Margaret and I would be setting up housekeeping in New York City. On Monday I would once again be a medical student.

Margaret and her family had the two days fully scheduled. At noon on Friday the Wilkins hosted a party including, in addition to Mom and me, Margaret's aunt and uncle Morrill, my college roommate and best friend, Geoff Nowlis, and Margaret's maid of honor Ginny Johnson, who she had lived with during summer school at Harvard and then during her year at Oberlin.

The lunch was in the Swett-Isley House on 4 High Road in adjacent Newbury, built in 1670 and over the three centuries used as a candy shop, tavern, candle maker, printing shop, and private home. The long dining room had a single table, limiting conversation. The Wilkins had seated Mom safely between Aunt Katharine and Uncle Tony Dodge. Curious, straightforward, and warm, they were able to fill Mom in on the cast of characters and the history of Newburyport, and they also kept Mom safely away from Aunt Frances, who would have spent the entire meal complaining about her frailties, having never recovered from being dragged from her home in the south to the frigid New England wilderness.

On Friday afternoon William Dowd, a harpsichord-maker from Cambridge, Massachusetts, set up a harpsichord in the family parlor that a local quartet would rehearse on later in the day for the music they would perform the next afternoon. Dowd stayed for an hour after tuning the harpsichord to give an impromptu concert.

After a quick change of clothes, we were off to the Morrill's High Street house for a cocktail party and reception for everyone who had made it to Newburyport by then. That house—where Margaret's mother grew up—was even larger than the Wilkins' house, again with parlors on both sides of a central hallway and staircase, and also furnished with beautiful New England antiques. Dr. and Mrs. Wilkins' best friends—many of the same people who had attended the engagement party—were there, along with a few of my medical school friends who had come up from New York City a day early to tour Massachusetts' North Coast. The Wilkins' good friends Jane and Justin Dart had come from California, donating 10 cases of Schramsberg champagne along with a wedding gift of 100 shares of Rexall

Drug, the company that Mr. Dart was president of, worth about $3000, for "a trip to Europe or a down payment on a house."

I found Aunt Katharine and asked her if I could fetch a gin and tonic for her, one that actually had gin in it. She laughed and said she was already two down and finished for the night.

Margaret escorted Mom and me from group to group to introduce us. The conversation was friendly and limited—none of the Newburyport guests had any stake in getting to know either Mom or me beyond a polite introduction. Margaret and her family were the centerpiece of the evening, which was what I had imagined and hoped for. I was already in a daze and my cheeks were tired from all the smiling.

I managed not to say anything weird, or at least nothing that got back to me.

The next morning Margaret's family and the wedding party went to Aunt Katharine's and Uncle Tony's house, almost as old as 4 High Road, with low-ceilinged rooms and several fireplaces that had been used for cooking, six feet wide and six feet high. I have no recollection of that breakfast beyond Mom's delight and amazement in having a chance to be in a house nearly 300 years old. By now Aunt Katharine and Uncle Tony were her favorites.

Margaret, her sister and her mother disappeared for the rest of the morning and early afternoon. I watched the catering company set up tents in the backyard, set out tables and silver chafing dishes and more tables with silver trays and crystal punch bowls. The quartet came around 3 pm to rehearse one more time. Bertrand Steeves, the minister from the First Unitarian Church, came early to check out how the ceremony would be sandwiched just inside the front door, with people looking in from the hallways and the two parlors. Jeff and I changed into our suits.

I had thought that the tents were superfluous, but fortunately the caterer had insisted and, as the time for the wedding came, a storm was brewing in the western sky.

At precisely 4 PM the quartet began to play and in pairs the wedding party descended the steep staircase, I with my mother, then Bobby with Margaret's mother, then Mary, then Ginny Johnson with Jeff. There was a pause before Margaret, wearing her mother's and grandmother's wedding dress, descended on Dr. Wilkins' arm. People strained to get a glimpse through the parlor doors and from the crowded hall.

Margaret and I had met with Reverend Steeves in the spring to plan the service. I was an onlooker as Margaret snipped away some of the more oppressive language in the traditional wedding service; then she pressed him to leave out the usual references to supernatural beings—she was from that branch of the Unitarian Church that believed that the origin and meaning of life could be discovered without needing to refer to a narrowly conceived Christian god. She also declined to "obey."

The minister had not found it in his conscience to fully comply, and—as though an offended spirit sent down an "Ahem"—when Reverend Steeves intoned, "We are gathered together in the presence of God," an enormous flash of lightning and deafening blast of thunder drowned out the service. Hard rains began. There were nervous giggles. Geoff, a thorough-going atheist, raised his arms in a wide V above his head like Moses receiving the tablets from the skies, and everyone began to laugh. It only took a few more minutes for the "I do's", the exchange of rings, the kiss, and then our pivot to look at everyone peering in from three directions. It was over in five minutes:

"Margaret Dodge Wilkins, oldest daughter of Dr. and Mrs. Robert W. Wilkins, of Newburyport, Massachusetts, a recent graduate of Harvard College and Oberlin College married Gordon Lee Noel, also a graduate of Harvard and currently a medical student at Columbia University in New York City, son of Leah and Robert Noel of Missoula, Montana, were married on the afternoon of 17 July in the Wilkins home in Newburyport, Massachusetts, followed by a catered lawn party."

The storm had left the lovely gardens behind the Wilkins' house cool and green and fresh. A soft warm breeze blew in from the west carrying the faintest smell of the salt marshes. There was, of course, no crab, but there were lobster rolls and lobster Newburg and fancy sandwiches on white bread with the crusts cut off, huge trays of cheeses and crackers and three kinds of punch and dozens of bottles of Schramsberg being raced about by skinny men in skinny black pants, white jackets, and gloved hands, trays of glasses on one upturned hand and a Champagne bottle in the other, held by the bottom high above their heads.

There was a toast where Dr. Wilkins welcomed me to the family. He seemed sincere, but possibly also a little tipsy. Geoff offered a lengthy toast and managed not to say anything either blasphemous or comprehensible.

The wedding was at 4:00. The Wilkins had indicated that they didn't like long parties, and we had scheduled our flight to New York City from Boston at 8:30 PM. The Wilkins had thought it would be indecorous for us to leave their house and drive up High Street in a car decorated and dragging cans, so we had arranged for Margaret's car to be hidden a short distance away. By 7:00 we had changed clothes and descended from the second floor together, our feet barely touching the stairs. Margaret and I were both in suits, mine grey, hers green. We were young and willowy and excited. In a shower of rice my friend John Baker drove us away to the airport.

We learned afterwards that when most of the guests had dispersed Geoff spent the evening hammering out songs on the harpsichord and the family sat around in the guest parlor talking about the wedding. I later heard from the Wilkins that they had really enjoyed getting to know Mom, and she said the same about them. The Wilkins had put on a wonderful day for us.

We landed at LaGuardia at 9:30 on a steamy, stinky, hot July Saturday night. We still had the smell of the freshly rained-on back yard and salt marshes of Newburyport in our heads, but now everything smelled familiarly of melting asphalt and airplane and automobile fumes.

The taxi ride to our new home in the Bridge Apartments took only twenty minutes and soon we were deposited on St. Nicolas Avenue with our suitcases. We took the elevator to the 28th floor and I rather awkwardly carried Margaret through the apartment door. I had arranged the furniture that had come down from Newburyport a week before, but her clothes, her books, cooking gear given to her by her mother and everything I had moved out of my Bard Hall room was in boxes. I had made up the bed and put towels in the bathroom just before I left for the wedding.

I suppose that wedding nights are often different than imagined beforehand. Ours was bizarre: at about 2 AM we were awakened by the distant sounds of fire trucks and police cars and ambulances. Through our shadeless windows we could see flickering orange light. A five-alarm fire was raging across the East River in the Bronx. We slept fitfully.

I was used to waking early and was up making a small breakfast from a few groceries I had laid in when Margaret appeared, sleepily. She disappeared into the bathroom, and a few minutes later sat down at the table where I was eating cereal.

I was in full project mode, thrumming happily at the prospect of making our first home: "I thought we should wash out all the cabinets and the refrigerator and the bathroom medicine cabinet before we unpack. The renters before us didn't do a very good job of cleaning."

Margaret burst into tears. In a little while, she said: "For two weeks I have for the first time in my life felt like a princess—feted at showers and luncheons, wrapped up in planning, unwrapping and taking notes on gifts. The wedding and the parties were heavenly. I don't want to come down from that feeling. I don't want to clean out cabinets!"

On Monday morning thirty-six hours after the wedding, I began my surgery specialties clerkship. Margaret was no longer a princess, and I had turned back into an ordinary medical student.

CHAPTER 10

Internal Medicine Clerkship

For three months I had been learning the ropes of being a clinical clerk, first on neurology, and then on surgical subspecialties. For those of us who were thinking that we wanted to be a physician who takes care of sick adults rather than becoming a surgeon or an obstetrician or pediatrician, the internal medicine clerkship, twice as long as any other, was both our most comprehensive introduction to physicianship and the gateway to a good residency. Even for those not planning to be internists, doing well in the medicine clerkship was critical to being competitive for residencies in surgery and most other specialties.

In October, thirty of us started three months of medicine. We washed and ironed our short white coats over the weekend and on Monday morning we lugged our heavy *Cecil and Loeb Textbook of Medicine* in one hand and our microscope in the other to a conference room on the 9th floor of Presbyterian Hospital. At 7 AM we were "oriented" by Dr. Tapley, a slender 50-year-old physician with silver hair, a faintly British accent, and an inscrutable Cheshire-Cat smile. He gave us our ward assignments and steered us to the student laboratories on the eighth and ninth floors where we set up our microscopes, cubby-holed our books and bags of physical examination equipment, and stowed away our gear for doing blood counts. I put my sack lunch in the suspicious smelling refrigerator among the cardboard sample boxes of this morning's stool and urine collections. Then in tens we walked a few dozen feet to the three wards that would be our working homes until Christmas. Taped to the glass window of the nurses' stations we found the list of patients assigned to us, whose blood samples we now needed to draw for blood counts, chemical analysis, and cultures.

My team's wards were Eight and Nine West, each with twelve beds divided between the two sides of a long room, separated from each other only by a curtain that could be pulled around the sides and foot of the bed. Our patients knew that at seven they needed to be fasting and ready for the swarm of students to invade the room with a tray of vacuum tubes and an array of needles and syringes to draw their blood.

As our bunch of green students trickled into the room, the patients were looking at us with expressions varying from indifference to dismay: for days or weeks they had gotten to know the students who preceded us, and they guessed correctly that we would not yet be proficient in finding a good vein and managing to draw blood with just a single stick.

My first patient was a woman all but mummified by her white hospital gown, white sheets, and white blanket. There was no arm in sight. She avoided looking at me by burying her face in her pillow.

I addressed her only visible part, her left ear. "Hello. I am Gordon Noel. I'm your new medical student."

She grunted but said nothing.

"May I draw two tubes of blood?"

No answer.

Her name was Maria Garcia. It dawned on me that perhaps she might not speak English. I introduced myself again, this time in Spanish, and asked her name. She didn't answer, and I realized that my three years of Spanish in high school and college had not prepared me to ask even the simple question, "May I take a tube of blood?" I managed to ask her if I could possess her blood, perhaps close enough, but still she did not answer. I reached for her arm and tried to gently pull it out in front of her so that I could act out the motions of taking blood, but she pulled her arm away.

Then the lady in the next bed called to me: "She is stone deaf and hasn't heard a word you said."

No one had told me. There was no sign over her bed.

By eight o'clock we had gotten the bloods drawn and were all hunched over our microscopes doing blood counts and urinalyses. I had trouble drawing blood from two of my patients and with embarrassment had to ask Bruce Goldreyer and Oscar Garfein, our very smart and very cocky interns, to draw the blood for me. They made it clear that this was a one-time assist that they didn't expect to have to do again.

At ten sharp our attending physicians arrived for rounds. Dr. Alfred Fishman was a pulmonary physiologist and Dr. Sydney Werner was a practicing endocrinologist specializing in thyroid disease. We were told to listen carefully to Drs. Goldreyer and Garfein, who would briefly present a summary of each patient because, beginning tomorrow, we were expected to present a succinct, well-organized progress report on each patient and to know every lab and imaging result. Dr. Werner— whose bulging cheeks and bulging eyes gave him the look of an elderly chipmunk wearing a tie and long white coat—said that, since we were new to internal medicine and had not yet gotten to review the charts of our patients, we should ask questions about anything we didn't understand.

Fifteen of us—ten students, two interns, two attendings, and the resident—walked from bed to bed down the left side of the ward. After the intern's presentation, Dr. Fishman or Dr. Werner spoke with the patient, performed a brief exam, and then turned to us with questions or an explanation of some aspect of the patient's illness. The patient in the fourth bed had severe hyperthyroidism, Dr. Werner's specialty. He got quite exercised demonstrating the physical signs of high levels of thyroid hormone, and then quizzed the interns on the proper dosing of a drug called Tapazole. I had no idea what the drug was, or how hyperthyroidism was treated.

Taking to heart Dr. Werner's admonition to ask questions about anything we didn't understand, I asked, "Dr. Werner, what is Tapazole?"

He glared at me. "Sonny, if you don't know what Tapazole is, you have no business being here."

He might have looked like a chipmunk, but he was a vicious chipmunk, and I faded to the back of the group of students and kept out sight for the rest of rounds. I looked up Tapazole when I got home. We had been taught only generic names of drugs, and were encouraged to not use trade names. Tapazole was the commercial name of a drug I did know about, methimazole, although even then I didn't know much about it.

The interns—three months out of medical school but P & S graduates—were impressive. The West Team had beds for eighteen women patients on the ninth floor and eighteen men on the eighth floor. Not all our beds were full, but in less than two hours we rounded on 25 patients, spending four or five minutes with most, a minute or two with a patient that was progressing smoothly and needed no change in treatment, and about ten minutes each with two patients who had been admitted since yesterday's rounds. Without reference to notes or a chart, Drs. Garfein and Goldreyer presented a thumbnail sketch of each "old patient" in a few lines, and then the update:

"Mr. O'Reilly is the 62-year-old bus driver admitted twelve days ago with antero-lateral st-segment depression after three hours of crushing chest pain. His enzymes and ESR and white count all rose and are beginning to return to normal. He is on complete bed rest with a dental soft diet and stool softeners and he is chest-pain free without morphine or nitroglycerin and says he is in good spirits because he survived his heart attack and outlived his dad who died when he had his first heart attack at 55. He has no new complaints."

Dr. Fishman was overseeing all the male patients and stood at the head of the bed on Mr. O'Reilly's right. Oscar, who was the male ward intern, stood on the patient's left, and the ten students stood in an arc like a choir of angels around the end of the bed. Dr. Fishman took a stethoscope out of his pocket and listened to Mr. O'Reilly's chest and heart, asked him if he had any questions, and then turned to Oscar, asking "What's your plan?"

"Well, it is an uncomplicated MI. So, three weeks of bed rest with gradual mobilization. He probably has had untreated hypertension, and if that develops in the hospital, I would start him on a thiazide diuretic, and then discharge him home to see me in my clinic in three weeks. If he is free of further pain for six weeks, then he can return to work."

"What is his work?"

"He drives a city bus in Queens."

"And if his pain recurs?"

" Nitroglycerine. He'll have to stop work unless we can prevent it."

In 1965, that is what we had to offer. If a patient survived a heart attack we tried to manage the one risk factor for which we had decent treatment, hypertension; routine catheterization with imaging of the heart's blood supply was still a half-decade away, and routine coronary surgery or dilating the coronary arteries with a balloon catheter weren't yet available. Based on concern that the spot in the heart where muscle had died resulted in weakness in the cardiac wall that exercise might cause to rupture, patients were kept at complete bed rest for four to six weeks. When they finally got out of bed they were as weak as kittens and often needed another week or two in a nursing home to recover basic functions like walking to the bathroom or climbing a flight of stairs. There was nothing else to do but hope that another episode of infarction—death of heart muscle due to inadequate delivery of blood to a section of the heart—did not throw them into heart failure or a life-ending abnormal rhythm.

The reason that in 1965 our two interns could each take care of eighteen patients was that we kept patients so long. If a patient needed ten days of antibiotics intravenously, the only way they could receive them was in the hospital. New diabetics stayed in the hospital until their self-administration of insulin was producing fairly smooth blood sugar control. To facilitate getting tests done, patients with mysterious, hard-to-diagnose problems stayed in the hospital until a diagnosis was made even if they were receiving no treatment and could have cared for themselves in their homes.

Every morning at 7 AM all thirty internal medicine students arrived at the hospital to draw bloods, review the nurses' and any doctor's notes on our patients, perform the laboratory tests, and do any procedures that the interns ordered, like spinal taps or thoracenteses (removal of fluid between a patient's lung and chest wall). Although the patient's intern was never more than a few minutes away, we did these procedures by ourselves after they watched us once.

Other hospital staff members could tell what role young doctors played simply by looking at our clothes. Male students wore short white coats over wool slacks and dress shirts with neckties. The women wore white coats over dresses—women in pants were rare. Our male interns and residents and even the chief resident, wore "whites"—short white coats over white pants with a button fly. Women residents wore white skirts with sensible low heel leather shoes. The attendings wore long white laboratory coats. No one wore scrubs, which were reserved for the operating rooms. Our shoes were leather and stiff; there were no sneakers or clogs.

Interns were on every other night and every other weekend—arriving at 7 AM on their admitting day, and leaving around 4 or 5 the next evening. Patients were admitted through the night, so interns were rarely functioning on more than ten hours of sleep every two nights.

Students were on in pairs every fifth night. We admitted every patient, took a complete history and did a comprehensive physical examination, drew all the admission blood tests and performed any needed procedures. The next morning we presented the new patients, from memory, our hands behind our back, standing in the interns' position on the patient's left hand, speaking to the attending and the arc of students. We knew all of the laboratory data, all the medications and the doses. When they were admitted we reviewed the patients' old records—sometimes no more than a few pages thick, sometimes no more than a few pages thick, sometimes multiple volumes as high as a foot or two. Each of us would admit one or two patients overnight. The interns, residents, and sometimes even the students easily clocked 100-hour weeks and thought it was normal.

Outside the hospital we had no expectation of more than survival activities for those three months, other than an occasional weekend day off.

Interns and residents had call rooms to sleep in, although much of the time they were up all night. On rare quiet nights, students slept a few hours on the hard couches in the solariums, large, glass windowed rooms at the end of the wards that in earlier decades had been used for "open-air" care of tuberculosis patients. In the winter the clanking cast iron radiators were not up to the task of heating that vast, frigid space and we shivered under a thin cotton blanket that sometimes a friendly nurse would autoclave to give us a warm start.

The central skills that students learned on the medicine clerkship were taking the comprehensive history, performing a detailed physical examination, and recording both. The write-ups were often six or seven hand-written pages long. This was the most complete data base for the patient, a permanent part of the record, and scrutinized by the interns, resident, attending, and consultants. We were expected to know every detail of a patient's medical life: if the patient spoke good English and had a good memory, the history could take as much as an hour. The chart review took as long as necessary to go all the way back to the patient's first visit to the Medical Center—sometimes as much as five or six hours. We took the physical examination very seriously—along with the history, simple lab tests, and simple X-ray images, we had nothing else to formulate a list of possible diagnoses and create a hypothesis from which we proposed a course of treatment. The patients were undifferentiated—that is, no senior doctor had seen them first and admitted them with a diagnosis and set of orders: that was the residents' job. Although patients might have pneumonia or a heart attack, we took a step back and presented them as "cough, sputum, and fever" or "chest pain" to encourage everyone hearing the presentation to think of all the causes of those symptoms, to not jump to the obvious diagnosis and miss the possibility that something more unusual might be going on.

The students were with the patients for 12 hours every day. We had each other and our interns and resident as role models, and most of the patients were with us for long enough to know if we had gotten the diagnosis and treatment right. Usually we had: most of the patients had straightforward infections of the lung or urinary system, or exacerbation of chronic lung disease, or heart failure, or out-of-control diabetes or coronary artery disease. Once we had become familiar with the common problems, we savored the diagnostic dilemmas: fever without a known cause, unexplained weight loss, inflammation of the heart, inflammatory arthritis, rheumatic fever, abdominal pain, anemia, leukemia, meningitis, seizures, nodules in the lungs that could be cancer or tuberculosis or sarcoidosis.

The written workup was not only the central document of our participation in our patients' care, it was the text from which we were tutored. Twice each week in groups of six we met with our preceptor, Dr. Earle Wheaton, who at each meeting read through one of our workups out loud, asked questions about what additional information the other students would like to have, what diagnoses came to their minds, what connections with other aspects of the patient's history might serve as clues in separating one possible cause from another. Then the six of us and Dr. Wheaton visited the bedside, where he talked with and examined the patient. From watching him we learned more about history-taking and examination.

Dr. Wheaton had been a student and resident at Columbia, so he was deeply familiar with the traditions and expectations. His presence was extraordinary: tall, slender, quiet, and calm, with the demeanor of the actor Jimmie Stewart. He instilled in our patients and us instant confidence while in no way flashing his knowledge or making us uncomfortable because of what we did not yet know. He practiced in a suburb about forty five minutes away, and twice a week for three months he taught us for an hour and then spent the afternoon caring for uninsured patients in Vanderbilt clinic—all with no salary, just for the love of the program and the expectation of giving back some of what he had gotten as a student and resident.

The vast majority of our faculty and half the residents had also been Columbia students. New interns who came from other medical schools—typically from Harvard, Hopkins, Cornell, or the University of Pennsylvania—were tutored in how to write up their histories to the Columbia standards; in a few weeks they couldn't be told from P & S graduates.

The high priest of the P & S history, Dana Atchley, met with all thirty students once a week and drily read one 0f our workups out loud, criticizing everything from bad handwriting and poor grammar to incomplete or contradictory information. No matter how much detail we included, he always found troves of unasked questions, the absence of which he said made our workups incomplete: if we said that a patient woke up at night with abdominal pain, Dr. Atchley complained that we didn't describe what the patient had for dinner. He was so crotchety, humorless, and monotonous that keeping our attention on him was hard. No one ever missed a session because the department treated him nearly as a deity whose devoted patients, including Elizabeth Taylor and a raft of other celebrities, had just contributed a new private practice building in his honor.

Someone told me that Dr. Atchley drove a taxi for a summer in the roaring mining town, Butte Montana, when he was in college. That made him seen more approachable. Hoping he might warm up to me, I mentioned it to him one afternoon after his dreary session, after saying that I had lived in Butte for a few years. He looked at me as though I had worms crawling out of my eyeballs and wordlessly shuffled away.

I sometimes had that effect on people.

I swore that I would never stay in a teaching hospital if I were approaching his level of physical decrepitude. I was young and had some attitudes that I would later amend: in time I met many other clinicians his age who were brilliant and vibrant and exemplary.

Columbia was a place where tradition—much of it admirable—infused everything we did, from the textbooks we chose to the way we wrote our notes and presented. The faculty and the residents and most of the students (with no basis in data) believed that Columbia was the best medical school in the United States, and in the world second only to Oxford; we couldn't imagine why anyone would want to be anywhere else.

Our interns changed every month, so in the three months of the clerkship I met half the intern class. Most of them were smart as hell, and many of them were smart-asses, quick to let you know how dumb you were and, by inference, that you weren't in their class. Dealing with ten students at a time, I don't know if they ever praised or encouraged anyone. I never heard an intern or resident say, "When I was a student, I had no clue what I was doing; don't feel bad, you're getting it." They carried themselves as though they were proficient from birth. I was unable to imagine them fighting forest fires or working on a farm during their college summers, or taking a night off in medical school to go dancing or spend a night watching Bogart and Bacall.

Every day it was clear to me that those of my classmates who had been quietly booking it from sunup to sundown seven days a week during the first two years were better prepared for what was expected of us. Almost all of the best had been pre-meds or science majors and came to our early lectures already familiar with biochemistry and physiology and anatomy. None of them were among the dozen of us with raised arms confessing to being liberal arts majors; none of them had thought that a "lesion" was a "legion," or that "bilirubin" was a Jewish biochemist. The questions asked at the bedside by our attending physicians were rarely stark basic science facts; they were clinical questions that we would not yet have been taught the answer to, but might be able to figure out if we could apply our basic science knowledge. The students who were soaring had been reading their pharmacology or pathology texts in the second year and simultaneously their *Cecil-Loeb Textbook of Medicine*, learning clinical medicine as they learned basic science, immediately putting the basic science to work. That had not occurred to me, and had it been suggested, I doubt I would have had the time or the discipline to do what they were doing, because I had not yet become motivated to devote every minute to memorizing science and reading about what I would need to know a year or two into the future.

By the time I got to the Internal Medicine clerkship I had mostly set aside my disappointment over the unpleasantness of the preclinical years, but I keenly felt that I was underprepared. Now I was spending every waking minute taking care of my patients and reading about the other 90% of patients on our team. I came away from conferences like Team Rounds where residents presented two difficult patients, inspired by listening to a faculty member skillfully dismantle the patient's history and data to create a framework of pathophysiology that explained the symptoms and led to agreeing with the chosen treatment or correcting it. The presentations were the best part of the week and the faculty members left me in hopeful awe.

The most useful hour of teaching that had the longest impact on me was done by John Brust, another P & S graduate who would complete three years of medical residency and then another three years of neurology residency. He delivered a list of mandates that went something like this:

Get help from everyone but don't trust anyone. The patient is your responsibility and you need to be sure you are doing the right thing—so consult, but also confirm.

Write down everything you don't know; before you go to sleep look up everything.

Keep a notebook. Write down the useful references, formulas, lists of differential diagnoses.

Before you leave the hospital be sure that you know the results of every test, every X-ray, every consultation.

Don't wait for the x-ray report. Go to radiology and review the X-ray yourself.

Never leave a problem for someone else to figure out because you failed to address it.

Never pretend you know something that you don't know. Just say you don't know, and make sure you know it next time.

Place a check in red in front of every test result so you know you have seen it. Circle abnormal results in red.

Listen to the nurses. Seek out each of your patients' nurses and find out if there is anything they think is being overlooked or needs to be changed. They are smart and they spend more time with the patients than you do.

All idols have feet of clay. Even the most-perfect-seeming attending or resident will be wrong some of the time.

Write legibly, especially orders.

What he didn't say was that perfection comes at a high price.

Every Wednesday Dr. Bradley, the Samuel Bard Professor of Medicine and department chairman made professor's rounds for an hour, during which three students presented a patient to him. Famous for his impatience, humorlessness, narrow clinical knowledge, and total absence of charisma, he was disparaged by the residents as the failed successor to the most revered chairmen in Columbia's history, Robert F. Loeb.

The rules for Dr. Bradley's rounds were that all patients had to be bathed, covered with a sheet and propped upright in their beds when he arrived for rounds. The nurses rushed to get the patients ready by 9 AM. All thirty students assembled just outside the doors of the ward; the nurses in their white dresses and caps stood in a hushed line, like privates assembled for inspection. We entered the ward and the nurses closed the doors behind us. No one was allowed in until the rounds were completed. The students clumped three deep around the bedside of the first patient to be presented, many of them more interested in what disaster might befall their classmate than what they might learn from the Samuel Bard Professor.

My turn came about six weeks into the clerkship. I had been taking care of Miss Brawling, a black woman in her fifties, with low-grade fevers, several types of skin rashes, renal failure, weight loss, and multiple-joint arthritis, who still did not have a firm diagnosis after two weeks in the hospital. One possibility was systemic lupus erythematosis, a rare and usually deadly disease that is most common in black women, affecting the connective tissue, immune systems and eventually every organ.

The most definitive diagnostic test available then was the LE prep. On her first day I drew a tube of blood and carried it in my shirt pocket to keep it warm and stirred. After an hour I did a blood smear; the test is positive for lupus if, on searching through the smear, white cells are found that have consumed other white cells. I was sure it would be positive.

It was negative.

My intern told me to do a daily LE prep, but every day the tests were negative. After three failures I found time to sit in the medical library and read all of A. McGehee Harvey's 75-page monograph on lupus in the journal *Medicine*. There were no copying machines, so I wrote copious notes and day-by-day I went back to Miss Brawling's bedside looking for all of the features of lupus mentioned by Dr. Harvey. She had so many of both the common and rare manifestations of lupus that I was convinced that she had lupus, but I couldn't prove it. In my readings I came across a modification of the LE prep, reported by Israel Snapper, a physician practicing in the Bronx, New York—the "Snapper test." Dr. Snapper had observed that if he added his own normal plasma to the blood of a patient he suspected of having lupus but who never had a positive LE prep, the test might become positive. A few days before I was planning to present Miss Brawling to doctor Bradley I did what Dr. Snapper described. After incubating the tube in my shirt pocket for an hour, I drew a tube of my own blood, spun it down, separated the plasma and added it to her blood. I finished rounds with the tube in my pocket, skipped lunch, and made a new smear of her blood. Almost breathless and convinced that I would see LE cells, I brought the slide into focus and saw something as spectacular as those photos of the cosmos showing millions of stars: virtually every white cell was trying to eat one or two or three other white cells. Either she had lupus, or I did! There was a lot more going for it being her than me.

For a few days every student on Medicine and few from other rotations asked to see the LE prep, my one week of medical school celebrity.

On the morning of the presentation I put on a clean white coat that Margaret had ironed the previous night. From my not-spectacular collection of neckties I chose my best. On the ward that morning I visited Miss Brawling, reminded her that she would be one of the patients presented to the "chief professor," and asked if she was still okay about that. She grunted an assent. Ms. Brawling was skinny, without much muscle mass. Her hair was thin and missing in patches randomly around her scalp, she had a dark, scaling rash over her nose and under her eyes, like the mask of a wolf, which is where the name lupus (wolf in Latin) came from. She was stiff and some of her joints hurt, as usual. She never said much and nothing suggested that anything had changed since the previous day.

At precisely 9 AM Dr Bradley arrived. The patients were sitting up in their beds; the nurses were waiting for us to enter so that they could close the doors behind us. Harry German had volunteered to do his presentation first, but as we walked down the left row of beds, we saw that his patient's bed was empty. Dr. Bradley exploded, red faced in a full-on conniption: nurses were commanded not to allow patients to leave the floor when he was about to make rounds. A nurse murmured an apologetic explanation, Harry squirmed, the other students were uncomfortable for Harry—a relaxed, funny, unpretentious guy who had made a living for many summers walking on to tennis courts wearing mismatched and faded tennis clothes, with the demeanor of a schlub, asking if anyone wanted to play a money match against him, not knowing that Harry had been a star on the Princeton tennis team. He played just well enough to always win without it becoming clear that he was an Ivy League champion.

Miss Brawling's bed was directly opposite us; since the third student's patient was on the men's ward one flight down, I volunteered to present first while Harry's patient was retrieved from the radiology floor. The herd of students turned around and ambled across the narrow space toward her bed, but now the curtain was drawn around her. I called in, "Miss Brawling, are you ready? May we pull back the curtain?"

In a thin voice she said we could, and students on each side whisked back the curtains to reveal Miss Brawling, totally naked, sitting bolt upright on a full bedpan. Dr. Bradley scowled, turned pale and walked away. The two nurses with us gasped and ran to clean and cover her. She was totally unaware of the thirty students and the Samuel Bard Professor of Medicine.

The student who was to present third raised his hand and said he could present his patient, and everyone departed to the eighth floor.

I helped clean Miss Brawling up. As I talked to her I realized that she was acutely psychotic, hallucinating and disoriented.

In twenty minutes the students and Dr. Bradley came back. In that short time Miss Brawling had returned to her baseline and said she was fine with being presented. Dr. Bradley moved to stand on her right hand and I presented her history, which was complicated; the very long list of test results seemed to irritate Dr. Bradley. I began to demonstrate some of her physical findings and told him that, if he wanted, he could see rare abnormalities characteristic of lupus in her retinas and offered him my ophthalmoscope, but he said he didn't need to do that. I was waiting for him to ask me what I thought the diagnosis would be. Instead, he asked me something about which he was expert, Starling's curve and the mechanism of the failing heart and how digitalis worked. Beside Miss Brawling on her bedside table, two feet from him was my microscope with the dramatic LE prep in focus for him to see. I had imagined this to be my gateway into a residency at Columbia: that I had diligently pursued the question of her diagnosis, and now had a dramatic answer after two weeks of futile efforts by the residents, our attending, and even the rheumatology consultants. Impatient with my floundering answers to his heart failure questions (totally unrelated to her), he impatiently turned to Harry German and asked him to present his patient. I slumped to the back of the group, humiliated at my total flubbing of his questions and robbed of a brief moment of success, of which so far there had been very few in medical school.

For the next day, the other students, either out of kindness or embarrassment, did not make eye contact when they passed.

When I got home that evening Margaret asked how my presentation had gone. I told her that I would never be a resident at Columbia and that a career in internal medicine probably was now going to be impossible: word would go out through the network of department chairs that I was the hapless student who unveiled a fully psychotic naked woman perched on a bedpan in front of the Samuel Bard Professor of Medicine, the oldest and most distinguished professorship in American medicine.

About once a month a visiting professor was invited to discuss the cases at Team Rounds. On 9 November the chairman of medicine at Washington University School of Medicine, Dr. Carl Moore, was discussing a patient with multiple myeloma in front of a packed audience of faculty, residents, and students. Suddenly the amphitheater went dark, with only three dim orange bulbs indicating where the exit doors were.

Dr. Moore, a brilliant, but relaxed, teacher said into the total darkness, "well, I knew I was bad, but I didn't think I was that bad."

We assumed the problem was local—in our amphitheater, or an entire floor or two of the medical school. We slowly stumbled out of the amphitheater and began the walk to our wards a hundred feet away: the hallway between the school and hospital was totally dark. A few of us took out the pocket penlights we used to inspect throats and pupillary reflexes. When we got to the entrance of ward Eight Center we realized that the hospital was dark as well. A nurse told us that the entire city was dark, and that the elevators and overhead paging system were dead. We filed through the ward to the solarium and could see that all of Manhattan was dark from where we were at 168th street all the way to the southern tip of Manhattan. A stream of cars coursed up the Henry Hudson parkway, lit only by headlights. Across the river, the New Jersey shore of the Hudson River was brightly lit from Palisades Park as far south as we could see, but the towns north of that were dark.

Word spread rapidly that there was a power outage affecting much of the Northeast, as far as Canada. The students were immediately put to work, checking on our patients and taking over for the useless motors on the iron lungs: the Medical Center's emergency generators kicked in at once, but there weren't enough "red plugs"—outlets where the emergency power could be tapped—to support the operating rooms where surgeons were in the middle of cases, and all of the medical equipment like respirators and refrigerators for blood and medications that required uninterrupted electricity. The iron lungs were large cylinders sealed at the patients' necks, with bellows at the foot. A motor pulled back the bellows about 12 times a minute, but the bellows could also be operated by pulling an attached handle, somewhat like a giant accordion. And so for hours a few dozen of us pulled handles to keep the patients alive, trading off every ten or fifteen minutes.

Around 10 PM I imagined that Margaret probably would have been able to get home from her teaching job in New Jersey, just across the Hudson from the Medical Center. No one had portable phones in those days; when I called the apartment phone there was no answer. Worried, I asked if I could walk the ten blocks to our apartment to be sure Margaret was safely home. The scenes on the streets were stunning and inspiring. In the absence of stoplights and streetlights people had taken on the tasks of directing traffic with flashlights, depending on a bright full moon and cars' headlights to make themselves visible. The mood was cheery, as though New York City had just won the World Series. Shops along the way were candle-lit and people were gathered on the streets talking because there was nothing else to do: restaurants couldn't cook, bars were dark unless they happened to have some candles, hair salons and fruit stands and grocery shops were shut down, the subways weren't running.

When I got to our apartment on St. Nicholas Avenue I checked our mailbox to see if Margaret had left me a note. She hadn't. We lived on the 28th floor and I began to trudge up. Votive candles that some thoughtful person had placed illuminated each landing. The supply of candles apparently ran out on the fifteenth floor; I climbed the next thirteen in the dark using my penlight, which was already becoming dim. On the 28th floor there was no evidence of life, and our apartment was empty. I left Margaret a note, since I had no other way of communicating with her, and began the long descent. I returned to the hospital and took over someone's iron lung handle.

The power came back around 7 AM, when we would ordinarily have been showing up to start rounding on our patients. We were a ragged, haggard lot, unshaven and stinky, like we had just finished a workout. We tried to round as though nothing had happened, but rounds were surreal as every nurse and every student and every resident had a story to tell: we had admitted new patients and examined them and written our notes by flashlight, we had groped our way to bathrooms, climbed stairs from the ground floor to the ninth floor because the only elevator connected to emergency power was being run manually and was reserved for moving patients. For weeks we felt bonded to each other, not just to the hospital staff, but to strangers on the street, as though we had all survived a hurricane or a blizzard by helping each other out.

Nine months later a story got started that there was a sharp spike in births, as people, having nothing else to do, made love. I told people that story for years, but it was apocryphal.

Contrary to expectations, the night of November 9th had the lowest rate of crime in New York City history.

The rest of our clerkships, in Obstetrics and Gynecology, Surgery, and Pediatrics were taught on a very different model. On Medicine the students were responsible for their patients in a way similar to interns—we did everything the interns did, only more slowly and for fewer patients. Because we stayed with our resident for three months, we became progressively proficient in fulfilling his expectations. On the other clerkships we were mostly observers, trailing around behind a preceptor. We didn't take our own histories or even get to talk with most of the patients. In the operating rooms we held retractors and tried not to fall into the open surgical fields, as occasionally happened when a student fainted: we were warned to faint backwards, not forwards, but fainting people have other things—or nothing—on their minds.

During two weeks in the labor and delivery suites we got to catch babies from the "multips"—multiparous women who were having their second, third, fourth, fifth baby. These women often progressed quickly. The nurses would pop into the small conference room where the students hung out and say, "Come fast!" We would throw on a gown and race into the room, where the mother was already on her back, her widely spread legs in stirrups. The nurses would point to a stool, give us gloves (which we did not always get on) and remind us not to drop the baby. Our gowned lap was like a basket and the slippery babies would end up in our laps more often than our hands. Then one of the nurses would cut the umbilical cord and we carried the baby over to a bassinet where we guessed at the Apgar score, giving 0, 1, or 2 in each of five categories to estimate the baby's health at birth.

Three or four days into the labor and delivery block I delivered a Puerto Rican mother's eighth baby. The baby's head was already crowning as the woman arrived in the emergency room; she was taken straight through to the elevators and from there directly into the delivery room. I was summoned and caught the baby and handed him off to the delivery room nurse who cleaned and swaddled him while I delivered the placenta. In Spanish I told his mother that she had a son without looking over the drape tented across her knees. The nurse said, "She didn't hear you. She is sound asleep. Probably the first time she has had any peace and quiet for a while."

She had delivered easily; there had been no need for an episiotomy or any stitches. I picked the baby up out of his bassinet and cradled him in my arms while the nurses cleaned up his mother and got information from her so that they could admit her to the postpartum ward. I walked over to the windows overlooking the Hudson River. It was just dusk and the peak of rush hour. We were on the 19th floor and I could see a stream of headlights on the Henry Hudson Parkway, all the way down to the business district; the lights of New Jersey and downtown Manhattan office and apartment buildings were brilliant; there was a thin, new moon on the horizon. In a low voice I sang a lullaby, "All the Pretty Little Horses", content in the thought that this little boy could become anything—he could end up as a doctor or teacher, a policeman or factory worker or lawyer. He had the same biologic potential, I supposed, as any baby born at the medical center that day, the rich ones whose mothers would have a private room in the

Harkness Pavilion, or the poorer mothers, white or brown or black, who would bed down in the Presbyterian Hospital maternity ward with only cotton curtains for privacy. I knew very little about Puerto Rican culture: the patients we saw at the Presbyterian Hospital frequently were first or second generation, many living in homes where only Spanish was spoken and would be the only language that the children were exposed to until they began school at 5 or 6. The Puerto Ricans were the latest wave of arrivals in Upper Manhattan—the successors to the refugees of the Second World War, and before them the Irish, the Italians, and the Germans. The Puerto Rican families I saw in the hospital usually had many children, and most of the time the fathers were the only wage earners at largely basic labor jobs. At that moment I felt the vast difference in probabilities for the little bundle in my arms compared to what mine had been in Missoula Montana twenty-five years earlier. I became somber: biologically he might have the potential to go to college and become prosperous, but the odds were heavily against his being the driver of one of those cars on the Henry Hudson Parkway streaming toward suburban homes in New Jersey or Westchester County 25 years in the future.

CHAPTER 11

The Internal Medicine Subinternship

I had started the third year of medical school excited but unpolished in every way: even after two years I was still awkward with many of my classmates, I supposed, in part, because of the wide difference between the Montana and East Coast cultures in which we had been raised, and in part because of my narrow experience of socialization with students as diverse as those I met at Harvard in Cambridge and now at Columbia in New York City. My diffuse and eclectic college experiences were not focused on medical sciences. At Harvard I got by in the relatively narrow confines of my literature courses and with a limited number of friends. I rarely struck up friendships with students in my classes. I didn't join any organizations or play any group sports, which would have exposed me to a wider range of students. Near the end of my junior year I began spending a lot of my time with Margaret, and when my roommates of three years, Jeff and Ted, left to spend a year in Germany, I lived in a single room by myself and spent nearly all of my free time with her. I had not grown up in a sprawling family where conflict and adaptation would have given me more practice of situational and emotional awareness. In medical school, learning how to navigate New York City, the unrelenting necessity of mastering the vast body of medical knowledge, and my inexperience with the diverse cultures of my patients and colleagues sometimes left me feeling immature and insecure.

Medical educators talk about students' fund of knowledge—what students can bring immediately to play in understanding the mechanisms of diseases, their diagnosis, and their treatment. My fund of knowledge continuously fell short of what I observed in the most brilliant of my classmates, the only ones against whom I chose to compare myself.

In comparison to memorizing dozens of pages of anatomy or biochemistry or pharmacology during the first two years, taking care of patients came more naturally to me. I enjoyed meeting them, taking their histories and examining them, and digging through their often-mammoth old records that went back for years, sometimes for decades. The tedious process of abstracting that history and turning it into a coherent and chronological narrative seemed easier for me than for some students, perhaps whatever skills and interests I had that led me to be an English major now at last proving useful.

I had decided that I wanted to become an internist: while there were a few surgeons and obstetricians and pediatricians I respected, even admired, I resonated more with the physicians in internal medicine who more frequently embodied the traits that I had imagined wanting to have as a physician: their expectation of constant availability, their drive to dig deep to solve problems that others had failed to correctly diagnose or treat, their insistence on knowing the most current evidence about therapeutic efficacy and pathophysiology, and their respectfulness and grace as they cared for patients of every background. It was not that I thought I had those qualities, but I admired them and they represented the point on the horizon toward which I wanted to navigate.

In June and July of the senior year, the medicine sub-internship at Goldwater Memorial Hospital was the starting line for many Columbia students hoping to get very competitive residencies. Columbia staffed two large wards for patients with chronic diseases who were there for months or even the rest of their lifetimes. Senior students were their only caretakers, under the supervision of a single staff physician, Dr. Arthur

Wertheim, a legendary teacher who over decades had disproportionately influenced the development of large numbers of Columbia students who aspired to be internists.

Ten students were selected to go to Goldwater for the first block of our senior year. Six of us were planning to apply to internal medicine residencies and four were planning to be surgeons. They were the best students in our class and once again I felt that I was, if not out of my league, much less likely to make it to the championships than they were.

Between the last day of May and the first day of June we went from being clinical clerks carrying out the instructions of residents, to students taking care of patients as though we were interns. The genius of the American model of clinical training is a gradual increase in responsibility beginning in the final two years of medical school and continuing through all of the years of residency. That model has not changed substantially for more than a century. As subinterns we were on our own to perform the initial history, physical examination, chart review, and laboratory data review and come to a conclusion about the diagnosis and needed treatment. As third year clinical clerks we had done this after the residents had already made a tentative diagnosis and started treatment. Now, everything was our responsibility and when we had made our decisions Dr. Wertheim listened to our presentations and plans and either approved them or suggested modifications.

Each day we arrived before 8 AM, making the long and complicated commute from Washington Heights by subway and cross-town bus to the East River, and then walking out the Fifty-Ninth Street Bridge—not yet immortalized by Simon and Garfunkel—and descended a stairway from the bridge to Welfare Island far below.

As subinterns we graduated from short white coats to white coats over white pants. There is something about the whites of medical education that function like the costumes in a period play: dressing for the role helped us play the role—if we looked like Falstaff, it was more likely that we could pass as Falstaff. As students in short white coats surrounded by residents in whites and faculty members in long white laboratory coats, no one expected as much of us. In full whites, we looked like our patients' doctors, and at Goldwater we had no competition for that role.

As soon as we arrived we read the nursing notes in our patients' charts and then rounded. There were rarely more than a few admissions a day; there were no nighttime admissions; our patients seldom changed dramatically from day to day.

Rose O'Brien was my first patient and also my first encounter with a patient who was used to receiving narcotics and firm in her intention of continuing to get them. She had chronic rheumatoid arthritis so severe that she couldn't walk; her spine was so stiff that she couldn't sit up without help; she barely had use of her arms and hands. She had been at Goldwater for years—as she said, "Before the Irish landed at Plymouth Rock."

I walked up to her bed where she was propped up on pillows eating oatmeal using a spoon with a handle the size of a toilet paper tube so that she could fit her deformed fingers around it. She eyed me with undisguised skepticism. I introduced myself, but not until she had gotten her mouthful of oatmeal out of the way did she answer.

"You're not going to be one of those doctors who tries to take away my codeine, are you?"

"What?"

"I go through this every two months. I get a new student and either he lets me keep taking my codeine, or I make his life miserable. I always win. You might as well not even try."

She slowly worked her spoon down to her bowl and scooped up a bit more oatmeal. I had no idea where to go with this, and since I really didn't know her history at all, I told her that I would like to talk with her for a while and examine her.

"What's to examine? Here I am. There are sixty physical exams in my chart already—six a year for ten years—take my word for it, you're not going to find anything new."

This began 61 days of compromise with Mrs. O'Brien. She let me listen to her heart from the front but only with my eyes closed. She let me listen to her breathe from the front, push a few places on her tummy through her

The Internal Medicine Subinternship

nightgown, and for everything else she said it was too hard for her to move. Being thorough and attentive to detail I asked if I could do a pelvic exam. She told me that I also wouldn't find anything interesting there, and besides that, what was I trying to save her from. I spent three hours going back through her old records and she was right: every two months for ten years a new student wrote a frustrated account of being refused access to most of her body. Those who tried to taper her off her codeine gave up by the third or fourth day.

Once she had assured herself that she had tamed me, she warmed up and told me short stories about growing up poor and Irish on the Lower East Side, about meeting Mr. O'Brien and having eight children. She told me she didn't know how he had fathered eight children, since he was rarely both sober and at home at the same time. Three sons died in the War, two daughters had moved back to Ireland, and her three other children lived some distance from New York City and visited rarely. Her rheumatoid arthritis had burned out, but she talked about being one of the first patients to get cortisone shots, about the ravages that aspirin and cortisone exacted as the price for reducing her inflammation, about learning how to cook with hands that couldn't wrap around a frying pan handle, and how she had to stop using makeup because her fingers weren't flexible enough to grasp a lipstick tube. She had been sent to Goldwater Hospital after she was hospitalized for pneumonia. After three weeks in bed, she was too stiff and too weak to walk; her physical therapists had given up even trying to do passive motion. Her entire life was her bed, her bedside table, and a locker from which the nurses could fetch her few belongings.

I asked her if she ever wanted to move back to her apartment; she told me that there no longer was an apartment or furniture or photographs.

I tried to imagine a life where each day was exactly the same as the one before, in a white-walled hospital ward with 20 other women in beds enameled white, under white covers. Over several months I succeeded in understanding more about her life, with growing respect for the tenacity it took to live with only the hope that tonight's sleep would be better than last night's and that her new student wouldn't make life worse for her.

On our daily rounds we walked by every bed, stopping where a patient had important changes, all of us crowding around the bedside with Dr. Wertheim, our attending. Once the student had finished, he quizzed us on everything we should know about the patient, whether it was our patient or another student's. This, he told us, was why rounds were important—our own direct experience was limited, but by hearing about our colleagues' patients, looking up what we didn't know, trying to prepare ahead of time for everything we might be asked the next day, we would learn ten times as much. He knew the patients intimately: each day he read our notes, visited the patients he thought needed a more senior evaluation, and sought us out if he had suggestions.

Every night one of us was the only "doctor" in the Columbia wing. We had the sole responsibility for the patients, which was a little daunting, although most of our patients were stable. If we needed help we could call Dr. Wertheim at home, or in a pinch, Dr. Curran, the senior physician. For the first six weeks my nights were uneventful—a constipation crisis that absolutely couldn't wait until tomorrow morning, rewriting a nighttime sedation order, evaluating a patient with chest pain or fever or abdominal pain.

During my last overnight call the nurse called me at 3 AM to tell me that one of my own patients, Mr. Jimenez, had been drowsy after dinner and now was unconscious. Mr. Jimenez had a rare disease, progeria, which is premature aging and calcification of all the soft tissues. His joints barely moved, his skin was as hard as belt leather, he had trouble opening his jaw, and his esophagus was so rigid that he could only swallow a liquid diet. He had had diabetes since he was a child, and as a young man had become blind.

My examination confirmed his nurse's observations: no amount of shouting or moving his limbs aroused him. I thought he probably had had a stroke but I couldn't be sure that he didn't have meningitis. One maneuver to detect meningitis is to try to bend the patient's head forward, or flex his legs onto his chest—when the meninges are inflamed, the

The Internal Medicine Subinternship

patient is often very stiff. When I tried to lift Mr. Jimenez's head from his bed his entire upper body lifted up like a plank, but that was always true because of his progeria. Since he was unconscious, I couldn't evaluate muscle strength or sensation, and because of his rigidity he didn't have reflexes. By now I was anxious and tense: I couldn't be certain that he didn't have a reversible condition. I thought that he needed a spinal tap, but I was afraid that if he had increased pressure in his head because of bleeding, a spinal tap might kill him. My one chance to eliminate this possibility was to examine his optic nerve to see if there was swelling because of increased pressure inside his brain. I was usually very good at using an ophthalmoscope and began to examine his eyes. His pupils were midsize—a good sign— but did not react to light, a bad sign. For fifteen minutes I tried to see his optic discs at the back of the eye, but I couldn't. I asked the nurse for drops to dilate his eyes but after ten minutes his pupils were fixed at the same size. The senior nurse had now come into the ward and was watching me, and then started to laugh.

"Mr. Noel, Mr. Jimenez has glass eyes. They cannot be dilated."

I wish I could have laughed at myself, but I was too flustered to think it was funny, and I was deeply embarrassed. He was my patient; I had reviewed his history when I took over his care and had asked him why his own eyes had been removed. In my panic, I had totally forgotten. I had been attempting to see the optic nerve of a man with glass eyeballs, a medical first.

The spinal tap attempts also failed. To widen the space between vertebrae to facilitate inserting the long spinal tap needle, a patient needs to be curled up, but Mr. Jimenez couldn't be curled, and the needle kept hitting bone, or the calcified ligament between the vertebrae.

Mr. Jimenez never recovered. For two days he remained in coma. When I came in on the third day his bed was empty. At 23, he had died the death of a man three or four times his age.

There was no debriefing his death, and no black humor. Although at our rounds the next morning I reviewed what had happened and explained the impossibility of doing a lumbar puncture, I never told anyone about trying to do an ophthalmoscopic exam on my own patient, who I had forgotten had glass eyes—I already felt dumb too much of the time.

Occasionally we would receive a patient who was admitted both because of disability and for a research study. The most unusual was a woman assigned to my classmate Richard Mackler. Richard had been a classical language major at Harvard; he was small of stature and long on sarcastic New York City humor. Mrs. Kravitz had been bedridden at home for years because of profound obesity. She was so heavy that she had to be in a special bed that was extra wide and extra strong and that had a motorized head lift since no nurse was strong enough to hand-crank up the head of her bed. For her ambulance trip to Goldwater, the fire department had been called in and had sent four of their strongest men. She told us that they used a steel stretcher, since she would have torn through the bottom of a canvas stretcher, and that when they were executing the corners in her staircase the four had to lift the stretcher above their shoulders to get her over the newel posts; she said that they were grunting and sweating by the first flight and sat exhausted on the curb after getting her into the ambulance.

She was admitted for a green bean diet. A physician who specialized in nutrition had concocted a theory that a person who ate only green beans—in any quantity—would lose weight and not give in to hunger. Our job was to weigh her accurately, feed her as many green beans as she wanted, and weigh her again after a month. Because she was too heavy for the hospital patient scale, which topped out at 250 pounds, we had commandeered the kitchen meat scale, which could weigh up to 800 pounds.

It had taken seven nurses and the motorized patient crane used to raise and lower paralyzed patients to move her from her wheelchair into bed when she was admitted. When we asked the nurses to help us get her out of bed, they refused and left Richard to assemble a team to help him. Six of us got the lift's canvas sling under her, attached it to the lift, and were holding the edges of the sling while Richard operated the crane. When she was about a foot above the bed, we tried to rotate the crane 90 degrees while pulling it away from the bed. The crane tipped over and the sling and Mrs. Kravitz crashed to the floor, dragging all of us with her. She was howling on the floor, not hurt but surprised, when we realized that Richard had disappeared—we had no idea where. Someone spotted his bent glasses beside her, and as we lifted the edges of the sling, we found Richard flattened beneath her, her weight making it impossible for him to get enough air in or out to speak. By now the nurses had rushed into the room, and the dozen of us managed to get Mrs. Kravitz back into bed and to rescue Richard, who was both emotionally and physically crushed. We postponed the great weighing until we could get a forklift.

Richard requested swapping patients with me, taking over two of my patients if I would take care of her. I agreed, and sat down beside her to review her history. At home her diet had been very strange: each day a friend brought two loaves of day-old unsliced white bread, two pounds of ground pork, a large onion, two large bags of potato chips, and twelve bottles of Coca Cola. The friend sliced the loaves in half lengthwise, shaped the ground pork into two oblong patties the size of the loaves and fried them with the onion. She put the patties between the sliced loaves and delivered them to her bed with the Cokes and chips. That was her only meal each day. She performed her ablutions and eliminations once a day in the bed, which she hadn't left for months.

The student who took over her care after I left at the end of August said that by the third week she began to refuse the green bean diet. The nurses found potato chip fragments in her sheets. They staked out her room and caught her friends smuggling in contraband hot dogs. She ultimately left for home where she could eat "normal food".

Goldwater was a critical experience for me. It tested my assumption that I wanted to be an internist, and it was an opportunity for me to demonstrate my potential as a resident. I had no way to judge how well I was doing in comparison with the other nine students. Most of them had impressive clinical knowledge immediately accessible when questioned on rounds. On the other hand, I had many occasions to read their progress notes at night when I was covering, and our notes were about the same. That summer I learned about the honors organization *Alpha Omega Alpha*, to which the top 5 percent of the class were elected at the end of the third year: four of the students with me at Goldwater had been selected for junior AOA.

I thought that I was a middling student in internal medicine, but it was the field that fit me best. While I had no confidence that I would successfully compete for one of the top residency programs, I didn't feel discouraged: there was simply too much of the fourth year yet to come to be able to predict.

On my last day I stopped off to say goodbye to Mrs. O'Brien. I told her how much I had enjoyed spending time with her. As she had predicted, nothing happened during the two months that required a change in her care. Nonetheless I was hopeful that she would say that she had appreciated my twice-daily visits. She didn't say a word, the first of many patients whose feelings about me they kept to themselves. Over time I found out that if what doctors were looking for was a steady stream of gratitude from their patients, they were going to be disappointed frequently.

Decades later when I was teaching in Japan, I heard high school students who had spent years preparing for the college entrance exams say, "*Ganbarimashita*," "I did my best!" Had I known that phrase when the two months were finished, I think I could have honorably said, "Whatever my grade, I did my best," but in my heart I was disappointed that my best wasn't better.

CHAPTER 12

Honeymoon

After finishing at Goldwater at the end of July, Margaret and I took a month-long trip to London, the Lake Country and Wales, Paris, Venice, Florence, and finally Rome. Margaret's generous, elderly cousin, Virginia Hamilton, had given us a wedding gift of a thousand dollars that covered our plane tickets, which were just over five hundred dollars each on Pan American Airlines. We used *Europe on Five Dollars a Day* by a not-then-famous travel writer named Frommer to book our hotels, with an occasional "big splurge" from the ten-dollar-a-day selections, including a dinner at the famous Simpson's in the Strand in London where the waiters looked terminally bored wheeling the silver domed carving trolleys from table to table, serving rare roast beef with horseradish sauce, beef-fat roasted potatoes, and Yorkshire pudding onto enormous plates. We left feeling stuffed, drowsy and unpleasantly touristy, as we did after taking high tea at the Ritz or Claridge's, I can't now remember which.

In England we visited several inns in Wales and the Lake Country, visited Nottingham to check out the area from which the Noels were said to have emigrated to the United States in the 1700's, and spent half a day each at Cambridge and Oxford universities.

During our 5 days in Paris we ate way above our budget. I wanted to go to the three-star Maxim's, but regarded it as too fancy to visit without training, so I arranged for us to have dinner at the Hotel Plaza Athénée, which had only 2 stars for cuisine, but 3 knives and forks for the beauty of the restaurant and the elegance of the china, crystal, and decor. The interior dining room was closed during the summer and we ate in the lovely central garden, just outside the dining room windows. I spotted a wine I had tasted in college, Chateau Margaux Margaux 1959, at only $10.00 US, a bargain, and asked for a bottle. We started with sherry and cream soups and then had filet mignon with the wine. We ordered soufflé Grand Marnier and when the table had been cleared, three waiters in black tuxedos marched out, one holding the soufflé above his head, the other two holding doors to be sure that the soufflé wasn't jiggled so that it collapsed. In a great puff of steam the soufflé was incised and delivered unto our plates. When I scanned our bill, which was in French, I thought that the sum was high but I was too tipsy to figure it out and too intimidated to ask.

As we walked back to our hotel near the Arc de Triomphe along the Champs-Elysees I took it to mind that I needed to leapfrog over 20 or so parking meters, jumping a dozen before I failed to clear one, nearly neutering myself.

In our room we were horribly sick from sherry, a full bottle of wine, and very rich food. We each threw up, grateful that the French knew that a bidet would be useful for that purpose.

The next morning, hung over, I recalculated the bill from my recollection of the prices on the menu and decided that we had been overcharged by $10.00 US, the big splurge budget for an entire day's expenses including meals and hotel. I asked Margaret to go back to the Plaza Athénée with me so that I could recoup the overcharge from the maitre d'. As we entered La Cour Jardin in the late morning, the same maitre d' dressed in his black tuxedo walked quickly toward me and asked if he could help me. I said that I thought we had been overcharged for our wine. He protested that the charge was perfect, that he had checked the bill personally, and with that he disappeared back into the dining room. In a minute he returned trailing 20 feet of adding machine tape that he was rapidly pulling through his fingers as he approached. With triumph he found our charges near the middle of the tape and then showed them to us. Indeed, the charge for the Margaux Margaux was $20, not $10.

"Ah, then I was correct, the wine was listed in the menu at $10!"

"Ah no monsieur! You ordered a full bottle of the Margaux. $10 was the half-bottle price. The charge for your entire meal was precisely correct."

Humbled, I had no recourse but a discrete retreat. A half bottle would have made much more sense, and I had demonstrated my ignorance in the very place in which I was trying to feel that I knew what I was doing.

However, the dinner at Chez Maxim went off smoothly. It was a much less classy restaurant; our food was excellent but in spite of its extra star, less good than the Plaza Athénée.

We spent five days walking in Paris, seeing the original paintings and drawings and sculptures that we had grown up knowing through high school and college courses and reproductions in the bookshops around Harvard Square. We tracked down the bistros where Camus and Sartre argued over coffee and the sites we had read about in the novels we read in high school and college. Looking at a photo in its lobby, I realized that the Hotel du Bois where we were staying had been used to depict a brothel in a new wave gangster movie I had seen when I should have been in Bard Hall studying.

We visited Venice next, and then Rome and Florence. In Venice we stumbled on an obscure villa on the Grand Canal owned by Peggy Guggenheim, a member of the famously wealthy art-collecting family. *Frommer's* mentioned that her house was sometimes open for people to see her collection of modern art. When we passed by, the house was quiet; it didn't look like a gallery or a museum, and nothing indicated whether it was open or where we might enter. We walked into its ungated courtyard from a narrow walk along the Grand Canal and were admiring the notorious Marino Marini statue of a horseman whose erect penis could be unscrewed if religious dignitaries were visiting. A woman in a caftan and turban surrounded by a cortege of Lhasa Apsos walked out onto the terrace where we were standing. She asked if we would like to look around. We said we would and spent an hour admiring the collection. In a small room near the main entrance were a dozen pastel drawings of men and women in various states of sensual relaxation, with a small sign saying, "Works of Pegeen Guggenheim, for sale."

We liked one of the paintings and wandered around the villa until we found the woman in the caftan to ask if we could buy it. She told us that Pegeen Guggenheim was her daughter. I asked if she would take a check. She said she would and then she wrapped the large, framed, glass-covered painting for us. From Venice to Rome to Florence to New York's Idlewild, we walked out onto the tarmac with the painting, handed it to the luggage handlers, and fetched it on landing. With the cancelled check taped to the back, it still hangs in our living room.

In Florence we stayed in a big splurge hotel, the beautiful hotel Berchielli that overlooked the Ponte Vecchio. On the second day we arrived at the Uffizi Gallery at about 3 PM and began slowly exploring its enormous halls. As had happened in Paris, it seemed that nearly every famous statue or painting we knew about was suddenly in front of us. The crowds were small because most Italians had taken to the hills and shores for their vacations; post-war international tourism had not yet begun to grow. One of our guidebooks said that if we went to the final chamber on the top floor and walked all the way to its end, and then looked carefully at the paneled wall to our right, we would find a hidden door that we could push open. We doubted it, but looked—and found it! Certain that we were transgressing, we slipped inside. The book said that this was a secret workshop for the goldsmith Benvenuto Cellini, but that in reality, it was a room that looked down at the chamber in which the Florentine Council met in which Cosimo Medici could plant a spy to detect plots against him.

On our hands and knees, we were looking down on the room through a grate in the floor, when we heard a loud slamming of heavy doors and the receding footsteps of one of the galleries' guards. It was 5 PM exactly, and without knowing that we were in the small chamber behind the panel, the guards were clearing the room. We popped out into the empty gallery and ran toward the double door into the next gallery as it was being closed. We opened the door and entered the next chamber just as its door was being closed at the far end. Still running, we caught the guard's attention. He stared at us as if we had suddenly materialized out of thin air. Although we didn't understand some of what he was saying, the gist of it was, "where in God's name did you come from?"

We didn't attempt to explain ourselves

A few days later, exhausted but euphoric we landed at Idlewild Airport. The trip was my first vacation longer than a week since I was in the fifth grade.

The next day Margaret resumed teaching high school science in Leonia, NJ, and I began a pediatrics subinternship and the process of applying for internal medicine residency programs.

Chapter 13

My Year of Loving Everything

Our pediatrics experience as third year students was passive, mostly watching faculty members and residents take care of patients or listening to classroom presentations by our classmates. Once a week we saw newborns in the well-baby clinic, but we never had direct contact with a sick patient in either the hospital or clinic. Whatever interest I had in becoming a pediatrician had faded by the end of the clerkship.

The subinternship in the fall of my senior year was altogether different. I was the senior resident Frank Stroud's subintern on a combined kidney and cancer ward; there were no other students to compare myself with and Frank gave me as much responsibility as I could handle. The children were heartbreakingly sick; most had been in and out of the hospital for more years than I had been a medical student. Frank and I rounded together at 7 each morning with the senior nurse, who brought us up to date on anything that had happened overnight. Parents rarely were able to stay overnight, so we saw the children, ranging in age from 3 to about 11, without them. After rounds it was my job to draw blood, a tricky procedure with the terrified, squalling kids doing everything they could to keep their arms out of my reach. I always won, but sometimes at the price of having to swaddle them to keep them still enough to get a needle in and the blood drawn. Most couldn't eat well because of inflamed mouths or nausea or vomiting; most had an IV running that also had to be replaced every day, if not more often.

As hard as it was to care for a child who was actively resisting, it was even harder to be with the sickest children who were so beaten up by surgery or chemotherapy that they offered no resistance at all; it took all of their energy just to answer my few simple questions.

At the best moments some of the kids were wonderful. I enjoyed talking with parents; I admired the skill and patience of the young women who were their nurses, most of them graduates of Columbia's School of Nursing. I admired Frank Stroud's knowledge and kindness, and I was attracted to the laid-back demeanor of the other residents and the faculty.

Although I had decided to apply for an internal medicine internship, I began to wonder if it would be better to be a pediatrician. When I got my grade for the subinternship, an A, I was interested enough to ask to meet with the chair of the pediatrics department. Dr. Curnen was a kindly, gentle, cherubic looking man. I asked him if I could do a medicine internship and then become a pediatrician. Many residencies outside of medicine and surgery did not have their own internships then, and moving from an internship in medicine to a pediatric residency wasn't regarded as a problem, and certainly a medicine internship would be great training. He said it was done all the time: "It just takes some people longer to see the true light. If you make up your mind that you want to be a pediatrician let me know. Shouldn't be a problem."

"Good grief!", I thought. Had he just offered me a residency? Had I finally progressed from being a liberal arts major who the professor of biochemistry thought didn't belong in medical school to a student that the chairman of pediatrics thought would be a good resident?

My next subinternship was two months of obstetrics and gynecology. As a third-year clerk I had enjoyed delivering babies and I was looking forward to a full two months more of obstetrics, but I was caught off guard by how deeply engaged I was during the first two weeks, assigned to the septic abortion ward. Other students had asked for the gynecologic surgery wards, but I had asked to take care of the young women admitted from the emergency room after alleyway and kitchen-table abortions. They were largely Puerto Rican, pregnant without being married, with families that would have been disgraced or abusive if it were discovered that their daughter had premarital sex. They had not sought counsel in the Catholic Churches they attended because they knew that they would be told that they had to keep the babies and that they would be forced to leave school.

Legal abortion was still years away, and the women—many of them girls of 14 or 15—resorted to trying to abort themselves, or have a friend or sister or the man who got them pregnant do it, or they would find a shady doctor working outside of a hospital or clinic that would do it in his office. Some of the girls had inserted knives or coat hangers or knitting needles or rubber catheters into their uteruses, resulting in incomplete abortion or perforation that led to infection and sometimes to systemic sepsis—bacteria in the blood. Others had used turkey basters to inject turpentine or alcohol or potassium permanganate through the cervix into their uterus. When the result was bleeding or infection that brought them to our emergency room, they and their friends did whatever they could to conceal their hospitalization, which left us in a pickle if they were too young to give permission for procedures. If they were successful in concealing their situation from their families and were on the verge of death, a senior physician would give consent in the absence of a parent, and the girl was rushed to the operating room.

In two weeks we lost three patients from overwhelming infection; another four or five were saved by surgery, their massively infected uteruses removed. We would never know, but probably a few who didn't need surgery would be unable to conceive because of damage to their uterus and fallopian tubes.

More than half of our nurses were Italian or Irish Catholic, but whatever their beliefs, they were sympathetic and understood the crisis these girls were in. I felt privileged to be the student doctor for these desperately ill and frightened young patients who were cared for without judgment.

The hospital priest was similarly low key and self-constrained—he gave last rites to any fetal tissue removed during an operation or curettage, he comforted the girls, he assured them that if they prayed and were truly contrite they would not go to hell, even though they had had sex out of wedlock and had had an abortion. If they spoke little English he would invite a Spanish-speaking priest he trusted to keep their secrets to visit with them.

We regarded the regular pages for a priest or rabbi or minister as part of the daily routine of the medical center. When the overhead speakers beeped and a voice announced, "Father O'Flanagan stat 19th floor" we knew he would be hurrying up the elevators to baptize a stillborn or struggling newborn baby.

I watched Father O'Flanagan do this once. He walked over to the delivery room sink and wet his finger with a drop of water, then touched the tiny infant's forehead. I was shocked.

"Father O'Flanagan," I said, "I thought to baptize someone you had to dip them in holy water, but that water came out of our sink and it was just a drop."

He pursed his lips, making a good attempt at taking me seriously. "Ahh, that is one of the abiding mysteries of the Church—that if I touch the water, it is holy, and if you touch it, young doctor Gordon, it is not. No offense of course. And my job is to anoint the babies, not drown them."

The resident on the obstetrics service was glad to have an internal-medicine- bound student manage the ward. I rounded on the patients at 7 am and then met with him to review plans. After that he went off to the operating or delivery rooms and I took care of the patients all day. My Spanish was good enough to have a simple social conversation. My medical Spanish was almost nonexistent, and the patients' medical English just as limited. I did a lot with sign language or drawings or with the help of another patient who could translate.

When I finished the two weeks on the septic abortion ward, I moved to the delivery room. I was never happier as a medical student than when I was delivering a baby. The senior students got to deliver many of the easy patients. As far as I know the women were never told that the gowned and masked body delivering their baby had only a few weeks of experience and had been reading Shakespeare and fighting forest fires just three years ago. When there weren't babies to catch we assisted in the operating rooms with Cesarean sections and cancer operations, neither of which excited me much.

After two weeks of gynecologic surgery and pre- and postpartum clinic, I found myself more relaxed, more comfortable, less exhausted than I had been on my medicine subinternship at Goldwater, perhaps because the stakes were lower. But something else had changed: in directly caring for patients and carrying out my responsibilities for histories and physical exams and writing progress notes and talking with patients, I felt as competent as other students. There was less continuous evaluation by the residents and faculty. Because the residents and faculty knew that most of us were not planning to enter their field, there was not an implication that we should already know what they were teaching us. To patients, I was just a young-looking doctor, but they had no one else to compare me with: on our morning and afternoon rounds the residents came and went in minutes, and the faculty members were barely involved except in complex cases.

I began to think that I would enjoy a life of delivering babies. Somehow the fact that the entirely-male faculty doctors were in the hospital all hours of the day and night and had committed themselves to delivering their private patients' babies at any hour of any day escaped me, or seemed natural. It certainly didn't turn me off, since my expectation no matter which specialty I chose was that my job in life would be to attend—to be present when my patients needed me, at all hours and almost every day.

Once again, I scheduled an appointment with the department chairman at the end of the two months. He told me I would be getting an A.

"I am heading for an internal medicine internship," I told him, "But I have loved taking care of these patients and delivering their babies. Could I apply during internship if I decided to do Ob-Gyn?"

"Of course, just let me know. A year of medicine would be fine preparation. We would be happy to have you apply here, or help you if you want to go someplace else."

My last subinternship was two months of surgery at Roosevelt Hospital, a few blocks south of Columbus Circle on Manhattan's West Side. The hospital had once been the primary residency teaching hospital for the College of Physicians and Surgeons, but when Columbia University decided to build a new medical center in the 1920's that would combine the medical and nursing schools with a new hospital near the north end of Manhattan, Roosevelt declined because of Columbia's insistence that medical students would have to be allowed to participate in the care of patients, and because they did not want to move to a deserted end of Manhattan away from their prime location near Columbus Circle. The idea of having medical students involved with their patients horrified the Roosevelt clinicians, who regarded medical students as rowdy drunkards who were too unrefined to be near their well-to-do patients, and they voted to stay put in midtown. But Presbyterian Hospital was eager to have students, who they thought would stimulate their physicians and contribute to the care of their patients, most of whom were poor. They agreed to build a new hospital and move from their current site. By the 1930's Roosevelt had become a less important Columbia teaching hospital; by the 1960's it was no longer an elite residency program, and a town-gown attitude developed among its faculty and residents, who cynically called Presbyterian Hospital "The Mother Church". Of course, in time Roosevelt did accept medical students, and it remained a popular site for senior students.

I hadn't found surgery appealing during my clerkship and didn't have high hopes that it would be an enjoyable way to spend the final two months of medical school. Still, I wanted to learn the basic surgery skills I would need like suturing, wound care, and placing intravenous catheters. I also wanted to understand what the operations my medicine patients might undergo for ulcer or gallbladder disease or cancer would entail.

My Year of Loving Everything

I was delightfully surprised: as a subintern, I loved surgery. Like the residents in obstetrics and gynecology, the surgery residents were glad to have someone interested in the daily care of their pre- and postoperative patients so they could comfortably be in the OR without being hassled by the floor nurses about IV and pain medication orders and patient complaints. As a third-year student I had been a passive observer in the OR, but at Roosevelt I was the second assistant surgeon, actively retracting, trying to answer the stream of questions from the attending or resident about what the blood vessel or structure they had draped over a clamp was, where it originated, where it went, and what its function was. They taught me how to put in the closing sutures and how to change dressings and how to write post-op orders.

No student heading for surgery would have put off the surgery subinternship until the last few months of school: the clerkship and subinternship evaluations and letters of recommendation from the surgeons were an essential part of what had to be included in their residency applications three months into the fourth year. The two other students with me were headed for psychiatry and radiology, and for a change I probably was the stronger student. The residents quickly figured out that I could take care of the most complicated patients after their surgery and assigned them to me. I was in seventh heaven managing fluids and medications of patients with multiple failing systems or whose metabolic balance was in disarray because they had had large sections of bowel removed or were losing fluids because of severe burns.

One of my patients was admitted for resection of a tumor at the base of her tongue, where it attached to the anterior pharyngeal wall. This operation was usually debilitating because, as conventionally done, the lower jaw had to be split in the midline all the way into the neck. Her head and neck surgeon wanted to try a method that involved leaving her jaw intact and splitting her tongue all the way back to the tumor, resecting it without opening up her entire neck. My job postoperatively, I was told, was to keep her comfortable and her tongue and mouth sterile until healing had occurred. Every two hours I washed her mouth and pharynx with an antiseptic solution; I maintained her nutrition with a feeding tube inserted at the time of surgery and with that kept her diabetes and heart failure in balance with meticulous avoidance of salt loading and hourly insulin injections that required hourly blood sugars. She was in terrible pain, which I managed with narcotics, but which kept her semi-sedated and constipated. I practically lived in orbit around her for two weeks, until her tongue had healed enough that she could begin to swallow small amounts of liquefied food. Her ordeal had been terrible. When I discharged her, she was matter of fact about her experience: she remembered very little beyond falling from and rising into foggy, painful consciousness. She had few visitors and as best I could tell no family had come. Her room was devoid of flowers or cards or evidence that the world knew where she was or what had happened to her. She said that she hoped never to set foot in a hospital again. She didn't thank me. I don't think she thanked her surgeon. She might not have been cured, and I don't know what happened to her. My only feeling on her departure was confusion about whether in the end she had done herself any good by having the surgery—whether we had done her more harm than if she had turned down the operation.

The surgeons at Roosevelt seemed more colorful than their reserved, distinguished colleagues at Presbyterian Hospital. One of the middle-aged orthopedic surgeons—from Montana—drove a red convertible, had been married and divorced multiple times, and currently was dating a twenty-two-year-old nurse. He dressed elegantly and when in scrubs had a mop of red chest hair filling the V in his scrub shirt. Everyone assumed that, since he was from Montana and I was from Montana, we would be kinsmen and he would be my role model. Unfortunately, no one ever had expressed an interest in my chest hair, and because of poor planning or lack of imagination, a red convertible was not part of my life plan.

Another Roosevelt surgeon was a graying, lean, cigarette-smoking thoracic surgeon named J. Maxwell Chamberlain, who had been trained in Boston and Michigan and ended up in New York City. I thought it was ironic that a chest surgeon who spent his life operating on lung cancer patients would smoke.

Dr. Chamberlain was famous for developing methods of operating on patients with tuberculosis who had abscesses or cavities and were gradually dwindling away from chronic infection. He was one of the founders of the specialty of thoracic surgery.

He also was notorious for hazing medical students, and legend had it that he deliberately caused students to believe that they had killed his patients in the operating room. The story went that when a student scrubbed in on one of his cases, he was told that he had one job—to retract the ribs hard enough for Dr. Chamberlain to see clearly the root of the lung where it attached to the trachea in the middle of the central arteries and veins.

When he was close to removing the lung, Dr. Chamberlain would yell at the student to "pull harder, pull harder... I can't see what I am doing."

When the lung was about to be cut free—its vessels tied off and only the bronchus holding it in place—he would start yelling:

"Pull, you idiot. I can't see what I am doing! Pull harder... harder!"

At that point he would cut the through the bronchus, and the student, pulling the lung with fifty pounds of traction, would fly backwards through the room and land on the floor with the lung on his chest, and Chamberlain screaming, "You moron, you idiot, what the hell have you done... you've' ripped his heart out, you murdered my patient."

The residents and nurses had seen this before and knew what was coming, but their masks concealed their grins, and the students didn't have the courage to protest and allowed themselves to be thrown out of the operating room in the belief that a residency was now out of reach and jail was probably only hours away.

I would have been the perfect dupe: I scrubbed and retracted on one of his cancer cases, but other than a quiet request to change the angle of retraction, he left me alone.

A year later, after a long day of surgery, on his way to join his family in the country for a holiday, in the dim light before dark he was killed in a head-on collision. He was the preeminent chest surgeon of his time.

Whether it was because I had achieved a level of practical competence that was an asset to the residents or merely because medical school was nearly over, the end of the two months of surgery had been enormous fun. A bit dazed by the emotional turn-around since my third-year surgery clerkship, I wondered if I had been mistaken in not choosing a surgery residency. One more time I made an appointment with a department chair, this time the Valentine Mott Professor of Surgery, Dr. George Humphrey. I asked him if I could apply for a surgical residency during the early part of my medicine residency. And once again he said that would be fine, it was done from time to time. He told me to let him know by October.

CHAPTER 14

The Match

In mid-September of 1966, 8000 senior students in American medical schools applied for residency programs that would begin a few weeks after our graduation in June of 1967. The application process was done entirely through the mail: we filled out a form that summarized where we had grown up and gone to secondary school, where we had gone to college and what we had studied, and information about our medical school record. We struggled to write a personal statement that we hoped would reveal what we would add as a member of the residency program we would be joining. The medical school sent a transcript of our grades and a letter from the dean summarizing our performance as students. We asked faculty members to write letters of recommendation: mine were written by my medicine clerkship preceptor, Dr. Wheaton, by the director of my Goldwater subinternship, Dr. Wertheim, and by Dr. Bradley, the chairman of the department of medicine.

Some of the students in my class at Columbia who were from New York and wanted to stay close to their families requested interviews only in New York City and the close-by programs in Connecticut, New Jersey and Pennsylvania, but those of us who were seeking highly competitive residencies applied up and down the east coast in Boston, Baltimore,

Philadelphia, or further away in Cleveland, Chicago, North Carolina, and Virginia.

An on-site interview was a required part of the process. Plane travel was still a pricey luxury and most of us didn't own cars, so for interview trips on the East Coast or in the Midwest we took trains.

After several months of interviewing, the students and the programs would each create a rank list. Computers do the Match now, but in the 1960's it was done by hand. A complex algorithm matches each student's choices with the programs' choices. Students go to the highest program on their list that ranks them high enough to match. The Match is binding: neither programs nor students can change their minds.

I chose the internal medicine residencies I applied to casually, without any basis beyond reputation. We did not have faculty advisors, but from students ahead of us, from some of the residents, and occasionally from faculty members, we learned about the programs that were most highly regarded: in medicine they were at the Johns Hopkins Hospital, the Peter Bent Brigham Hospital, the Massachusetts General Hospital, the Harvard service at Boston City Hospital, and the University of Pennsylvania. I applied for interviews at most of those. Dr. Wertheim suggested Western Reserve in Cleveland and the University of Chicago. A few residents and faculty members said that the University of Rochester was famous for a very thoughtful, humanistic approach to patients and might be somewhat easier to get than the top programs on my list. Someone suggested that I have a "backup" on my list—a program that certainly would match me if none of the others did. I chose the University of Buffalo in Upstate New York.

From Columbia's corner of the galaxy, the internal medicine residencies at Stanford, the University of California at San Francisco, UCLA, and the University of Washington were out of sight, simply not in the experience or consciousness of our faculty, almost all of whom had grown up and trained on the East Coast. When a faculty member left for a position on the West Coast or the Deep South they were considered lost to civilization. Cornell Medical School across town was treated by some residents and faculty in the same snotty way as Harvardians treated Yale: "A lesser but still worthy institution."

I was surprised to get interviews at all of the places I applied to except Massachusetts General. I didn't feel that I was a strong enough student to be ranked highly by Hopkins or the other two Harvard programs, but I was glad to have a chance to at least see them.

My first interview was in November at my own medical school. One December afternoon was devoted entirely to the Columbia students. There was no tour or introductory explanation of the program: after living for three months cheek by jowl with the residents and faculty during our clerkship, it was assumed that we understood what we would be getting into. We were given a time to wait outside the department chairman's office. I had no idea what to expect. I was ushered into Dr. Bradley's woody, book-filled, austere office and was a bit set back to see the entire group of full professors seated like white-coated jurors in a semicircle around an empty chair for me in the middle. If they had worn hoods and had there been burning incense it would have fit what I imagined the Inquisition to have looked like.

One by one they asked me questions, for some of which I managed to produce credible answers, and some of which I flubbed totally. The questions were clinical. There were no moral quandaries posited, no probing for the worst moment of my brief, pathetic life as a medical student, not even inquiries about why I wanted to be an internist or do my residency at Columbia or had chosen literature and not biology or chemistry as my college major.

"A black man from North Carolina is admitted because of enlarged lymph nodes on his chest X-ray and new onset of joint pain. Can you think of several possible diagnoses?"

"Sarcoid. Tuberculosis. Hodgkin's Disease."

That seemed to satisfy the questioner. I looked in vain for a glimmer of approval from the encircling professors, but they were stone-faced.

A professor specializing in lung disease asked me to interpret several tests of lung function. I guessed chronic obstructive lung disease. I wasn't given a sign that I had it right.

Next, questions about the kidney, gut, heart, blood, and joints. I had to tell them that I didn't know the answers to several of the questions, missed one completely, probably got a few right.

I was dismissed with a formal "thank you very much Mr. Noel. Good luck."

A classmate was waiting in the hallway as I emerged. It was Walt Berger. He asked me what it was like. The sunofabitch had done nothing but study for 36 straight months. I told him he would do fine.

It would be hard to choose which day was the lowest point of the interview season and impossible for me to label any interview visit as successful.

My interview at Boston City Hospital occurred over the Christmas break, when Margaret and I were visiting her parents in Newburyport, an hour's drive north of Boston. Dr. Wilkins had advised me against applying to the residency in his department of medicine at Boston University: he thought it would be awkward for both him and me if I were not chosen, equally awkward if I was. All three Boston medical schools had services at Boston City, each with independent clinical and residency programs. The Harvard service was famous: the Thorndike Memorial Laboratory was part of the Harvard Service, and for decades a stream of fundamental discoveries in blood cell development, pernicious anemia, the effects of vitamin deficiency, the elucidation of beriberi heart disease, the treatment of infectious diseases, and the natural history of delirium tremens poured out from its faculty members.

The applicants and a half dozen faculty members and residents sat in a circle. We were told about Boston City Hospital's illustrious past as one of the first and greatest of the hospitals for the "underprivileged poor." The residents were proud of its legendary grittiness: they told us that we would be taking and reading our own X-rays at night and that we would pass out the evening and nighttime medications. When a patient was being admitted to our hospital ward from the emergency room, we would be pushing the gurney and running the elevator. If we were lucky enough to be able to go to our room for a few minutes of sleep, we should be prepared that the elevator only made it to the six-and-a-halfth floor. From there we would have to pull aside the door and crawl up onto the seventh floor to find a bed; the living quarters looked as though they were new shortly after the civil war.

We were made to understand that these deprivations were just a few of the things that made the Harvard Service at Boston City Hospital special.

The interviews were as a group. Each of us was asked several questions about why we were interested in Boston City Hospital and what our goals were. Fortunately, Dr. Wilkins had done his post-medical school residency on the Harvard service at Boston City and I had been hearing stories for years about famous graduates and middle of the night miracle diagnoses. I talked about some of the discoveries made at BCH and about their storied history of caring for, as a former resident had once written, "Some of the sickest, poorest, saddest, and often drunkest people you can imagine." I was not insincere when I said I was attracted to training in that institution, caring for that population.

A few days later I was interviewed at Women's and Brigham Hospital. Dr. Wilkins had informed me more than once that the he didn't think the Brigham was up to the standard it had when he was a medical student—that the department was not as strong with clinicians or researchers as it made itself out to be. Over the entire time I knew him, Margaret's father was down on Harvard because he felt that Harvard had an unfair advantage over the two other Boston medical schools just because it was Harvard, and that Harvard faculty regarded with indifference, if not disdain, any Boston scientist or clinician without a Harvard appointment. He told me the story of working hard to get a mid-career BU faculty member from the legendary Boston Lowell family promoted to full professor with tenure and appointing him as his pulmonary medicine division chief, only to stand by helplessly while Harvard recruited him as a non-tenured associate professor. When Dr. Wilkins tried hard to persuade him to stay at BU, he was told, "I'm sorry Bob, but a Lowell really belongs in a Harvard institution, don't you think?"

The Brigham employed a gauntlet interview to sort out its applicants. There were ten of us, each given a card with a different starting location on a circle of labs and offices, in each of which were one or two Brigham physicians. The interview was ten minutes per stop, with five minutes to walk from place to place. At each stop I was asked a medical question: not once did anyone try to find out anything about me beyond what I had written in my application. At my first stop I was asked a series of questions about heart failure, at the next questions about kidney stones, and after that the unsmiling interviewers visited my meager knowledge of the liver, iron metabolism, and arthritis.

My last three stops were two total wipeouts and one modest success. In a laboratory that smelled like a brewery in which hundreds of Petri dishes were incubating the world's most hostile bacteria, I failed to explain the mechanism of action of several antibiotics. In exasperation (or dark humor), the investigator asked, "so, Mr. Noel . . . Alright. Hmmm. How many rings does tetracycline have?" I actually had to work on that (tetra = four and cycline = a six-sided ring), but I got it right.

At the next stop two men sat in their laboratory's Dutch doorway with a board at desk level in front of them. One was all beard below and billiard-ball bald above, and the other had a muff of blood-red hair and pink cheeks puffed out as though inflated. That one asked, "what do you know about uric acid metabolism?" I knew about gout and kidney stones, but missed the next three questions about the enzymes that took proteins apart and facilitated the excretion of uric acid. I felt sorry for them wasting their time on me.

The last stop was the chair of the department, George Thorn, the Hershey Professor of the Theory and Science of Physic. His question was fascinating, a test both of knowledge and reasoning.

"Imagine that Boston has been hit by an atomic bomb and all the power has been lost. However, a half-million people have survived, thousands of them with hormone deficiencies for which they need replacement drugs. There is no refrigeration, and none of them can refill their prescriptions. In what order, and after how many days, would patients with each of the deficiencies become symptomatic and who would die first?"

I reasoned that the diabetics who required insulin would get in trouble first, in a matter of hours or a day or two. People with adrenal insufficiency would also become sick quickly, perhaps in one or two days if they were stressed, as would patients with diabetes insipidus—loss of the hormone that helps the kidney hold on to water. Pure pituitary failure would take longer, as would thyroid failure, since the manifestations of those problems even when full blown sometimes take weeks or months, and death comes even much later than that.

I couldn't tell if he was satisfied, but he must have been because it would not be my last encounter with him.

On my way back up to Margaret's home to continue our Christmas holiday I imagined the summary note scrawled across my file by the uric acid twins: "Dumb as a stump, about what you would expect of an English Major who spent his winters reading Medieval poetry and his summers running chain saws and throwing dirt at burning trees."

Dr. Wilkins asked how I liked my interview. I said it was fine (it wasn't). He confided once again that the Brigham wasn't up to its reputation. I'm sure the interviewers thought that Columbia's medical school also wasn't up to its reputation based on their encounter with me.

A few days later Margaret drove me to South Station where I got on an overnight train for the ten-hour trip to Baltimore. A winter storm watch was on for the East Coast, but I expected all winters everywhere to be snowy and cold and thought nothing of it. I arrived at Baltimore's deserted Union Station at 7:40 AM. I had planned to take a taxi up to Hopkins for the 8 AM start of the interview day. In front of the station nothing was moving: there were two feet of new snow on the ground and there were no cabs, no shoveled sidewalks, and no plowed streets. Snow was continuing to fall. I had no choice but to walk up the hill in the Brooks Brothers blue suit and black wingtips I had gotten married in. It was a long slog. The snow had fallen over packed snow and my leather shoes slipped on icy patches every few steps.

When I walked through the Hopkins' front door my shoes were soaked through, I couldn't feel my feet, and my pantlegs looked like accordions. I smelled like a wet dog. No one seemed to notice.

Half of the interviewees didn't make it. I was taken on rounds by a resident who informed me that Hopkins was hell and then presented enough information to confirm that and double it: interns were on call for eleven months straight on the same inpatient team. They had to live in an apartment building across the street, married or not. They always covered their own patients day and night and they took every other admission. All notes had to be typed. They had one day off each week.

I was used to residency being hard and thought Columbia had that covered—our interns were on every other night and every other weekend, the residents every third night and weekend. A Columbia intern might get two or three admissions and be awake all night, but then could sleep uninterrupted in his own bed the next. I had been taught by a few Hopkins-trained faculty members whose skills and knowledge were outstanding, so I knew that the residency was among the best in the world and, although it was hard, it was survivable.

I was in a quandary. I had been to four legendary residency programs: I felt outmatched at all of them.

After that I made train trips to Cleveland, Ohio, Rochester and Buffalo, New York, and Chicago, Illinois. What I remember most about Cleveland and Buffalo, both waning industrial cities, were the faded Sheraton and Hilton hotels with their threadbare carpets, peeling wallpaper, and stained sheets.

The programs all seemed good enough, but only at the University of Chicago did I feel that they were enthusiastic about my visit. They made

The Match

an effort to convince me to come there, pointing out a long line of previous Columbia students who were or had been their residents.

My final visit was to our cross-town rival, Cornell, on its last interview day. At the end of two months of interviewing, they seemed as worn out as I felt.

At the end of January we listed the programs in the order of our preference, and the residency programs submitted their rank lists. And then began the long wait to learn where we would be spending the next three or four or five years.

The most desirable programs usually got their top applicants, and the strongest students usually got one of their top two or three choices. Weak students who had not applied to enough programs for which they were competitive might not match at all, but a few days before the match results were made public, the deans' offices in all of the medical schools got a list of unmatched students and a list of programs that had not filled all their positions. The unmatched students were summoned to the Deans' offices; calls were made to the programs with remaining spots that were most appealing to the students; and the students accepted one of the programs that offered them a spot. By Match Day almost all of the 8000 US medical students would have an envelope with the name of the residency to which they would be going.

Match Day was in the middle of March. We assembled in the ninth floor amphitheater where we had our first lecture by Professor Rittenberg, who had suggested that students who hadn't majored in science might as well quit right then; now we were about to find out if he was right. For two years we had spent several hours a day transcribing lectures in that ancient room. This is where we had learned of President Kennedy's assassination in Dallas, and this was where we were listening to Professor Moore expound when the great New York City blackout began. Now we were there to receive a white business envelope that would reveal what nearly four years of hard work had netted us.

The amphitheater was packed well beyond the number of seats. Many of the students had brought their parents or girl friends or wives or younger brothers and cousins who aspired to one day attend P & S. Margaret had taken the morning off from her teaching job to join me, her first visit inside the medical school buildings.

At precisely noon the Dean of Students, Dr. Perera—trim in a grey vested suit, black wingtips, and expensive tie—walked into the lower level of the amphitheater with two secretaries who each carried a shoebox full of envelopes. One by one they handed him an envelope and he called out the name of the student typed on it. It would take a long time to get to N, and nervously I watched as students opened their letters. Chuck Balch, one of the driven, surgery-bound students who seemed to have been born with the plan for his life encoded in his DNA whooped when he opened his letter: "Duke! I got Duke!" It was strange to see him jumping up and down and waving the letter announcing his match—usually he was uptight and stolid. David Brewster got surgery at the Massachusetts General and Frank Bragg got Columbia internal medicine, neither of those choice spots a surprise to any of us. Richard Mackler passed out, as he often did. Someone picked up his letter from the floor and called out "McGill." Richard was a pacifist and was planning to move to Canada in order to avoid being sent off to the war in Vietnam.

Most students quietly told those standing nearby where they would be going, the information spreading to a few adjacent people until the next student ascended the stairs with their letter. My anatomy partner Ken Nakano was called down before me; as he passed he told me that he would be training in Neurology in Boston.

During the weeks between my last interview in January and today I had been dreading not matching at all. My mind had been kept busy as a sub-intern on the Obstetrics and Gynecology Service, but during my daily ten block walk between the Medical Center and our apartment I worried that none of the Internal Medicine programs I had visited for interviews had been enthusiastic or encouraging—at each place I felt that I was not going to be at the top of their list. I decided that I would rather not match than go to my "back up" program, the University of Buffalo, and so I didn't rank it. It hadn't helped that on my interview day Buffalo was buried under three feet of snow, with a daytime high temperature of 12 degrees.

I feared that my envelope might say "No Match." I didn't know that three days before Dr. Perera had found spots in residency programs that had not filled for the two Columbia students who had not matched.

My rank list was:

Columbia-Presbyterian in New York City

Women's and Brigham Hospital in Boston

Johns Hopkins in Baltimore

Boston City Hospital, Harvard service

Cornell in New York City

Western Reserve in Cleveland

University of Rochester

Cleveland Metropolitan General

University of Chicago.

I took my envelope from Dr. Perera, but didn't open it. I climbed the stairs back to where Margaret was standing at the top of the amphitheater. I opened the letter, my hands shaking. I read the words on the letter but still had no idea of where I was going: it said, "The Billings Hospital and Clinics." I hadn't applied to the Billings Hospital. The only "Billings" I knew was in Montana, and if there had been a residency in Montana it would have been the Internal Medicine equivalent of being sent to Siberia. I looked again and beneath the crease in the letter were the additional words "of the University of Chicago."

I had matched into my last choice. The other programs had passed me by. Only the University of Chicago had wanted me.

I took Margaret's hand and left the room so that I didn't have to talk with anyone.

"For god's sake, Chicago."

The other people I admired who were heading into Internal Medicine had gotten stronger programs than I had: Dick Winickoff, Frank Bragg, Willy Lee, and Sandy Ackley (who I didn't admire but did respect as a student) would be four of the twelve interns in Medicine at Columbia. No one had gotten the Massachusetts General or the Brigham internal medicine programs, and no one was going to Hopkins. Walt Berger was going to the University of California in San Francisco for medicine, the most prestigious of the West Coast programs. Bob Clark would be going to the University of Washington in Seattle. Tony Imbembo, Dave Brewster and Bob Sloan were all heading to the Massachusetts General surgery residency in Boston.

My friends who had attended our wedding had done well: Bob Grossman had matched in internal medicine at the University of Pennsylvania, Bill Johnson would be going to Cornell for Neurology, Bennet Kolman to the University of Virginia in internal medicine.

My feelings oscillated: I was relieved that I had matched, disappointed that I wasn't staying at Columbia, and ashamed that I wasn't good enough for eight of the nine programs that interviewed me. I was ashamed, not angry, because I agreed with those residency programs' decisions: I also didn't think I had been strong enough to match at the Harvard programs or Hopkins or my own medical school.

We were going to have to find a place to live in a city I knew only from passing through when switching train stations traveling between Montana and Boston, and from a four-day convention I had attended in high school.

Margaret left to finish her day at Leonia High School. I took the A Train to Times Square; at a kiosk named "News of the World" I picked up the *Chicago Herald Tribune*. On the subway back I began to read the classified ads for apartments near the University of Chicago.

I stumbled through the rest of the day at the hospital. A junior resident who had been my intern for a month, who was bright but not warm, asked me where I matched.

"University of Chicago," I said, trying to look positive.

"That's about what I would have guessed," she said.

Good grief!

My friends, all more excited about their matches than I was, were supportive and enthusiastic about the University of Chicago, but I wasn't

The Match

having any of it. They were nice people. What were they going to say—that I was going to a shitty place, too bad but not surprising? My mood was grey and I felt that this was the worst day of my life.

I decided that the University of Chicago must be a terrible program if they had to accept me to fill.

Medical school graduation fell short of being even anticlimactic. We had all become doctors in practice if not academic degree months earlier. Unlike college and high school, there was no mystery or uncertainty about our future: residency and what it led to were well understood and loomed ahead of us not as an obstacle or opportunity, but as the obligatory next step on the long and well-travelled path to becoming a practicing physician. There were glimmers of excitement about being done with medical school, but the last year with eight months of subinternships had been like an internship and the step up to residency wasn't that big, more a matter of greater intensity than acquiring entirely new skills. Most of us felt a nervous energy when anticipating our first weeks and months as doctors who would be writing orders and making decisions with much less direction from older doctors. I felt that I didn't have enough experience to deal instantly with an emergency, but I expected that I would have one or several residents with me at those times.

That turned out not to always be the case.

On the day of graduation I donned the Columbia blue robes and the green hood that signified a medical doctoral degree and rode the IRT subway to 116th Street, Morningside Heights, where we merged with thousands of other Columbia undergraduate and graduate school students and their families and friends, heard an nearly inaudible and totally unmemorable speech, and then returned to Washington Heights for the more intimate medical school celebration where we received our diplomas, threw our hats in the air, said goodbye to each other, and dispersed in every direction.

I didn't have a single pang of nostalgia or sadness. No one ever wished medical school to be longer.

Perhaps the unspecialness of graduation was why I had not invited my Mom or Dad to come to New York City, partly because of expense and distance, partly because I had grown even more distant from them over the years, and partly because there just wasn't that kind of joy in the air. By and large, medical students are as sentimental and celebratory as anyone else who has just spent eight years in university education. For some students graduating from doctoral programs in other fields, a job and a salary and a family are just around the corner. But medical school graduation isn't the end of anything; for us there would be at least three and often as many as five or six years of residency training and fellowship ahead; for a great many of the men there would be two years of military service, and even then we would not be done learning. Proficiency and skill develop rapidly during residency, but it would take years of practice and a few thousands more patients before we would have seen and done almost everything in our field. We might change jobs several times in our first few years of practice to find one that fit us well. Until then most of us would not have stable lives: we had moved like gypsies from one college room or medical school apartment to another, and it would be years before we had a home that we settled in to raise a family.

At the end of medical school the one thing we could be reasonably sure of was that we were ready to begin training as MD's and that our lives were going to be much harder than they had been as medical students.

BARD HALL, WHERE I LIVED AS A FIRST AND SECOND YEAR STUDENT

Learning the Art of Medicine—a Memoir

COLUMBIA PRESBYTERIAN MEDICAL CENTER.

P & S CLASS OF '65 YEARBOOK

Photos

THE NINTH FLOOR AMPHJITHEATER—BASIC SCIENCE LECTURE
P&S CLASS OF '65 YEARBOOK

DAVID RITTENBERG *You got a good grade for a liberal arts major—an F.*

Photos

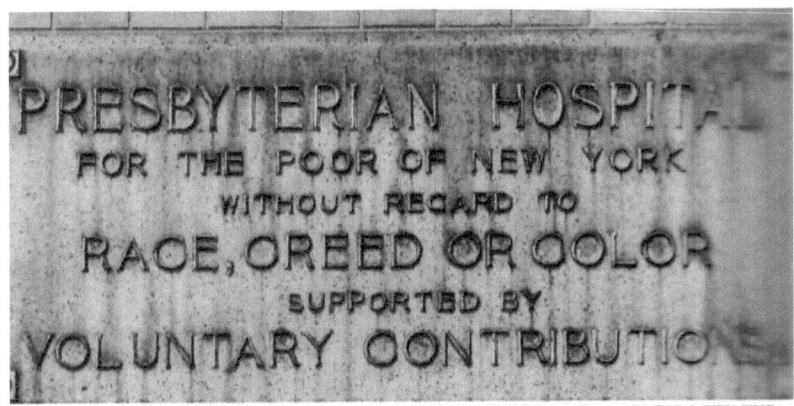

THE COLUMBIA UNIVERSITY COLLEGE OF PHYSICIANS AND SURGEONS MERGED WITH THE
PRESBYTERIAN HOSPITAL TO CREATE THE FIRST ACADEMIC MEDICAL CENTER IN THE 1920'S

P & S CLASS OF '68 YEARBOOK

QUIET SATURDAY AFTERNOON REVIEW OF THE WEEK'S DISECTION IN THE ANATOMY LAB

MARGARET STUDYING IN MY ROOM, 1963

GRADUATING FROM HARVARD, JUNE 1963, WITH MARGARET

Photos

MARGARET'S GRADUATION FROM HARVARD, WITH HER FAMILY, 1964

MARGARET, ON HER WAY TO CLASS AT HARVARD, 1963

MARGARET DURING HER MASTER OF ARTS IN TEACHING STUDIES AT OBERLIN, 1965

MARGARET, ENGAGEMENT PICTURE, 1964

Photos

ME, ENGAGEMENT PICTURE, 1964

WEDDING—MARGARET AND HER FATHER, DR. WILKINS, JULY, 1965

Photos

JUST MARRIED, WITH MY MOTHER ON THE FAR RIGHT, AND IN THE BACKGROUND MARGARET'S BROTHER BOBBY AND MY BEST MAN, GEOFF NOWLIS

CUTTING THE CAKE

Photos

DR. WILKINS WORKED FOR WEEKS TO MAKE THE GARDEN PERFECT

MARRIED. LEAVING FOR NEW YORK CITY

1965 Mrs. Gordon Lee Noel
Bradford Bachrach

Noel-Wilkins Wedding Held in Home of Bride

NEWBURYPORT — In Bermuda on their wedding trip are Mr. and Mrs. Gordon Lee Noel (Margaret Dodge Wilkins) who were married July 17 at a 4 o'clock ceremony held at the home of the bride's parents, Dr. and Mrs. Robert Wallace Wilkins, 299 High St. The bridegroom is the son of Mrs. Leah Noel of Missoula, Mont.

In a setting of western smilax, lilies and garden flowers, the Rev. Bertrand Steeves of the Unitarian Church performed the double ring ceremony.

Providing baroque music for the wedding were the following: Mrs. Robert W. Pearson, violin; Dr. Robert W. Pearson, 'cello, of Newbury; and Bernard Jones, harpsichord, of Rockport.

The bride was given in marriage by her father. She wore her grandmother's wedding dress of ivory satin and a fingertip length heirloom lace veil, and carried a bouquet of white daisies and phlox. The gown had carried pink tea roses.

Geoffrey Nowlis of New Haven, Conn., was best man and the bride's brother, Robert W. Wilkins Jr. of Newburyport ushered.

For her daughter's wedding, Mrs. Wilkins selected blue lace and wore a corsage of white phalaenopsis.

The bridegroom's mother, Mrs. Noel, chose pink lace and a corsage of green cypripediums.

For her going away costume the bride chose an aqua summer suit.

The bride attended Newburyport High School, Abbot Academy, Radcliffe College and Oberlin College where she received her M.A. degree.

Medical Student — The bridegroom attended Harvard College and is presently in his third year at Columbia University College of Physicians and Surgeons.

After Sept. 15 Mr. and Mrs. Noel will make their home at 1385 Nicholas Ave., New York.

GARDEN PARTY AT THE WILKINS' HOME

Photos

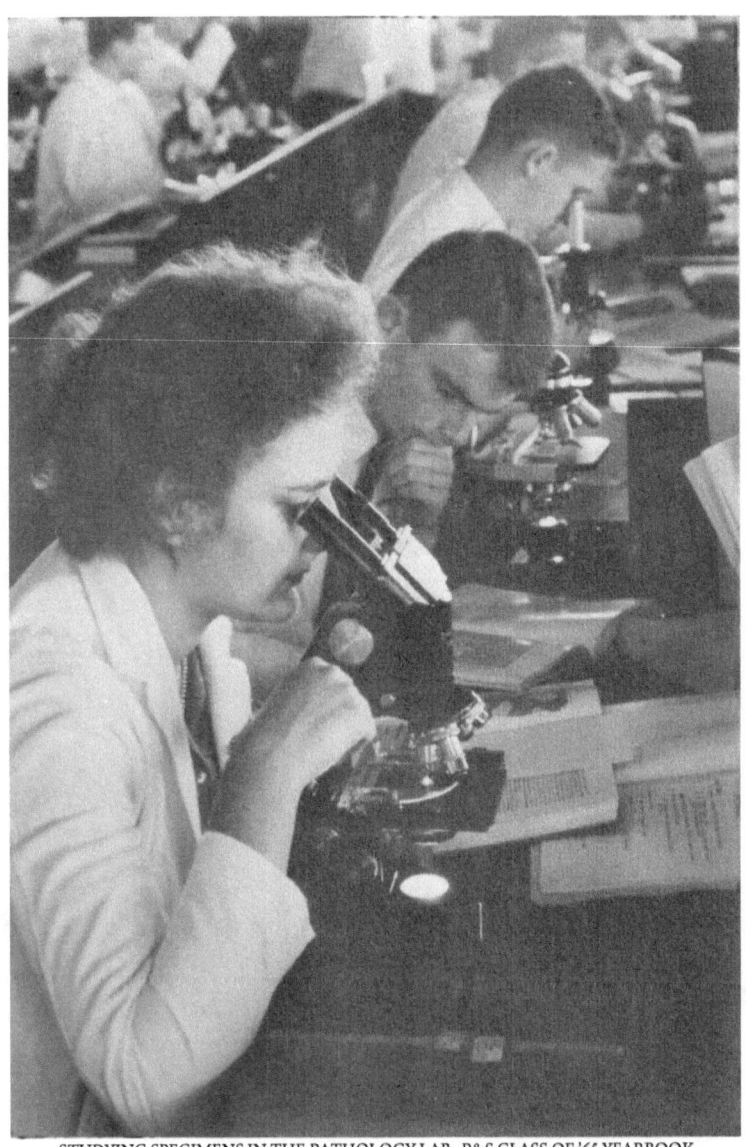

STUDYING SPECIMENS IN THE PATHOLOGY LAB. P&S CLASS OF '65 YEARBOOK

Learning the Art of Medicine—a Memoir

THE MEDICAL LIBRARY—THERE WERE NO COPYING MACHINES—IF YOU WANTED TO REMEMBER SOMETHING YOU WROTE IT DOWN.

Photos

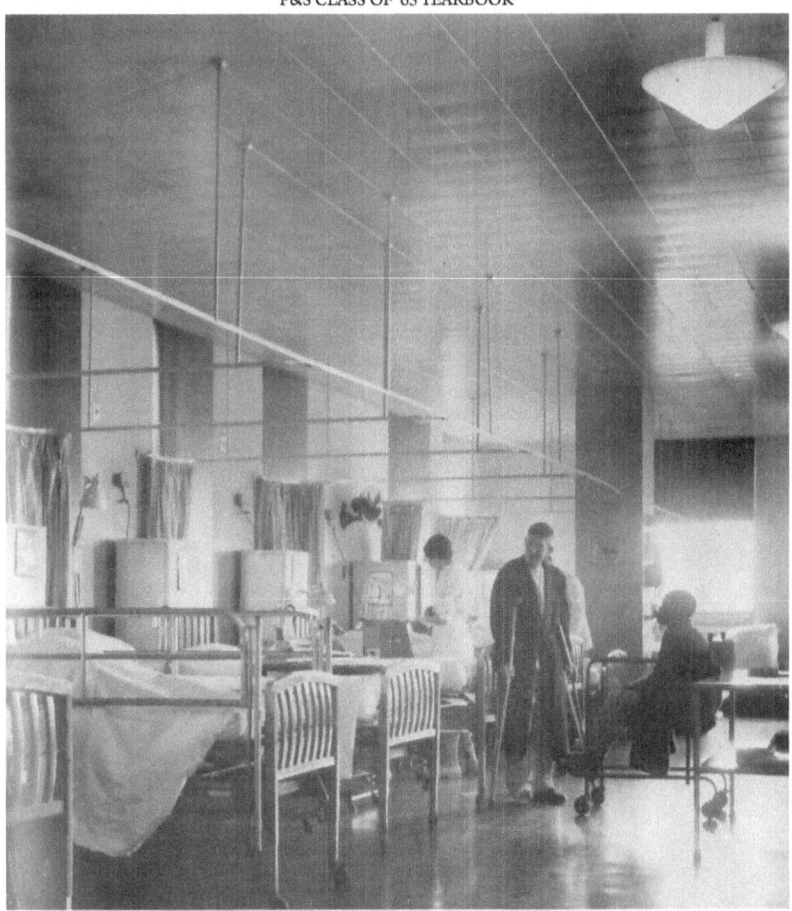

P&S CLASS OF '65 YEARBOOK

A WARD FOR MALE PATIENTS IN THE PRESBYTERIAN HOSPITAL. THE FIRST ACADEMIC MEDICAL CENTER IN THE 1920'S.

P & S CLASS OF '68 YEARBOOK

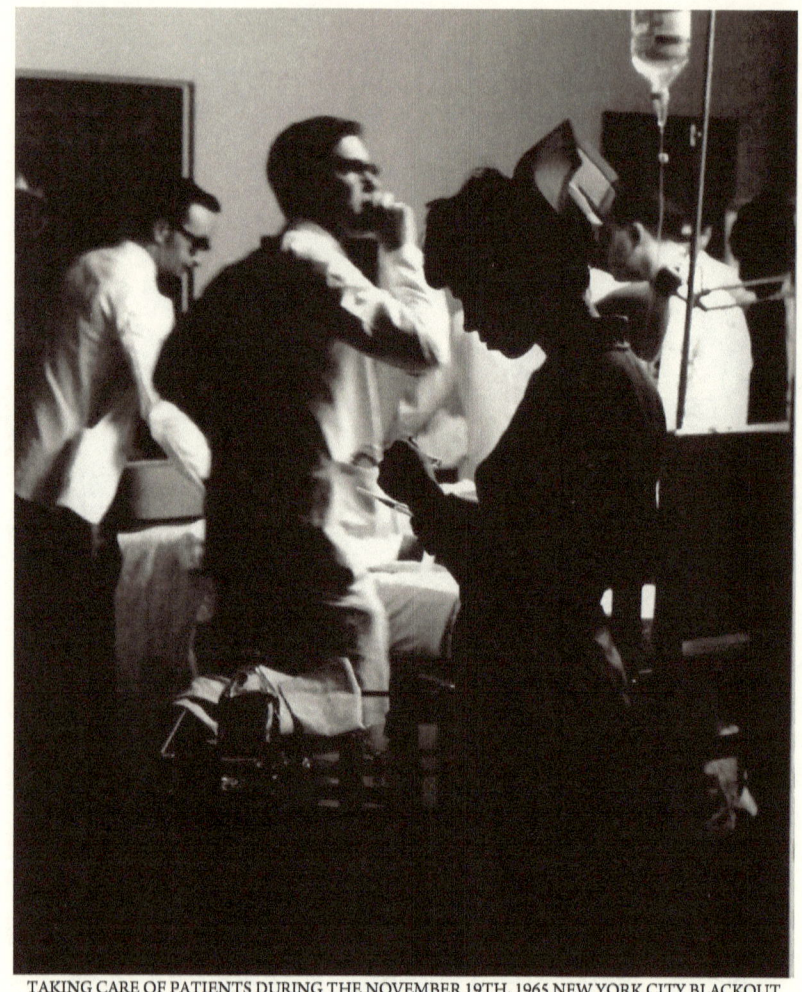

TAKING CARE OF PATIENTS DURING THE NOVEMBER 19TH, 1965 NEW YORK CITY BLACKOUT

SEVENTY-FIVE YEARS OF HEALING ON THE HEIGHTS

Photos

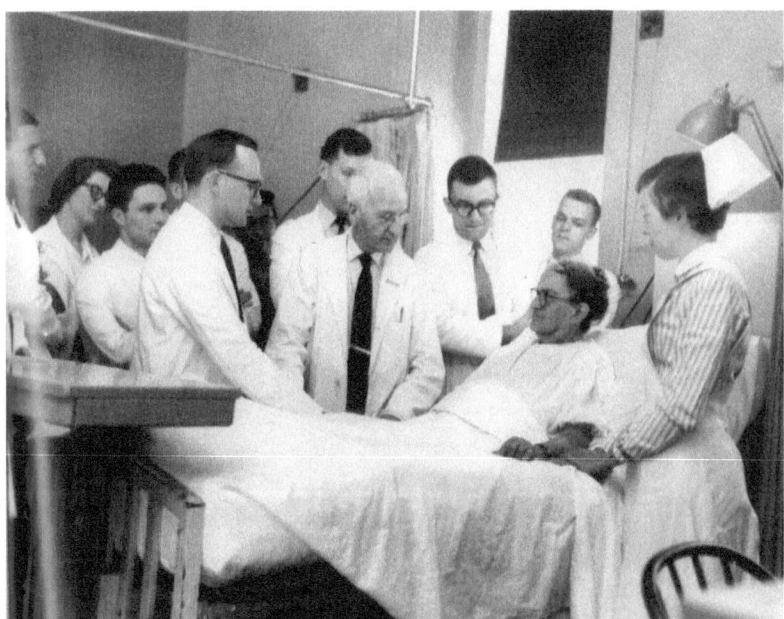

DR. DANA ATCHLEY MAKING BEDSIDE ROUNDS WITH THIRD YEAR MEDICAL STUDENTS IN THE PRESBYTERIAN HOSPITAL IN THE LATE 1950'S.

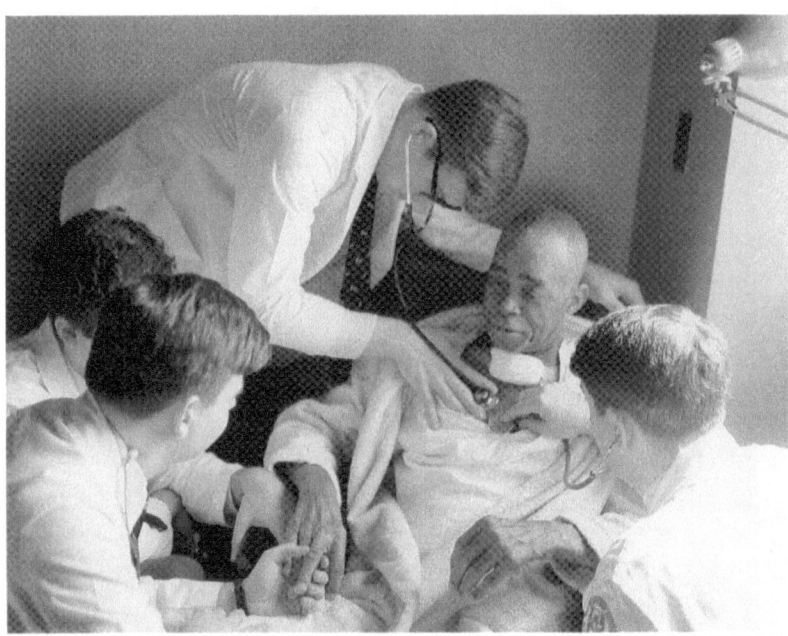

MEDICAL STUDENTS LEARNING PHYSICAL EXAMINATION—TWO ARE INSPECTING THE HANDS, TWO LISTENING FOR A HEART MURMUR FROM "SEVENTY-FIVE YEARS OF HEALING ON THE HEIGHTS"

Learning the Art of Medicine
Residency

1967 – 1972

CHAPTER 15

The University of Chicago

A few days after graduation the same moving company that had brought furniture down from Margaret's parents' house in Newburyport pulled up in front of our St. Nicolas Avenue apartment building. We felt that the furniture from Margaret's family was precious, and since the driver who did that move was really good at moving antique furniture, it made sense to have him drive it to Chicago. He was a respectable, sober, clean-shaven guy in his late fifties. He talked like a Newburyporter, a kind of Down-East/South Boston dialect in which "awe" becomes "aaahh," and "r" gets dropped, as in "Havad Yahd", or an "r" is attached to a vowel at the end of a word, as in "idear".

This was going to be a week-long move for him, and to avoid having to hire crew in two unfamiliar cities, he had brought along two scruffy helpers who were nothing much to look at: one had half his teeth missing, the gaps too random for him to have lost them in just a single fight; the other was scrawny, his skin cured and scented by smoking two packs of Camels a day.

Our building was home to a number of nurses from the medical center. Every afternoon they returned home from the day shift in a steady stream. As the guys stood waiting for the elevator between loads, they asked each of them if she would like to show a couple of out-of-towners around in exchange for a steak dinner and a good time. I predicted that their efforts to land a double date were hopeless; most of the nurses demurred, averting their gazes or saying "no thanks." After about a dozen rejections, one accepted and gave them her apartment number:

"I'll get my girlfriend to join us. Knock on 1221. Give us an hour and we'll be ready."

The guys weren't even surprised.

There have been a lot of times in my life when I glimpsed my own unworldliness. I saw that I knew absolutely nothing about picking someone up or guessing who might be attractive to whom or the transformative power of a free steak dinner and a couple of drinks.

A Columbia faculty member who was moving to the University of Chicago had gotten our names and we agreed to drive one of his cars to Chicago, loaded with the clothes we needed until our furniture arrived. As soon as I graduated I began to feel the enormity of what was now just a week away: I was going to be writing orders for acutely ill patients, many with diseases I had no experience with. I asked Margaret to drive while I paged through the thick *Washington Manual of Medical Therapeutics*, trying to memorize everything I would need to know, from treating drippy noses to managing constipation, coma, convulsions and cardiac arrest. I read the entire manual during that trip and arrived in Chicago with brain lag, no recollection of the scenery we had passed through, and badly shaken self-confidence.

A month after Match Day, Margaret had flown to Chicago to find an apartment and interview for several jobs. The Encyclopedia Britannica Publishing Company offered her a job in their educational films department. Close to the campus she found a new apartment building. The rent for our apartment in New York City had been $137 a month. With our combined incomes, in Chicago we could afford a two-bedroom apartment with a large living room, dining area, and two bedrooms for $250 a month.

During our second year on St. Nicholas Avenue cockroaches had worked their way up to the 28th floor. In the middle of the night Margaret went into the bathroom and turned on the light, startling a cockroach on the mirror that scampered out of sight. She screamed as though she had come face to face with a murderer. After that she and the cockroaches were locked in unequal combat. Our Chicago apartment was new and clean and Margaret was determined to keep it that way: when our boxes were packed in New York City, Margaret bombed each one with lethal doses of Raid for Cockroaches. When boxes were unloaded in Chicago, Margaret opened each one herself. She found dozens of corpses of stowaway cockroaches. The only one that had survived her fumigational fury she blasted with a half can of Raid as it staggered out of a box of pots and pans.

We never saw cockroaches where we lived again: word went out to the insect world, "Do not mess with Margaret."

The first day of residency the twelve new interns—eleven men and one woman— met in a medical school lecture hall. The chairman, Professor Hans Hecht, introduced himself and described the program's call schedule. Then he asked each division chief to introduce himself and describe in a few words what the experience would be like during our one-month rotations on his service. The final introduction was saved for the head of endocrinology:

"Well, the cardiologists will give you hearts, which are important—it's hard to get along without a heart—and the renal division will give you urine, which, while messy, is also important. What the gastroenterology division will give you is unmentionable. But endocrinology is best, because only endocrinology will give you sex."

There was thin, nervous laughter.

The entire orientation to internship lasted less than 30 minutes. Then we were turned over to the resident with whom we would work for the next month. Those on call were given an hour to go home to get a toothbrush and a razor. I was one of them.

And so it started: I began on the Nephrology service, caring for patients with severe bladder infections or kidneys that leaked protein so that the patients' feet and legs and often their abdomens were swollen with fluid. "Teddy" Pullman was our attending physician, in charge of me and a senior resident, John Growdon, one of my most fortuitous pairings: we became friends for life. John had been a student at Northwestern University's School of Medicine in Chicago, and was now in his last year of residency before fulfilling his draft obligation with a two-year assignment to the huge Air Force base in Guam. John was elegant, worldly, scholarly, funny, and ironic, with an air of cool sophistication: if he had ever been intense as a student or intern, he was entirely over it now.

The attending physicians at the University of Chicago were different than those at Columbia: they seemed less often to come from a world of wealth and privilege and manners and were more down to earth; while by no means humble, they were rarely pretentious.

Dr. Pullman made rounds with us every morning, hearing about our new admissions and reviewing our other patients' progress—or lack of it. The first day, John presented the new patients and progress reports since I had arrived just minutes before rounds. He told me that he would present our eight patients and any new admissions the next day as well. I told him that I could do that; he didn't doubt me, and from that point on John held back, filling in details I had missed or left out, and then listening as I presented our plans. After a few days John told me that it wasn't common for interns to be able to present until the second half of the year. I told him I had presented and written the notes on all of my patients for two years and that I would like to keep doing it.

It seemed as though the students from the two other medical schools that made up the majority of our intern class —Harvard and the University of Chicago—had been somewhat more observers as students, even in their fourth year. I checked with Bob Russell—the other Columbia student who was now an intern with me—and he confirmed that he too had taken on much of his resident's role. Two years of high responsibility patient care at Columbia had created a distinctive style: although we had spent less book time than many of our fellow interns, we had learned how to manage patients and organize a day's chores efficiently. For the first few months, when I was not on call I would usually leave the hospital by six. While most of the other interns were still a few hours away from finishing their new patients' admission notes and writing their orders, I was home reading. By halfway through the year we were all in the same place—my book knowledge had caught up with theirs, and their efficiency had caught up with Bob's and mine.

Almost from the beginning I was comfortable at the University of Chicago. There was a high level of support and an absence of elitism among the residents and faculty that quickly translated into my no longer feeling like an outsider: there was an assumption that all of the interns had the knowledge and skills we needed and that we would be successful. There was no grandstanding, no hot-shot residents who wanted to let you know how smart they were by facial expressions and tones of voice that implied how dumb you were, nothing like the hazing I had felt as a third-year student during the medicine clerkship. Unlike when we were students, we no longer felt that we were being constantly evaluated, and there was a tolerance for different styles of going about the daily work of caring for patients. In spite of my sense of comfort—or possibly because of it—I began to feel guilty that I wasn't working as hard as my classmates who had stayed at Columbia, who were taking call every other night and admitting many more patients. I was afraid that I would not be as good a doctor as they would be when we finished our residencies. Internship was supposed to be hard, and while mine had long hours, we only took overnight call every four or five days and there were fewer critically ill admissions.

In New York City, Presbyterian Hospital sat in the middle of a lower middle-class working neighborhood and many of our Irish and Jewish and Puerto Rican and black patients had little or no insurance. Everyone could be admitted to one of the Presbyterian Hospital wards, no questions asked about finances. The University of Chicago wasn't allowed to take care of the uninsured patient that came to its emergency room unless it would be dangerous to transport them crosstown to Cook County Hospital. The ward politicians wanted all the city and state funds for the uninsured to stay in the city hospitals where they controlled the budget and the hospital jobs that they used to reward constituents who turned out votes for them. They didn't want any of the city money to go to private hospitals like Northwestern or the University of Chicago.

A well-insured city council member I cared for who preferred the University of Chicago over Cook County for his own medical problems told me it went like this:

"So, I am out walking my district and stopping in at the little shops and calling on the priests and the policemen. I know all them guys. I find out what they need—a little help with an overzealous inspector, maybe spread some good words for their business, tell them about a city contract they might try for."

"A few days ago, I run into a friend I went to grade school with, we even took our first communion together, and we start talking. And after a while I say to him, 'so is your little girl Mary Magdalena doing okay in nursing school?' and he says 'sure is, she's a smart girl and gonna be looking for a job in a few months,' and I say to him, 'Jimmy, I appreciate the way you went to bat for me in the last election, you know that don't you, and I don't forget my friends. So you tell Mary Magdalena when she's ready to graduate she just needs to call my office—you know the number—and tell my new girl Annie who answers the phone that Mary Magdalena will be graduating soon. We'll have a job waiting for her at the County.' Then we laugh about a few of our old friends and we say goodbye and he'll be there for me in the next election. So that's what I can do for my people, and for the ones that gave money to my opponent, they won't get shit from me."

As a result, most of the patients that were admitted to the University of Chicago were the insured people living near Hyde Park or the more affluent suburbs. A huge African American community surrounded the University on three sides, but those people didn't feel welcome at UC. When the ambulances brought in someone who was too sick to be transported, we admitted them, but anyone stable enough to travel was sent away. As a result, most of our admissions were elective and arrived during the day, and usually I could get them worked up by the early evening.

The University of Chicago

My second rotation was neurology. As they had been at Columbia, the faculty members were scholarly, calm, and versed in the history of medical discovery. At the end of the month, our attending invited us to his Victorian Hyde Park mansion near the campus for a dinner party, where good wine and good food was served and conversation was spirited. I was in love with neurology; I had already learned a lot as a student, and I began thinking that when I finished my medical training, I should do another residency in neurology. The fact that John Growdon was planning to become a neurologist after his military service made the idea even more attractive.

After Nephrology and Neurology, I had a month on the Gastroenterology Service. The chief of that Division was J. B. Kirsner, a world-famous clinician and scholar who had one of the three largest programs in the United States for the care of inflammatory bowel diseases like ulcerative colitis and Crohn's disease. Dr. Kirsner's attention to his patients was legendary: as his interns we functioned more as caddies than as first line diagnosticians and managers. Woe be to the intern or resident who did not care for a patient exactly by Kirsner's all-encompassing guidelines and rules.

Dr. Kirsner's patients were devoted to him, but I found many to be demanding—often taking the stance of, "My sleeping pill is what Dr. Kirsner said I should take; if you change it, I'll tell Dr. Kirsner that you are a terrible doctor and I want someone else."

However, in the two months I was on the GI service I saw three times as many diverse presentations of inflammatory bowel and peptic ulcer diseases as I would have seen at Columbia in a year. His patients came from all over the world—and he attracted very strong post-residency doctors to train with him as gastroenterology fellows. The University of Chicago's expertise drew in patients who had failed in the hands of other physicians, including many patients who had repeatedly been operated on with resulting shorter and shorter bowels and marginal nutrition.

Some of his patients were admitted as emergencies with acute, life-threatening flares. One young woman, who had developed severe ulcerative colitis when she was 8, was rushed in for surgery because of fever, shock, and sepsis—bacteria in her blood—with a syndrome called toxic megacolon. Plain abdominal films showed a massively enlarged colon full of gas; she was too sick to have a barium enema to be sure she wasn't obstructed. Ordinarily she might have had proctoscopy, but her colon tissues were too friable and the diagnosis wasn't in doubt. The plan was to have her in the operating room within two hours of admission and my job was to update her history, do a complete physical examination to make sure she could withstand surgery, and order preoperative laboratory tests. With her admission orders from Dr. Kirsner was the instruction to make sure she didn't have a fecal impaction. She agreed to let me do a rectal exam. Because of her discomfort I did the exam with her on her back. As I inserted my finger a thick stream of liquid poop erupted. As usual I was wearing a white coat and pants, and for some reason I was wearing my second-best necktie, the one I wore when we left from our wedding two years earlier. The bottom of my tie was directly in the fecal stream. The rest of my clothes were spared—my tie had served as an expensive bib. I cleaned her up, grabbed my bandage scissors, bent over the wastebasket and cut off the lower half of my tie. We got her to the operating room within an hour; the patients I had yet to tuck in that night before going home did not comment on my half-tie.

Two days after her operation I visited her on the surgical ward. She was lying in bed, still frail looking and pale. She smiled weakly when she recognized me and told me how embarrassed she was.

"I thought you were too sick to know what happened," I said.

"I was terribly sick, but I saw you cut your tie off and guessed why. Was it an expensive tie?"

"Not any longer!"

She smiled again. "Can I buy you another?"

"No," I said. "I'm switching to bow ties. I owe it all to you."

She smiled weakly.

The University of Chicago

"I am so glad to see that you are better. "

She wished me good luck, and I wished her the same. For the next five decades I never again wore a necktie when I was taking care of patients.

Initially I wasn't enthusiastic about Dr. Kirsner's service, in part because he referred the care of his patients' non-gastroenterological problems to other specialists—simple problems like uncomplicated, stable diabetes or mild hypertension that at Columbia any internist could have cared for without needing the help of a specialist. By the end of the month my feelings about Dr. Kirsner's service had softened a little. I had no doubt that many of his patients were alive because of the expert care of Kirsner's staff and the University of Chicago surgeons.

In October, I was on a general medical service. My attending, Dr. Thompson, though a rheumatologist, had trained at Columbia and was also a good generalist. Only third year residents rotated on the general medicine service since they were considered more capable of handling a broad range of patients without specialist supervision. Mine was Howard Schacter, chosen to be the next year's chief resident. He was off on my first day and I rounded by myself and then presented the service to Dr. Thompson. The next day Howard was back and was surprised that I had seen half of the patients without him before he arrived. He felt that he had to guide me through what needed to be done. Somewhat famously as it turned out, I asked him to let me round alone in the morning while he made his own rounds, and then to meet with me before rounds to go over the patients to be sure he agreed with my updated history, exams, and plans. I never did my morning work rounds with a resident again. It got back to me that he was grumpy about this. On the other hand, since I had thrown out the next chief resident, for the rest of the year the other residents were prepared to grant me independence.

During the gastroenterology and nephrology months my concern grew that the University of Chicago had abandoned the notion of training great generalists in favor of training great specialists. Instead of getting over my disappointment at not matching at my top choices, I began to long for the programs at Columbia, Johns Hopkins, and Harvard's Boston City Hospital service where the focus was on training generalists with broad expertise.

The war in Vietnam was ramping up and during the 1960's total military personnel increased by a million. Every male doctor still in training had to plan on two years of military service. Many chose to do it after their internship, so occasionally a residency program would have a second-year position open in July. In September I decided that I would try to transfer from Chicago to one of the East Coast programs that had interviewed me for internship.

I applied to Columbia, the Brigham, and the Harvard service at Boston City Hospital. Our department of medicine asked all of the residents to let them know if we were planning to sign a contract for the next year. I told Dr. Hecht, the department chairman, and Dr. Tarlov, the residency program director, that I would like to apply for the second-year residency at Chicago, but that I would also be applying to several other programs. I asked Dr. Hecht if he would write a letter of recommendation to the programs that I was going to apply for, and he agreed.

There were no interviews or formal matches for residency positions after the internship. The internal medicine department chairmen had agreed that they would all offer any vacant positions on the 28th of October. Drs. Hecht and Tarlov told me that they hoped I would stay, and that if I did, they would like me to be their chief resident after my third year.

On the 27th of October the paging operator told me I had a long-distance telephone call. It was from Dr. Davidson, the chief of medicine of the Harvard service at Boston City Hospital, offering me a second-year residency. He reviewed the virtues of Boston City Hospital and asked me to let him know by the next morning. I was thrilled. Boston City Hospital had been my third choice; I loved its tradition; and I loved the idea of living in Boston, a city that I had fallen in love with in college and had never gotten over when I moved to New York City.

The University of Chicago

I finished up my day's work and bicycled home. With excitement I told Margaret, expecting her to love the idea of returning to Boston. She didn't. She was crazy about Chicago and had spent most of her life in or near Boston: it was no adventure for her to go back.

While we were eating dinner, our apartment phone rang: it was Dr. Bradley at Columbia-Presbyterian, asking me to come back for residency. I was speechless. CPMC was my first choice of the three. I had understood why four of my classmates had been chosen and I had not—they were heads and shoulders better medical students than I had been. Dr. Bradley seemed actually warm, and I didn't remind him that I was the guy who presented him a psychotic naked woman sitting on a loaded bedpan and that he had ignored my figuring out her diagnosis when no one else could. If I had been in seventh heaven when the call came from Boston City Hospital, I was in at least tenth heaven to be given the chance to return to Columbia. I reflexively told Dr. Bradley that I would come, although I hadn't told Margaret, who was in the next room.

The next morning while I was dressing the phone rang again. It was Dr. Thorn, the Hersey Professor of the Theory and Practice of Physic at Harvard, offering me a residency at the Brigham. I was stunned. In twelve hours I had been invited to my top three programs, in two cities I wanted to live in, and I already was beyond considering staying at the University of Chicago. Without any pause for longer consideration, I told him that I had already been invited to return to Columbia, and had accepted.

"Damn," he said. "I knew I should have called you last night, but I was playing by the rules. Well, I'm sorry."

I didn't tell him that the other two chairmen had called the night before.

That evening I laid it all out for Margaret. She listened quietly and said that she was prepared to go where I thought I would get the best training, although she loved Chicago— she found it much more accessible than New York City, and she loved her job at Encyclopedia Britannica. "If it were only my choice," she said, "I would want to stay in Chicago."

When I got to the hospital the next day I sought out Drs. Tarlov and Hecht and told them that I planned to leave. They were beyond gracious, congratulating me, and telling me that they were sorry that I would be leaving but they had assumed that I probably would and had made a tentative offer to an intern in another residency program who was hoping to switch to the University of Chicago.

Dr. Tarlov continued to be very supportive. He had an award from the Markle Foundation to pay for some of his time to mentor students and residents. Every few months over the rest of the year he invited me to have lunch in his laboratory and gradually shared his wisdom about leading a life in an academic medical center. He had no obligation to do this at all, and given my planned departure in the spring, he could have chosen to spend the time with any of the interns who were staying.

The setting was always the same: A few days before the date we had chosen, his secretary would find me and ask if it was still convenient to meet. It always was. Then she handed me a menu of sandwiches and drinks and desserts available from the hospital cafeteria, from which I chose. When I arrived in his lab a few days later, a space had been cleared on one of the benches, placemats and napkins and eating utensils laid out. He always started by asking me how my current rotation was going and then asked if anything could be better. He was not much taller than I, with a quiet face and calm, slow voice. He was always fully engaged; his secretary held phone calls. He didn't take notes but seemed to remember the details of our earlier conversations. We probably met four times, and each time he left me with some thought about a future career that perhaps he could see and that I could not.

His most useful advice was, "Never agree to serve on a committee the work of which you feel no passion for." He noted that universities had myriad committees, many of them required by regulation, and most of which would not be central to my interests and work. He went on, "When you are working on something at eleven at night for a meeting the next day, it should be something you care enough about to give up the sleep. You'll always be asked to do committee work, and if you are good at it, you will be endlessly asked. Sometimes you have to take on a project that is not of great interest to you but that is important to the institution. However, try not to have your time so tied up that you can't take on the projects for which you feel an aching enthusiasm."

That December was our first Christmas since I was a college senior that we hadn't spent at Margaret's family home in Newburyport. It was also the first time that I had real money in my pocket. Always loving to shop for Margaret, after an overnight call I showered as soon as I got home, slept for a few hours, and then about noon put on a suit and my good overcoat and best shoes and walked to the Illinois Central station to catch a train into downtown Chicago. It had snowed several days before and I was expecting a winter wonderland as I walked north from the train station to the fashionable stores on Michigan Avenue. With an icy wind in my face, block-by-block I got colder and colder and, worse, my leather shoes were a poor choice to navigate the slush that the combination of salt and snow had become. In medical school I had shopped for her at Bonwit Teller on Fifth Avenue in New York City once, and I was planning to find presents for her in Chicago's Bonwit, which occupied an elegant four-story building on Watertower Square next to Saks Fifth Avenue. I crossed the street and as I tried to push open the heavy front door an astonishingly lovely woman—at least six feet tall and wearing a long ruby red gown with matching shoes and candelabra earrings—pushed open the door for me and gently took my left arm.

"Welcome to Bonwit Teller. What a cold wet afternoon. Let me take care of you."

Needless to say, I had no ready, suave response. In fact, nothing came to my mind but reversing directions and fleeing out the front door. No woman matching that description had ever touched or spoken to me.

"Are you here to shop for someone?"

My face was stiff from the cold. "My w-wife," I stammered.

"Please let me take your coat. We will hang it in a special closet and it will be warm and dry when you are ready to leave." She had amazing eyelashes, like dense, dark daddy long legs' legs. I didn't know that there could be eyelashes like that, and I looked into dozens of eyes every day.

Without resistance I surrendered my coat and wondered what was next.

"Let's go somewhere more comfy," she said, and she hooked her arm in mine and slow-walked me to an elevator, where a tall blond in a long black gown and three-inch heels and more daddy-long-legs eyelashes took my other arm; together the three of us rode to the second floor. The door opened to a lush carpeted room strewn with deep easy chairs and lavish chandeliers in which sat a dozen slightly embarrassed-looking, portly elderly men, each chaperoned by a gowned young woman. The ruby-gowned woman disappeared and the black-gowned woman asked me what I was hoping for. This struck me as being a once-in-a-lifetime opportunity. Fortunately, I didn't say any of the first three things that came to mind.

"Well, a long nightgown with an empire waist and spaghetti straps, low cut, on the edge of, but not quite, transparent. And perhaps a wool sweater. And maybe a dress, high-waisted."

She bent down close to the chair and unlaced and removed my shoes, ignoring my damp socks and wet pant cuffs. From beneath my chair she pulled out a pair of fleece-lined leather slippers and gently tucked my feet into them.

"What can I get for you? I can give you anything you'd like."

Now my mind was racing. Why was she saying these things? I had heard that bordellos existed but never dreamed I would walk into one on Michigan Avenue while Christmas shopping for my wife.

Again, I barely managed to suppress myself. "Anything? Scotch and soda?"

"Of course."

She picked up my shoes and left the room. Now there was no escaping.

In a few minutes another gorgeous woman appeared with my Scotch in a weighty cut glass tumbler. I looked around the room and saw that there were now small racks of clothes pulled up beside most of the other men, from which more gowned women pulled clothes off the rack and held them high with one hand, draping the item over their other arm, the men nodding, or shaking their heads. Gradually a small collection was being made on another rack. Further away a woman was holding a black velvet pad on which she displayed one and then another and then another item of lingerie. I blushed and looked away.

In a few minutes the woman in the black gown returned with two other similarly garbed and eyelashed women who had armloads of clothes. I don't think I ever heard her name, but she had gotten mine and had learned my trade: "Dr. Noel, was this what you had in mind?" "Dr. Noel" was a title that still felt slightly fraudulent, but as the scotch warmed me I was becoming comfortable with the title and the place.

It crossed my mind that I wasn't going to get out of Bonwit's cheaply.

We went through a dozen sweaters, and I picked out two. And then I choose a single brown dress of soft wool, high-waisted, knee length. The practical items chosen, she began to take nightgowns off the rack. I immediately rejected the baby dolls and teddies and narrowed the selection down to two long gowns, one yellow, one white. Now a question bubbled up that I should have suppressed, but I was enjoying my disinhibition: after all, who was going to tell on me?

"I don't suppose someone about her size could try on this one so that I could see how it looks?"

Unfazed, the black-gowned woman skillfully redirected me: "No one would be exactly your wife's size or have her coloring, but she can try it on at home, and if you or she don't like it, she can bring it back."

"She can return it, even if she has tried it on?"

"Of course." She looked at me with a warm but faintly pitying smile, as though thinking that I was a nice but socially inexperienced and certainly unworldly young doctor. We were about the same age and she decided to advance my education.

Leaning close over me, her fluttering eyelashes lightly flicking the edge of my ear, she whispered, "Do you see all those gentlemen across the room?

They buy the most outrageous and skimpy lingerie and nightgowns for their wives, always two sizes too small and totally impractical. The day after Christmas the wives will all be downstairs at the return desk exchanging the presents for clothes they actually want to wear. The clothes these gentlemen choose are kind of a gift card. The men have a great time buying these things every Christmas and wouldn't at all enjoy buying what their wives actually end up with."

I had a choice here: to believe that I had chosen what Margaret would actually wear and I would enjoy seeing, or admitting that I might already be like the rich old guys across the room. I gambled. I asked her to have the gifts wrapped, and she whisked the four pieces through a little door at the side of the room. Then she and yet another gowned woman returned with my warm topcoat and dry shoes, tucked me into them, relieved me of my empty tumbler, and said that if I walked to the desk beside the elevator I could write a check for my purchases.

In a few minutes, with two Scotches on board and a Bonwit's shopping bag in each hand I wobbled out of the store with my hot shoes and not-too-hot presents and a warm glow of incipient customer loyalty. I smirked at a couple of old men walking in with rosy cheeks and dribbling noses, feeling superior. I knew I would go to Bonwit next Christmas, although at the Fifth Avenue store in Manhattan. Christmas shopping had never been so fine. I felt very grown up. I was also down half a month's paycheck.

In the early winter I took over the care of a man about my age who was an assistant manager at the Chicago Playboy Club. He had Hodgkin's disease, a form of cancer that was usually so responsive to radiotherapy that a high proportion of patients were cured. When discovered, his Hodgkins was both above and below his diaphragm and was more aggressive than most. Over the previous year he had received extensive radiation therapy, but the radiation had damaged his lungs and had caused inflammation of his small bowel. Just before I met him he had been admitted for spread of the disease to his brain.

The University of Chicago

I introduced myself to him and his girlfriend, who had been one of the Playboy bunnies. She sat on his bed with her back propped up against the headboard holding him in her arms, stroking his face and hair. With every breath he made a small groan as he inhaled.

I asked him if he could tell me about the course of his treatment. He refused to give me any history: "It's all in my record, volumes and volumes of it," he said. "Look it up."

I asked what I could do for him, and he said, "Nothing."

The nurses told me that he refused pain medication because he wanted to remain alert, to be aware of life, of his girlfriend, of his few visitors. He was wasted to the point where all his fat was gone, his muscles thin and stringy under his now pale, sagging skin.

I saw him twice a day. Every time I visited our conversation was the same: "Can I do anything for you."

"What can you do? Can you cure this?"

"Is there anything you think you can eat?"

"So that I can die four ounces heavier?"

Eventually, his girlfriend, now with him day and night, would say: "It's alright. We appreciate it. I'll take care of him."

The nurses hated being in his room because he was their age, because he was so sad, because of the torment he was experiencing, because of the faithful, boundless caring of his girlfriend, because of his crying out in pain with each breath.

After two weeks the head nurse told me that the nursing staff wanted to move him away from other patients and away from the nurses' station because it was so painful to hear his cries and pleading. Now he was calling out, "Won't somebody help me? I hurt so much! Why do I have to die? I don't want to die. Help me please, help me."

I entered the room. His girlfriend was holding him in her arms, her long hair falling over his face and shoulders, his face tucked into her shoulder and breast. She looked up at me and quietly said, "I think it will be soon. Can you give him something now, just a little, not enough to take him away."

I asked one of the nurses to give him a tiny dose of morphine. The ward hallways were deserted. The door to the nurses' station was closed, as were all the patients' doors. The only sound was his cries of pain.

I returned to the room and sat on a chair in the corner for an hour, until it was time for me to sign out to another intern. Gradually the morphine had taken hold, but he continued to quietly murmur, "I hurt so much, I hurt so much."

I said I would see him in the morning, but he didn't reply.

The next morning his room was empty, his girlfriend gone, all the cards and weary-looking flowers trucked away, the bed freshly made waiting for the next cancer patient.

I wish that I had known enough then to ask where his body had been taken, to have learned his girlfriend's and family member's names, to have called them, perhaps to have gone to his funeral.

I had known many dying patients much better than I knew him, and yet at that time his death was the most harrowing for me: I had watched a youthful life flicker out in the most miserable way possible, with incurable cancer and incurable pain, what all of us as nurses and medical students and residents feared most for ourselves and the people we were closest to. It is impossible not to identify with a young man our age—at the same stage in life as we were—and to not feel the fearful randomness of disease.

His death haunts me now as it did at the time.

Since the beginning of internship I had lived with the fear of hurting someone. In April I did my first rotation in the Emergency Room. For the reasons that I noted earlier, the ER wasn't busy at the University of Chicago. The pace was leisurely and in a month I only occasionally saw a patient with decompensated heart failure or shock or trauma or respiratory failure who required rapid intervention.

One afternoon the ER nurse told me that she had gotten a call from an ambulance heading for our emergency room bringing in a patient with asthma. The only information they had was that she was a student at the University of Chicago and was being transported from her dormitory. I hadn't seen severe acute asthma before and quickly reviewed in my *Washington Manual* what I needed to do. She arrived before I finished the section. I quickly examined her: she was sitting bolt upright, sweating, struggling to move any air at all. She couldn't talk and answered my few questions by shaking her head or nodding. Her face was flushed but her lips and fingernails were dusky; her pulse was 160 and her blood pressure was high. I asked the nurse to give her epinephrine while I listened to her lungs: there was very little air movement, and what tiny breaths she could make were associated with dense wheezes.

The resident who was supposed to be supervising me looked in. I told him I thought she was going to need to be admitted. He told me to give her IV theophylline and then for some reason left the emergency room. I told the nurse to get the theophylline and began to administer it. I knew that it was supposed to go in slowly, but I was tense about her breathing—the epinephrine had done nothing. I had administered about half the theophylline, hoping it would improve her air movement when suddenly she arrested: her pulse was unobtainable, she was no longer breathing, and the ECG showed ventricular fibrillation, an irregular, ineffective, and often-lethal rhythm. I yelled for more help and the emergency room exploded as residents flooded in from other parts of the hospital. Our attempts at artificial respiration were useless. It took minutes for an anesthesiology resident to arrive. His first attempt at intubation failed. Now she was blue. After multiple attempts the anesthesiologist finally got a tube in place, but she was so tight that he could barely move any air. We shocked her heart several times with no response and in another minute she straight-lined: her heart was no longer beating.

Her arrival, my initial treatment "from the books", and her respiratory and cardiac arrest had all happened so quickly that no one had had time to process that a nineteen-year-old college girl was dying before our eyes from an acute asthma attack. Now she lay on the white gurney sheet, her lips and fingers and toes purple, alone, with no friend or family with her, nameless. The profession whose mantle I was learning to wear had failed her. I felt something deeper than sadness: a sense of utter worthlessness, ineptitude, vulnerability, hopelessness.

I don't know who gathered the information from the ambulance drivers about where she had been picked up, who learned her name, who found out who her parents were, who contacted them. I never saw them come to the hospital, never got to tell them what happened, never got to comfort them—if comforting them would even have been possible, especially by me, who felt a terrible burden of failure.

Until then I didn't know that anyone could die from asthma. I had never treated a severe asthma attack and was working alone: my resident had abandoned the scene—I never knew why—and when we got the forces assembled to deal with her cardiac arrest, our inability to move air prevented resuscitation: I was afraid that the theophylline I was giving her when she arrested had killed her, that in my panic I had given it too fast.

At the end of my shift my resident reappeared, but he wouldn't look directly at me; he didn't say a word, and neither did I. No one ever asked where he was, why he had left me alone.

The tragic death of that young woman has also never left me. I can still remember every thing I found on my hurried physical exam: she was unable to speak, agitated, terrified. Her face was red from the effort of exhaling against resistance, her chest barely moved, she had no sounds of breathing beyond faint harsh wheezes, her pulse was racing. She couldn't answer any of my questions. I remember the nurse giving her epinephrine, my clumsy efforts to start a large-bore IV, my attempts to sound calm as I tried to reassure her, my starting to push the plunger on the syringe of theophylline, counting out the seconds between each cc I gave her, her eyes rolling back, and then the nurse calling out "we are losing her," my yelling for the electrocardiogram machine, and then "call an arrest, call the OR and tell them we need an anesthesiologist to intubate her!" Probably from her arrival on the ambulance gurney until her arrest was no more than ten minutes, a young life gone just like that.

Many years later the death of a young person from asthma in the emergency room would have triggered a careful analysis by the hospital:

was she treated correctly? was her bronchospasm so severe that she was one of the rare people who could not be helped? had something gone wrong in our care? where was the resident, who was supposed to guide me? why hadn't I asked for help sooner? why did the anesthesiology resident have to make multiple attempts to intubate her?

For days I expected to be called into the chairman's office and given a chewing out. But no one asked any questions or asked me what had happened or asked if I was okay. I definitely was not okay and months passed before I stopped continually replaying the entire event minute by minute.

The next day Martin Luther King was assassinated while standing on the balcony of the Lorraine Motel in Memphis, Tennessee. In the black neighborhoods on Chicago's west side and the Woodlawn neighborhood just south of the University of Chicago, massive rioting erupted. Hundreds of buildings were set on fire. There were enormous numbers of injuries among the rioters, bystanders, and thousands of police and soldiers. Every emergency room in the city was overflowing with people with gunshot, knife and broken glass wounds, burns, and broken bones. The riots started about the time much of our nursing and physician staff members would be leaving to go home. We were all told to stay for as long as it took to stabilize and treat the patients already filling every examination room and hallway and the waiting room chairs. Nurses and doctors that could be reached were called to come back if they could safely do so. Eleven people died during the riots, but as far as I knew none of those deaths were in our emergency room.

We worked through the night and through the next day and until late the next evening. The emergency room was beginning to clear out but there were still a few patients who had not been seen. One of our nurses asked if I could sew on a man's half-torn-off ear before I left. He was totally drunk and barely noticed when I injected the skin of the ear and his scalp with anesthetic. I put in about twenty stitches, stood back to admire my work, and then asked the nurse if she could wrap a gauze bandage around his chin and head to protect the injured area. I had gone into the nurses' station to write my "op note" when I heard loud laughing followed by, "Dr Noel, your patient is leaving." He was lurching toward the ER doors with the small pillow from his gurney attached to the back of his head. In my ineptitude or exhaustion I had managed to put half the stitches through both his scalp and the pillowcase. The nurses cracked up. We got him back into the examination room and I replaced the stitches.

When I had him sit up while the nurses redid the gauze wrap, he gave me a big grin and a thumbs up and said, "You're a helluva surgeon doc, never met no one like you." It was not the first time that a patient to whom I had given totally messed up care was more grateful than some of the patients for whom I had done something both correct and useful.

After John Growdon and I worked together in July on the Nephrology Service, we saw each other in the halls of the hospital and often stopped to talk. In the fall he invited Margaret and me to have dinner with him and his wife Elvira. In those days dinner parties were sometimes formal, even for residents, with silver and china and linen and an artistic style of food preparation, usually French. Margaret and I were dressed in the best clothes we had short of what we got married in, and Elivra and John were similarly dressed. John always wore a bow tie, as by then I did, and Elvira was in a long skirt. She was tiny, with long black hair, as bright and witty and refined as John was.

After that dinner we went out about once a month with them, when John's call schedule and mine gave us back-to-back weekend days off. We took tea in the Drake Hotel's elegant dining room; another time we went dancing at a hot jazz and steak restaurant just a few blocks off Michigan Avenue. In January, for Margaret's birthday, John and I went downtown to a branch of the three-star Paris restaurant Chez Maxim and over cigars and sherry negotiated a formal dinner with the maitre d', planned for the next Saturday. When we arrived food and drink were served without any further discussion with our waiter: dry sherry and raw oysters, followed by grilled flounder in a white wine reduction with a white Burgundy; tournedos of aged tenderloin served rare with asparagus and sauce Béarnaise, accompanied by a second growth Medoc, then crepes for dessert while John and I smoked cigars and Elvira and Margaret smoked cigarillos.

I have no recollection of the trip back to our Hyde Park apartment.

As spring ripened, we picnicked at the dunes of Lake Michigan with strawberries and champagne and oysters, and exchanged dinner parties. Although we were rushing the season—it was still cold and windy on the shores of Lake Michigan—there was something autumnal about our brief, warm friendship in the unspoken awareness that we were soon going in different directions—they to their Air Force posting on Guam, and we to New York City—that tinted our final outings in a chiaroscuro of sweet sadness.

In one year of interneship I too had fallen in love with Chicago. Life was more manageable and less expensive than in New York City: Margaret and I had opportunities to see plays and musicals, attend concerts and a baseball game, and go out for dinners at some of the small cafes close to where we lived. I could bike to the hospital in ten minutes and walk to a record shop and first-class supermarket in just a few minutes. Margaret enjoyed her daily Illinois Central commute to her work with the Encyclopedia Britannica and she loved the creative team she was working with. The pace at the hospital was slower than at Columbia, and the attitude of the residents less abrasive and intense. I found the faculty to be kind, the students to be treated with respect, and the interactions between nurses and doctors cordial and mutually supportive.

As the time came to leave I knew that I would miss the half-dozen residents with whom I had become friends, especially John and his wife Elvira.

Margaret wasn't happy to be returning to New York: she was going back to a city that she had found isolating and intense. I was probably insufficiently grateful for her sacrifice in giving up a really good job so that I could return to Columbia for training that I knew would be more demanding and that would make me less available to her, with the hope that the higher bar would make me a better clinician.

CHAPTER 16

Second Chance

Residency programs are unrelenting: there are no holidays or weekends or nights during which patients simply get along without their doctors. I was scheduled to start at Columbia on the first of July, and my internship didn't finish until June 30th. Fortunately, someone helped me out by swapping weekends and I had the last day off. On the 29th a moving truck pulled up to our Hyde Park apartment and by the time I got home late that afternoon they had boxed up our kitchen and lamps and clothes and books and moved out our furniture. On the 30th we flew to LaGuardia and spent the night in Frank and Jane Bragg's spare bedroom a few blocks away from the Medical Center.

I had forgotten how grimy New York City was, how the hot pavement and automobile exhaust created a unique and demoralizing stench. I realized that Chicago, swept by the winds coming across the prairies and Lake Michigan, usually smelled of grass and trees in the summer. I was again conscious of how much I had asked of Margaret, who had grown up with the bracing smells of the Atlantic Ocean and the salt marshes.

Frank was one of the four P & S seniors who stayed for internship and one of the nicest, least self-serving, and most ebullient members of our medical school class. He had been on overnight call the 30th. On July 1st, a few minutes after 8 AM, he walked into his living room where I was preparing to begin my first day on the Neurology Service. Although he had been awake since the previous morning, he looked as fresh as a spring daffodil and announced: "I loved being an intern. I would gladly do internship all over again!"

I felt the same way about internship, or at least the "loved" part: I in no way wanted to do it again. Loving one's internship was not a widely shared feeling. For a change I kept my mouth shut because I knew that my internship was easier than his.

My first stop was on the eighth floor in the Department of Medicine office where Mrs. Ryan handed me my pager and a large paper bag with three sets of white pants and three short white coats. In a few minutes I had changed into the esteemed uniform of a Presbyterian Hospital resident with a patch identifying me as belonging to the Department of Medicine, in my mind not only the oldest but also the best medical service in the country.

I couldn't escape feeling a bit of a fraud because I had not yet earned membership in this exclusive club that had passed over me a year ago. I had been deeply happy when I received invitations to return to Columbia and was also offered positions at the two Harvard hospitals, but it didn't seem like vindication for their not selecting me for internship. I bore no grudges. I could only hope that I had grown enough in my senior year and the year at Chicago to hold my own now that I was back home.

Outside the Department office I ran into David Perera, the son of the Dean of Admissions, who I had known slightly when I was a student. He had just finished his final year of residency.

He smiled. "I heard you were coming back. Have a great time."

"How was it?" I asked.

"It would have been wonderful if only I could have kept myself from feeling guilty all the time."

"Guilty? About what?"

"Everything! Mistakes, there always being more I could have read, or a patient who decompensated after I signed out, or a skimpy, hastily written progress note that didn't have all the information the resident covering for the night needed."

I laughed. "Well, that will be nothing new: I grew up in Montana. I was born feeling guilty."

As a second-year resident on Neurology I was paired with a first year Neurology resident who had finished a medicine residency elsewhere. I had already spent a month on the same Neurology service as a third-year student, and I had a year of subinternships as a senior student, so I was proficient enough to teach the new resident the Presbyterian Hospital methodology: the expected detail and organization of notes, the once- or twice-daily progress notes, and our role of being the primary physician for our patients, while the senior resident was our team's "consultant."

The majority of our patients were admitted with a stroke or brain mass or a chronic, undiagnosed degenerative disease like progressive muscle weakness, Parkinson's disease, cerebellar degeneration, or multiple sclerosis. The emphasis was almost entirely on diagnosis—very few of our patients' conditions could be treated medically. Patients with a mild stroke might get better over a year or two, but not because of pharmacologic intervention; the most we could do was to start them in a rehabilitation program. The first effective treatments for Parkinson's disease were still new and fairly primitive; multiple sclerosis waxed and waned on its own time course but its progression was otherwise unstoppable. There was decent treatment for seizures.

The neurosurgeons had a little more to offer: patients with brain hemorrhages from aneurysms were stabilized and then went to surgery, as did a few of the brain tumor patients.

The Neurology residents were amazing. John Brust, who had been my junior resident during the internal medicine clerkship, was now my neurology senior resident. Four of the senior residents went on to become academic neurologists; three became department chairs.

My reintroduction to Columbia-Presbyterian was gentle. The learning environment was very positive, since all the neurology residents and faculty members enjoyed teaching and didn't expect medicine residents to become expert with the more abstruse diseases. Rounds were comfortable. During my year as a medicine intern in Chicago I had become proficient with day-to-day management, I enjoyed problem solving, and I had plenty of time to read about diseases with which I was unfamiliar.

For the third time I wondered if I should finish my residency in medicine and then go on to become a neurologist. I thought it likely that I could get a neurology residency at Columbia, and I wrote a letter to Raymond Adams, the neurology chairman at the Massachusetts General Hospital, about the procedure for applying there.

In the end, I didn't apply, in part because I enjoyed being an internist and liked the broader range of disease, and in part because, while the neurologists were diagnostically and personally erudite and elegant, there was so little that could be done for many patients other than preside over their gradual deterioration or long slow recovery.

In August I was the resident on the endocrinology consultation service, seeing new patients throughout all of the Presbyterian Hospital inpatient services. Every third night I took overnight call alternating with the residents covering the hematology/oncology and cardiology consultation services. Our primary responsibility was to carry the "box", a portable EKG machine that we needed when patients had severe rhythm abnormalities or cardiac arrest. In 1968 EKG interpretation, cardiac catheterization to diagnose valvular disease, and restoration of normal heart rhythm by electroshock or drugs were the most common procedures done by cardiologists—echocardiograms, coronary angiography, and intracardiac electrical studies of heart rhythm were still in their early stages. While technicians came by during the day to do routine cardiograms, at night, the resident with the box was the EKG expert for all the patients not on the medical service, and no other services, not even the operating rooms, had EKG machines.

We spent our nights doing emergency hematology, cardiology, and endocrinology consultations on the non-medicine specialties like surgery and neurology, answering questions like, "Can I operate on this patient who has a low platelet count?" or, "Can you help us get this patient's diabetes under control so we can take her to the operating room in the morning?" There were no fellows in any medicine specialty available during the night; if we needed help we would wake up an attending physician at home for advice. If a patient was too sick to be managed on the surgery or neurology services, we transferred them to the medical service. We also were in charge of running all the pulmonary and cardiac arrest procedures throughout all the buildings of the medical center, spread out over seven city blocks.

Our call days were 34 hours long—7 AM until 5 PM the next day. The amount of work most nights was considerable. Over time I realized that if I had to consult on a patient in the middle of the night, I didn't fall asleep easily and I often wandered the halls seeing sick patients who had been admitted to the medical wards, or I dropped down to the emergency room to help interns with interesting or difficult patients. When I finally got home after call I felt a kind of mental fatigue bordering on walking coma—I struggled to stay awake on the subway and bus back to our apartment on East 79th street and I fell asleep within a few minutes of eating dinner.

One call night I stopped by to check on an intern who was taking care of a teenage girl who had been admitted with delirium due to hepatitis that rapidly progressed to coma. We could not yet differentiate between what were called infectious hepatitis (now hepatitis A) and serum hepatitis (hepatitis B) except by history. It was very unusual for infectious hepatitis to cause massive hepatic destruction and coma leading to death, which were more typical of hepatitis B. When she became comatose one of the attending gastroenterologists suggested that her team try to keep her alive by passing her blood through a pig's liver with the hope that we could keep her alive long enough for her liver to regenerate.

When I arrived, Christine, the intern, was gowned and gloved and held a huge syringe attached to a Y stopcock. On one branch of the Y was an IV line leading to a large needle in the girl's right arm, and the other branch led to a line that disappeared into the portal vein of a huge dark red pig liver that was immersed in ice water in a large galvanized wash tub. Out of the pig's hepatic vein another line returned blood to the girl's left arm. Every sixty seconds Christine withdrew 50 cc of blood from the girl's arm, flipped the stop cock, and pushed the syringe plunger to send the blood through the pig liver and back into the girl.

Christine had been doing this for several hours by herself; I took over for a while so she could eat and use the bathroom. Through the night we perfused the pig liver in fifteen- minute shifts. From time to time I got a consultation request and disappeared for an hour, then came back to relieve her. At seven she was joined by one of her medical students and I went to my call room to shower and shave and begin my day.

At mid-morning, after 18 hours of pig liver perfusion, the girl was still in coma—the pig liver had failed to do the job of a normal human liver, or the hepatitis virus had totally destroyed her liver and she would never recover. She died that evening.

Several weeks later we had a dinner party for the chief resident, Dick Byyny, and his wife Judy, along with John Brust, who had twice been my resident, his wife Meridee, and a nurse, Eileen Toohey, who I had become friends with during my neurology rotations as a student and resident.

The dinner was something like a coming out party, with residents who had been my teachers when I was a student and were now my fellow residents. In our Washington Heights and Chicago apartments we could serve four at a lovely Queen Anne round drop leaf table that the Wilkins had given us. When we moved to the bigger apartment on East 79th Street, they gave us an early 19th Century rectangular table that could seat eight, along with a set of matching Hitchcock chairs. For our wedding Margaret's mother had given us enough sterling silver for eight, I had given her china, and we had just bought Baccarat crystal wine glasses.

We planned a dinner of roasted filet mignon to be carved at the table and served with sauce béarnaise, an elegant salad, and the piece de resistance, poire Helene—a pear hollowed out and filled with bitter sweet chocolate and almonds and coated with dipping chocolate.

A dinner party on this scale was a big deal for us. Margaret and I had been up late Friday night preparing the dinner. By early Saturday afternoon, all but the final roasting had been done and I went out for a four-mile run along the East River up to Gracie Mansion, the mayor's residence.

When we sat down to dinner I was strangely without an appetite or my usual conversational energy, and I was very tired. The next day, on Sunday, I dragged around the apartment feeling listless. On Monday morning I took the bus and subway to the Medical Center and started to round on the endocrinology patients we were following. I felt nauseated and had eaten nothing for breakfast; I thought I must have some kind of virus. When I went into a bathroom I saw that my urine was very yellow—not ordinary dehydrated yellow, but nearly orange.

When a Presbyterian Hospital resident on any service was sick, the medicine chief resident helped us find a doctor and figured out what immediate medical care was needed. I paged Dick Byyny. He looked at me, thumped my right upper abdomen, which hurt, and said I probably had hepatitis. He drew a few tubes of blood, sent them to the laboratory, and told me to go down to the residents' quarters and take a nap while he contacted the endocrinology attending and told him that I wouldn't be able to see patients that day.

He came to the call room a few hours later.

"You have hepatitis. Your bilirubin is three-times normal, and your liver enzymes are too high to measure—they are doing a dilution and will let me know, but the actual number doesn't matter. You can have any of our faculty physicians take care of you. Who would you like me to call?"

Without hesitation I said "Jack Morris."

I was admitted to the seventh-floor isolation unit, ominously to the same room in which I had been perfusing a pig liver trying to save the life of the young girl who died of massive hepatic destruction just a few weeks before. Dick came by a few hours later to tell me that I had the highest level of hepatic enzymes he had ever seen, evidence that I now had severe liver damage.

There were always a few doctors and nurses who contracted hepatitis each year, but that year an unusually large number of residents had been hospitalized with hepatitis. Our precautions were minimal when examining patients—we only wore gloves for procedures and we often we didn't know when a patient we were caring for was in the early, undiagnosed phase of hepatitis or any other contagious disease. Because of its virulence, we assumed that the girl had serum hepatitis, which was much more likely to cause death than infectious hepatitis. The incubation time was about right for her to have been my source of exposure. She had died within two weeks of falling ill: I wasn't going to have long to wait before I knew what my fate was going to be.

When I was still a medical student many of us held a few residents and clinical faculty members in the highest regard. There was surprising unanimity about who was in that group. For those of us who stayed for residency our admiration was rarely diminished by anything we heard or saw as we crossed their paths. They were our best bedside teachers, the ones we called when we had tough clinical choices, and the ones we modeled ourselves after. I think that all of us admired Jack Morris. The legend was that Jack, who was both a Yale graduate and played tackle for the New York Giants for three years before beginning medical school, was academically an average medical student. But during his clinical years, what impressed everyone was how hard he worked. He would stick with a sick patient, sometimes for several days, without leaving the hospital, drawing every blood, running the medical students' laboratory tests like blood counts and urinalyses, starting the IV's, spending time talking with the patient. Only twelve interns were chosen every year, and the rumor was that Jack initially was not ranked high enough to guarantee his matching at Columbia. But the physicians who taught him were so impressed that together they asked the chair to move Jack up the list and he got in, probably over a lot of people who on paper appeared to be smarter.

As a resident, Jack continued to be dedicated. On his call nights Jack would rarely sleep, moving from team to team going over the new admissions with the interns, taking care of the patients who were crashing.

When he was a senior resident he was chosen chief resident, I imagined for his dedication, knowledge and grace.

At the end of the day Jack came by. He pulled up a chair and began to take the long, thorough history that every Columbia student and resident took and then he examined me. I had a huge, tender liver—not unusual in hepatitis—but he told me that the rapidity with which my liver had failed worried him.

For the first few weeks in the hospital I was too fatigued to read the medical journals I had asked Margaret to bring, and so I tried to read novels. I failed to penetrate John Barth's heady, fabulist novel *Giles Goat Boy*. I quickly discovered that I needed plot and not complexity to fill the few hours a day when I had the energy to read; I lived for the evening news and, for the first time in my life, I watched television dramas and comedies. I could eat breakfast but after that meat or anything fried or fishy that came up from the food service stayed on my plate. I asked for breakfast three times a day but steadily I lost five pounds a week.

When my bilirubin reached 30 and my enzymes had peaked at 5000, the concern was that there was little liver left to die. Jack asked two liver consultants to see me. They gathered in the hall outside my door; I heard them say in hushed voices that with massive hepatic destruction I might not recover. Steroids had never been found useful in hepatitis. Liver transplants were still decades in the future.

There was nothing for Jack to do for someone with hepatitis lying in a hospital bed—caring for me was like watching a cornfield gradually wilt during a prolonged drought. For five weeks we waited to see if I was going to live or die. It would have been easy for Jack to poke his head in, ask if I was okay, and move on. Every day I waited for him to finish up his rounds and come by. He was a big man—more than six feet tall, over 220 pounds, all muscle, with an ebullient presence that filled the little room. At his arrival the best part of my day began. "What's on the news?" he would ask with a big grin highlighted by a gold tooth that replaced one I supposed had been knocked out in football. "What are you reading?" "Who do you think is going to win the election?"—it was October, 1968 and Humphrey was running against Nixon. I even started watching professional football games so that I could talk with Jack about the New York City teams, the Giants and Jets, on Monday evenings. Our conversations would often last past 8 PM, and Jack was back in the hospital by 7:30 the next morning, rounding on his sickest patients before he began office hours.

By the fifth week I had lost 30 pounds. My appetite hadn't improved, but my bilirubin had dropped to the mid-twenties. Each morning one of the nurses came in to give me a bed bath and then a massage with lotion to protect my skin. I was barely strong enough to walk the five feet to the toilet, but at least I did that on my own. One morning as I sat down on the toilet I was so scrawny that I went right through the seat, my legs folded up against my chest, toilet water lapping at my butt. I was helpless. I couldn't get myself out of the toilet seat, and I couldn't operate the nurse-call button with my toe. After five minutes, one of the nurses, Cathy Coffee, came into the room to see if I was ready for my bed bath and saw me tucked through the toilet seat like a napkin in a napkin ring.

She started laughing: "I don't know whether to pull you out or take your picture," she said.

I called Jack's office and left a message. When he called back, I told him, "Jack, I think I want to leave. If I am going to die, I can just as well do it at home as here. There is nothing being done except waiting for me to get less yellow."

"Are you strong enough to get home?" he asked.

"We can take a taxi. Margaret says she can take a couple of weeks off. I think we might go up to Newburyport to her family's home. More appetizing food might help."

So, Jack discharged me. I weighed 110 pounds and looked like someone coming out of a prisoner-of-war camp.

Over the next three weeks my appetite did get better and I began to gain weight and strength. I was out of the residency for two months. When I returned just after Thanksgiving, my first clinical assignment was to supervise two senior students in a subinternship at the nearby city cancer hospital where I had worked in the blood bank as a student. Glenda and

John called me their skinny yellow resident. It took me months to regain my weight and stamina and for my skin to lose its yellow tint.

I learned a lot from that sickness, but the most important thing I learned was how much a doctor can give to patients by just spending time with them. Not one gram of my liver was saved by Jack's long daily visits, but, sick as I was, he cared about me enough to give up time just to keep me company. I cherished his visits, and I remembered them later when I cared for patients who were dying, for whom I could do nothing but sit beside them talking, helping them manage their pain, negotiating with the food service to prepare meals they could eat, and caring for their skin and bowels. Bit by bit, many of them told me the stories of their lives.

I never knew if the girl I had helped care for one night was the source of my hepatitis, or if it was some other patient to whom I was exposed. I was lucky to recover.

CHAPTER 17

The "House"

For reasons lost in obscurity, perhaps dating back to post-graduate training in England, residents were called house officers or house staff, and at Columbia the second-year resident managing an inpatient team was called "the House.'" At the beginning of the New Year I began my three-month stint as the House for the West Team. Jack Morris and Dick Byyny were concerned that I wouldn't have the stamina to handle the call, for good reason: we worked every third weekend from Saturday morning to Monday night; for the next two weekends we rounded on Saturday morning and didn't come back until Monday morning, when we had 48 hours of catching up to do. During our long weekends we were awake on both Saturday and Sunday nights supervising the three interns covering the East, Center, and West services. Since it was hard to sleep for more than a few hours when on call at night, we took care of patients for 56 hours straight. For those three months we averaged 120 hours in the hospital every week. In spite of the hours, leading an inpatient team was the high point of our Columbia residencies.

The interns worked even harder: they were on wards for a month at a time, but took call every other night and didn't go home after being awake most of the night until they signed out at 4 PM, and often later. Our twelve interns would each have six months of every other night call.

Half of our patients were admitted with a myocardial infarction or severe cardiac ischemia ("heart attack"), uncontrolled diabetes, pneumonia, respiratory failure because of chronic lung disease, or abdominal pain or bleeding because of peptic ulcer disease. Remarkably, a quarter of our patients were admitted because they needed a diagnosis; they would stay in the hospital for days or even weeks before all the tests and biopsies came back and treatment was started. There were no limits to the number of hospital days a patient could stay: since most of them did not have insurance, there was no review of the need for hospitalization by an insurance company eager to reduce the costs that they would have to reimburse.

When patients had a heart attack we kept them in bed for three weeks, on the theory—later disproven—that early exercise could result in the heart rupturing. We had no intensive care units: patients with shock or severe diabetes or active bleeding from the stomach or intestines were placed next to the nursing station in the twelve-bed ward so that the house staff and nurses could keep a close eye on them.

An intern usually had between twelve and sixteen patients. They began rounding at 7 AM, first meeting with the nurses and their co-intern who had covered their patients overnight to hear about anything that had happened, and then wheeling a chart rack from bed to bed to talk with and examine each patient and write progress notes until rounds began at ten.

At 9 AM the three residents met in Dr. Bradley's office to briefly discuss each patient admitted in the previous 24 hours. Dr. Bradley took a few notes on an index card, although he rarely asked a question or offered advice; the chief resident might add a few suggestions about diagnostic possibilities or treatment for any puzzling new admission.

At 10 AM seven days a week the attending physicians arrived to round on all the patients, both new and old, walking from bed to bed first on the 9th floor, and then on the 8th floor. Students presented both the old and new patients, the interns corrected or added information, and the resident quietly stood in the background until a question about the diagnostic or therapeutic plan exceeded what the students and interns could answer.

At noon when rounds ended, the residents and attendings left the wards for lunch in the doctors' dining room. In addition to eating, this was a time when we could track down specialists or surgeons to quickly get advice or request a formal consultation.

The tradition at Presbyterian Hospital was that the management of the patients was the residents' responsibility. Our attendings were consultants, and although they often had useful suggestions, they weren't in charge—they didn't write notes, and they didn't bill. Only the interns and residents wrote progress notes. We almost never called an attending to review our plans before rounds. That meant that it was our job to be sure that our decisions were correct.

The residents wrote a scholarly "House Note" for every new admission illuminating some aspect of the patient's history or course. We summarized our diagnostic or therapeutic plan, referencing the current literature. There were no copying machines then, and no quick way to discover articles. We all carried a concise pocket index, *Current Medical References*, that had a thousand of the most important articles about therapy and diagnosis, updated every year, and we used the *Index Medicus* to find references by topic, one year at a time: "tuberculosis, diagnosis" or "hypertension, crisis, therapy", going backwards in time—1968, 1967, 1966.

It was an arduous process. In order to write our resident's notes we had to hand-transcribe the information we were going to use. For a diagnostic dilemma, my note might be three or four handwritten pages long. When my classmates and I were third year students we swarmed the chart rack when we knew that our resident had just written a note on an unusual or complex disease, expecting to learn the most recent science underlying diagnosis and treatment. As students we thought that our residents were giants astride the world of medicine. As the House I wanted my notes to be as good as those I read as a student: after I put my note into the chart I sometimes glanced into the small doctors' room to see if a student had pulled a chart and was reading my note. I was rarely rewarded. The most common response to my House Note was, "can you tell me what this word is," my handwriting very little better at 28 than it was when I was 14.

When I arrived at 7 AM my first job was to check in with my two interns as they rounded to see if they had any questions or problems, and then to quickly evaluate all the patients admitted overnight. At each bedside I reviewed the intern's admission note, took my own history, and examined the patient, all before 9 AM. Since one of my interns was always on call, there were new patients for me to see every morning; after a weekend there might be as many as a dozen and I would stay late to write my notes, race home, sleep for a few hours, and come back for overnight call the next day.

The interns varied in their skills, resilience, and style. During the three months I supervised six of the twelve. Several would not continue beyond the first year because they were heading into a specialty that did not have its own internship: two became psychiatrists and one became a radiologist.

In knowledge and experience, I was behind the other residents who had been interns the previous year. The residents who had been medical students in other schools accepted me without fanfare and seemed indifferent to my joining them; several became close friends. My chief anxiety in returning to Presbyterian Hospital was that my four Columbia classmates would not feel that I was strong enough to join their ranks, and on the evidence of my first three years as a student that concern would have been justified. Six months into the year, one of my medical school classmates, Willie Lee, gave me what I suppose he thought was useful information as we stood in line outside of doctors' dining room:

"We were all surprised to see you come back. You turned out to be alright, not as pompous"—or did he say pretentious? — "As you were in medical school."

With that, he filled his tray and went off to sit at another table.

I was taken aback, but I did not disagree with him. I knew that I had been awkward trying to grow into the skin of a doctor that they seemed to more comfortably inhabit from the beginning of medical school.

Still, one doesn't get that kind of cutting-to-the-core feedback from a colleague very often and I took it at face value: I was much stronger as a junior resident than I had been as a junior student, but I knew that I still had a long way to go to achieve the level of knowledge, communication skills, and decorum of the best of our residents and faculty.

That, of course, is what a residency is for.

During March my two interns were memorable. Tom Jacobs was a lanky former Amherst College basketball player who grew up in a large Catholic family in Westchester County. He had gone to Johns Hopkins for medical school. Tom was one of the nicest people I met during my training—calm, thorough, responsible, self-effacing, funny, and generous. His patients adored him, as did the nurses and students.

On the nights when he was on call, Tom didn't bother to go down to the residents' quarters to sleep after he had finished taking care of all his patients and any new admissions. Instead; he found a gurney and laid down on it, falling asleep in minutes. He slept so deeply that he didn't stir no matter what was going on around him. One night a student and I removed one of his beat-up shoes and his sock and tied a mortuary tag around his great toe, then covered him head to foot with a sheet, as we did with patients who died on the ward. He slept that way for a few hours. I was going over a new admission with another intern when a nurse signaled that he was waking up. From a spot where he couldn't see us, we watched him pull the sheet down, calmly look around for his shoe, read the mortuary tag, grin, and then get up and start his morning rounds.

Lennie Chess, like Tom, grew up near New York City. He was intense, very bright, efficient, and blunt. He and Tom made a great team, instantly friends from the beginning of internship, but quite different in character. Both were excellent doctors. Lennie already knew more medicine than I did and I rarely had anything to add to his evaluations and plans. One night Lennie, a third-year student and I were sitting in the isolation ward's nurses' lounge that reeked of yesterday's scorched coffee that had been boiling down since the evening shift began. Lennie was haggard and eager to get to bed. Since I never slept much on call, I was leisurely leading the student through a differential diagnosis of their patient's lung disease that presented as several weeks of a cough that produced yellow, blood-streaked sputum. An admission x-ray showed fluffy white patches obscuring large areas of his lung on chest x-ray. He had been admitted to the isolation ward because of concern for tuberculosis. I was encouraging the student to think of other causes of his cough and sputum—pneumococcal or klebsiella pneumonia, fungal disease, and so on, each less likely than the one before.

"So, Keith, what else could this be?" The student looked at me blankly—after four or five good guesses he had run out of ideas.

I said, "So, does he own a parrot or parakeet?"

Lennie, who had been quietly fidgeting, waiting for this to get over like the internship equivalent of bad sex, exploded: "For Christ's sake, Gordon, this guy doesn't have psittacosis, or coal miner's lung, or sarcoidosis, or any of the other things you have been talking about. He's got tuberculosis. It's 3 AM and I'm going to bed," and he stomped out. The poor student didn't know whether to stay or leave, I was chagrined, and Lennie ignored me when I walked by as he was writing his final orders before going down to the call rooms.

By this point in my residency it was easy for me to quickly determine what intervention was needed for a patient with a crashing blood pressure or unexplained seizures, but it was a new experience for me to do on-the-spot teaching of a beginning medical student side-by-side with a seasoned, smart intern just a few months away from doing my job.

Lennie was right—I should have recognized that he didn't need to sit through this elementary discussion. I should have excused him to get some sleep, talking to the student separately.

The principle that I was trying to demonstrate to the student was that doctors should never take their first impression as correct: we wanted the students to consider other possibilities and know the evidence for and against each possibility. After more than one tired intern wanted to get on with his or her work I learned when to go through the diagnostic possibilities and treatment just with the student, who would present the patient on rounds in a few hours and would be expected to know what other diagnoses and treatment had been considered.

The "House"

The educational environment—what had made Columbia highly regarded for preparing students for residency, and residents for practice as generalists—was self-sufficiency: there were no night-time attendings in the house and I cannot remember ever being encouraged to call one at home. We were responsible for taking a thorough history, doing an accurate physical examination, formulating the diagnosis and plan, and implementing it. Only when a patient needed acute surgery was there anyone else to call.

At night X-rays were done with a portable machine, with the patient propped up in bed for a chest X-ray or lying flat for an abdominal film. Frequently one of us put on a lead apron to hold an unconscious or weak patient in the right position. The expectation that the residents would review every image was taken as a commandment and as soon as a film was developed we went down to the third floor with the students on call to read it with the radiology resident that we had shaken out of bed, grumpy but helpful. As a result of our being there to read the film, the radiologist was never asked to work without a context. If a radiologist misread a film leading to an incorrect diagnosis and we had accepted the diagnosis without going over the image with him, we considered the error ours, not the radiologist's. The same was true for histories and physical examinations—the student and intern and resident would all do their own complete evaluations and compare notes, never relying on someone else's work.

There was a subtle pleasure in unlocking a diagnosis missed by others or resolving why a treatment had failed and finding a successful one. The clues were often buried in reviewing the old record, or going back to a patient's bedside to repeat the physical examination or to dig deeper into the patient's history. Thoroughness, responsibility, and reading current clinical research articles were our key tools and they were what made us useful to our colleagues in surgery and neurology and psychiatry when they asked us to see one of their patients. There was a lot of Sherlock Holmes in our processes, but also a great deal of emphasis on repetition: if at first the patient was missing the clues to a heart valve infection, we would go back twice a day to look for tiny hemorrhages beneath the fingernails or in the conjunctiva of the eye, for showers of red blood cells in the urine or dot-like hemorrhages in the skin. When a discovery of a new diagnostic sign was made, other students and residents would come by to look, so that a single patient might be training a dozen or more learners. The open wards facilitated that: the patients were used to seeing five or ten of us at their and other patients' bedsides honing our skills at detecting murmurs with our stethoscopes, palpating an enlarged spleen, or detecting vascular changes in the retina of the eye. It could take us days or weeks to make a diagnosis that is now quickly made with an echocardiogram, advanced imaging techniques, or vastly improved laboratory tests.

Some of what John Brust and other residents had taught us when we were students informed our work and teaching as residents. Perhaps the most important were, "Get help from everyone but don't trust anyone," and, "Write down everything you don't know; before you go to sleep look up everything." If someone advised a drug we weren't familiar with, we checked to be sure we had been told the right dose and that there weren't reasons for our patient not to be given it. If the report from radiology was that the chest x-ray was "normal" in a patient whose history and examination suggested pneumonia, we went down and looked at the image with the radiologist. On call we didn't go to bed until everything had been done, and when we signed out we tried not to leave anything for someone else to do.

Because we were in the hospital most of our waking hours, we did not yet recognize how large a price a life in medical practice founded on almost constant availability, the thorough consideration of every diagnostic possibility, reading all of our patients' x-rays, not missing critical laboratory or history or physical examination results, and understanding and responding to our patients' concerns and needs might extract from us and our families in the future.

CHAPTER 18

The Private Service

I finished my three months as the house resident on the West Team at the end of March. My next rotation was in the Harkness Pavilion, the private practice hospital of the Medical Center.

In the Presbyterian Hospital where the teaching wards and clinics were housed, neither our attendings nor the hospital expected to be paid: the care of the patients was "voluntary"—that is, the attendings' time and the cost of care were free for patients who had no insurance.

The staffing of the Harkness Pavilion was nearly the reverse of that: patients were admitted by their private physician, not by residents. Most of the attending physicians saw their patients in their offices before admission, or in their hospital room shortly after they arrived and usually the private physician had written orders before the patient was admitted. If a private patient was unstable the nurses called the resident first, who examined and treated the patient until the attending arrived.

On my busiest day in Harkness I admitted 18 patients. I wrote full admission notes and orders on half and brief notes on the others, starting at 8 AM and finishing around 9 that evening. Usually Harkness was substantially more gentle than that, and, because we were not managing the patients, also far less educational. At the same time we could do more in-depth reading about diseases that we were encountering for the first time and we could attend the two main weekly conferences—team rounds and the combined conferences where faculty members from different disciplines provided comprehensive updates on disease diagnosis and treatment—without frequent interruptions.

Occasionally we met celebrities. One day while I was seeing a patient on Harkness 3, Dick Byyny paged me. "Gordon, you need to go see the patient Dr. Cosgriff just admitted, Lester Young. In fact, I want to see him too. I'll meet you outside my office."

Dick's office was a cubbyhole on the 8th floor of Presbyterian Hospital, and Mr. Young was on the Harkness 11th floor in one of the rooms reserved for the wealthy, famous and elusive. For some reason Dick was in a hurry and we ran up three flights of stairs, crossed over into Harkness and charged down the long hall to Mr. Young's room.

Dick knocked. A quiet voice responded, "Come in," and Dick pushed open the door. Sitting up on the edge of the bed facing us, wearing nothing but a silk lounging robe, was the famous comedian, Bob Hope. Dick, who was from Los Angeles and more star struck than I, but short of breath from running, barely managed to gasp out our names by way of introduction.

Mr. Hope took in the scene—two breathless young doctors with their white coat pockets stuffed with notebooks and reflex hammers and stethoscopes—and ad libbed, "You guys are in worse shape than I am, and you're planning to take care of me?"—his eyebrows arched with incredulousness. Dick, still short of breath, said, "We just wanted to make sure you are comfortable."

Hope rejoined, "Would you like me to move over so that you can sit on the bed and recover your breath?" Dick gave him a brief summary of his Los Angeles life, going to college and medical school at the University of Southern California, and his long service as a lifeguard. Hope smiled pleasantly, Dick realized that we looked foolish, and we excused ourselves. Dr. Cosgriff had just admitted him for a checkup; there was nothing we could do for him, and a few days later he left. Half the nurses on the floor managed to get his autograph.

The Private Service

Later that month I was called urgently to the 11th floor to see a patient that I hadn't admitted, and whose name I didn't immediately recognize.

I asked the head nurse what his problem was.

She said, "Mr. Gunther was admitted with pneumonia and he is in an oxygen tent, but insists on smoking. Could you please tell him that he can't smoke in an oxygen tent; he won't listen to his private duty nurse or to me."

I walked down the hall, knocked on the door, and walked in. It was midday but the curtains were partially drawn and the room was gloomy and dark. A big form humped up the rumpled covers that disappeared into a clear plastic tent behind which I could barely make out the unshaven face of a deeply short-of-breath man. It is hard to talk with someone in an oxygen tent, so I turned off the oxygen and opened the front of the tent, putting my face close to his.

"Hello, Mr. Gunther. I'm Doctor Noel. The nurses are worried about you and asked me to stop in."

"They won't let... me smoke," he said in a gasping, scratchy voice, "I'm going crazy. Turn this... damned thing off... I'll smoke... then she can... turn it on... again."

I explained why he couldn't smoke with the oxygen on, and that he was so short of breath that it was dangerous to turn off the oxygen. He told me he insisted, and I told him I would call Dr. Cosgriff.

When I went back to the nurses' station the head nurse said, "You know who he is, don't you?"

I said I didn't.

"That's John Gunther, the author. He wrote *Death Be Not Proud* about his son, who died here when he was just a teenager."

I was barely aware of the name, mostly because of his famous journalistic books *Inside Europe* and *Inside U.S.A.*

I called Dr. Cosgriff, who said that under no circumstances could we let him smoke or turn off the oxygen.

About an hour later my pager began to beep and there was an overhead page used to call staff to a medical crisis: "Arrest, Stat, Harkness Pavilion, 11th floor! Dr. Gordon Noel, Stat, Harkness Pavilion 11th floor!"

217

I ran up five flights of stairs, turned the corner into the corridor, and a nurse called out, "It's Mr. Gunther."

I went into the room while several other residents piled in behind me. Acrid smoke filled the room. The oxygen tent had a large ragged hole burnt into its front and sides. Gunther was facing me, his eyebrows burnt off, his hair singed, and his lips and cheeks charred. His frazzled nurse said that when she left the room to get his medications he lit a cigarette inside the oxygen tent and it blew up.

He was more stunned than injured; the burns were superficial.

He had been a lifetime heavy smoker; most of the photos of him throughout his life showed him with a cigarette in his right hand or dangling from his lips.

The next morning, he told me that if he couldn't smoke, he would rather die.

He had reported all over Europe before, during, and after the Second World War. He had written eight novels and twenty books of nonfiction. I felt incredible sadness for him—that Gunther himself—this active, creative man, who had spent his life traveling in every part of the world during the run up to wars, during the wars, and during America's and Europe's reconstruction and return to prosperity—should spend much of the last few years trapped for months in a narrow, gloomy gray hospital room just a few hundred yards from where his son died of a brain tumor at age 17.

Mr. Gunther survived his near-incineration and pneumonia, but died a year later of liver cancer.

The next week Dick Byyny called me to say that one of the attendings had admitted an "extraordinarily beautiful" woman to a private room. To ensure that the best resident physician admitted her, he decided to call on the chief resident. Although that was not ordinarily a responsibility of chief residents, Dick did not decline. Being ecumenical, he let me know in a few words that she was indeed beautiful and that she had an interesting heart murmur, for which she had been admitted for evaluation. I doubt that Dick felt that, for either my education or her benefit, I needed to listen to her heart murmur, but it was a slow morning. She was sitting up in bed in a white nightgown reading a novel that she put down when I walked in. She smiled warmly, and said, "Another one! You boys certainly are thorough." I guessed that I wasn't the only resident who Dick had talked with. I was too embarrassed to carry on the charade. I introduced myself as the Harkness resident, asked if she had everything she needed, and excused myself.

Although there were occasional stories of resident encounters with seductive patients, they were rare, and this young woman certainly was not seductive. But the situation was as close as I ever got to a patient being exploited. I never heard of anyone—student, resident, or attending physician—engaging in inappropriate behavior. Perhaps this was a reflection of my own innocence and being out of any gossip stream and not because it was a more honorable time.

Dick also introduced me to his daily "well-nurse rounds." The internal medicine residents had no fixed home as we moved from rotation to rotation. Our patients were scattered over eight floors of the Harkness Pavilion and three floors of Presbyterian Hospital, Vanderbilt Clinic, and all the other floors housing obstetric and gynecologic, surgery, neurology, and ophthalmology patients. The private patients who were admitted frequently got to know the nursing staff well. Those who were grateful gave the nurses boxes of chocolates like Whitman Samplers and Stouffer's Chocolates, or coffee cakes, or cookies. Dick would make his morning rounds briefly seeing the new admissions on the Presbyterian inpatient medicine wards and then cross over to Harkness, going from nursing station to nursing station to "check in." He was good-looking, friendly, and helpful. The nurses were glad to see him and they always steered him to any food that had been brought in, pointing out that he would be doing them a favor since they claimed to be on diets. While I was on Harkness, Dick would drag me, not unwilling, along. Since I too knew all the nurses, well-nurse rounds were like strolling the neighborhood. Although they were giving away the food, they also appreciated the socializing and over time I found that our relationship meant that they would go out of their way to help when there were urgent patient issues.

The best candy, doughnuts, and coffee cake were on the top three floors of Harkness, where the most expensive rooms were. After a while—and well after I was no longer the Harkness resident—I would get overhead pages: "Dr. Noel, call Harkness Ten nursing station." Whoever answered would say something like, "Dr. Noel, we saved two maple walnut chocolates for you. They are in a napkin in the fridge."

By April of my first year back at Columbia I was beginning to feel comfortable both as a clinician and as a teacher. The essence of the Columbia model of internal medicine residency training was being personally responsible for patients, with only arms-length faculty supervision; caring for large numbers of patients in order to have exposure to both rare and common problems; being thorough and persistent when a diagnosis was elusive; searching in-depth both current and classic medical literature; and teaching students, interns, and other residents constantly.

In contradistinction to the lecture-based memorization during our basic science years, clinical education for clerks and residents is an excellent model of how adults learn best: we wanted to know something because we were both curious and had the full responsibility for our patients' lives; we determined the best method for our learning, usually reading the most recent articles and textbooks and talking with consultants; and we put the learning immediately to use. Information we acquired in the setting of taking care of patients stayed with us for years.

My month on the private service where the attendings were making the decisions gave me my first look at the high level of skills that physicians who trained at Presbyterian Hospital had developed after decades of practice. The best of them were in the hospital at all hours of the day and night, which their patients, the nurses, and the residents appreciated. They served as wonderful examples of the art of medical practice.

These were the giants I emulated. But my view was two-dimensional. I knew nothing about the rest of their lives.

CHAPTER 19

Family Life

Parenthood arrived in our lives by a circuitous route and, as it often does, more by chance than by planning.

When I was eighteen I and all the other eighteen-year-old males were required to register for the draft. In order to assure a sufficient number of engineers and doctors and lawyers, the draft deferred full-time college and graduate students; as long as we were in school we weren't likely to be drafted. Medical school counted as graduate school, but residency beyond the first year did not because the military services required a steady supply of general medicine officers, for which an internship was adequate preparation.

Newly graduated doctors had three choices: If they were eager to get military service out of the way or did not want their training to be suddenly interrupted during residency because they had been drafted, they could volunteer to go into one of the services at the end of internship as Air Force flight surgeons, Navy ship's surgeons, or Army general medical officers. The tours were two years, with a high likelihood that one year would be spent with the fighting forces in or near Vietnam.

Our second choice was to not to volunteer and hope that the draft passed us by. If residents had very low lottery numbers they could continue their training and go directly into practice without much fear of being drafted.

The third choice was to ask for deferment until the completion of training, a program called the Berry Plan. The hitch was, in exchange for not having your training interrupted, you had to go into one of the services.

Because the secretary of my draft board in Missoula, Montana had made it clear that she would draft me the minute I became eligible, it seemed likely that if I did nothing to prevent it, I would be drafted at the end of my internship.

I chose the Berry Plan and in the fall of my internship at the University of Chicago I had to report for a physical exam before I could be commissioned. On a cold February day I took the train into downtown Chicago to the National Guard Armory, where I lined up with a hundred other young men for hearing and vision tests and then a mass physical exam. The legend among doctors was that if we had one working eye, one working arm, one working leg and one working testicle, we could be drafted.

In groups of 25 we undressed and then were lined up side-by-side along a yellow tape, facing forward, each holding a card with a number. I was number 17. Some poor doctor who was probably playing out his second year of service after returning from overseas stood in front of us, a cigarette hanging from his lip, a stethoscope around his neck, flanked by a sergeant with a massive clipboard with our numbers along the side and categories along the top.

"Stand on your left foot," the doctor commanded.

We all stood on our left foot. Everyone had a left foot, no one fell over. Check.

"Stand on your right foot!"

Another check.

"Right hand above your head, left hand above your head." Check! Check!

He walked to the far left of the line and with only one of the earpieces in his ears, he put his stethoscope on the left side of our chest, listened for two heart beats, and called out to his sergeant, "ok." One of us could have had a cement mixer churning at high speed in his chest and that doctor would not have heard it.

He had no idea I was a doctor. I thought to myself, "My gawd, I don't, don't, don't want to spend a year doing what he is doing."

There was worse to come.

When he reached the last man on the line, he called out, "spread your legs!"

Cigarette smoke drifting up, glove on his right hand, he walked back along the line checking with one finger that we each had at least one testicle, no hernia bulge, and nothing gross going on. He wore the same glove for all 50 testicles.

At this point I was writing letters of protest to my congressman and to the Secretary of Defense.

"Turn around. Spread your cheeks with both hands. Bend as far forward as you can."

He walked down the line bent forward and only spoke twice. "Hemorrhoids, 12!" The sergeant scored a big X in that column. "Hygiene 24!" That got a double x.

That was it. I don't know the results of anyone else's eye or hearing checks, or whether the guys with bad hygiene or hemorrhoids were now on the path to "4F," unfit for duty.

I toyed with the idea of calling out to him, "check my arches." I have very flat feet and I wondered if that would earn me a dismissal from the lottery, but I figured it was useless.

I felt strangely violated.

As I walked back to fetch my clothes from a locker, 25 more naked men were lining up along the yellow tape.

The next step for me was to select which service I wanted. I hoped to be chosen for the Public Health Service, which would have meant that after completing residency I would be at the National Institutes of Health or the Center for Disease Control learning how to do research. Needless to say, residents hoping for basic-science research careers in a medical school coveted these positions, and evidence of research experience or training increased the chances of riding out the war in Washington DC or Atlanta. Two of my medical residents when I was a student got NIH appointments; both went on to win Nobel prizes.

In a month I found out that I was not chosen for the NIH. The price of my gamble was that, since I had volunteered, I now had to join one of the military services. The Navy seemed exciting to me, and as a fully trained internist I would more likely be away from battle zones in evacuation hospitals in SE Asia, the Philippines, or San Diego. Margaret was unhappy with the idea of my being away for a year, and the number of state-side postings in the Army was higher than in the Navy or Air Force. So that settled that.

A few months later I received a letter from the Department of the Army congratulating me and telling me I was a 2nd lieutenant in the U.S. Army reserves. I was given three years of deferment to finish my training, although I would only need two.

From the doctors' draft evolved an entirely different life than I could ever have imagined.

Just before my month on the Harkness service, the management of our apartment building on east 79th street sent us a letter telling us that our lease would be terminated on June 30 because the building was converting to a condominium. We could buy our apartment if we wished, but we would have to leave if we didn't.

This presented a dilemma. The rule of thumb was that owning a house or an apartment for three years was the minimum time needed for its increasing value to cover the real estate, mortgage, and lawyer fees. My deferment gave me time to finish residency and do one more year of training beyond that, but the most we could count on was two years to recover our closing costs, so buying a condo or a house was a gamble.

Two other events coincided with the "buy or leave" mandate from our apartment house's management. Margaret had loved working with a team of more senior colleagues at Encyclopedia Britannica in Chicago. She had never before made educational materials and she enjoyed the creative work of matching the text she wrote with images for schools to use in teaching. It meant that she had to learn about the subject herself, and then figure out how to explain it. Her managers at EB liked her work and saw an opportunity to open a New York City office where she could hugely expand their catalogue of topics. But instead of being part of a team, she worked alone in Brooklyn Heights; the few other people in her office were doing entirely unrelated work. While it was exciting for her to work with a photographer to gather images of longshoremen loading and unloading freighters and to fly over the waterfront in a helicopter, she wasn't happy with her isolation or the hour-long commute by subway to and from Brooklyn.

The transition back to New York City had been hard on Margaret in other ways. In order to shorten her commute to work, instead of finding an apartment in Washington Heights near the Medical Center, we had moved to midtown on Manhattan's east side, with the result that instead of my having a ten-minute trip to work on foot or by bike, I now spent two hours a day commuting. To get to the hospital at 7 I left the house at 6 AM. I rarely was home before 6:30 or 7:00, which gave us about two hours to eat dinner, clean up, and get ready for bed. Our time for conversation was mostly limited to the basics of daily living.

While I was immersed in a residency program and gradually was developing friendships, she had no other friends in the City other than her sister Mary, who was working as an assistant in the art department at New York University. Margaret spent a lot of her time by herself, reading. We did occasionally go out, usually to a local German or Hungarian or pizza restaurant, and we went to movie or a concert every few months. Without a car, an outing in one of the Adirondack parks or at the beach was out of the question.

We also found apartment life strange. Growing up in Montana and during college, and medical school I always had some contact with my neighbors. In our East 79th Street apartment we rode the elevator silently, everyone wrapped in a cocoon of privacy. When I walked out of the elevator or waited for it with a neighbor, they totally ignored me and everyone else. Neighbors never introduced themselves. Only the doormen acknowledged our participation in the apartment house community.

One February night we came home late from a concert. When we arrived at the 16th floor the door opened on a half-naked, screaming man crawling toward the elevator, dripping blood from multiple stab wounds. I told Margaret to get out and call an ambulance from our apartment. I dragged the man into the elevator. On the first floor I dragged him out and began looking for any wound that was gushing blood. None were, and while his clothes were soaked in blood that continued to ooze, he had a decent pulse. The aghast doorman clucked about the mess he would have to clean up. Once the city ambulance arrived and the crew loaded him on a stretcher, I went back to our apartment and found a trail of blood leading to the apartment next door. That apartment and ours shared a wall, and we had often heard laughter and music from what seemed to be partying, but we had rarely seen the two young women who were living there. It quickly unfolded that they were someplace on the high-class hooker spectrum; we never knew what had gone on that led to the stabbing.

They—and the blood-stained carpet—were gone by the next evening. We were a little unnerved.

A few nights later Margaret and I were sitting at our dining room table trying to decide what to do. Should we buy our apartment or find another apartment closer to the Medical Center for the two remaining years of my deferment? Should she look for another job, perhaps as a teacher in one of the Manhattan private schools? Should we have a baby? Our decision hinged on whether Margaret wanted to quit her job and whether this was a good time to start a family. She was 26, and I was 28; some of the other residents were starting families; a few of my high school friends already had one or several children. If we were going to have children, how long would it take for her to become pregnant, and how big an apartment would we need? Should we try to find a small house in Riverdale, a short distance away in Westchester County, or across the George Washington Bridge in the close-by towns of Teaneck or Leonia, where some of our faculty lived?

On the spur of the moment, I asked her if she wanted to stop taking birth control pills. She said something like, "Maybe." I walked into the bathroom and picked up the several packets and raised my eyebrows in inquiry. With a slight tilt of her head to the left, she eyebrowed back, "Why not?" Our kitchen had a double-hung window that looked down on a sidewalk sixteen stories below; I opened the window and we watched while the packets sailed into the darkness. Perhaps the pills were eaten by the pigeons that scampered underfoot eating anything that dropped onto the sidewalk. A little pigeon birth control didn't seem like a bad idea.

In early May, in the time-honored way, she told me with a little smile that I was going to be a father: she had missed a period. I knew almost nothing about babies, and what little I knew I had learned during my pediatrics clerkship in the well-baby clinic: that babies were efficient vectors of infectious diseases, and not to wear a good necktie when removing a little boy's diaper.

Margaret and I had begun to look for a new apartment before we knew that she was pregnant, but now with a July 1 move only two months away we had to decide if we were going to rent an apartment or try to buy a house. Buying a house depended on being in a training program for at least two more years—and, better, for three more years.

I had nothing planned when I finished my residency in a year. I called Dr. Frantz, my teaching attending during my Harkness month, and asked if I could come around to his office to talk with him. I knew that he sometimes took fellows and perhaps he could help me sort out some way to stay at Columbia for at least one year after I finished residency.

Andrew Frantz was a small man with a slightly curved spine that he partially masked with carefully tailored suits. He had grown up in a Columbia-Presbyterian family: his mother, Virginia Kneeland Frantz, was a pathologist and the first woman promoted to full professor at the medical school. She was famous for her contributions to clinical pathology—the microscopic study of tissue biopsies and post-operative specimens. His Uncle, Yale Kneeland, had been an early member of Dr. Loeb's faculty during some of Columbia's most luminous years in the twenties, thirties, and forties. Late in his career Dr. Kneeland had severe rheumatoid arthritis. When I was a student he was our sole teacher of physical diagnosis that he demonstrated with such elegance and clarity that, had this been Japan, would have led to him being designated a Living National Treasure.

Andy was born in the delivery room at Presbyterian Hospital and grew up in a penthouse apartment at 1185 Park Avenue, living alone with his mother. He attended a private elementary school in Manhattan; as a teenager he attended St. Paul's School in New Hampshire, followed by four years as an English major at Harvard. After Harvard he returned to Columbia for medical school and residency, then spent two years in the Navy. When he finished he came back to Columbia looking for a job. Dr. Loeb told him, "Go someplace else and learn something we don't do here, and then come back and I'll hire you." Andy went to the Massachusetts General Hospital and joined a lab studying the contribution of growth hormone to normal and abnormal human development with a recently developed growth hormone immunoassay.

As a purely teaching attending, Andy did not have to review my plan for the Harkness patients, or keep up with their progress. The cases I chose to present to him were good examples of classic diseases being well managed by their private physicians. Gradually our conversations turned from discussing the patients to literature, sociology, theater, music, film, and medical history. Although I had a warm relationship with Dr. Tarlov at the University of Chicago, my discussions with him were about my experiences taking care of patients and his advice about navigating a career in academic medicine, and I listened much more than I talked. My conversations with Andy were the first time that any faculty member had heard my thoughts or told me his on subjects not related to the practice of medicine.

Andy's "office" turned out to be a screened off corner of a large research laboratory where a couple of technicians were pipetting and weighing. Without his long white coat, Andy, in suit pants and a starched white shirt, still managed to look formal. He motioned me to sit down on a couch too littered with journals and papers to actually be available for sitting. Noting this, he moved one pile of papers on top of another pile of papers, and I tucked myself into the narrow space.

I explained my situation with the Berry Plan—that after my final year of residency I still had another year of deferment—and asked if he ever took fellows.

"Why yes, Gordon, I do take fellows. Are you interested?"

"I am. What would I have to do to apply?"

"You just did. So tell me more about yourself."

This is a dangerous thing to say to me. I think and talk in stories and metaphors, and it can be troublesome when I get started, which is probably why people seldom ask me an open-ended question a second time.

I told him about growing up in Montana with a single parent—my Mom—about my brother and father and his new family living a short distance away, about spending three years in Butte, Montana but then coming back to Missoula and ending up at Harvard. He told me that he too had been raised just by his mother.

For Andy, mine was a romantic story in the way that accounts of hiking the Alps and swimming the Caspian Sea and living with Swiss goat herders were for the 19th Century Romantic poets and their land-and-convention-bound readers. He talked enthusiastically about small town culture, about the honesty of westerners, about Grange Societies and fraternal organizations and the Kiwanis and Rotary clubs, and the virtues of living close to the land.

I knew the Kiwanis and Rotary clubs well and had never found anything whatsoever romantic or even interesting about them. I was surprised that he knew about Grange Societies, since I knew nothing, although I had frequently passed Grange meeting halls in small towns.

We talked about our different responses to King Lear, about Fitzgerald and Faulkner and Hemingway.

After an hour I thought I needed to leave so that he could get on with his day. I stood up, planning to ask him how long it would take for him to decide whether I could spend a year with him, but he took a shortcut: "Well, Gordon, see you next year."

We shook hands, and I went back to work. I had no idea what Andy did in his laboratory, or what I would be doing. But I now knew we could stay in New York City for the last year of my deferment.

I began to talk with other residents and with a few faculty members for their advice: apartment vs. house, Upper West Side or Riverdale or a close New Jersey suburb on the Hudson River. We saw a two-hundred-year-old house in Tappan, New York, that was barely more than an antique chicken coop with indoor plumbing, and we saw two-bedroom apartments in Riverdale and the Upper West Side that cost twice what we were paying on East 79th Street.

Then someone told me that one of the oncology fellows who had expected to stay at Columbia was moving to the University of Pennsylvania. During the last year of his fellowship, Peter had been assured that his boss had the power to hire him at Columbia, and the previous summer he and his wife had bought a house in Teaneck, New Jersey, where they planned to have a second child and settle down for a long time. That turned out to be incorrect—something had fallen through and there would be no position for him at Columbia. Their house was in good shape, the commute by car was twenty minutes at 7 o'clock in the morning, and there were frequent buses to and from the George Washington Bridge bus station that was only a ten-minute walk from the Medical Center. The price we settled on was $37,500, and Peter, who had spent three years in the Public Health Service at the NIH, could transfer his VA loan to us. We used savings bonds that Margaret's father bought for her education and a $3000 wedding gift of stocks from a friend of Margaret's family for our down payment. A silvery-haired lawyer named Fitzgerald closed the house sale for us, and only a few months after we decided to try having a family, we owned a house.

CHAPTER 20

Senior Resident

The same day I started the third year of my residency we moved into our house in Teaneck, New Jersey. As we progressively lived in larger places with each of our four moves, Margaret's family generously sent us more of the New England antique furniture that they collected and that Dr. Wilkins restored. Our first child wasn't due until January, but we now had three bedrooms, larger dining and living rooms, a full basement, and a third-floor room under the eaves that could be used as a playroom.

Living in the suburbs, we could no longer depend on subways and buses, so we bought a new, two-door lime green Ford Fairlane, for about $3000. We had no experience with babies and failed to consider paying a little more for to get a four-door model with easy access to the back seat. Somehow, we came up with the money to pay the mortgage for our house, the move from Manhattan to New Jersey, and a car on my salary of about $6000 a year and Margaret's salary as a substitute science teacher at Leonia High School, where she had taught when I was a medical student.

With the house came a small front yard, a small backyard heavily shaded by large trees, and a garage, all of which made me realize that even before the baby came our lives were rapidly shedding the flexibility and freedom of our first four years of marriage. A yard required mowing and watering, and therefore the buying of hoses and a lawnmower, fertilizer to perk up the neglected grass and, with the fertilizer, a spreader. On a hot, sunny July Saturday I drove to Gangerie's Garden Center the next town over and came away with a trunk full of garden equipment and flowers: hose, a mower and fertilizer, a spade, a rake, hand clippers, hedge shears, a hand trowel, eight rose plants in big pots and little pots of marigolds and zinnias and geraniums. It all cost a small fortune. As I drove home, on the car radio I could hear Simon and Garfunkel singing "Homeward Bound." I was feeling happily domestic, far beyond anything I had experienced moving into a new dorm room or any of our three apartments.

I had weeded and edged and mowed and raked and watered gardens since the sixth grade, often under protest, but I had also grown up in a place where everyone had flowers in their front yard and a vegetable garden and some fruit trees in their backyard. I had spent summers in my grandfather's paradisiacal flower and vegetable gardens and orchards at Flathead Lake. Although I was expected to do garden work for my mother and grandfather, I had also made money when paid by Missoula neighbors to do these chores. Now, the owner of a small patch of grass and dirt, my inherited growing and gathering gene expressed itself, and by midsummer I had converted much of the front lawn to a flower garden raging with hip-tall roses and zinnias and underplanted with groundcover flowers I had never heard of like alyssum and ageratum and moss roses and vinca and impatiens.

Some days I took the car to the hospital, others I took the bus from Teaneck to the George Washington Bridge bus terminal and walked to the medical center. I quickly found that the bus provided time to read—the *New England Journal* and the *Annals of Internal Medicine* and *Medicine* in the morning, and *The New York Times* at night. With some remorse I realized that I had nearly stopped reading novels, that the English major in me had gone dormant.

The third year of residency at Presbyterian Hospital was entirely different than the second year: we had no further rotations as the house resident for the inpatient wards; instead our time was heavily focused on consultations for the hospitalized patients on the surgery, ob-gyn, and dermatology services (called the "infield" because they were housed in the same building as the Medical Service) and neurology, psychiatry and ophthalmology services (called the "outfield" because they were in three separate buildings).

As consultants, we were entirely on our own—no attending reviewed our consultation notes or saw patients with us each day. When we were stuck with a problem that was beyond our experience, the specialists were always ready to help us: if we had a complex anemia that needed sorting out, we could ask the hematologist covering medicine inpatient consultations to review the case with us, and similarly we had access to the cardiology, gastroenterology, endocrinology, and infectious disease faculty. We could also ask the chief resident to review a case with us. It was both an expectation and a matter of pride that we would do everything we could to recommend the correct management before we asked for help so that we never depended on a specialist to teach us the basics, only to help where the diagnosis was obscure or the treatment novel or unavailable or risky. When we felt that a patient was too complex to be managed on the surgery or ob-gyn wards, we transferred the patient to the medicine wards: when that happened, our care up to that point was under fierce scrutiny, and since that could happen in the middle of the night or on a weekend when we were off, we made sure that our notes were complete, up-to-date, and based on a review of contemporary current practice.

Many of my second-year resident classmates had left at the end of the second year to begin military service: their plan was to get that out of the way and then come back to Columbia, or go to another institution for their third year, or "fast track" into a fellowship without ever doing a third year. As a result, there were only five third-year residents, including several who had returned from military service, and we took overnight call as the hospital medical consultant and the emergency room senior resident every fifth night for the entire year, a substantial improvement over every third night call as a junior resident.

The emergency room was managed entirely by the internal medicine residency staff, with three medicine interns and one surgery intern who took overnight call in pairs every other day. There was no attending physician working with us in the emergency room, but every department had a designated resident or attending physician who would come if we needed help. The first residencies in emergency medicine would not begin for another few years. At Columbia it was more than a decade before board certified emergency medicine physicians were hired.

Patients poured into the emergency room day and night, mostly for problems that could have been taken care of in an office or clinic visit if the patient had established care and could get a same-day appointment. As the patients entered the emergency room they passed by a nurses station, where a secretary or a nurse asked their complaint and called for their record or started a new one. They took a seat in a large waiting room more like a bus station than a medical clinic. Kids ran around, waiting patients and their families smoked, people were strewn around on stretchers or in wheelchairs. The front door opened onto Broadway, steaming and stinking in the summer, intermittently letting in gusts of icy wind in the winter. There was no guard and it was very rare that there was a need for anyone to manage an unruly patient.

When the old records were received from the file room they were placed in a wooden box on wheels that looked homemade. The interns grabbed the next chart in the order in which the patients had arrived. If the nurses thought a patient was urgent they put the chart in the front of the box. We didn't argue with them.

If patients came in with acute abdominal pain or shock or chest pain suggestive of a heart attack or a high fever the nurses rushed them into one of the six examination rooms. Several of us would drop what we were doing and stabilize the patient. If we thought the patient had a surgical problem we paged the surgery resident on call, who quickly came to the emergency room, examined the patient, and made a decision about admission. If they thought a patient was "non-surgical" but acutely ill we took them on medicine. Women in labor were seen by one of the Ob-Gyn residents and either sent home if they were not close to delivering, or admitted to the labor room.

Almost every day patients would arrive with a heart rhythm problem—tachycardia, a fast rate unable to sustain an adequate blood pressure—or bradycardia, a very slow heart rate. We would start care in the emergency room but a few times a week a patient was in such severe condition that we called a cardiac arrest, which brought more nurses, the second-year resident covering cardiology, and an anesthesiologist who would intubate the patient if they needed support breathing. If the patient had ventricular fibrillation—sustained random writhing of the heart, which was almost always fatal—we shocked them, trying to reestablish a normal rhythm. Since we didn't have intensive care units, the emergency room became the ICU until we were able to move the patient to a medical ward, often with one of us doing chest massage and another compressing an elastic Ambu bag connected to the tube in the patient's airway to keep the patient alive while being wheeled to the elevator and through the hallways to the medical ward.

One muggy August late afternoon a young man from the neighborhood was brought in with acute chest pain that had developed on his job carrying bricks and mortar up ladders. He quit work and walked the few blocks to his home; his sister insisted he come to the Medical Center. After she paid for the taxi, she told a nurse that he had never been sick a day in his life. The nurses rushed him into a room and as I was examining him and an intern was hooking up the leads of an electrocardiogram machine he suddenly became unconscious. His blood pressure and pulse were undetectable. I yelled to the nurses' desk to call an arrest and I began cardiac massage. He was blue by the time we had intubated him; his rhythm was coarse ventricular fibrillation. We shocked him without effect. He was big and muscular and our external cardiac massage wasn't effective in creating a palpable pulse. A surgeon who was in the next examination room wandered in, saw the patient's massive chest and told us that we would never be able to do effective cardiac massage—his chest wall was too far from his heart. He asked if we wanted to do open chest cardiac massage and within a minute he had split open the man's left rib cage and was compressing the patient's heart with his hand. While the anesthesiologist continued to bag him, the patient's face and fingers became slightly less blue. The surgeon was squatting at the head of the table, invisible except for his hand disappearing into the patient's chest.

An excitable infectious disease fellow who was moonlighting as a triage doctor looked into the room from the man's right side, and, seeing no one doing chest compressions, pushed his way into the table and began compressions, somehow not noticing the open chest. The surgeon's forehead and then full face slowly rose above the other side of the table like the rising sun.

"Would you mind stopping that?"

The fellow staggered backwards, taking it all in. Neither he nor any of us around the stretcher had seen a chest ripped open for direct cardiac massage. He apologized and meekly disappeared.

I asked the surgeon to stop briefly to see if his rhythm had converted, but there was still only ventricular fibrillation. We shocked him several more times, his body jerking with each discharge, but he never developed a functional rhythm. After a half hour we called an end to the resuscitation. All of us were spattered with blood, the young man's chest was a gaping excavation, a few students were leaning against the walls of the examination room in shock and dismay.

I found a nurse and asked where his sister had gone. The nurse pointed toward the entrance of the emergency room where she was in a pay phone booth frantically trying to contact her parents. When she saw me, she dropped her hand and the phone away from her face and just stared at me, covered with blood and probably ashen myself. She stepped out of the booth, dropped the hand piece, from which, swinging on its cord, the voice of whomever she had called was faintly audible. She didn't say a word; her eyes teared up. She turned and placed the phone receiver back on its hook, and then turned back to me. My hands were too bloody to touch her clothes, but she propped her forehead against my shoulder and we stood that way, both in tears, for minutes.

I whispered that I was sorry. She nodded, and then shrugged, both eyebrows raised, as if to ask, "Now what?"

That night never came together. Neither the two interns nor I had experienced a patient our age having a cardiac arrest and dying in spite of our efforts, of watching a chest opened by a surgeon with nothing more than a scalpel and sterile gloves, of watching ribs being wrenched apart by brute force, of watching a sister try to cope with the horror of her brother's death and the sight of his bloody corpse lying motionless on an examination table, his eyes rolled back, an endotracheal tube protruding from his purple lips.

We worked all night seeing other patients, but all of us had haunted, hollow-eyed faces. We barely talked with each other beyond reviewing cases. At eight the next morning, the night interns went home. I had showered and changed clothes after the arrest; in the morning I went back to my call room to shave. I spent the rest of the day doing consultations on the surgery service.

No one ever talked with any of us about the event. No chief resident came to ask if the interns or I were "alright," whatever that means after this kind of emotional trauma. We probably didn't even think of it as emotional trauma, only as part of the gritty reality of being a doctor in an emergency room where patients sometimes came in after being shot, where old people came in with advanced lung or heart failure and died shortly after we admitted them.

There was no review of the case.

It was clear that the surgeon knew that his last-ditch effort was probably going to be futile. When I saw him a few days later I thanked him.

He said, "For what? It's what I do."

It wasn't out of the ordinary for him. He opened chests and abdomens every day and he had seen many trauma patients die in the emergency room and on the operating room table during surgery.

"You do what you can do. Sometimes it works, more often it doesn't."

Around Christmastime I was helping the interns late one evening when a taxi driver rushed through the front doors and asked the nurses to bring a gurney out to his cab.

"I gotta girl in the back seat and she's having a baby."

The nurses grabbed a delivery kit—examination gloves, a cord clamp, and some towels. The cabbie had pulled into the ambulance ramp and left the cab running, the back door open and the lights on. By the dim dome light I could see a woman scrunched up against the passenger-side back door, her knees spread apart, and a bulge in her underpants which turned out to be a fully delivered head. I put on the gloves and delivered the baby easily—it wasn't her first. I clamped and cut the umbilical cord and handed the baby off to one of the nurses, who swaddled it, declaring, "it's a handsome little guy." I flipped the clamp up onto her abdomen, and with the nurses lifted her up onto the gurney. The cabbie stood outside the back door peering in over the nurses' backs.

As she disappeared into the emergency room, he looked into the back seat. "I hope she didn't make a mess of my cab! Oh hell, she didn't pay me."

"Has this happened before . . . have you had babies born before you got them to a hospital?" I asked.

"Yah. A few times. Most of the time we make it to the hospital before the baby comes out, but once when I was just starting to drive a taxi, just out of high school, a woman dropped her baby in my cab and I didn't even know she was having a baby, she just said she had cramps and needed to go to the hospital. Then I heard this crying in the back seat and I knew she didn't have no kid in her arms when she got in the cab. I almost went nuts getting her there. Came out all right though. Got to the hospital and the baby was between her legs on the seat. Come to think of it, she never paid me, neither."

I looked at the meter and gave him what I had in pocket change, $1.35, and invited him in to get some paper towels to clean his cab up.

No other department had a resident in the emergency room, but as their contribution to the Medical Service for running the emergency room twenty-four hours a day, every department let their residents know that when the senior medicine resident called them, they had to drop what they were doing. When kids came in, the on-call pediatrician came to take care of them. We saw all the surgery, obstetrics, neurology, and psychiatry patients first, and then contacted the covering resident to take over. It was an amazing education for us, since we usually saw patients early in the course of their illness and got to do the initial history and physical exam and order tests and X-rays. Most of the time patients didn't need to be admitted; we made a diagnosis, started treatment, and scheduled an appointment for the patient to come back for follow-up.

In the course of a week we would see multiple patients with sickle-cell crisis, acute upper and lower GI bleeding, pneumonia, tuberculosis, meningitis, stroke, profound anemia, diabetic ketoacidosis, severe hypoglycemia, acute heart attacks, shock, malignant hypertension, pyelonephritis, urinary tract infections, pelvic inflammatory disease, appendicitis, gallbladder disease, liver failure, delirium tremens, drug overdoses, highly contagious infections and septic shock, gunshot wounds, fractured arms and legs—and much more.

One night a man came into the ER looking ill and complaining that his skin hurt and was covered with blisters. We got him into an examination room and he undressed. He was covered with large and small red blisters, some of which were peeling off with thin flaps of dead skin. His lips and eyelids looked as though they had been through a meat grinder. In most of the residency programs at Columbia Presbyterian at least one resident stayed overnight, but the dermatologists took call from home. I asked the paging operator to get in touch with the on-call resident and a few minutes later the head nurse called out, "Dr. Kammerman's on the phone."

I described the patient, and asked him to come in and admit him to the small dermatology inpatient service.

He replied, "Admit him to medicine and we'll see him tomorrow."

"Look, this guy is incredibly sick. This is a dermatologic emergency, not a medical one. I want you to come in."

He snorted, "I went into dermatology because there aren't dermatologic emergencies. Nothing we are going to do overnight is going to change anything. We'll see him tomorrow."

"I think you know that the senior resident in the emergency room can admit a patient to any service. I am admitting him to dermatology. I'll let Dr. Nelson know."

Dr. Nelson was the distinguished, gentle, silver-haired chairman of the Department of Dermatology. With the dermatology resident still on the phone, I called over to the head nurse, "Would you please get Dr. Nelson on the phone?"

The resident muttered, "Oh for God's sake. Don't call Dr. Nelson. I'll come in. But would you keep him there for an hour: I'm already in bed, I live in the Village, and the subway is going to take a while at this hour."

"Sure. The poor guy will be glad to see you."

A few weeks later a young man came in with a diffuse rash covering his entire body. After examining him I asked the dermatologist on call to come down to see him with me. When he arrived, I took him into the examination room. I asked the patient to hold out his arms; I cradled his hands and turned them over so that the dermatologist could see that the rash involved the palms of his hands. I noted that the dermatologist was keeping his own hands behind his back and standing well away from the patient.

"It looks like secondary syphilis to me," I said, feeling pleased. Once common but now rare, I had never seen a patient with secondary syphilis before.

"Yup, you're right about the rash. Probably has secondary syphilis."

"Don't you want to examine him?"

"We usually don't touch patients who have secondary syphilis unless we put on gloves. They are incredibly infectious."

I almost never put on gloves unless I needed sterile gloves to do a procedure. Now I felt like a total dope: I had entirely forgotten that patients with secondary syphilis can infect other people from the skin lesions.

The dermatologist took over and made arrangements for the patient to receive penicillin and warned him against any form of contact with other people.

For months I worried that I was going to get syphilis, just as I had gotten hepatitis from taking care of a patient. How would I explain that to Margaret!

I had better luck this time.

The ambulance system in New York City operated by a flexible set of rules: Patients could tell them which hospital they wanted to be taken to, but the ambulance drivers would make up their own minds. In acute, critical situations they often went to the closest hospital. If a patient was already established at one of the teaching or private hospitals, the ambulances often would comply and go where the patient wanted.

Because Columbia Presbyterian was not a city hospital, it was under no obligation to admit every patient who walked or was carried through the ER front doors. The hospital tried to take care of as many patients as it could from the Washington Heights neighborhood, whether or not they were established patients and without regard to their ability to pay. When patients came in from the Bronx or Queens or from near Harlem or Bellevue hospitals, we could admit them if we thought they were good teaching cases, but we could also "LCH" them—send them to the local city hospital.

On a warm spring evening an ambulance brought in a man in his mid-sixties who had chest pain. We did an ECG which showed that he was having "cardiac ischemia"—insufficient blood getting to the heart muscle—which could evolve into myocardial damage. While we gave him nitroglycerin and a little morphine, I took a history and found out that he had been having chest pain on and off for months and was being treated at Harlem Hospital. That evening he had been visiting his daughter in the Bronx, and when particularly severe chest pain began, his daughter called an ambulance; they took him to Morrisania, a local city hospital in the Bronx.

He told me that at Morrisania they did an ECG, determined that he was having a heart attack, but decided that they wouldn't admit him because he lived in Harlem. They put him back in the city ambulance and sent him to us at Presbyterian Hospital.

I called the emergency room at Morrisania and asked why they sent him to us—they either should have admitted him there, or sent him to Harlem Hospital, where he was already a patient.

The resident on the other end was a total smart ass.

"You guys dump patients on us all the time that you don't want to admit. I figured PH was closer to where he lived and that I'm tired of your sending patients to us that you don't think are interesting enough for your delicate little interns."

At this point I should have simply hung up, admitted the patient, and called the chief of medicine at Morrisania Hospital the next day to complain. But for some reason I let vanity and righteousness take over. Probably the worst of the two was my vanity. The interns and residents covering the wards were constantly hammered by admissions; they regarded some of the senior residents as "sieves," admitting everyone if they didn't want to go to the trouble of caring for them in the emergency room. A few were overly sympathetic. Howard Baker was considered to be a sympathetic "sieve" who would admit anyone for whom he felt a twinge of sympathy.

Howie was soft spoken and nebbishy; his phone calls were dreaded and typically went like this: "Hello, this is Dr. Baker. I am sending you a lovely elderly lady who just hasn't been feeling well for a couple of days. She has lost her appetite and thinks something bad is wrong with her."

"Did you find anything on her exam?"

"No, her exam was normal."

"And lab?"

"Well, I thought you should do that. Even if her labs were normal, she reminds me of my grandmother, who also lives alone, and I just can't bear the thought of sending her home. So, she is coming up."

This happened once or twice every night Howie was on, and invariably the patients had nothing wrong that we could discover and were sent home the next morning. The interns and residents held Howie in high disdain.

I on the other hand had cultivated the reputation of being the "Ironman at the Front Door," and fancied myself as appreciated for being tough and protective of the interns, often admitting patients to the overnight ward and working them up myself if it wasn't yet clear that they needed to be in the hospital, or if the interns were overwhelmed by earlier admissions.

Beyond my vanity was the issue of maintaining the right of the Medical Center to decide whether patients not in our own neighborhood and who were already being cared for in another hospital—and, in particular, a city hospital—would be admitted or transferred. Since we could not take care of every patient who was sent to us or came to our door, the admitting resident had the responsibility of making decisions to admit or transfer.

So, the Iron Man at the Front Door decided to protect his interns from the admission of a patient having cardiac chest pain, of whom we already had a great many, who was medically stable, and who should have been kept at Morrisania or transferred to Harlem hospital.

I was conflicted about sending a patient with active chest pain in an ambulance to Harlem hospital, as I should have been.

I went back to talk with him and asked him how he was feeling. We had relieved his pain with nitroglycerin and morphine, and he said he didn't mind being transferred to Harlem Hospital. We had no way of duplicating records quickly, so I ran another cardiogram, circled the changes indicating ischemia, and gave him an envelope with the cardiogram and a note explaining that I thought that he was stable and could be safely transported to his "home" hospital. I asked the nurses to call the city ambulance and to let the nurses in the Harlem Emergency room know that he was coming.

A half hour later I got an irate telephone call from a staff physician at Harlem Hospital furious that I had transported a patient with active cardiac ischemia. I said that he should have been kept at Morrisania or transported directly to Harlem Hospital, since he was not a CPMC patient. The staff physician would have none of it and said he was going to call my department chairman, Dr. Bradley, the next morning.

We had no interventions for active ischemia to prevent acute myocardial infarction other than controlling blood pressure and reducing anxiety. The risk in transferring him was that he would have a cardiac arrest in the ambulance, rather than in our ER or on our ward.

Epiphanies arrive in many forms. There was no doubt whatsoever that transferring him was both dangerous and inhumane, an act of spite because Morrisania had sent him to us instead of admitting him, and an act of selfishness—my effort not to tarnish my reputation of protecting the exhausted interns against too many admissions.

I expected to be called into Dr. Bradley's office the next day, but I wasn't. Our chief resident at that time was Dick Baerg, who I liked a lot and who later became a good friend. Dick found me and said that Dr. Bradley had received the call, and while he thought that my decision was questionable, he agreed with upholding the right of CPMC to determine who we would admit and who we could transfer. My "ironmanness" didn't come up for discussion, beyond Dick saying that it had been risky to transfer him and that, while he understood my concern for our residents, he personally would have admitted the patient.

Our mistakes teach us more than our successes: I had never been rebuked during internship or residency—not even because of my handling of this patient— but I should have been. I had been humbled by medical school and the Match, but gradually I had allowed myself to become arrogant and more than a little impatient with file room clerks and laboratory technicians when they were slow to produce a record or an X-ray or a lab test. A rebalancing occurred that day. I had been let off the hook and the patient was safely now at Harlem Hospital, but I was chastened, and like a set in a play changing between acts, I changed in a matter of hours. I began thanking people for their work, became considerate about what their world was like, got to know their names, and treated them as I always should have treated them. And I never again treated a patient as a pawn in the turf wars between private and public hospitals.

Some things that happened in the emergency room could be funny. One evening as I was working side by side with the interns trying to clean out the box—a hopeless proposition—I pulled out the chart of the next patient, a neighborhood woman. The nurses clipped a small note to each chart as they triaged patients: the note for her said, "Problems down there."

I thought extreme modesty had prompted the nurse to not be explicit, but it turned out that the patient knew no English and just kept pointing "down there."

Using the overhead speakers, I called her: "Maria Galvez to booth 4 please."

No one appeared.

"Maria Galvez, booth 4."

No one stirred, so I pushed back the curtain separating my booth from the waiting room and called again. A woman in about her mid-thirties stood up and walked toward me, trailing a small boy who I guessed was about 7 years old. I found a chair for him, motioned them to sit down, and began my history-taking.

"So, why did you come to the hospital tonight?"

She looked at me and shook her head. "No ingles."

"Ah. Porque viene usted a la hospital, por favor?"

She smiled and started talking a blue streak, not a word of it comprehendible to me.

I excused myself and asked the several nurses at the screening desk if any of them spoke Spanish. None of them did. Both of my interns were busy.

I returned to the booth and asked the boy what his name was. It was Miguel, and he said he spoke English.

"Can you ask your mother why she came here, Miguel?"

Turning his face toward her, he said basically the same thing I had asked. She started talking fast, using a lot of motions, several of them pointing down to her lower abdomen.

"I can't understand. I don't know English for those words."

I took a wild guess. "Ask her if she missed a menstrual period, please."

"I don't know what that is."

I was pretty sure that "vaginal bleeding," "vaginal discharge," and "when was her last period" were not going to work either.

"Blood down there. Sangre down there. Has she had sangre down there?" I pointed to her abdomen.

Miguel looked dazed. He had no idea what I was talking about. The workings of his mother's reproductive system were as much a mystery to him as they were to me.

I asked one of the nurses to take her into an examination room so that I could do an abdominal and vaginal exam.

She was about four months pregnant. "Usted tiene un bebe." This apparently was not a surprise to her. All that she wanted was to make an appointment for an obstetrical pre-partum checkup. I don't think the ER visit with me was going to qualify.

In spite of my total inability to communicate with her, about five months later I got a page to call the delivery room.

"A patient here, Maria Galvez, has named her baby after you. Congratulations."

"What? I don't know a Maria Galvez." It flashed through my mind that someone was trying to blackmail me by saying that I had fathered her child.

"Yes, you do. You diagnosed her pregnancy in the Emergency Room last fall. She must have either liked you or your name. She had a girl, Noel Maria Galvez. At first she wanted to call her Doctor Noel Maria Galvez, but one of our gals persuaded her to drop the doctor part for now."

As a senior resident I had developed a large practice made up mostly of patients I had taken care of in the hospital and my weekly clinic tended to sprawl, beginning before noon and finishing after 5 PM.

I met one of my more colorful patients when he was admitted to my team with poorly controlled diabetes. Augustus Duncan was an enormous, muscular African-American, built like a football fullback; he had spent twenty years in prison for murdering someone as a paid hit man. He probably had diabetes undetected for years, but when it was discovered he was already mostly blind and he was afraid of needles and reluctant to take insulin. Shortly after he was paroled he was admitted to our team for out-of-control diabetes, and in caring for him in the clinic I struggled to get him to follow a diet. A nurse came to his house once a week and loaded seven syringes with the insulin that he would then administer by jabbing his leg through his pants leg every morning. Because he was blind he couldn't check his urine for glucose.

He always came to the clinic with his appropriately huge German shepherd guide dog, Caesar, who coiled up at his feet and growled at me when I touched Augustus—whose response was, "Don't bite the nice doctor, Caesar, or he'll cut your tail off."

One day Augustus talked his way into clinic a week before his next appointment. I assumed he was having trouble with his diabetes, but he wanted me to examine Caesar.

"Doc, could you take a look at Caesar's left ear. He keeps pawing at it and rubbing the side of his head on the floor."

"You want me to look in Caesar's ear?"

"Yah Doc, please do it. Sumpin in there's bothering him."

Caesar was scary under the best of circumstances, but Augustus was a professional hit man and I was more reluctant to cross him than Caesar.

"He isn't going to like it!"

"I'll tell'im not to chew on you, Doc."

I wasn't convinced, but I took down the otoscope from the wall, put a clean speculum on it, squatted down, and gingerly lifted Caesar's floppy ear while Caesar rumbled a warning growl.

I pushed in the tip of the speculum carefully and peered in. Staring back at me was a large bug, both of its feelers waving inside the speculum.

"Cockroach!" I said.

"Again? Damn! I figured as much. They like to climb in there because it is warm and dark. Can you get it out, Doc?"

"I dunno. What do you think Caesar?"

I found a nurse and asked for a long forceps or a straight clamp.

Caesar behaved himself while I put a clamp in the ear canal blindly, closed it, and dragged out the furiously kicking cockroach by a feeler.

"Should I feed it to Caesar?"

"Naw, he don't like cockroaches Doc. Shoulda got me a cat."

Moreno Gonzalez was my most exasperating patient: I first met him when he was admitted to our team two weeks after a previous team had discharged him. He was a grumpy, elderly man who spoke very little English and had a problem list as long as my arm, including severe diabetes, congestive heart failure after multiple heart attacks, lung disease because of a two-pack-a-day smoking habit, bad vascular disease that had resulted in the amputation of one foot already, severe vascular disease in both eyes resulting in near blindness, kidney failure, hypertension, and at least one stroke.

In the previous six years he had been admitted multiple times for severe heart failure and during my three months as house our team admitted him three more times. We would give him diuretics for four or five days and get ten pounds of water off of him, we would review how he was to take each of his eleven medications, and we would have a Spanish-speaking nurse review how he was to avoid sugar and salt. He would resist discharge for three days or a week after that, accusing us of trying to kill him, and within a week he was back in the emergency room. If he made it to my clinic, I tried to review his medications with a translator, but he could never remember their names or what he was supposed to take when. His vision was so limited that he couldn't read the labels on the pill vials.

Finally, I got a set of tuning forks and asked him if he could tell the difference between three tones.

He could.

Then I asked the pharmacy if they could put his medications in bottles grouped by time of day. A few blocks from the medical center there was a sewing store that had small bells in different pitches that could be sewn on clothing. Using a rubber band to attach the bells, we grouped vials of his early morning pills together with a low-pitched bell attached to each, his midday pills in vials with higher pitched bells, and his evening medications in vials with very high-pitched bells.

It was an imaginative, but vain, effort. I saw him in clinic nearly every week that he wasn't in the hospital and on the first visit I discovered that he had totally mixed up which pills were in which bottle. But the greater problem was that he ate salty food, and nothing we were giving him was sufficient to counteract that. Every week or two he would be readmitted. With each admission the student admission notes began with steadily ascending numbers: "This is the 37th admission of this 67 year old blind, diabetic man with congestive heart failure, peripheral vascular disease, renal failure, chronic obstructive lung disease, " and the list went on and on. The current history was essentially the same for the past five or six admissions:

"Mr. Gonzalez says that he has become short of breath in the nine days since his last admission and so he came to the ER and was found to have gained eight pounds and to be in heart failure." With each admission the four-foot-high stack of old charts was brought to the floor and some poor student would be expected to go back through all of them to find some clue that would unlock how to keep him out of the hospital.

In the end, my efforts to make his medications audible were subverted by his confusion, and nothing we could do to reverse his heart failure worked since he would not follow a salt-restricted diet. He needed continuous care in a nursing home, but there was no funding to pay for it. After several more admissions I got a message that he had been brought into the emergency room with a spreading leg infection that led to an amputation. He never left the surgery service, dying of infection and kidney failure. He had spent nearly 200 days in the hospital in the year and a half I took care of him.

I took care of hundreds of patients as a resident, but now, fifty years later, I remember in detail only a few dozen of them. Although Mr. Gonzalez was one of the most challenging patients that I took care of — and easily the least grateful—I have never stopped thinking about him. His medical history included almost every complication of diabetes, all present at the same time.

Medical education has always been associated with the care of the poor. For a century, it was practically the only way a person with little or no money could get care in a big city. In my experience, the tradeoff was beneficial for the patient: Mr. Gonzalez got the best care we had at that time, in no way less expert than our attendings' private patients next door in the Harkness Pavilion, and hundreds of residents and students learned from taking care of him.

Dr. Bradley was the Bard Professor of Medicine for twelve years. He never achieved the stature and adulation of his predecessor and mentor, Robert F. Loeb, who stepped down and withdrew from the medical school at age 60 to avoid becoming antiquated and an obstacle to change.

Dr. Bradley's style was to maintain the traditions of the Loeb era. He tended to block new developments. He refused to create a dialysis program for moral reasons: renal transplantation was in its infancy and most patients with kidney failure would not recover kidney function; to allow dialysis would put physicians in the position of making life-and-death decisions based on arbitrary choices, since the number of dialysis machines could only treat a tiny percentage of the patients with chronic renal failure.

He also continued Dr. Loeb's refusal to allow any internal medicine faculty member to be purely a specialist, emphasizing the centrality of every internist being first and foremost a great generalist. At the University of Chicago and many other academic medical centers, nearly every internist was a specialist. I came back to Columbia because of its emphasis on training broadly competent physicians and appreciated the perpetuation of the generalist model, but the price of that was that Columbia was not especially attractive to graduating residents who wanted to become specialists; there were few fellowship programs and limited opportunities to build nationally recognized divisions of gastroenterology, cardiology, or oncology. Dr. Bradley had failed to recognize that internal medicine was evolving toward specialization, and under his leadership Columbia was falling behind.

Out of view of the residents, because of his refusal to allow change Dr. Bradley had gradually accumulated enough enemies in the Department of Medicine and in the medical school administration that he was asked to give up the chairmanship.

While the residents had never been great fans of Dr. Bradley in spite of the fact that he was invariably supportive of the residents and very committed to their training, many of us felt that we had to give him a warm send off. I had learned from Margaret's father of Dr. Bradley's long and successful research career that had culminated in his being chosen as editor of the *Journal of Clinical Investigation*, the most prestigious research journal in the world, and his quite diverse interests outside of medicine. Knowing that I knew a little about him, Dick Baerg, the Chief Resident, asked if I would take charge of buying Dr. Bradley a gift and collecting money from the residents. I discovered that he was fond of the novels of Henry James, fortuitous, since I too was a Henry James fan. I had the great fun of exploring the musty bookstores of lower Manhattan looking for the original editions of James' complete set of writings. At a ceremony a few weeks before the end of the resident year we gave him the yard-wide collection, for which he was appropriately grateful and embarrassed.

I felt sorry for Dr. Bradley. I knew none of the behind-the-scenes issues that led to his unseating, but I felt that being forced out must have been humiliating. While I, like everyone else, was somewhat aware of his limitations as a leader, clinician, and teacher, I recognized that his ascendance to the chair had occurred under the worst possible circumstance—he was succeeding a beloved leader who had created a very successful department, an almost impossible act to follow: better to take over a department in decline headed by an unpopular chair, with everyone desperate for a new leader, than to try to take the place of a legend.

I savored the irony that the debacle of my presentation of Miss Brawling to Dr. Bradley, after which I was convinced that my career in medicine was over, had ended up with my organizing the residents' farewell tribute to him. I never asked if he remembered that presentation, and I was deeply grateful that he had invited me to come back to Columbia to finish my residency. After he stepped down, he became a fleeting shadow in the remote regions of his old research labs. My primary feeling about him was sadness, because he seemed never to have been able to express the joy of caring for patients and presiding over a high-spirited, talented faculty and residency program.

It never occurred to me to ask him if he would talk with me about his life in medicine, or to ask his advice: many years passed before I learned the value of talking with more senior physicians or became aware of the satisfaction they might feel in being useful or simply interesting to a younger colleague.

Margaret's due date was the middle of January. Gender prediction was mostly witchcraft—if the baby was very active and had a fast pulse, chances are it would, be a boy; a calm baby with a slow heart rate was probably a girl. We didn't have a clue. The pregnancy had gone along smoothly, although with the expected discomfort and loss of mobility. I had switched my January rotation with another resident so that I wouldn't be in the hospital overnight when she went into labor. We had laid in the necessary gear—or rather Margaret did, since I had no idea what it would take to care for a newborn beyond a diaper bucket. We had chosen names for both a girl and a boy, referencing a book that Margaret's mother had owned called *What to Name the Baby*. We avoided continuing the tradition of Margarets that went back to Margaret's grandmother; instead, we thought of people we liked, focusing on Margaret's family, since the few adult women's names from my childhood—Nonie, Leah, Ruth—didn't appeal to either of us. We had liked Margaret's great aunt Katharine a lot—she supported Margaret's marrying me against the prolonged opposition of Margaret's mother, father, brother, and sister; her great aunt Julia Redhead had also been supportive, but the name Katharine seemed more elegant, perhaps a halo effect of the great actress Katharine Hepburn. I pushed for the random name Elizabeth as a middle name, again perhaps for elegance —no one we knew had that name. Katharine Elizabeth Noel scanned well. For boys I wanted to avoid the name Robert or Bob, both of our fathers' names, and came up with Christopher Andrew Noel, again because it scanned well, although I was friends with no Christophers. Margaret didn't like names, the initials of which were words— "CAN" didn't appeal, and her mother said it sounded Irish Catholic, which to her was low class. I thought a boy nicknamed "Topher" or "Chris" would be cool. The women and, as it turned out, genetics outvoted me.

The predicted date came and went and I was running out of time before my next overnight call rotation. I decided to take Margaret to the then-notorious movie, *I Am Curious Yellow*, on the assumption that certainly she would go into labor just at the scene that had earned it an X rating—a nude woman sitting in a tree—but she fell asleep during the movie and no baby emerged. We read books that suggested jumping ropes—hard to pull off in frigid January—or driving on bumpy roads, which we tried but that resulted only in my getting a traffic ticket when I failed to yield to a New Jersey highway patrolman at a traffic circle.

Finally, on the twentieth of January I woke up in the middle of the night and found Margaret missing. She had gone into labor and, knowing that the contractions were far apart, she simply moved into the other bedroom to wait it out. Later that day I took her to Columbia-Presbyterian. As was the custom then, her obstetrician, Ed Bowe, said he would deliver her whenever the baby came, unless it was during one of his two weeks of vacation.

It was still relatively uncommon for fathers to be in the delivery room when their children were born, but we made the decision that I should be there. Spending hours with Margaret in the labor room left me feeling helpless: this was nurse territory. As a student we met the patient when they got to the delivery room, where we had a role to play, if only a small one. I was used to fixing pain or making diagnoses or leading patients through decision-making, but in the labor room there was nothing I could do hour after hour as Margaret pushed other than encourage her, which didn't seem nearly enough.

On 21 January, Margaret's birthday, Katharine Elizabeth Noel was born: Margaret had been in labor for 18 hours. When Katharine was handed to me after she had been wrapped in a blanket, I was stunned that Margaret and I had made this little creature, that now we were responsible for her, that her future happiness was in our hands. Before medical school I had never held a very young baby in my arms. I knew nothing about being a father. I wasn't anxious, only puzzled that I wasn't.

In time we decided that the name Elizabeth didn't have any familial resonance and added Margaret's sister's name: Katharine became Katharine Mary Elizabeth Noel.

Margaret took to mothering as though she had prepared her entire life for it. The one thing she was clear about was that she didn't want Katharine to have any bottle-feeding and would nurse—a generational shift since our mothers' time, when bottle feeding was considered a form of liberation and nursing was thought to be lower class by some. Margaret loved the novels of George Eliot, her model of an emancipated woman, and I had bought her a complete early 1900's set of the novels. When Katharine woke up at night, Margaret moved into the small bed in the room where Katharine's crib was and read Eliot while nursing. I was back on 36-hour call every fifth night and Margaret did a nearly flawless job of not disturbing me: I rarely woke up.

After Katharine was born our house became the center of our time together. Between my continuing residency responsibilities and having an infant, now we never went out. We had neighbors with teen-aged children, but it was a long time before we entrusted a babysitter to care for Katharine for even a few hours. When I was at home on weekends I spent much of my time reading medical articles. Margaret was a full-time mother and housewife. We ruefully discovered the inconvenience of putting a baby into the back seat of a two-door sedan.

Senior Resident

Now a father and focusing on life beyond residency, the spring of 1970 was a halcyon time. After four years of medical school and my two years of residency at Columbia Presbyterian I felt like I knew everyone at the medical center. All but one of the other P & S students who had been interns at CPMC had left for military service or practice or advanced training; Willie Lee and I were the only graduates of P & S '67 left. I had learned the advantages of being calm and considerate rather than intense and imperious. I was proud of the training program and enjoyed the opportunities to teach students and interns.

On the 30th of June, the last day of the residency year, I was on call with Glenda Garvey and John Bilizekian, who had been my students at Delafield two years before when I came back from three months of hepatitis still yellow. We decided to celebrate the end of their internship by taking the beat-up wheeled wooden box that nurses put the waiting patients' charts in up to the 19th floor roof of Presbyterian Hospital, lighting it on fire, and dropping it on Broadway. During the day we had the whole internship class come by and carve their initials in the wooden sides of the box. At 6 AM on July 1, after being up all night taking care of patients, we pulled the charts out of the box, piled them on a chair, and rolled the box into an elevator. When we got to the roof it dawned on us that a flaming wooden box hurtling 19 stories down toward Broadway at 6:15 AM might be spectacular, but also lethal. We returned it to the ER and for the next dozen years the initialed box collected the carved signatures of dozens more interns, a perhaps more useful tradition.

Chapter 21

Prolactin

On July 1, 1970, after my last night in the emergency room, I went back to my call room to pack up the few things I had been keeping there for showering and shaving. I was now a fellow . . . but I had no idea what that meant. I had not yet been issued the two long white coats that faculty members and fellows wore, or turned in my "whites"—the button-fly white pants and short white coats I had worn for two years—to be washed and passed on to a senior student for his subinternships.

I went to the public cafeteria for breakfast—toast, tea, scrambled eggs, two pieces of bacon, orange juice, 75 cents—and then walked over to the new research building given to Columbia by William Black, the founder of the Chock-Full-o'Nuts coffee empire. Andy Frantz's labs and office were on the 9th floor.

Andy kept very regular hours, arriving at P & S from the east side by taxi just before 9 AM. He was already in his shirtsleeves when I walked in.

"Good morning, Dr. Frantz."

"Ah, you're here!" Andy was beaming.

"So, what am I going to do?"

"Well, Gordon, you're going to become an endocrinologist and we're going to discover prolactin!"

"Uh, you're an endocrinologist?"

"Yes, of course. That's what I do, and that's what you are going to do."

I had no clue. In Dr. Bradley's prohibition about specialization, no one labeled themselves: we were all internists, some interested in the gut or in the heart, but first and foremost, internists who were expected to take care of the entire range of medical problems without limitations. Andy had after all been my attending in Harkness, where patients had every manner of disease, and only rarely did they have endocrine problems other than diabetes. And nationally, at that time there were not even board exams for any of the medicine specialties except cardiology and chest-medicine.

I also had no clue that I would be doing hormone research. The fellowship with Andy was a holding action before going into the Army: a future in research or discovering a hormone had never been part of my life plan, although it would probably be more accurate to say that at that point I had no life plan other than using up the extra year of deferment I had been given in the hopes that the war in Vietnam would be deemed a mistake and cancelled. I didn't know what I would be doing or where we would be living a year from now.

Andy introduced me to the several people already at work in the lab: Robert Sundeen, a technician who taught me how to pipette and use microbalances; Alan Robinson, who had been a second-year resident when I was a student and who began a fellowship with Dr. Frantz after spending two years in the Air Force; and a neurologist, Earl Zimmerman, who was doing basic science research in Andy's lab and who, like Alan, would go on to a long, productive research career.

What Andy had in mind for me was to continue the work that a previous fellow had been doing, trying to isolate and measure the hormone prolactin in human pituitary glands. The prolactin molecule is nearly identical to the growth hormone molecule, which Andy had participated in measuring during his fellowship training at the Massachusetts General Hospital. In cows, sheep, and pigs, prolactin had already been isolated and assays developed to measure it—in part because it was more abundant in those animals than in humans, and in part because there was a strong

Prolactin

interest in studying a hormone that could stimulate milk production in cows, which could have enormous economic significance.

It appeared that in human's prolactin had proved difficult to isolate, both because it is much more similar to the growth hormone in humans than in animals, and because in the non-pregnant, non-lactating human pituitary it is present in tiny amounts compared to growth hormone. By all the biochemical means available, no one had been able to separate the small amount of prolactin in a human pituitary from the huge amount of growth hormone. Because lactation occurred naturally in women and could be compensated for by bottle-feeding if lactation was inadequate, no one had bothered to isolate or study human prolactin.

Andy had made this his mission because he had come in on the tail end of studying growth hormone once it became measurable by a sensitive technique called radioimmunoassay. He was just a beginning fellow at the MGH when another fellow, Mitch Rabkin, who was a year ahead of Andy and was deep into studying what stimulates growth hormone secretion, confronted Andy one morning.

"Andy, what big event begins in Boston tomorrow?"

Andy guessed the start of baseball season, although it was July. He then guessed the beginning of the oyster season, but Mitch pointed out that it wasn't an "R" month.

"Andy! The circus! The circus Andy!!"

Andy, ever agreeable, responded, "Why, yes, the circus. Of course. Are you going?"

"Andy, what does the circus have?"

Andy was baffled, having no idea what Mitch was hinting at. "Well, I guess elephants, and lions, and clowns. And cotton candy."

"Andy, think about it. What about the human acts?"

"Well, I already said clowns. Acrobats maybe? And lion tamers?"

"Andy, Midgets! Midgets!"

"Well of course, midgets."

"Andy, why are midgets, midgets?"

Andy assumed, along with the rest of the medical world, that midgets were genetically small, some kind of hereditary misadventure that produced miniature people. It had never crossed his mind that midgets' hormones needed to be studied.

"Andy, what if midgets are midgets because they don't make growth hormone. Our lab is the first to measure growth hormone. We can be the first to see if midgets are normal-stature people who don't make growth hormone and wouldn't be midgets if they did."

Andy was chagrined that it had never crossed his mind. A day later he and Mitch Rabkin were at the circus, trying to talk a few of the Ringling Brothers' little people into being subjects for measurements of growth hormone.

Andy was well into telling me this story, as excited as an explorer who had just made an important discovery. I was worried that I wasn't as excited as he was about the physiologic mysteries underlying the various kinds of dwarfism.

Andy went on to write more than a dozen papers about growth hormone in normal-stature and short-stature people. Now he wanted to establish the first foothold in understanding how prolactin works in humans: what triggers lactation during late pregnancy and during nursing, why abnormal lactation (called galactorrhea) occurs in people who are neither pregnant nor nursing—or, rarely, were men. The first step would be to separate prolactin from growth hormone, then create an immunoassay for it, and then measure it in humans. This would be Andy's vehicle for becoming a pioneer in the elucidation of a hormone not previously studied in humans, and I was to be the chief crewmember.

Fifteen minutes earlier I had been eating bacon and eggs and knew nothing about midgets or prolactin or my destiny.

With great excitement, Andy asked me to follow him to the Black Building elevators, which took us to the top floors where there was a zoo that, after 7 years at Columbia, I had not known existed: under the care of veterinarians were monkeys, rabbits, dogs, rats and an odd cow or two—

even pigs and sheep. Who knew that there were cows living in the penthouse of a research skyscraper?

Andy introduced me to the veterinarian and told him that I would now be in charge of the mouse colony. I didn't remember signing up for this when I asked Andy if he ever took fellows and I wondered what he would pull out of his starched sleeve next.

It didn't take long to find out.

"Well! Gordon, every three weeks we will get a new batch of thirty virgin female mice. On the first day you will expose them to male mice—you will be able to tell the difference because the males' tails are dyed blue. You leave the male mice with the females for the day, and then remove them. Most of the mice will become pregnant. You will be able to tell which ones are pregnant after a week. You separate those not pregnant and put them with the next batch of virgin mice. At three weeks you will anesthetize the pregnant mice in this glass bottle that has ether in the bottom. Then, you will open the skin on their chest and remove all of the breast tissue. "

He showed me the sterile dissection kit and where to find a sterile beaker to place the mouse breasts in. I was then supposed to put about an inch of a sterile tissue culture fluid that the mouse breasts could live in.

A week later the first batch of virgin mice arrived, I conducted the mating ceremony, and three weeks later Robert Sundeen, who had been doing the tissue cultures, showed me how to anesthetize the mice and dissect out their breast tissue. He made no secret that he was glad to be turning this task over to me—four years of college, another four years of medical school, and three years of residency and I was now doing mouse mastectomies and hanging out in a stinky rat and mouse dormitory.

Andy and David Kleinberg, the fellow who had preceded me, had developed a mouse bioassay for the presence of lactogenic (milk production stimulating) hormones. In the presence of sheep or cow prolactin, the mouse breast tissue, primed by three weeks of rising estrogen and progesterone levels because of the mouse's pregnancy, would then begin to make milk in the cultured breast tissue. With each increment of prolactin or growth hormone, the tissue would gradually produce increasing amounts of milk, which could be detected when the tissue was embedded in wax and sliced thin and stained for milk proteins.

For several weeks I was given slides to read from cultured mouse breasts to which Robert had added carefully measured amounts of sheep prolactin, to teach me how to correlate what I could see under a microscope with known levels of the hormone.

Human growth hormone was also lactogenic, and the effect on the tissue cultured breast tissue was indistinguishable from the effect of sheep or cow prolactin.

It took four months for me to learn how to manage the tissue cultures and read bioassay slides.

Andy had been asking physicians who were caring for women who were nursing or had pituitary tumors that caused lactation to collect a small amount of their blood. Robert separated the blood from the serum and froze the samples. When I used small amounts of serum from the nursing mothers in the tissue culture, the mouse breasts reacted as they had with sheep and cow prolactin—the tissue filled with mouse milk, and using this we could roughly guess how high the serum levels of lactogenic hormone would be. The problem was, since growth hormone did the same thing, we could not yet state that what we were measuring was prolactin.

Our next step was to make large amounts of antibodies to human growth hormone in sheep. Again using the mouse breast bioassay, we could culture the tissue with human growth hormone and, in some of the samples, add antibodies to human growth hormone. The bioassays were positive when growth hormone alone was present in the culture fluid, but there was no milk protein manufactured when anti-growth hormone antibodies were added.

The final step was to use serum from patients with galactorrhea or who were pregnant or nursing both with and without antibodies to human growth hormone in the tissue culture fluid. Without or with the antibody present, the mouse breast tissues filled with milk. We had crude evidence that the lactogenic hormone present in women with pituitary tumors or who were pregnant or nursing was not growth hormone.

Prolactin

About this time Henry Friesen, an endocrinologist in Canada, developed a method for separating the tiny amount of prolactin from the much larger amount of growth hormone in normal human pituitaries that were collected from people after death who had volunteered to donate their bodies "for science." He needed evidence that the polypeptide he had collected in tiny amounts was in fact prolactin. Since we had developed a method to block the effect of growth hormone, he sent the small amount of prolactin he had collected to us.

Again, using the mouse bioassay, we were able to demonstrate that the material he had sent was powerfully lactogenic and that its effect was not neutralized by antibodies to growth hormone.

We had demonstrated that normal humans made prolactin, which had been suspected but never proven.

We had bought the Teaneck House on a gamble that the three-year deferment I had been given before entering the Army could be extended to four. The formal requirements for being certified as an endocrinologist were still being figured out, but they would include at least two years of training. The first board examinations were scheduled in 1972.

Once I had started working with Andy it seemed that the best plan was to try to extend the deferment for a year to get the two years of training needed to sit for the endocrinology board examination, but I didn't know how to request an additional year. Someone—probably Andy—suggested that I get in touch with whoever was in charge of endocrinology in the Army's five teaching hospitals. I called the Army's chief medical manpower distribution officer. He was a grumpy conscriptee like I would soon be and more or less told me I should do what the Army told me to do when it got around to telling me. I ignored him and was able to find out who the head of endocrinology was at Walter Reed, the Army's main teaching hospital, and in a telephone call he agreed to let me visit him in Washington D.C.

Jerry Earle turned out to be a relaxed, pleasant Midwesterner who had trained at the University of Iowa. As the Army's consultant in endocrinology, he was responsible for a steady flow of endocrinologists into the various teaching hospitals to act as consultants and to train residents. He said that the only endocrinologist at Walter Reed that focused on pituitary gland disease would be leaving about the time that I would finish my training; he volunteered to ask the Army to extend my deferment for one more year so that I could be fully trained. As to whether I would be allowed to go to Walter Reed, Dr. Earle said that was more complicated but he could try to make that happen.

Within a few months he said that the Army had agreed with him to let me be fully trained as an endocrinologist. So here I was, an accidental endocrinologist for whom serendipity seemed to be in charge of my planning, now with a guaranteed three years in our Teaneck house, long enough that we would at least break even on our closing costs when we had to leave.

By June of 1971 I had spent a year being a mouse biologist and a human endocrinologist. The shift from being an internal medicine resident had been sudden but undramatic. Nine months after Katharine was born, Margaret was again pregnant, with our second child due in August.

There were three other endocrinology fellows; we were on the consult service every fourth month. My nighttime duties were few—occasionally I would get a telephone call from a resident asking my advice about the management of a severely ill diabetic or the rare patient in thyroid storm or adrenal crisis and I would go back to teach the intern and students how to treat these rare and life-threatening conditions. In two years I went back to the hospital fifty times in the middle of the night, about twice a month. With that little nighttime work, regular daytime hours, and most weekends at home, Margaret and I had entered a different phase of our life in which we could plan vacations at Flathead Lake in Montana and make occasional trips to Margaret's family in Newburyport. My salary was $7000 a year; the purchasing power of $7000 in 1970 was equivalent to about $44,000 in 2020. It was enough to pay our mortgage, keep a car, take vacations, and eat well. To augment my salary, every few weeks I moonlighted as the screener in the Medical Center emergency room from around 5 PM when the daytime resident left, until about 10 PM. As the screener I called patients to a small booth to find out why they had come to the emergency room and to determine if I could take care of their problem so that a resident didn't have to see them, like refill a prescription or help them understand how to use a medication. I took care of the easier cases and got some of the more complex patients started with imaging and laboratory tests so that by the time the intern saw them they had a complete data set.

Our home life was simple. I woke up around 6:30 AM and by 7:30 I had eaten breakfast and was on my way into the city. In the evening I got home around 6:30. Margaret did almost all the cooking and grocery shopping in addition to taking care of Katharine. The couple from whom we had bought the house had equipped it with new appliances and there was rarely anything that needed fixing beyond replacing light bulbs and unclogging drains. Our neighbors were mostly one-job families with teenage children—the mother staying home, the kids in the Teaneck public schools, the men working at mid-level jobs in insurance companies and retail stores and car dealerships. The houses were modest, two-story affairs with three bedrooms and small yards. We were on friendly terms, but I can't recall that we ever socialized with them.

CHAPTER 22

Prolactin Part Two

Once we had established that the hormone the Canadian scientist Henry Friesen had isolated was human prolactin, he worked for several months to separate enough prolactin from growth hormone for Andy to be able to develop a radioimmunoassay using some of the small amount of purified prolactin as a standard.

I was set to the task of running bioassays on samples of Andy's "library" of frozen serum while in the other lab Bob Sundeen was doing the first immunoassays. With this we were able to state that what our lab was measuring corresponded to bioassay-confirmed mouse breast tissue lactation. We were able to tell the physicians who sent those samples whether their patients had elevated prolactin levels and might therefore have a pituitary tumor for the first time.

Professor Friesen was a physician by training but he worked as a full-time scientist. In his small teaching hospital in Winnipeg he did not have access to the large population of patients with pituitary tumors and galactorrhea that we did in New York. Collaboration between our two labs was established: Professor Friesen would provide us with most of his harvest of prolactin and in turn we would use it for clinical studies in which we would reference him as co-author. There were others who were eager to get some of Professor Friesen's prolactin to jump into the frenzy of "first discoveries" and Henry provided it to them—most notably William Daughaday at Washington University School of Medicine in St. Louis, who had been one of Andy's chief competitors for years.

Our race to be first was on.

Andy had three resources possibly unique to him and our laboratory. First, Andy was independently wealthy and was willing to bankroll human volunteer studies. Second, there were few rules regulating human volunteer research studies at that time, so there was not a long delay between asking a question and beginning a study to get the answer. Third, having just finished a residency, I knew hundreds of students and nurses: while I was polite and avoided any coercion other than money, I was comfortable asking them if they would be interested in providing blood samples during normal activities that were safe.

There was a well-established pattern for studying newly discovered human hormones. The first step was to replicate studies that had been done in animals to see if what stimulated prolactin release in animals would be the same in humans. If pregnancy and nursing were associated with high prolactin levels in sheep or pigs or cows, would that also be true in humans? In the mouse bioassay we knew that serum from nursing women caused tissue culture formation of milk. Now that we could measure prolactin accurately, we could accurately measure serum prolactin levels in pregnancy and during the phases of nursing.

The second step would be to determine whether situations that caused the release of other pituitary hormones also released prolactin. Growth hormone and ACTH—the hormone that stimulates the adrenals to produce cortisone—are released by stress and severe low blood sugars. We were curious about whether stress also caused prolactin release. Rarely men lactated and now we could determine if they had high prolactin levels indicating that they had an undetected pituitary hormone. Would breast stimulation in women who were not postpartum cause prolactin to rise?

Because we could measure prolactin accurately by radioimmunoassay, we put the mouse bioassay to sleep: it was cumbersome, expensive, and delicate. If there was a small lapse in sterile technique all the tissue culture

Prolactin Part Two

specimens of an assay run could be infected and worthless. The results were at best crude.

Blood samples from women with galactorrhea with or without pituitary tumors began to arrive in Andy's lab: we collected histories on the patients from whom the samples had been drawn and began a several-years-long study of the causes of high prolactin levels.

The natural question for me to study at this point was to find out what happened to prolactin levels during pregnancy and nursing. Margaret had stopped nursing Katharine six months before we had the immunoassay ready for large numbers of samples, but she was now pregnant again. Most of our friends were the doctors I had trained with as medical students or residents, whose wives were also having babies. Several among our very few women residents were also about to have babies.

Margaret's second pregnancy had gone smoothly, with two exceptions. The first was being eight or nine months pregnant and trying to put a squirming one-year-old in the back seat of a two-door sedan during the muggy, hot New Jersey summers. The other exception was a short vacation we had planned close to her due date. We had foregone the long flight to vacation in Montana. Instead, I had the bright idea of returning to Bermuda, where we had gone for a short first honeymoon. In early July Margaret flew up to Boston with Katharine on the Eastern Airlines shuttle and gave her mother a quick refresher course in infant care. We met at LaGuardia Airport at the end of her return flight and left for Bermuda, only 2 hours away; by evening we had moved into a little bungalow at Pink Beach. We sunned and read novels for two days; and then I had another bright idea: renting mopeds for a day of touring around the island.

The mopeds were motor assisted bicycles—for the flat and downhill areas we pedaled, but when we encountered a hill the motor kicked in. Neither of us had any experience on motorized bikes. Margaret had ridden a bike to commute to her Harvard classes from her Radcliffe residence. I hadn't ridden a bike regularly since I was 14. We also had very different levels of risk-avoidance: hers was normal, mine nearly non-existent.

With an eighth-month belly in front of her, she gamely sped over the nearly empty roads while I trailed behind so as not to go faster than she would be comfortable with. At an intersection where there was a car waiting to turn, Margaret stopped and planted her right foot. I did not anticipate her stop and ran over her foot.

I don't recall how we got her, her foot, and two mopeds back to where we had rented them. We found a first aid clinic where her foot and ankle were wrapped in an Ace bandage.

I called back to Columbia and asked to be connected to the chief of orthopedics' office to see who might examine Margaret's foot when we got back. The secretary said that Dr. Stinchfield would see her whenever we got to the hospital, it didn't matter when and we didn't need to call ahead.

I was stunned—I had not expected the world-famous department chair to care for Margaret's banged up foot.

"Really. Isn't he awfully busy?"

The secretary replied, "When you want a good job done, get a busy man to do it."

That afternoon we took a taxi from LaGuardia and Margaret limped painfully into his examination room. In half an hour she emerged on crutches with a cast on her foot.

What a mess. Katharine was in Boston, Margaret was on crutches, I was scheduled for a clinic the next day with a long list of patients, many of whom did not have a telephone in their home. In a decision that was both an example of the times and a demonstration of Margaret's determination, she flew to Boston. Her parents met her at the airport with Katharine and walked with her across the tarmac to board the Eastern Airlines shuttle. At the foot of the stairs from the tarmac to the plane door Katharine was handed to a flight attendant. Margaret hobbled up the stairs, took a seat, and was handed Katharine.

At the LaGuardia end, I walked out to the plane when it landed and Katharine was delivered to me while Margaret hopped down the stairs and then, new to crutches, made her way with me to the car park.

Prolactin Part Two

From tough New England women like Margaret, pioneer women were derived. It remains unclear exactly what is derived from goofy Montana men.

A month later, on the 5th of August, Margaret went into labor. The labor with Katharine had lasted eighteen hours. Margaret expected this to take much less time. We had arranged with various neighborhood girls or mothers to take care of Katharine when the time came. When Margaret's contractions became stronger and more frequent, I called to the neighboring house of the high school girl we had warned the evening before, and called Margaret's obstetrician, Ed Bowe, to tell him that I was taking Margaret to the hospital.

Because many of the medicine faculty members were on vacation, I had volunteered weeks earlier to lead chief of service rounds for the students, something generally done by the most senior faculty. We got Margaret to the labor floor about 6 AM, by which time she was nearly fully dilated and Ed was on his way in. By 8:30 I was holding Little Margaret in my arms in the delivery room, and at a quarter past nine, only 15 minutes late I was standing at the bedside of a patient eight floors down on the medical wards, listening to a student doing the first of three bedside presentations for thirty other students, the teaching clock and my responsibilities ticking on without the slightest deference to the doubling of our family.

The concepts of paternal leave had not arrived yet and our advanced plans for caring for two children had not included any change in my work hours or responsibilities at home, except for my making more of the runs to markets and stores during the evening and weekends and solidifying that I always would be commuting by bus so that Margaret had the use of the car.

During her pregnancy, I had been drawing blood samples from Margaret every few weeks and freezing the serum. When Margaret Lea was born, I began to study what happened to prolactin levels during nursing. During breast-feeding there is a phase called "milk let down" in which milk starts flowing from the breast. This can occur just with the thought of nursing, or even looking at another woman nursing or hearing a baby cry. In animals a hormone called oxytocin is responsible for let down, but let down had not yet been studied in humans, nor had the role of prolactin in stimulating milk production and breast enlargement during pregnancy. A mother's milk might not come in for the first few days after delivery, but again the role of prolactin in starting milk production was unclear. Margaret agreed to be the first human in whom the physiology of lactation would be studied and reported, along with a half dozen women who were our friends who also volunteered to be studied over the next half year.

While prolactin rose steadily during pregnancy to quite high levels, in most women it was not until after the massively elevated levels of estrogen and progesterone fell at the time of delivery that lactation began. Nursing mothers' prolactin levels remained quite high for weeks after nursing began, but gradually fell to lower levels while milk production remained steady. Once nursing was stopped, prolactin levels returned to pre-pregnancy levels within a few weeks. Prolactin did not suddenly spike up before the initiation of suckling—that is, prolactin had no role in milk let down.

I don't know what the men whose wives I was studying thought. However, most of them were doctors and they drew the four blood samples I needed. For friends with non-doctor husbands, I would travel to the mother's house, or she would come to ours, and I would measure prolactin a half hour before nursing, just as she was preparing to nurse, and then several times afterwards. It was an odd way to spend a few hours with these healthy and normal young women after years of the intense care of severely ill patients.

There were well-described cases of women who had never been pregnant being able to nurse babies, and even reports of men nursing babies. Andy, who was intensely shy, had in me the perfect co-conspirator. If I said, "Andy, do you think we could get a woman who has never been pregnant to lactate?" Andy's face would light up and he would pull out his wallet. "How much do you think it would cost?"

Prolactin Part Two

"How about twenty-five dollars a day for two weeks?"

"Sure."

In the mad free-for-all of being the first to accurately map the role of prolactin in humans, I now had a group of medical students' and doctors' wives and nurses who were glad to volunteer for the kooky studies we devised.

Exercise raises the levels of a number of hormones and we wanted to see if hard exercise would raise prolactin levels. I asked four nurses who exercised regularly to run up and down eighteen flights of stairs in the medical research building, drawing a tube of blood at the bottom before and after each lap, repeating it four times until they were exhausted. Prolactin levels didn't rise.

One of the nurses who had taken care of me when I had hepatitis was now living with her boyfriend, a surgical resident. I asked if she would be willing to have him draw bloods after thirty minutes of breast stimulation, four times a day for two weeks. She was willing. They rented a cabin in upstate New York, went into honeymoon mode, and returned with forty tubes of blood that had been kept on ice. Katie neither lactated, nor did continuous breast stimulation change her prolactin levels. Andy paid $350 of his own money for that study.

In sheep and cows, mating caused prolactin levels to rise. The most eyebrow-raising study I proposed was to find out if sexual intercourse caused prolactin release in humans. I posted signs in the medical student locker room asking for couples to volunteer to draw bloods on each other before, during, and after having sex, $25 for the man and $50 for the woman. Within a few hours two women who were medical students married to other medical students and three married male students had called me to sign up. The next morning word had spread throughout the medical school that princely sums were being paid for students to have sex and one after another, single male students were calling me: apparently their fantasies of going to medical school and being asked to participate in scientific studies by having sex with beautiful nurses had suddenly gone from fantasy to reality.

The calls all went like this:

"Hello, my name is Steven and I am a first-year student and I would like to volunteer for your study. I don't have a partner, so you would have to find one for me, but I'll be glad to do it for free."

I thanked each of the eleven randy male students who had called by 10:30 AM and then went to the locker room to take down the sign. Calls continued in diminishing numbers for the rest of the week. It should go without saying that I assumed that it would require a larger incentive to enlist women than men, and the failure of any single women to volunteer if I could find them a partner probably confirms the accuracy of my assumption.

The difficult part of the experiment was that the students were all in the first or second year and had not yet had any experience in drawing blood samples. Of course, the non-student partners were in a similar boat. Seventy-five dollars was a lot of money in 1971, enough for three to dine in New York's finest restaurants if they ordered three courses and a second-growth Bordeaux rather than Chateau Haut Brion. None hesitated to say that they would let me teach them how to get the samples and that it would not be a problem.

The plan was for each partner to draw a tube of blood before beginning to have sex, then a second tube after ten minutes of caressing, then have sex and draw bloods within moments of orgasm, and then draw a final tube fifteen or twenty minutes later.

I had assembled seven couples, and during the next few days students dropped by with the blood samples and a record of times and activities. Many of the couples after the first two were rounded up by a woman medical student who went on to a residency at Harvard and then became a world expert in breast cancer. I fancied that this was her first experience at helping to organize a clinical trial, although the ones she led in the future perhaps were more useful.

A few days later, I was assaulted by Ron Drusin in the doctors' locker room. Ron was a lanky, sardonic cardiology fellow who I had known since I was a first-year student.

From the other side of the locker room, he called out, "Gordon, what the hell kind of research are you doing?"

"Huh?" My mind was on other things.

"Are you doing sex studies?"

"How did you know that?"

"Last night I was watching television, and one of the students who lives on the same floor knocked on my door. He was in his pajama bottoms, bare-naked from the waist up, with dried blood that had run down his arms, his hair messed, and he was in a panic. He said, 'Would you be willing to come to our apartment and draw blood from Kathy. I'll explain later.'"

"I start out the door and he tells me to grab a book or the Sunday *Times*. So I go into his apartment and he takes me into their bedroom, and here is Kathy lying flat on her back, the covers pulled up to her chin, both arms on towels, with huge bruises on her arms. He asked me to draw a tube of blood from Kathy, which I did, although I had no idea what kind of game I was participating in, and then Kenny says, 'Please wait outside, it'll be a few minutes. Sorry!' and closes the door."

"Well, there is some muted noise on the other side of the door and I waited and started reading the paper and Kenny reappeared and asked me to draw blood on both of them. He was easy, but Kathy had little tiny, rollie veins and it took me more than one try. They both looked terrible, Kathy was wearing a nightgown that was sprinkled with blood, and the bed covers and pillows were strewn around the floor. He asked me if I could come back to their apartment in about fifteen minutes, and when I knocked on the door, they were both dressed and wearing t-shirts and I drew blood again."

"I asked him, what's going on? And he told me he and Kathy were doing an experiment for Dr. Noel and that he didn't realize how hard it would be to draw Kathy's blood, and she was terrible at getting his. He promised me a bottle of wine when he got paid, and I said, Dr. Noel is paying you for this? And he said 'yes, a lot.'"

By the next day Ron had informed the entire hospital and I was cornered by the less dignified junior faculty and quizzed. When one of them passed Ron's story on to Andy, Andy apparently turned a deep shade of maroon and stuttered out some kind of explanation that apparently included references to sheep and goats and dairy cattle that entirely avoided the mention of sex.

When Kenny stopped by with the samples, he left off his bloodied flow sheet with the following information:

—"Took five attempts to draw Kathy's first blood, three for her to get my blood (I finally drew blood on myself).

—"Dr. Drusin drew remaining blood samples on both of us but did not stay to watch.

—"Orgasm: me yes, Kathy, no.

—"Additional information: Kathy wouldn't talk to me this morning. We had to cancel dinner with Reverend and Mrs. Peters so that they wouldn't see her mutilated arms and think that I was abusing their daughter, which would not have been far from the truth."

At the same time, we were studying exercise and intercourse we also studied other situations in which pituitary hormones were sometimes released: insulin induced hypoglycemia (a potent stimulus for growth hormone and ACTH release), surgical stress in anesthetized patients, and patients having sigmoidoscopy, which at that time was done without sedatives or anesthesia with a rigid scope and was extremely painful.

A few years later we published a paper in the *Journal of Clinical Endocrinology and Metabolism* with our results," Human Prolactin and Growth Hormone Release during Surgery and other Conditions of Stress." The abstract read:

"Human plasma prolactin, measured by a homologous radioimmunoassay, has been found to rise significantly in a number of situations associated with stress. The greatest elevations, averaging approximately five-fold, were seen during major surgery with general anesthesia. Absolute levels of prolactin were higher at all times during surgery in women than in men. Smaller but significant elevations were found with gastroscopy, proctoscopy, and exercise. In all situations except exercise the prolactin rise was as high as, or higher than, that of growth hormone. Hypoglycemia induced by 0.2 U/kg of insulin produced significant prolactin elevations in all of seven normal women. Major elevations of prolactin, but not growth hormone, occurred in a minority of normal women following sexual intercourse; prolactin did not rise significantly in their male partners. It is concluded that prolactin in human beings is at least as responsive as growth hormone to release by stress in most situations; the two hormones differ significantly, however, in their response to other stimuli. The release of prolactin in some women following sexual intercourse may be related to stimuli, as yet undefined, other than those associated with stress."

One of the reviewers returned the manuscript with the wry comment that in his experience, he would not equate sexual intercourse with surgery or proctoscopy. We decided not to disabuse him of the notion by pointing out that the woman in whom the prolactin rose substantially was Kathy, and that her experience was essentially surgery without anesthesia.

Kenny was a first-year student when we did the study. He graduated three years later and went on to residency in internal medicine. I saw him at graduation and he assured me that Kathy had resumed conversations with him a week later, and that they were still married. She, however, did not think kindly of either Dr. Frantz or me.

The fellowship years were relaxed in comparison to medical school and residency. Because we were tethered to our Teaneck home by first one, and then two, babies, we rarely went out. I loved working in our small yard and eventually had converted half the lawn into flower gardens.

The house originally had a small kitchen at the back, overlooking a grass lawn, but at some point in the 1950's an enclosed sun porch was converted into an extension of the kitchen large enough to hold a small dining table. It had windows on three sides and a long bench with cushions on which we could sit and watch winter storms and the trees sprout fresh green leaves in spring that turned to flames in the fall.

I spent a lot of evening and weekend time in the sun porch reading. Online searches for medical articles were three decades in the future. Our primary exploration of older literature to find important papers required going to the library and pulling the massive bound annual volumes of the *Index Medicus* off the shelf. For the current literature, most of the residents and fellows "tore" the journals we subscribed to as they arrived: we read articles that we wanted to use for teaching or to guide our patient care in the future and then tore them out. On weekends I perched myself on the bench on the sun porch and tore pages from the *New England Journal*, the *Annals of Internal Medicine*, and the *Journal of Clinical Endocrinology and Metabolism* while Katharine and Margaret Lea played or slept, perhaps a football game or classical music playing in the background. I developed a filing system with three hundred folders, stapled the article pages together, and stored them away for future use. Copying an article at that time was primitive—one black-on-grey sheet at a time—and expensive. I probably read, tore, and filed twenty medical articles a week during fellowship. Like a squirrel hiding acorns in the fall, I saved more than I would ever use.

We had been living with a small portable black and white television set that had rabbit ears antennae since we got married. Although we rarely watched television, the signals we could get in our home gave us excellent pictures. Occasionally we watched the news or an episode of Julia Childs' "The French Chef" on public broadcasting.

In February of 1972 the Winter Olympics were in Sapporo, Japan. We decided that we were watching enough television that it would be nice to own a color TV. The model I wanted was a Sony Trinitron, which cost $400, equal to 16 dinners in three-star restaurants, much more than we had in savings.

I called my Dad in Montana and asked if his First National Bank would give me a loan, expecting it to be an easy decision. But Dad never passed up an opportunity for a put-down:

"Jeez, you don't have enough savings to buy a TV set," he asked?

"Dad, on a resident's salary, with a mortgage and a car and two kids, no I don't."

"That's a helluva excuse."

"It's the only one I've got. Do you want to do it or not?"

"I don't know. I'll think about it."

The loan came through, and at $11.50 a month, we paid the loan off in four years.

The Olympics were spectacular, and "Sesame Street" was much more interesting in color and on a big screen.

Now that we owned a home and had children, dinner parties with other couples were the way we saw our friends. Since at least one member of every couple was a physician, our few days off overlapped only on weekends. The idea of getting together for a hiking afternoon or a picnic with one or two babies was too complicated, or simply not a part of the New York City ethos, and meeting in restaurants would have been too expensive.

At that time brides were given china and silver and crystal, with the expectation that they would be entertaining. From the beginning we had dining tables that would accommodate guests—four in our Washington Heights and University of Chicago apartments, six in our East 79th Street Apartment, and twelve in our Teaneck house. All of us were interested in food, and most owned one of Julia Child's French cooking books, or the *Gourmet Cookbook*, or the *New York Times Cookbook*.

Margaret had grown up in Newburyport eating plain food not that much different than what my mom prepared in Montana. Her mother had a woman who cooked and sewed: the meals were standard American fare, with an emphasis on simplicity. From the time we were married, I was intrigued with the more complex cooking of Italy and France, based in part on a wine-tasting group that I had belonged to as a senior in college. Margaret was game to try dishes like veal Prince Orloff or roast suckling pig or complicated side dishes.

Although neither of us were drinkers—the ten bottles of liquor we brought back as our custom's quota from Bermuda lasted for fifteen years except for the gin and scotch —we liked wine, but only drank it at dinner parties. It was not until a cabernet sauvignon from Stag's Leap Vineyards beat all the French wines at a Paris competition in 1976 that California wines appeared in New York stores and on dinner party tables. After reading about the Stag's Leap wine that won the tasting, I bought some the next day for around five dollars a bottle for several of our parties. Second growth Bordeaux were about the same price—in short, affordable for special occasions. On a fellow's salary of $6000 a year, we were able to live a comfortable life

From the first days of my endocrinology fellowship I began teaching as a general internist. A requirement of the NIH training grant from which Andy was paying my salary was that I was to spend 75% of my time doing research and no more than 25% of my time as a clinician or teacher. I was in violation from the first months because, in addition to my weekly endocrinology and general medical clinics, I also precepted students in the general medicine clinic another half day a week, did the usual endocrinology consultation months, and had asked to do inpatient attending rounds three months a year. As a student and resident I had loved the daily attending rounds on the medicine wards with a research-focused attending paired with one of the physicians in private practice at the medical center. Now as an endocrinology fellow, some months I was paired with a senior clinician, other months with an investigator. Our obligations were only two hours a day: we rounded from 10:00 AM to noon 7 days a week for the entire month, but invariably I spent time out of rounds reviewing the residents' notes and the incoming flow of consultations and data from the laboratories and radiology. I often went to the library to expand what I knew about disease or drugs that I had not yet encountered.

I loved to now be standing on the patients' right side while a student stood on the left and everyone else formed an arc around the foot of the bed as the student presented and either I or the other attending examined the patient and questioned the students. I immediately discovered that I had not forgotten how it felt to be a medical student. Overall, the tradition at Columbia was that the teaching attendings were consultative and not confrontational. While some of the interns and residents could be arrogant and blunt, rarely as a student and resident had I experienced attending physicians who were rude or dismissive. Attendings seldom put residents on the spot: it was clear enough through our interactions with the student when an attending felt that the diagnostic workup or care might have fallen short. While the team was clearly held accountable, it was done in a way in which words or facial expressions were not used to humiliate anyone. This was particularly important since we did not want the patients to lose confidence in their doctors.

After a half year of teaching senior students in the general medical clinic, I realized that there was no didactic curriculum in outpatient practice at all: the students each worked up one patient a day, five days a week for two months. Teaching came in the afternoon when they presented and examined their patient with the preceptor for that day. There were no student lectures or assigned reading, so there was no coordinated method for teaching them practical therapeutics and the skills of doing a diagnostic assessment for patients who were not hospitalized.

No clinical faculty members at Columbia were paid to teach or to manage educational programs: they contributed their time. There was nothing like a departmental education committee since the student programs had been running on automatic pilot for decades and the only management of the clerkship was writing a schedule for which students would be where. Beyond that, our faculty members, who had often been students and almost always been residents at P & S, knew what they were supposed to do and there was no expectation that anything needed to be improved or eliminated.

Dr. Tapley was still the faculty member who oversaw the student programs. When I approached him to ask whether I could hold a voluntary weekly seminar on clinical practice before the students' clinics, he agreed. I suggested that I use the billiards room in the residents' sleeping quarters, a rarely used space which had served as the all-male residents' living room during the years before and immediately after World War II when residents were required to be single and to live in the hospital.

The students had never had a course in basic clinical therapeutics that was systematically organized—they learned randomly one patient at a time and learned extensively from handbooks like *The Washington Manual* and the two major textbooks of medicine.

I had only the sketchiest idea of what I was going to do when I met those students the first time, but I had a good idea of what they didn't—but should—know.

Nearly all of the students showed up for my first session. I asked a question: "If you were called to an elderly man's home because of fever, cough, and sputum production, what would you do to make a diagnosis, how would you treat him, and what would you need to have in your black bag?"

By using a simple case of pneumonia that did not require an emergency room visit or hospitalization, in an hour we talked about the treatment of the common cold, flu, bronchitis, and uncomplicated pneumonia in an otherwise healthy patient. Beyond how to make a diagnosis without laboratory tests, we talked about managing fever, cough, shortness of breath, and the usual antibiotics used for common respiratory infections. At the end we talked about what would be the circumstances in which a patient with pneumonia should be hospitalized and not treated at home. Since all their experience had been with hospitalized patients, they had never seen that subset of pneumonia patients who did not need around-the-clock nursing care. They had little idea of what warranted admitting patients to the hospital rather than treating them at home. I asked them as a group to figure it out: my questions to stimulate their participation were, "What do you think? " "What else might you do?" "What would you worry about?" One by one they sorted out which factors put a patient at risk if not hospitalized.

The next week I started the session by describing a young woman with symptoms of a urinary tract infection: "A 20-year-old female college student comes to your clinic complaining of burning pain during urination and frequent urination. What history do you need, and what parts of the physical examination would you do?" As a group they filled in all the other data they would want and together they outlined what the possible diagnoses were and what they needed to do before they treated her. Then they pieced together how to treat uncomplicated urinary tract infections.

The course went on for eight weeks and after that I repeated it for the rest of the year. It got the title, "The Doctor's Black Bag."

Coming back to the laboratory from one of the sessions in a state of high spirits I greeted Andy one morning. Andy was incapable of mustering a glower, but in his formal, tactful and highly indirect way, he reminded me that I didn't have to spend so much time teaching, but he never insisted that I give up my inpatient attending or the course, or my long nights in the hospital with students taking care of patients with endocrine emergencies.

After Dr. Bradley left the chairmanship, one of our senior, highly respected clinicians took over as acting chair. Henry Aranow looked like a Viking senior statesman—tall, dignified, and fair with a ruddy complexion and white hair. He exuded clinical wisdom, diplomacy and warmth. He had trained at Columbia and Johns Hopkins and had become an expert on thyroid disease and a rare illness called myasthenia gravis. He had served on many advisory boards because he had the capacity to both listen and to quietly and effectively change the direction of a decision.

Dr. Aranow had heard at a meeting of internal medicine department chairmen a speech by the chair of medicine at Emory, the eminent cardiologist J. Willis Hurst, describing a new way of organizing the medical record and daily progress notes to make more accurate decisions and ensure that all aspects of a complex case were attended to. One of my friends, Bill MacLean, had returned to the residency program after a two-year stint in the air force and had been designated as the next chief resident. Dr. Aranow sent Bill and me to a workshop run by the originator of the problem-oriented record, Dr. Larry Weed and we cheerfully flew to Cleveland.

Learning the Art of Medicine—a Memoir

I already knew Dr. Weed: when I interviewed for a residency at Cleveland Metropolitan Hospital, a city hospital affiliated with Western Reserve, the chairman of medicine required that every candidate meet personally with Dr. Weed, who spent the first ten minutes telling me about his years of choral singing with the Robert Shaw Chorale, and then quizzed me to ascertain if I would be totally compliant with his program of converting the traditional medical notes to problem-oriented notes: he and his chair were searching for acolytes who would follow orders.

Dr. Weed's workshop was the equivalent of a religious revival meeting, missing only a tent and a gospel choir. He paraded out converts who told us how the miracle of problem-oriented records saved lives and malpractice suits. We were there to learn the true faith, and then, on returning to our hospital, to proselytize.

Though we were skeptical of the style of the presentation, Bill and I quickly agreed with the goals of the problem-oriented record. Even at Columbia, where comprehensive history taking and physical examination were taken as sacred commandments, the organization of the hundreds of pieces of data in the written note was sometimes chronologic, sometimes organized by problem, sometimes random. The organization of the history bore no relationship to the organization of the physical examination or the laboratory results or the plans for the patient.

What Drs. Weed and Hurst were urging was breaking the history into problems, so that for a patient who has diabetes and heart failure and mild kidney failure, the student or resident or practicing physician would take the gathered data and organize them by problem:

Problem 1: Congestive heart failure
    History
    Physical examination'
    Laboratory and imaging data
    Plan
Problem 2: Insulin-dependent diabetes mellitus
    History Physical examination

Prolactin Part Two

Laboratory and imaging data
Plan

The convention at the time was to write all of the history in one place, followed by the head-to-toe physical examination, and then the data. The Weed method put the heart failure history, data and plans in a block, then the diabetes history, data and plan in another block.

Not only was the first office or hospital admission note to be written this way, so were the progress notes. With that organization, it would be easy to see what the physician in training was thinking, and also easy to track the course of a single problem over time without having to wade through masses of information about other problems to pick out what was critical for a particular problem.

A by-product was that consultants could speed through the record looking just at what was essential for their consideration, instead of searching through all the daily notes where the information for four or five problems was tossed together like a salad. A cardiologist trying to find the key information about the patient's heart, for example, could rapidly go through the record to review the course of the patient's heart failure without slogging through the information about half a dozen other problems.

Part of Dr. Weed's method was to have a few faculty members who would first introduce the problem-oriented record at a departmental conference, and then make chart rounds guiding interns to change their note writing.

When we got back from Cleveland, we told Dr. Aranow we thought that Larry Weed was rather like a cultist, but that his methods seemed like a good idea. With Dr. Aranow's support I created two new hospital record forms, a blank problem list that was to be inserted at the front of the chart, and a blank flow sheet that allowed doctors to track data over time—something I had done in my own note writing but that was made much easier with a pre-printed table of blank column and rows that new data could be added to each day. This was particularly useful because laboratory data that accumulated over time came back as individual small chips of paper that we glued into the chart: there was no place where one could go to see a year's worth of blood counts or kidney or thyroid tests.

Bill and I started making problem-oriented record rounds: it only took a few visits to any intern for them to get the gist of this. Every three months we met the new clerkship students on their first day, and they caught on quickly.

Within a few months problem-oriented notes had replaced most of the notes on the Medicine teaching services, although it took some years before other specialties adopted them. Drs. Weed and Hurst had been right—the problem-oriented record forced doctors to both think and record systematically and made it much easier to avoid losing track of abnormal data or to fail to pay attention to all of a patient's problems.

In my second year of fellowship I was asked to help with the weekly Chief of Service rounds with all thirty students. Dr. Bradley had done these while he was chairman, but once Dr. Aranow took over he asked other senior faculty members to do them. One student from each of the three teaching services presented each week, twenty minutes each for a total of an hour. One of our distinguished senior clinicians, Hamilton Southworth, had been asked to do these rounds, but he felt a little uncomfortable in this unfamiliar task and I was asked to join him, I imagined because I was comfortable working across the wide variety of cases on the medical service and used to teaching that was focused at the student level.

One of our cases was an elderly woman who presented with confusion, a complicated medical regimen, and several serious medical problems. There were many potential reasons for her confusion and I thought that this might be a good opportunity to teach the students how to approach a problem with many possible causes in a system-by-system review. I hadn't planned to do this teaching—we never knew the cases we would be seeing in advance—but after bedside presentation I shepherded the students to the Nine East solarium where there was a black board and asked them to name the systems which might contribute to her confusion—could it be a structural change in her brain, for example, and if so, what brain problems would produce this? Could it be diminished circulation, caused by perhaps a stroke or decreased blood pressure? Could it be an endocrine problem? Could it have been a medication she was taking? Or could she have failure of her kidneys or liver.

In fifteen minutes we were ready to go back over her history and fit her particular problem into the many possible causes. In the end it seemed likely that her confusion had been caused by her blood pressure medications lowering her blood pressure too much, in the presence of several drugs that tended to cause confusion in the elderly—a sleeping medication and Benadryl.

Dr. Southworth complimented me on the extemporaneous teaching session. He was one of Columbia's most distinguished and famous clinicians, a man of considerable gravitas and reserve whose practice was reputed to be made up of celebrities, titans of business, intellectuals, politicians, and other doctors. He was entirely dedicated to medical practice and to Columbia's teaching programs.

As I was approaching the last months of my fellowship, I received a page from him, asking if we could meet. He invited me to join him in practice when I returned from the Army, along with my friend Bill Maclean, who by then would have completed a cardiology fellowship at the University of Alabama. Doctor Southworth said he wasn't sure how long he would be able to remain in practice and he wanted Bill and me to take over his practice when the time came, and in the meanwhile he would refer patients to Bill and me that he was too busy to add to his practice.

Dr. Southworth was at that moment the President of the American Board of Internal Medicine. I felt as though I had been asked by a deity to become his heir apparent. I was stunned, surprised, and pleasantly overwhelmed.

Admitting privileges to the private service at the Medical Center were given out with parsimony: rarely was more than one of the graduating residents or fellows invited. A few days later Dr. Aranow asked Bill and me to meet with him. He asked if we wanted to accept the offer from Dr.

Southworth. If we did, it would have to be approved first by the members of the department of medicine, and then by the board of trustees of the Presbyterian Hospital. He assured us that we would have his total support, and since it was Dr. Southworth's wish, was likely to sail through.

In the spring I received a letter from the Department of the Army's physician who managed the distribution of physicians, telling me that I would be inducted on 1 August at Fort Sam Houston, in San Antonio, Texas. I made one last pitch to stay out of the Army, writing back that my laboratory at Columbia had developed a radioimmunoassay for the hormone prolactin, which we suspected might have a role in the causation of breast cancer, and that it was vital that I continue doing research outside of the Army, to save millions of lives. The only thing that was true in that sentence was that we were able to measure prolactin, but there wasn't a trace of evidence that prolactin had anything at all to do with breast cancer.

He wrote back informing me that I had enlisted and that I would be assigned as an endocrinologist, where I would do more good for the world than studying prolactin. I contacted Jerry Earle at Walter Reed, who said that he would do what he could to get me assigned to Walter Reed.

With that we began planning to sell our Teaneck house and move to whatever godforsaken place the Army banished us to.

Before leaving I presented several papers at national meetings, first at the Endocrine Society, and then at the American Federation of Clinical Research in Atlantic City. There was a good deal of interest because these were the first studies that elucidated the role of prolactin in women and suggested that prolactin was a marker of pituitary tumors in men and women who spontaneously lactated.

I mourned leaving New York where, for the first time since I was eighteen, I had established a home and friendships that felt durable. I loved teaching and caring for patients at Columbia and wished that I could simply stay and cross the street from the research building to the Atchley Pavilion to begin practice with Dr. Southworth.

Prolactin Part Two

Once again, as luck would have it, my inability to avoid military service radically changed where our family would end up in the future, but of course I couldn't see that and would have disbelieved it if it had been revealed to me in a glass ball or by a fairy godmother.

WITH MARGARET, CHRISTMAS DAY, CHICAGO, 1967 WITH A SWEATER
I BOUGHT HER AT BONWIT TELLER

Learning the Art of Medicine—a Memoir

INTERNS, ALL SPECIALTIES, UNIVERSITY OF CHICAGO, MAY 1968. I'M 22, SECOND ROW, 5TH FROM THE RIGHT SIDE OF THE PHOTO

Photos

MARGARET IN OUR EAST 79TH STREET APARTMENT IN MANHATTAN

Learning the Art of Medicine—a Memoir

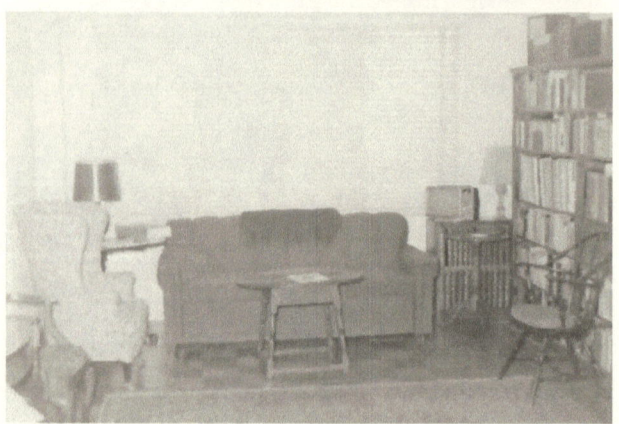

THE EAST 79TH STREET APARTMENT

Photos

OUR FIRST HOUSE, TEANECK NEW JERSEY, SPRING 1971

MARGARET AND HER PARENTS WITH KATHARINE AT MARGARET'S SISTER'S WEDDING, 1970

KATHARINE AND MARGARET, CHRISTMAS 1971

Learning the Art of Medicine—a Memoir

KATHARINE IN NEWBURYPORT, SUMMER 1971

Photos

KATHARINE IN THE TEANECK HOUSE GARDEN

PRESBYTERIAN HOSPITAL INTERNAL MEDICINE RESIDENTS, JUNE, 1972. I'M THE GUY WITH A BOW TIE STANDING NEXT TO DR BRADLEY, THE BARD PROFESSOR AND CHAIR OF MEDICINE (LONG WHITE COAT). TOM JACOBS IS IN THE BACK ROW ON THE FAR LEFT

DURING MY FELLOWSHIP—MARGARET LEA WITH ME IN TEANECK HOUSE, 1971

Photos

MARGARET LEA IN THE TEANECK HOUSE GARDEN, 1972

PORTRAIT OF ANDY FRANTZ, MANY YEARS AFTER I WAS HIS FELLOW. HE FAVORED MARTINIS

The Doctors Draft and the American War in Vietnam

1972 - 1975

CHAPTER 23

The Army Medical Corps

Although I had tried to talk the Army out of dragging me away from New York City in support of a war that I vaguely understood and equally vaguely felt was a bad idea, in May, Les Berger, the Medical Corps assignment officer at the Pentagon, called me to say that after basic training I could go to Walter Reed, but I would have to give them a third year. My obligation was for two years; had I said that I wouldn't extend my tour, I would have been sent to one of the numerous Army hospitals in the United States or around the world. Walter Reed was a plum assignment, not very different from taking a job at an academic medical center as a clinician, teacher, and researcher. I was disgruntled, but Margaret thought that Washington D.C. would be a good place for us and our young family, and many of the hospitals I might otherwise have been sent to were in small towns near Army training facilities in the Southeast and Southwest.

The Army had me over a barrel: I agreed.

We put our Teaneck house on the market as soon as we heard that we would have to move; it sold within a few weeks with enough of a profit to more than cover the closing costs. The new owner was a man who was doing at-home dialysis; he and his wife felt that the sun porch at the end of the kitchen was a perfect place for him to look out at the world while going through the several-hours-long procedures three or four times a week.

It was not hard to find a house in Maryland. A large portion of the population of Washington, D.C. and its Virginia and Maryland suburbs is tidal: as administrations come and go, thousands of people—the political appointees and the departing and newly elected congress members and their staffs—come and go with them. The Washington branches of corporations that do business with the government also turn over their Washington staff members, many of whom move to Washington for a few years for particular projects and then return to their home bases. We learned quickly that most of the people who became our friends had not grown up in Washington and many wouldn't be staying beyond a few years.

That was our expectation as well.

I knew that I would be commuting to Walter Reed on Georgia Avenue, so we looked for houses that were close to Georgia, Connecticut, and Wisconsin Avenue, the roads that feed into D.C from the close-in Maryland suburbs Rockville and Silver Spring.

Our choice was not quite bizarre, but certainly seemed quixotic: we bought a house on Norbeck Road on a fairway of a country club because it had a half-acre yard, beautiful old trees, and lots of lovely mid-century houses surrounding it. We had to take out a membership in the club; because we didn't play golf or tennis, its chief attribute was the swimming pool and lots of room for the girls to run around.

When my Army pay began in August, I would be making more than twice as much as I had as a fellow, with a fully paid insurance program and a housing allowance. We also had commissary privileges that could reduce some of our clothing and grocery bills when we wanted to deal with the commute and erratic selection of what was available. We had bought the Teaneck house for $37,500 and sold it for more; the Rockville house cost $50,000, which would not be hard to handle on my larger salary. There was no way to get to Walter Reed except by driving, so we would need a second car. Our budget would be tight, but we felt that moving to the Maryland suburbs was a step up from New Jersey.

Our new house felt very rural compared to the Teaneck house. Norbeck road connected downtown Rockville with Georgia Avenue;

The Army Medical Corps

traffic could pick up in the morning and late afternoon, but most of the time it was just a neighborhood street. North of us the Maryland countryside opened up, with a few new houses scattered here and there. Olney, just a few miles away, still had a blacksmith shop, a wholesale feed store, and a handful of general stores and antique shops of the variety that sold old country furniture that had never aspired to sophistication.

It cracked me up that where Norbeck Road crossed Georgia Avenue there was a booming retirement village named Leisure World, built conveniently adjacent to the Gates of Heaven Cemetery. I figured we were too young for Leisure World and that I would never meet the admission requirements to pass through the gates of heaven.

Our immediate neighbors were once again a good deal older than we, closer to grandparent age, but many of the families along the fairways had young children and most of the older couples had grandchildren. The swimming pool turned out to be a great place for our kids.

It wasn't possible to use the dense woods behind the house because it was dark and filled with dead branches and leaves. After we had gotten the furniture settled and boxes unpacked, in the month I had before leaving for basic training, I rented a chainsaw and a chipper and took down half of the twelve huge hardwood trees. The trees were 75 feet tall—oak, hickory, honey locust, and a few soft tulip poplars.

It took about a week to fell the trees and buck them up into fireplace sizes. It took another week of running an incredibly noisy chipper to turn all the branches and bark into coarse mulch. No one had ever taught me about hearing protection during the years I used chainsaws in the Forest Service and it would be another twenty years before I figured it out. This was nothing unusual—I never saw anyone my age use hearing protectors and in an increasingly rackety world a lot of us would end up with high-frequency hearing loss in our fifties.

By the time I left for Texas the remaining oaks and the one hickory were spaced far enough apart that the sun had begun to penetrate to the ground. By autumn, in advance of rains and snowfall, I plowed and raked and seeded the ground and by the next spring our lawn ran continuously from

Norbeck Road to the golf green and the individual trees could now be appreciated in their autumn colors and brilliant spring foliage.

On the last day of July, I flew to San Antonio, Texas. The Army told me to bring casual clothes and suggested a dozen motels that would accept what my per diem paid, most of them along commuter highways strewn with fast food restaurants, gas stations, payday loan shops, and used furniture stores. It was a dreary scene. On the first evening the temperature was 105. I checked into the motel, unpacked my clothes and books, and changed into running clothes. A few blocks from the motel I found a winding side street that led me into a neighborhood lined with neat one-story ranch houses with good-sized yards and double garages. It was still the summer school holidays and yet at 6 PM there was not a soul to be seen outside, no kids, no bicycles or tricycles on the porches, no one tending a garden. It was like a deserted village.

After a mile of running I recognized the problem: it was too hot to be running around outside or gardening. When a car arrived at home, an automatic door opener raised the door, the car drove in, and the door closed: people went from air-conditioned house to air-conditioned car to air-conditioned store or office. I wondered how people doing street repair or construction survived.

I ate a bleak dinner in a chain Mexican restaurant 300 feet away and 3000 miles from home and my family.

The next morning I drove my rental car to Fort Sam Houston to begin the Officer Basic Leadership course. With a war underway in Southeast Asia, major evacuation hospitals in Germany, Thailand and Italy, and tens of thousands of soldiers enlisted or drafted every month, the medical operations of the Army were huge. As Army doctors we would be serving everywhere from major medical centers in Hawaii, Tacoma, San Francisco, Washington DC, and San Antonio, to the hospitals and infirmaries in two dozen Army training posts throughout the United States, many of them in

The Army Medical Corps

the South, to the front lines in Vietnam and the European and Korean frontiers where we were in standoffs with Russia and China.

About sixty of us arrived for the doctors' version of Officer Basic training. The first thing we discovered was that we had only two things in common: a grudge about being in the Army and a grievance against training in San Antonio in the August heat. We were surgeons, internists, psychiatrists, pediatricians, orthopedic surgeons, radiologists, anesthesiologists and obstetricians—the full range of what the Army needed to take care of the massive medical and trauma casualties of the battle zones, and also to care for the families left behind in remote Army towns when their fathers or mothers were overseas.

For most of us the Army was not going to be our career: our military service was an unwelcome detour from the lives we had been leading, far from what we wanted to be doing now that our training was completed.

We spent our first day completing dozens of forms about our education, our dependents, and a day-by-day account of our life activities that, ostensibly, would be scrutinized by the FBI for any evidence of anti-American or criminal activity. We had a three-minute interview with a bored psychiatrist who asked how we were doing and if we had any problems we wanted to talk about other than that we didn't want to be at Fort Sam Houston or in the Army. That completed, our induction exam could be stamped "mentally fit." We submitted to a dental exam and a weirdly useless physical exam that concentrated on whether we could walk a straight line, stand on our toes, and had a right arm functional enough to be able to salute. We hypothesized that if we had an amputated left arm we would be fine, but if we had no right arm, we couldn't salute, and we would be relieved of our obligation.

Our first assignment was to get uniforms.

Officer uniforms were available from many private shops that dealt in nothing else. We were given several afternoons off to buy the green wool Army service uniform for everyday work, the Army khaki uniform for hot weather, Army fatigues, army combat boots, socks, several forms of Army hats, an Army raincoat, and a handful of Army shirts. As far as I can recall,

I didn't have to buy Army underwear or pajamas. We weren't measured for any of these items unless we were buying hand-tailored custom uniforms. A skinny old man who looked like he had a three-pack-a-day habit sized me up, turned to a long rack of jackets and pulled one off its hanger. He got the fit right on the first try, made a note, and sent me to a dressing room full of other men to try on a pair of pants with to see if the waist size was okay. Then he pinned the cuff on those and told me that he would alter the summer uniform to the same length, showed me the shirts, threw in a Navy-blue tie and a khaki belt and told me to come back in two days.

We were told to wear our fatigues and our combat boots until our summer uniforms were available.

While in college in Boston, I wore Ivy-League/preppy clothes: wool slacks, Harris Tweed jackets, Brooks Brothers suits and blazers, and paisley and regimental-stripe neckties. In medical training my clothing gradually became a symbol of my professional role: a short white jacket as a student—and in residency a white jacket and white pants—diminished our individuality, leaving only our choice of shirts and ties as an expression of our taste. But I was proud to wear those uniforms.

Putting on the Army uniform with sixty other amateur soldiers had a demoralizing effect. Now we were all dressed exactly the same, down to our socks and shirts and belts and ties, as though we had surrendered all individuality and character. To me it felt as though we instantly had transmigrated to interchangeable choresmen: "I need eight docs for Army helicopter evacuation units in Saigon—we're gonna draw straws." It dawned on me that was exactly what the Army wanted: subjugation, obedience to authority. Putting on the uniform meant taking off our habits of autonomy and self-authorization.

I suppose this had happened in residency as well. After all, we all put on the white coats and pants of residents with a sense of accomplishment and pride, we had no control over our schedules and were expected to work whatever number of hours were needed to provide the care our patients required, and we worked hard to achieve mastery of the same, vast medical canon. But while we were interchangeable, somehow, we managed to

The Army Medical Corps

maintain our individuality, sometimes to a disturbing degree—and, importantly, we were volunteers: we wanted to become practicing physicians, but at Ft. Sam it was clear that almost none of us wanted to be soldier-doctors.

Leadership training consisted of long boring lectures and weekly examinations in which there were three obviously wrong answers and one obviously right answer: apparently, knowledge or practice of leadership were less important for doctors than teaching us how to wear the uniform and not disgrace ourselves as Army officers. Question: how do you acknowledge the approach of an enlisted soldier: (a) ignore him and keep walking; (b) shake hands; (c) yell at him to get out of your way; (d) make eye contact and wait for him to salute, and then salute back.

The military history subjects included the history of knightly tradition—how the salute evolved from armored warriors raising the visors of their helmet to look in the eyes of the man they would kill or be killed by. Chilling information.

We restlessly listened to talks about the organization of the Army Medical Corps, the organization of battle field and evacuation medical care, the roles of support personnel in battlefield medical stations—what they knew and could do, how they were supported by physicians using walkie-talkies—and the methods of medical evacuation by helicopters and transports.

The doctors slated for assignment in Southeast Asia would have another six weeks of training in managing acute trauma, the pharmacology of the drugs they would be using, the epidemiology of tropical infectious diseases, wound management, and battlefield minor surgery.

We spent three days entirely devoted to war games—one game that terrified the teachers and one that terrified the doctors. We were bussed the 150 Miles from San Antonio to Fort Hood for our field training and put up in officer's barracks, eating in a mess hall and lunching on MCI (meal, combat, individual) rations. The first game was to learn how to shoot the M16 rifle. In the morning we saw scratchy movies of the M16 in action—a sergeant field stripping a gun to clean it, and proper gun handling—the chief message of which was not to point the sucker at anyone you were not planning to kill.

Thousands of troops lived at the vast Ft. Hood, training as drivers and gunners in tanks. Bombs, heavy artillery, mortars, and machine guns could be heard exploding in the distance almost every day. The M16 rifles were like peashooters in this environment, but our instructors assured us that they were more afraid of being shot by the doctors than anything they were exposed to from the heavy artillery. The rumor was that the sergeants drew straws to select the three or four losers who would have to spend a day with us on the target range. Occasionally one would settle up a poker debt by taking over someone's assignment.

After field stripping and reassembling the weapon, we were trucked to a firing range for two hours of target practice, the one constantly repeated message being "don't point the rifle anywhere but toward the target." Within five minutes one of the docs from New York City wanted to ask a question and turned around with his rifle pointing directly at the instructor's prominent belly. The instructor threw his hands up and yelled at the confused doctor, "Drop your weapon captain! Drop your weapon!"

At that point we were all lectured again.

I had been pretty accurate at target practice with a .22 rifle as a boy, but manning a M16 was to a .22 as a jet fighter was to a Piper Cub. And accuracy wasn't the issue: they didn't really care if we could become marksmen. Those who were going to Vietnam were never going to carry a rifle, because their neutrality under international laws of war required that they be noncombatants. The Army knew that everyone, including the doctors, would be safer if we never picked up a rifle again. The training in part was to give us a sense of what our patients would have experienced, a tiny taste of what war was like. We only needed enough skill to be able to pick up and use a rifle if our medical facility was under attack and we needed to defend ourselves.

Officers were allowed to carry pistols, and in combat countries required to. Doctors were excluded because when issued pistols they often accidentally shot themselves or someone else. They also regularly turned over jeeps and crashed motorcycles.

The other reason we were brought to Ft. Hood was to teach us orienteering, in case we got lost walking between our housing and the hospital. We were given an elementary introduction to reading topographic maps and using a compass, and a brief introduction to what to do if we were lost in a jungle in deep darkness, surrounded by Vietcong, with only a knife, compass, book of matches, two C-rations, and a topographic map.

One of the master sergeants started off the session by showing slides of the map we would be using and pointing out the contour lines, creeks, drainages and roads.

"So, were any of you docs in Boy Scouts?"

A few people raised their hands.

"Have any of you learned how to orient and read a map?"

Two hands went up—mine and one of the Boy Scouts. This was a stupid thing to do, I quickly learned: never raise your hand in response to a question from an Army master sergeant.

"Major Noel, how did it happen that you learned to read a map?"

I had reached a point in my life in which I no longer concealed that I was born in Montana and had decided that there were some pretty cool things about growing up there.

"I grew up in Montana and spent five years fighting forest fires in the Rocky Mountain wildernesses," I said.

A few eyes shifted to look at me as though I had just sprouted antlers.

The other guy had been an Eagle Scout.

"Major Noel and Major Habersham will be two of the squad leaders. The third squad will draw straws for a leader."

"We will meet at nineteen hundred hours in front of your quarters. You will be wearing full fatigues and your government-issue boots. You will be assigned one order of rations for each man, a canteen, a compass, a map of one sector of Ft. Hood, one flashlight, and one squad-level first aid kit in a backpack. The squad leader will be issued a 5-inch pilots' knife appropriate for cutting throats, sawing down trees, and treating rattlesnake bites. You each will be responsible for your own kit, including toilet paper. For reasons that by now should not surprise you, you will not be issued guns."

"And get this straight: the squad will stay together, and the leader will make the decisions. If you are not at the meeting point by dawn we will send out a search party to bring you in. If you are lost, find a clear area and spread out the red-cross flag in the first aid kit so the search helicopter can find you."

At twenty-one hundred hours we had assembled in our stiff, new fatigues with our last name monogrammed on the pocket, in boots that were even more stiff and not broken in. Three tan Army troop trucks were rumbling in the lot beside our quarters; silently we climbed into them and took up seats on the benches inside.

We drove for about an hour, first on a paved road, then on a dirt road that wound around a gradual uphill. The trucks with the other two squads had turned off at the end of the paved road.

I had tried to orient myself to figure out which direction we were going from the point where the trucks split apart, but soon lost track as the truck turned left and right dozens of times on curves or intersecting roads, I couldn't tell which.

Finally, we ground to a halt. We clambered out of the truck and gathered around Sergeant McKnightly. He spread the map out on the ground, oriented it with the top pointed to the north, and shined his flashlight on it. He pointed out where we were, at the top of a rounded hill. A large red cross marked the field where the three squads were to meet. To give us an incentive, he told us that the first to make it back would be bought beers by the other two squads the next evening. With that, Sergeant McKnightly climbed up into the truck cab and it lurched out of sight.

My quick look at the map had shown that we would cross three ridges and descend into three drainages before we got to a creek that led to the meeting place—it looked like a distance of about six or seven miles. We had no idea what the terrain would be like and we didn't have the benefit of a moon. It was hot—at least 90 degrees—and in the distance we could hear the faint rattle of machine gun fire coming from a tank night-training exercise.

One of my squad members asked, "Are there snakes?"

I had no idea. A few people volunteered that there were rattlesnakes everywhere in Texas in a tone that implied that we were all about to die. I had checked the inventory of our first aid pack, which included three snakebite kits and enough surgical equipment to remove a spleen.

No one but me questioned my competence to read a map and follow a compass. We headed off down our hill and broke our way through scrub cedar and live oak. Most of the time we walked silently in single file, since there was no clear trail. I used the flashlight to find breaks through the wooded areas where we wouldn't have to claw our way through brush.

I had chosen not to go on a direct line to the meeting grounds, but to cross the ridges and then follow the third drainage to the meadow.

When we hit our first drainage there was a swampy but shallow trickle of a stream with a high limestone bluff on the other side that took us a while to scramble up. After the first ridge we descended into the second drainage. There was heavy brush on the other side. I decided that it was worth going down the drainage until we could make out a part of the opposite bank that looked penetrable. Some members of the squad had buddied up and were talking among themselves, but so far no one had objected to my pathfinding among the trees and brush and through the two creek bottoms. It was past midnight and the sky was brilliant with stars. On the far side of the second stream I stopped and asked if we should take a break. People broke out their C rations and canteens and we sat on the ground and chatted. For most of us this was a mildly annoying but harmless introduction to the Army. We knew that we were to do what we were told, no exceptions, even when something seemed unlikely to be useful to us if, as was the case for many of us, we were going to be posted stateside. We also knew that some of us would be heading to Vietnam and we had been hearing stories for our entire training of evacuation helicopters that had gone down in the dense forests in which any village was as likely to be hostile as friendly and that for some, trying to get back to a base when there were no landmarks wasn't just an exercise in plotting a straight line.

Around 2 AM we headed over the last ridge, which was the highest and required some backtracking to get around cypress trees too dense to penetrate. Several squad members had swollen eyes and were sneezing from the pollen knocked out of the cypress branches. We made the creek bottom in about an hour and began to bushwhack down a low bank on the other side, dense with trees, fallen logs and brush. I had estimated that we were an hour from the meadows, but it took longer. I began to worry that I was off track. When finally we broke into a clearing we could smell a campfire and hear a couple of low voices laughing.

My squad began to chatter among themselves.

I was into it now! "Major Noel and Alfa Squad reporting, Sergeant."

"Whatd'ya know, McKnightly, we got one that we don't have to send out helicopters to find. You got all your docs, Major?"

I turned toward the other guys: "Roll call!"

Sergeant Brennan called out the names. We were all present. I hadn't thought to question that.

It was half-past four. We had been bushwhacking for about five hours.

"Okay," Sergeant Brennan called out. "Pull up some sagebrush and have a nap. The other squads should be coming in and the other trucks will be back to take you to the mess hall about oh-seven-hundred."

But only the Eagle Scout's Bravo Squad made it back. Our two squads went back on the troop trucks and by the time we got to Ft. Hood we saw three helicopters heading for the sector the other squad had disappeared in. We had been told to find a mountaintop or meadow and stay there if, at dawn, we hadn't found the field where we were to meet the trucks. Charlie Squad had hiked all night, ending up on a ridge top about a quarter mile from where they started out when they finally gave up.

The Army Medical Corps

In the officer's club that night we drank free beers —"long necks"— that tasted about as bad as a beer could possibly taste to wash down nachos mounded with gloppy cheese.

The next day we were bussed back to Fort Sam Houston and completed paper work to document reimbursement for our expenses.

We were each given an envelope with our assignment and asked to sign it. I opened mine:

"Walter Reed Army Institute of Research, Washington, DC, August 1, 1972—July 31 1975."

When I had heard on the phone that I would be assigned to Walter Reed there was no date associated with the term, although I was told that I would have to extend my enlistment.

Here it was in black and white. I walked over to the administrative lieutenant colonel and told him that I didn't want to extend to a third year, hoping that at this late stage that might be negotiable.

"Major Noel, you either sign or we will find you an assignment in Nam. You should consider yourself grateful for what you have been assigned. There is no shortage of people who would jump at that assignment."

Like telling the Army I shouldn't have to serve at all, that the future of millions of women was at stake because surely prolactin was the key to breast cancer, my last-ditch effort to shorten my tour was useless. We had moved to Washington, D.C, bought a house, and thinned a small forest to make room for sunshine and flowers. I wasn't about to stick my middle finger in Uncle Sam's eye.

I signed.

CHAPTER 24

Walter Reed

The drive from our house on Norbeck Road to Walter Reed was only 11 miles, straight down Georgia Avenue. I bought a two-door navy-blue Celica sedan, Toyota's concept of a sports car, with a five-speed stick shift. It was fun to drive, but no better a kids' car than Margaret's. Children's car seats were more elemental then, but even so, it was a strain to cantilever the girls in and out of the back.

I had never been a car commuter. The pleasure of shifting made the stop and go traffic on Georgia Avenue more enjoyable in a little car that could easily weave in and out of traffic. More interesting was that I now had an FM radio and three classical music stations I could listen to.

The September weather in DC was still hot and humid, but this car had air conditioning—another first. When I expressed surprise that air conditioning was not optional the Toyota salesman said that they would never be able to sell a new car in Washington DC without air-conditioning. Even Jeeps, he said—my idea of the no-frills, rough-terrain car—came with air-conditioning. When we bought our Ford three years earlier in New Jersey, the option of air conditioning was never mentioned.

At Fort Sam I had been wearing fatigues, but on my first day reporting for duty at Walter Reed I knew that fatigues would not be appropriate. I put on my summer khaki uniform. Even with air conditioning, by the time

I arrived at Walter Reed and hunted around the many streets looking for parking, my uniform was stained with sweat on my back and under my arms.

The Main Hospital at Walter Reed was a huge Georgian style red brick building opened in 1909. For decades it was the largest military medical facility in the United States, with at one-time 5,500 beds on its 137-acre campus in Northwest Washington DC. I was assigned to the Endocrinology Research Unit at the Walter Reed Army Institute of Research (WRAIR) not far from the hospital. I parked about a ten-minute walk away and decided it was too hot to be wearing my Army hat. Within three minutes I had problems. As I passed enlisted soldiers and medical personnel in uniform their arms flew up in salute. Whatever my training at Ft. Sam had taught me, I still hadn't grasped that I wasn't in New York City anymore: this was the Army, and I was expected to act like an officer, returning salutes when saluted. About the fourth salute came from a guy wearing the wool Army Green Uniform. I thought, "Whoa, this guy's nuts—that's way too hot for this sweltering weather."

He apparently outranked me: "Major! You're not inside. Where's your cover?"

I had no idea what he meant by "cover." I wasn't a book, and I certainly wasn't a bed.

"Sir?"

"Your cover, Major, your hat. When you are not inside you have to have your hat on. You must be a doctor, right?"

"Yes sir."

"First you are a soldier. Second you are an officer. After that, you can be a doctor. This isn't 'Let's Pretend' Major. Are you assigned here?"

"Yes sir."

"The summer uniform isn't authorized in Washington DC. You need to be wearing greens."

I was assembling an argument: if swampy, subtropical Washington, DC wasn't the most logical place outside of Saigon to be wearing the short-sleeve khaki uniform, then why was I forced to buy it?

As though he was reading what I was about to say, he continued, "Soldiers go to hot places. They don't take their uniforms off, Major. They don't wear just whatever they want. 'Uniform' implies uniformity, come hell or hot weather."

I had always thought that hell and hot weather were the same thing, but apparently he could tell them apart.

"Yes sir."

In that single conversation I said "sir" more times than in my entire previous life.

Now feeling like a conspicuous target for everyone I passed, I hurried to the building housing WRAIR. It was blessedly air-conditioned. My khaki shirt was now entirely soaked through.

Inside I found Len Wartofsky, the second in command of the Endocrine Research unit. He was wearing the Army green wool uniform and shirt and tie and eyed my summer khakis with skepticism.

"Any trouble making your way from the parking lot?"

"Yes, I think I took a few incoming rounds from the enemy."

"I'm not surprised. Who did you run into?"

"A guy who thought that my officer basic training didn't quite do the job."

"Did you see his name?"

"Moncrief."

Len's eyebrows arched. "Did he have stars?"

"Yes."

"That was your commanding officer, Major General Moncrief."

"Is my Army career over?"

"It isn't that easy to get out. If it were, everyone would do it. The only surefire way to get out is to do something that gets you thrown into prison."

"I thought about that option. My wife wasn't excited about it."

I had been cocooned in the increasingly comfortable microcosm of the Columbia University College of Physicians and Surgeons for eight of the last nine years. Columbia, with two hundred years of history, had a distorted view of all places non-Columbia, and New York City had the same myopia with regard to the rest of the world. While I had clung to Columbia's door frame trying to resist being dragged into the Army, like a child in a tantrum refusing a trip to the dentist, I had been dropped into the best posting I could have hoped for, and still I was coping poorly with the gift I had been handed.

There was no part of me that wanted to submit to the military rituals. Just as I had tried and then rejected the unquestioning faith of both high church and low church Christianity, I felt that there was a vast gap between the myth of American supremacy and goodness, and our support of autocratic governments around the world where democracy was a fraud and we were trying to protect American commercial interests and those of our allies that were trying to hold on to their colonies. Growing up I had believed in the righteousness of our belated entry into World War One and certainly our involvement in World War Two. I understood that the war in Korea had been a continuation of the Chinese Communist revolution that pushed out the nationalists as the allies were defeating the Japanese, and that North Korea was the battlefield between a free and democratic Korea and the drive by the Communists to control all of Southeast Asia.

The war in Vietnam seemed different—how different I only learned decades later, but it seemed from the beginning—and certainly proved to be—unwinnable, and, in my view, immoral. We had entered the war as France, seeking to restore its pre-World War Two control over Vietnam, was defeated by the North Vietnamese army led by Ho Chi Minh, who then tried to reunite North and South Vietnam with Chinese and Russian Communist support. America and its allies took over the war to keep Communism from spreading into South Vietnam and then through all of Southeast Asia.

And so here I was, an unwilling servant of what I regarded as a mistake, trying to fight a ground war in Asia to prevent Vietnam from throwing off colonization that extended back centuries. If I had been sent to a posting in Vietnam with real warriors—people who believed that might was right, that the USA was infallible, that loyalty should be unquestioning, that killing enemies was the highest calling a man could hope for— I would have been desperately unhappy. At Walter Reed, by good fortune I had fallen in with a bunch of Army docs, conscriptees like me, who were outspokenly liberal but had figured out a way to live with the contradictions of their situation.

Len Wartofsky had been in the Army for a while and was already a lieutenant colonel. He had grown up in DC, living above his immigrant parent's grocery store. He went to medical school at George Washington University, trained in internal medicine at Washington University in St. Louis, and in Endocrinology on the Harvard Service at Boston City Hospital.

Dick Dimond, like me, was a major but a few years my senior, with training at Einstein Medical School in the Bronx, New York. The chief of endocrinology and a colonel, Jerry Earle was a relaxed Midwesterner who had trained at the University of Iowa and was making the Army his career.

It was an interesting set up. WRAIR had evolved as a research program focused on specific military issues—most notably creating new treatments and vaccines for the parasitic and viral diseases that American troops encountered in their wars and postings all over the globe. In the early nineteen hundreds the government created a military medical school near the Washington Tidal Basin, with a full faculty that held professorial ranks. The medical school eventually closed but the research units that had been created remained, with larger experimental and vaccine development programs at Ft. Dietrich north of DC in Frederick MD.

The infectious disease programs made sense, but why there was endocrine research was more mysterious: thyroid, pituitary, adrenal, and gonadal diseases and new onset diabetes were neither infectious nor common in soldiers or likely to be caused by war, although working out the role of hormones in stress had been important in earlier decades.

My first assignment was to propose a research project. WRAIR had its own funding, which made it relatively easy to get a project started. The state of the art in endocrinology for the previous fifty years had been developing accurate methods to measure hormones circulating in the blood. The steroid hormones like cortisol, aldosterone and estrogen and androgen were made in great abundance in humans and animals and had been measured for decades. The physiology of what stimulated their release and suppression had been worked out in the 1940's, 1950's, and 1960's.

It had proved harder to measure the protein hormones like insulin and growth hormone that were comprised of strings of amino acids. Two researchers at the Bronx Veterans Administration Hospital, Solomon Berson and Rosalyn Yallow, made a series of revolutionary discoveries using antibodies to insulin to create a sensitive and specific assay, allowing for the first-time accurate measurements, which led to the discovery that there were two forms of diabetes, one that typically occurred in childhood or adolescence due to insulin deficiency, and the other in adults caused by the body's resistance to insulin. Soon they and others developed a radioimmunoassay for growth hormone, parathyroid hormone, and thyroid stimulating hormone and the field of hormone research was revolutionized. Dr. Yallow received the Nobel Prize for her discoveries with Dr. Berson, who died shortly before the award was announced, one of only six women who had ever won a Nobel Prize in any field at that time, one of two in medicine.

When I left for the Army, Andy Frantz had urged me to return to Columbia afterwards, not as a practitioner in the Atchley Pavilion, as Dr. Southworth had offered, but as a researcher. Although I was not planning to return to Columbia as a researcher, I needed to have a research program at Walter Reed for the next three years and I didn't want to completely reject Andy's desire to keep me in his lab. We had agreed on a plan for continuing the studies in humans of what stimulated and suppressed prolactin secretion. By now Professor Friesen in Manitoba had been able to sequence the amino acids in prolactin, demonstrate its very small differences from growth hormone, and had begun to synthesize it. Prolactin was now available in small quantities so that medical scientists at several other universities could create their own radioimmunoassay and they were now in competition with Andy's lab for discoveries and publications.

Len Wartofsky and Jerry Earl had assumed that I would be setting up my own radioimmunoassay at Walter Reed and they were disappointed when they learned that Andy opposed that: Andy knew that it would take a long time to create antibodies and set up a new radioimmunoassay of my own, but he also wanted to maintain his authorship and productivity by having me continue to be his partner: I was adept at organizing clinical studies and his lab was ahead of everyone in the world at precisely measuring prolactin. He didn't want me to become another competitor and I had no interest in being one.

Over the three years I was in Washington I performed studies of the blood levels of prolactin to determine whether, like other pituitary hormones, prolactin rises and falls in humans when awake and when sleeping. I recruited normal volunteers as well as women who had been referred to us with galactorrhea—non-pregnancy related lactation—who had elevated levels of prolactin. In these studies nurses and I drew blood samples on the women in their homes every twenty minutes for twenty-four hours.

We spent a few expensive nights studying the impact of drunkenness: three of us holed up in Dick Dimond's cellar with two bottles of fine Scotch whisky while a non-drinking fellow drew blood samples to measure our alcohol and prolactin levels. No profound discoveries were made beyond testing the limits of our ability to consume whiskey.

We did extensive studies of the effect of the hypothalamic thyroid releasing hormone, discovering that it was a potent stimulator of prolactin release as well. Inadvertently, we noticed that Margaret had the greatest response of any of our subjects, from which we deduced that she had mild hypothyroidism.

This was what I called "bricks and mortar" research. We weren't making concept-changing discoveries, but filling in the blanks about what prolactin did in the normal human beyond stimulating milk production in pregnant and nursing women.

Of all the Army docs I met during our induction at Fort Sam Houston, I had far and away the least military-relevant duties.

After my first year at Walter Reed, Jerry Earle received word that it would be nice if Major Noel were doing something useful for the United States Army. The head of research at Walter Reed Army Institute of Research had to make a yearly report to the Pentagon and Congress about what they were getting for their money. They found it hard to explain why the United States Army was studying prolactin levels in breastfeeding, drunkenness, and sleep.

It had been demonstrated years earlier that fear caused a number of hormones to increase, among them growth hormone, the adrenal steroid hormones, and adrenalin. Continuing my string of goofy studies, I decided to see if fear also increased prolactin levels in normal (and clearly not lactating) men.

I prepared a simple proposal to study paratroopers who were making their first jump, assuming that at least some of them would be scared. Whoever reviewed the proposal raised no objections, and a few weeks later I found myself on a commercial airline flight heading for the Army Airborne School at Fort Benning Georgia.

I was met at the Columbus airport by an Army Sergeant who saluted me so violently that I thought he was going to throw his shoulder out of joint. In the casual military environment of Walter Reed, there was very little saluting inside the buildings and it always caught me by surprise when I passed a junior officer or enlisted man who saluted me. My mind usually in some other place, I was often well past them before I remembered that I was supposed to salute back.

"Sir. Jenkins Sir! Welcome to the Airborne Training School, Major!"

I was nearly blown back by his enthusiasm, but managed not to shake his hand or tell him to loosen up.

Sergeant Jenkins loaded the two dozen insulated containers that we would use to ship frozen serum to New York City into the back of his jeep. We drove down a highway crammed with pawn and payday loan shops, bars, fast food joints, and strip clubs. The few patches of ground not taken up by those places were used car lots. I had never seen anything like it.

He drove me to my lodging at the officers' quarters that faced a large oval parade field where troops were drilling.

"I'll be waiting here sir. Your appointment to see Lieutenant Colonel Hazard is at fifteen-thirty sharp, Sir."

"Okay."

"One thing, Sir. With your permission, Sir. Lieutenant Colonel Hazard is by the book, Sir, if you know what I mean. You might want to look to your shoes and uniform. No offense, Sir."

I had no idea what he was talking about.

Sergeant Jenkins gave me a skeptical eyeing over when I returned to the jeep. For ten minutes we drove through a maze of buildings and fields and barracks and pulled up at a World War Two era gymnasium. On each side of the doorway were armed soldiers at attention. As I approached them they raised their guns straight up, the barrel touching the brims of their helmets and snapped "Sir!" in unison. I took a wild guess that I was supposed to salute and not throw my arms up in surrender.

The door entered directly into the gymnasium's basketball court. A square US Army field commander's tent was pitched under one of the backboards, its square front flap held parallel to the floor by two giant African spears. Under the flap Lieutenant Colonel Hazard in khaki shirt and knee-length shorts, pith helmet, and combat boots sat on a canvas director's chair, a table strewn with notebooks and sheaves of documents in front of him.

He glared at me, returned my salute without standing, and told me to get out. "You need a haircut, Major. Go get one and then come back."

"I just got a haircut, Sir."

"At Walter Reed? Get a real haircut Major. You're a disgrace to the uniform."

Sergeant Jenkins was standing behind me, apparently aware from the moment he met me that I was going to need a ride to the post barbershop.

The haircut didn't take long—a bored looking civilian ran an electric razor over my scalp leaving nothing longer than a half inch. I had not previously known how lumpy my skull was.

Back at the field commander's tent I gave what I took to be a snappy salute.

Lieutenant Colonel Hazard tilted back in his canvas chair until the front legs were six inches off the ground.

"What the hell do you want to do to my soldiers, Major. I have read your protocol. I believe in science. I have volunteered for every medical experiment that came along. I have landed in a combat zone with a wire up my ass, I have jumped out of planes with EKG's strapped to my back. I have parachuted hanging upside down with wires going everywhere. I have been scoped and x-rayed and purged and I have given a sample of everything more times than you have kissed your mother. But why the hell do you want to measure a hormone that makes breast milk in my soldiers!"

I had not expected to encounter any resistance to the study at this point, but his questions were entirely reasonable. I couldn't tell him that I needed some kind of research project that had a military purpose. So . . . I calmly told him the story of mother love hormone.

"Well Colonel, prolactin does a lot more than stimulate the production of breast milk. May I ask, sir, if you have children?"

He did.

"You may remember what happened to their mother—your wife—and you may have heard other men talk about this. Prolactin is the hormone that causes nesting behavior in mice and rabbits and squirrels and cats and dogs. In pregnant women, as the time of delivery approaches, they begin to want to repaint rooms and lay in baby supplies—diapers and diaper buckets and wipes and bottles and nipples—all that stuff. In fact, it is infectious."

Lieutenant Colonel Hazard was now nodding in agreement, his forehead wrinkled and his lips pursed.

"Their behavior stimulates all their lady friends to buy them stuff for the baby—group nesting behavior, the baby shower, all that. Women want to hold the baby and cuddle the baby, and make cooing sounds. Just imagine a squad entering a combat zone full of mother love hormone—we wouldn't want that!"

"Well, Colonel, we have discovered that prolactin goes sky high when people are afraid, sky high. What we think, sir, is that we can't measure prolactin levels just before men go into combat, but we can find some part of their training that might be pretty scary. Like jumping out of an airplane for the first time."

By now Lieutenant Colonel Hazard was leaning forward with his mouth half open, a semi-stunned look on his face.

"I had no idea, Major. Really." He paused for a long time. "I never would have thought about that."

No sane person would have thought about it, but I pushed on.

"We know that fear and anger can raise levels of other hormones, and we suspect that prolactin goes up too. But it is possible that the high levels of prolactin in new mothers may be the cause of maternal aggression, leading them to defend their cubs against a threatening intruder. That would be worth knowing, that a high prolactin level in men going into combat wasn't filling them with mother love, but with rage."

Hazard took a deep breath, tipped his chair back again, folded his arms across his chest, and scowled for a moment.

"So, you have said that you want 30 volunteers to have bloods drawn in the evening before their first jump—that would be tonight—and in the morning at breakfast, and then in the transport as they circle around toward the jump zone, and then on the ground as soon as they land, and then about two hours later. Right??

"Yes Sir."

"You got it, Major. Here's what we can do. Jenkins, listen up! We won't have any trouble getting volunteers. Our men will volunteer. We'll have the medics draw their blood tonight as they leave the mess hall. They don't eat before they jump—some of these recruits don't have much flight experience, and if it's bumpy it can get kind of messy in a C-123—but we can get them at the airfield before they load. All the volunteers will be in the first plane, Major, and we can send medics up with them to draw blood in the air. We will put out three large red-cross targets that we use for evacuation helipads and the jumpers will aim for those. The volunteers will be wearing red cross armbands to identify them. On the landing grounds we'll have the medics go right to them and draw blood after they take off their harnesses. And we'll do the final blood draws as they enter the mess hall for lunch. Got that Jenkins?

"Yes sir."

"Thank you, Colonel Hazard. Much appreciated. What would you like me to do?"

"We'll do everything, don't worry about that. But you might want to go down to the barracks and talk with the jumpmasters so that they will know what we will be doing. Jenkins can show you which building. Go now. It's nearly chow time."

I thanked him again and walked out of the gymnasium with Sergeant Jenkins. "Three streets down," he said, " Building 183. Ask them to get the jumpmasters for you. I'll pick you up at 0700 tomorrow to take you to the landing area."

I strolled down the street with my mind a few thousand miles away, found the entrance of the barracks building, walked up a short flight of steps at the top of which sat three enlisted men at a desk, quietly talking. One glanced at me and shot up from the table, shouting "Officer!" as though he had just seen a dragon. The other two shot up with their right hand against their forehead, all three rigid as icicles.

It was like I had set off a spring trap. Here were three men frozen into salutes and I had no idea what to do. I saluted back. They continued to salute.

I thought, "How do I get them unsaluted?" I quickly thought back through all the war movies I had seen as a kid: no answers there. I briefly thought about asking them what I should do, but abandoned that.

I gave, "At ease, soldiers" a try.

They dropped the salute, but still stood bolt upright, staring ahead without eye contact.

"As you were."

That worked. They clasped their hands behind their backs and spread their legs slightly, but they remained averbal, staring straight ahead.

"I would like to talk with the jumpmasters. Can you find them?"

When I got back to Washington, I told the story to the other doctors in the Endocrine Unit. Len Wartofsky said, "They probably had never seen an Army major that close, before. Officers don't walk into enlisteds' quarters. To them you were a space alien just off of your flying saucer. They probably had less of an idea what to do than you did."

The next day went flawlessly. All but one of the volunteers had five tubes of blood drawn. As arranged, the Fort Benning Hospital laboratory spun down all the blood, froze the serum, and shipped the coded tubes in dry ice to Andy's lab.

A few months later I wrote to Lieutenant Colonel Hazard.

"I want to thank you and your men for making our study successful. As we had hypothesized, average serum prolactin levels rose four-fold above baseline immediately after the jump. However, the levels reached were modest compared to a woman about to give birth or nursing a baby. Although prolactin may be the mother love hormone and may be partially responsible for aggressive maternal protective action, it seems unlikely to pose a threat or to be of benefit to US troops."

I never heard back from him.

The three years in Washington DC passed comfortably. We had a very nice family life with very few late evenings for me at the hospital, and with all of my weekends free to be with Margaret and the girls. Every morning I listened to classical music on the public broadcasting station WETA as I drove the half-hour to Walter Reed, and every evening I listened to a brand-new radio news program called *All Things Considered*. I was usually home by 5:30 or 6:00 and helped with dinner and putting the girls to bed. The lawn that I had seeded where there had been thick trees when we moved in had become lush. I set up a jungle gym for the girls, built a few stone walls to create raised garden beds, and planted spring bulbs and roses.

When Christmas came around Margaret suggested that we take the girls to an afternoon family Christmas service. She and I didn't have any religious affiliation after our wedding, and although I was skeptical about all things churchy, I agreed. I had an ill-informed and narrow opinion of her childhood religion, Unitarianism, but agreed to go. In spite of my disbelief in the most literal interpretations of the Christmas story, I loved the music and traditions of Christmas and looked forward to the usual carols and readings. I was dismayed that the Unitarian Church she had picked out of four in the Washington, DC area—the Unitarian Church of Rockville —chose to act out winter religious celebrations of a dozen other faiths, with very little about the Christmas story. I grumped at her the entire way back to our house, as though this was her personal failure: "For Christ's sake, can't the Unitarians relax for one day and just do a traditional Christmas service?"

Nonetheless, a seed was planted that ultimately had far-reaching consequences. Margaret wanted the girls to have exactly the broader religious exposure that the Rockville Church provided. First she, and then both of us began going to Sunday services. Gradually, we began to meet people at UCR we wanted to invite to dinner or go out with.

I was already invested in creating the gardens in our New Jersey and Rockville homes; when a church member donated money to landscape the large grounds at the church, I volunteered to organize the plant purchases and installation, on a scale far beyond what I could do in a private home. Our planting went on for months, often before or after church, or on Saturdays, and I noticed that while I wasn't good at walking up to church members and striking up a conversation, in spite of the church's efforts to encourage it, when working together outside it was easy to talk, easy to learn names and interests. It was my first recognition that churches were not just places for spiritual renewal, but could also become a community that went far beyond that.

In the foreground of our lives were two enormous societal conflicts: the withdrawal of the United States military from Vietnam with the eventual collapse of the South Vietnamese government, and the Watergate scandal. Living in Washington, DC and reading the *Washington Post* rather than the *New York Times*, the great struggles of those years were not just national news, they were our local news.

I was working in an Army Hospital, surrounded by combat soldiers and officers, often caring for patients wounded or stricken with infectious diseases during their Southeast Asian tours. During my summer basic training in Texas, the presidential campaigns of George McGovern and Richard Nixon seemed to pivot around whether the United States could win the war in the face of steady losses to the North Vietnamese, or whether we should even be in the war. McGovern's position was that the US should immediately withdraw, which he promised to do if elected, leaving the fight to the South Vietnamese. Under the pressure of strong and growing protests, particularly on college campuses, and a general sentiment that the US should get out, in 1968 President Nixon began bilateral negotiations with the North Vietnamese for a cease fire and a withdrawal of American troops.

I had hoped that a rapid end to the war would satisfy my hope that the maiming and slaughter of both Americans and Vietnamese would end. Unfortunately, over the next two years, the US provided massive aid to the south, periodically carrying out bombing campaigns against the North. The negotiations broke down repeatedly. By 1973, with the gradual withdrawal of US ground forces, the South Vietnamese army continued to lose ground even faster, and it became clear that the South was going to be overtaken by the North Vietnamese, eventually resulting in chaos as the Catholics and Royalists who provided the bulk of the support for the South Vietnamese government tried to escape to other countries.

In April of 1975 the US began to withdraw the last of its diplomats and military advisors, and in the ensuing bloodbath the North Vietnamese entered Saigon on 30 April, 1975. With that, the American conflict in Southeast Asia that had framed every step of my education and daily life since I had left Montana at the age of 18 with a draft card in my wallet came to an end. I was 34.

The American war in Vietnam had been the headline on the right upper corner of the front page of the *New York Times* and the *Washington Post* for the previous six years, but before Americans had any sense of relief the headlines were swiftly replaced by the investigation of an apparently unsensational break-in at the Democratic National Committee offices in the Watergate Hotel. Details leaked out for months as a growing list of associates of the Republican presidential campaign and many of President Nixon's White House staff were identified as being involved in a poorly executed effort to disable the already wobbly McGovern campaign. Senator McGovern had lost the election by the largest majority in history—520 to 17 Electoral College votes.

While the robbery itself could have ended up with a half-dozen people going to jail for a short time, the cover up of the connections between the burglars, the White House staff, and the president himself were a crime of foundation-shaking magnitude, with each of Nixon's maneuvers leading to ever increasing, and finally successful efforts by the Democratically controlled House of Representative to initiate impeachment hearings.

During a May, 1973 beach vacation at Kitty Hawk with friends who unilaterally declared our cabin a news-free zone, I snuck out several times a day on "errands" so that I could sit in my car and listen to the nationally broadcast impeachment hearings.

For months I had been sending letters to the White House telling Nixon to resign, listing a long string of his lies and his many wrong-headed ideas. This was a tricky thing to do: as an active-duty military officer I was forbidden to express any political sentiment while on duty or in my uniform. But as a private citizen, I could. After writing letters for several months I noticed that our mail no longer arrived as individual envelopes, but as a packet with a rubber band around it; sometimes mail seemed to have taken a longer time to reach me than seemed normal. I checked with neighbors to see if banding the mail was just a habit of a new mailman, but their letters were being delivered without bundling.

When reports circulated about Nixon-dissenters' mail being opened, screened and saved to FBI files, I concluded that I was on a watch list and figured that they would quickly learn that I was an active-duty officer. I stopped writing letters. My paranoia about Nixon was widely shared; there were frequently circulated predictions that if the Congress impeached him, he would declare a national emergency and suspend the Constitution.

After the House Judiciary Committee passed the first of three articles of impeachment, citing obstruction of justice, the Republicans, who controlled the Senate, counted noses and concluded that there were enough votes in the House to pass all three articles and send them to the Senate for a trial, where again it was predicted he would lose. The Republican leadership warned Nixon that there were probably enough votes in the Senate to convict him.

On 8 August, 1974, two years into my Army service, Nixon became the first US president to resign. His vice-president, Gerald Ford, became president. The nation was deeply preoccupied with this political drama, and in Washington DC the latest developments were the news we woke up to and fell asleep with for several more years.

A few months after Nixon's departure, my mail was no longer bundled.

In the fall of 1973, an escalating conflict between the United States and the Middle-Eastern oil producing nations exploded when Egypt and Syria attacked Israel, trying to force them out of Arab land they had occupied after the Six Day War. The United States supplied military equipment and support to Israel's forces, leading the Arab countries to embargo shipments of oil to the west to try to force the United States to give up its support of Israel.

The oil supply from the Middle East fell to 25% of its pre-conflict levels; in the United States there was immediate havoc as oil and gas rationing for automobiles and trucks was imposed to assure adequate supplies for critical industries, schools, hospitals, and home heating. All around the country gas stations would open at 7 AM with a hundred people in line, some having slept overnight in their cars to be in the front of the line. Supplies rarely lasted more than a few hours. Fights broke out when people cut in front of those already in line. Massive carpooling was begun, although the effect on consumption was barely noticeable. The price of gas skyrocketed.

Gas was slightly more available and also less expensive in the District than in Montgomery County. On one occasion I squawked at Margaret because she passed up a station still pumping gas in the afternoon while driving from Washington DC to home because she didn't want to sit in line for two hours. She told me that her time was more valuable than the few dollars she would have saved and we went to bed mad. It was like that in our friends' households as well: for all of us, there were no alternatives to commuting by car.

The country was in turmoil as high fuel prices and low supplies resulted in layoffs; much of discretionary spending by consumers dropped as their dollars went for gas rather than clothes and entertainment and household furnishing. Restaurants, shopping malls, and movie theaters had calamitous declines in customers, as did tourist destinations. Some states banned commercial window and billboard lighting and Christmas tree lighting. In England Prime Minister Heath asked people to heat only one room in their house during the winter.

At the same time, the United States government cut itself free of the gold standard, shaking confidence in the value of the dollar, and that—coupled with the gas shortage and falling business revenue—produced a dramatic crash of the stock market that lasted for more than a year.

In 1973, when Margaret Lea was two and Katharine was three, Margaret began looking for part-time work. A friend at the Unitarian Church told us about a girl in her late teens who was living on her own and needed a job. When Margaret went to work for a guy named Muldoon whose business was just inside the District of Columbia, we hired Jackie as a live-in nanny who did babysitting, drove the girls to preschool, and did some housekeeping.

Muldoon was a consultant to businesses that were trying to obtain government contracts. Margaret's work for Muldoon was to prepare proposals that the firms would submit. Her salary was small, and Muldoon was a difficult employer, expecting Margaret and the several other women who worked there not only to do their assigned work, but to make coffee, fetch lunches, and pour wine during his meetings with clients.

One day Margaret came home from work furious. At noon when she took a break to go out to buy something for lunch, she had asked Muldoon if she could pick up lunch for him. He declined. A few minutes after she ate and had resumed work on a proposal with an approaching deadline, he told her to get lunch for him. She refused, reminding him that a half-hour before she had offered to pick up lunch for him and he had declined. He ordered her to get his lunch, or he would fire her. Already annoyed with Muldoon because of the way he treated her and the other women in the firm, she told him he didn't need to fire her because she was quitting.

It didn't take Margaret long to radically improve her situation. While searching for other possibilities, she discovered that Montgomery County School System was mandated by the Maryland state government to teach high school students about sexuality, pregnancy, and family planning but was dissatisfied with what was available commercially and had decided to make its own curriculum. Margaret applied for the position, acknowledging that she had never created a curriculum but pointing out that she studied biology at Harvard, had a masters' degree in teaching, had taught high school science, and that she had a year and half of experience producing educational slide-tapes for Encyclopedia Britannica.

She was given the job, which involved not only mastering the biology of reproduction and the data about each of the methods of contraception, but also creating a curriculum that would meet the objections of those parents who were passionately opposed to contraception and school-provided information about sexuality. Over the next two years she met with dozens of groups that had an interest in what was to be put before students and gradually she negotiated a curriculum that won approval of the parental advisory groups on both sides of the issue. It quickly became a standard for other school systems. Margaret was largely on her own clock, the drive was much shorter and the people she worked with were supportive.

After Jackie had been living with us and taking care of the girls for six months, we decided to go on our first trip without them, taking advantage of one of the "fringe benefits" of military service, travel to other parts of the world in planes of the Military Airlift Command. Many of the other doctors had done it and portrayed it as simple and cheap: all we needed to do was pack our suitcases and drive to Dover Air Force Base in Delaware, park our car, walk into the small passenger terminal and request that we be put on standby for flights to Germany. The flights generally left late at night. We arrived about 6 PM, signed in, and showed our passports and my military ID. We were told that we could get a room in a close-by officers' lodging building for eight dollars and should return to the desk about 8 PM. At 9:00 we were told that there were seats on a huge C5A transport that could hold six Apache helicopters or six Bradley fighting vehicles or two battle tanks, as well as seat 70 troops on its upper deck above the cargo hold. As we boarded a small bus for the two-mile drive to where the plane was parked, we passed through a file of armed soldiers and German shepherds. There were more dogs and armed soldiers at the steep stairway to the cargo deck, and from there we ascended a ladder to the upper deck. Once seated on hard metal benches, an Air Force sergeant introduced himself as our "stewardess" and handed out two boxes of rations to each of us, plus heavy-duty earplugs and life jackets. He told us that we might have trouble knowing when the plane had left the ground and was in flight, but he would tell us when we could get out of our benches to use the latrines. After an hour we could feel the aircraft was moving. That went on for a long time and then for two hours we were motionless. The earplugs were effective and we could hear almost nothing. We dozed uncomfortably.

When our stewardess appeared again, he motioned for us to take out our earplugs.

"My apologies to officers, troops, and family members. We are going to offload you. We had a delay getting flight and landing clearance and the crew cycled beyond their flight time limits. We are back where we started. Please check with the passenger flight desk to get information about when the next flights might be."

We had never gotten off the ground.

We headed back to our quarters and fell asleep at 3 AM,

The next night we returned again and went through the same drill, except this time after crossing the airfield in the bus, loading into the cargo hold and climbing the ladder to the upper deck, the C5A began to move it steadily rolled out the several miles of runways, turned, and without much of a force pushing us back into our benches, at some point we were airborne. The sense of motion and the noise were the same as they had been on the runway.

It was late; there were no amenities on the plane and it was up to us to make ourselves comfortable. The seasoned soldiers fell asleep quickly; a few played cards. We slept fitfully on the unpadded steel seats without pillows or blankets or headrests.

There were no windows in the passenger deck; the only indication that we had entered into European airspace and that it was morning was a message from out sergeant that we would be landing at Rhein–Main Air Base near Frankfurt hour at zero-eight-hundred hours.

We had taken off on the trip with very little planning. Having been to Europe eight years earlier, we had assumed that we would arrive at an airport, exchange our travelers' checks for Deutsche marks, and take a bus or local train into Frankfurt, where we would change to the German train system to travel to Munich.

Every assumption was wrong. We landed at an enormous US Airforce Base where the language was American, the money was American, the food was American, and there were neither an airport building nor a clear way to get into Frankfurt. We knew that we would need German currency to use local transportation, but there was no obvious place to change money.

A helpful clerk inside the tiny arrival building told us that if we stood on the road outside a bus would come by periodically that made stops around the base and then at the commercial airfield to the east.

We had only the slightest idea of how to tour in Germany. I was still in my Army uniform and quickly changed when we got to the civilian air terminal, while Margaret found a currency exchange and directions to the Frankfurt train station where we could get tickets for Munich.

It was mid-afternoon by the time we started or journey. Our first look at Germany was from the windows of our coach. I was stunned to discover that every small plot of land on either side of the rail tracks was filled with small vegetable gardens fenced off from each other and neatly laid out, each with a small hut for tools and storage. It was winter and only the tops of root vegetables and heaped rows of straw gave a hint of how much they would grow as the season advanced. I was surprised to see that, mile after mile, every square foot of soil was utilized, apparently with no concern about the trains whizzing by no more than a few dozen meters away.

The trip took us through Nuremberg and finally, after four hours, into Munich Central Station. I had made reservations in an inexpensive hotel not far from the central station that I had found in a guidebook. We searched for fifteen minutes around the street listed in the guidebook, but saw nothing that resembled a hotel. Finally, we spotted a wooden door with a small placard with the hotel's name. We rang a bell, and a buzzer indicated that the door was open. We climbed up to the second floor in what we had taken to be a small office building, and found a tiny waiting area and desk in a very modern space; a young man who spoke fluent English quickly checked us in. Our room was very clean, very modern, and very small, with neat wood paneling and furniture, a tiny bathroom, and a tiny window looking out at nothing but the building next door.

We were asleep in fifteen minutes.

Our first morning in Munich we had a simple breakfast of bread, apricot preserve, and tea in the lobby and then went out in search of the Munich

Cathedral, the Frauenkirche. It was a weekday and we hadn't expected there to be crowds going in or out, but in fact there wasn't a single person in sight. We climbed the stairs to the main entrance and pushed on the massive door to open it—but it was locked, and on the door had been tacked a slip of paper with the words, "Geschlossen für Fasching".

This meant nothing to us and we circled the cathedral looking for doors that were open, but there were none.

We walked through the city to the art museum, the Alte Pinakothek, but found it closed too, and again there was the "Geschlossen für Fasching" sign. The streets now were full of people, but in casual clothes, and when we went to a beer hall to try the fabled Bavarian beer, wursts, and dark bread, every table was jammed: no one seemed to be working, and most were totally schnockered. Beer hall after beer hall, it was the same: crowded to barely even standing room, and it was still an hour until noon. We wondered what kind of country this was. Where were all the industrious, disciplined Germans? We couldn't spot even one who was sober, on a work day!

We inquired at the hotel about the signs and found that we had stumbled into Munich's Fasching, or Karneval, the equivalent of Mardi Gras; everything was closed and would be for days: schools, churches, museums.

The temperatures had hovered around freezing all day, and with light winds the cold was piercing. Discouraged, we went back to our room and thought about our options. When we left Dover we had been told that it could take several days to get a flight back, because there were troops and officers who had been pulled out of Vietnam and the Pacific airfields, naval stations, and supply posts trying to get back home. I suggested we give up on Munich and return to Frankfurt and get our names in a queue for return flights.

The next day at Rhein-Main Air Base we checked in and were told there would be nothing available until at least the next day. We also discovered that although I was a major, I would be outranked by all the more senior officers who signed on after me, and by anyone traveling on orders rather than holiday.

We decided to spend the rest of the day in grey, stolid Frankfurt and spent chilly hours wandering around a grey city. We were able to visit a museum and the city hall, but clearly late February wasn't high tourist season there either.

The next morning as we began our wait for flights, Margaret called Jackie to check that everything was going well and to give her our plans for returning. On the phone Jackie sounded cheerful but then disappeared and, in a few minutes, came back on the phone sounding shook. She had been starting a bath for the girls and when she answered the phone left the bath running until, while talking to Margaret, she heard a little voice calling out "Jackie" with some urgency and found the girls, two and a half and four, sitting in water that was getting very high and that they couldn't get out of the tub by themselves.

With that we felt desperate to get home, and trapped. We went back to see what our chances were of getting out. Finding that the situation wasn't hopeful, we explained our situation to the enlisted woman manning the desk, who suggested that we try going over to the Frankfurt Airport to see if we could get on a Davis Air flight, a contract airline that offered low-cost flights between Europe and the United States for families and other military personnel not traveling on orders. For $190 we got tickets. We boarded and sat for a long time until it was announced that the flight was delayed until the next day. Davis Air put us up in an old chateau, fed us an excellent dinner, and bed us down in high-ceiling, antique furnished rooms with hot baths and the best smelling soap I had ever encountered. We got breakfast the next morning after sleeping in pillowy beds.

All in all, we probably had close to the worst possible experience with hitching a ride on a military transport except, of course, for the poor guys being carried back to the states broken and those who were heading out for tough postings.

The kids were okay when we got back, but we had lost our confidence in Jackie and equally had lost any further interest in taking off without the girls with us.

To this day I can call up the smell of the soap and linen and pillows in that German Chateau.

My day-to-day responsibilities at Walter Reed fell short of the level of teaching and clinical practice that I wanted. As a staff member of the research institute, I didn't automatically have an opportunity to take care of patients in the general medical clinics or attend on the wards teaching the residents and the Georgetown medical students who were doing medicine clerkships at Walter Reed. Our only clinical responsibilities were to staff a clinic where we saw patients with endocrine disorders and to attend on the inpatient endocrinology consult service two months a year.

I learned that I would be welcome making teaching rounds on the Howard Medical School wards at D.C. General Hospital and twice a year I attended there, encountering a level of complexity similar to the inpatient teaching services at Columbia-Presbyterian, but with patients who had even fewer health care resources and lower incomes.

As a clinician and teacher, I longed to get back to New York City.

With most evenings and all my weekends free, we were meeting people outside of the hospital and building a community, largely through our regular attendance at the Rockville Unitarian Church. The catalyst that got me back into a religious community was the non-creedal nature of Unitarian- churches: we were not told what to believe—what was right and what was wrong, or that there was just one way to understand how life came to be, or only one way to discern truth. We were not required to believe in a listening, intervening god, or in the divinity of Christ, or the certainty that there was an afterlife that we had to earn or that already had been awarded or denied. Unitarian congregations encouraged members to figure out for themselves what they believed in. The services explored, endlessly, the contradictions of our culture, the nature of people's search for truth and meaning, and the conflicts between what was delivered as true about America's values and the palpable reality of the injustice and inequality in our imperfect country. Our minister, Bill Moore, had marched in the south with others in the civil rights movement, as had a number of our congregation. Social action was very much part of the Rockville and the other Washington, DC area Unitarian churches. While I had been aware of the civil rights struggles over the previous ten years, my attention was overwhelmed by being a medical student and resident. It was only now, with much more time to experience what was going on in the country, that I began to wrestle with some of the deficits and fallacies in my understanding of the United States.

After I forgave them for taking Christmas out of the Christmas service, I enjoyed the low-key provocations of minister and congregation alike. In medical school, residency, and fellowship, almost all of our friendships were with doctors and their partners. Although I don't remember being aware of it at the time, the Rockville church was my first experience of a community to which I was not connected by school or work, a community in which it didn't matter where I had gone to school or what my profession was. The people in the church spent very little time asking about our lineage or where we had traveled or vacationed—or where we had grown up. In time I found that our friends there were teachers and secretaries and lawyers and dieticians and engineers and government employees; a lot were working mothers and many were single parents, men and women raising children by themselves.

I learned how to hug people and how to be hugged without stammering and blushing. We were invited to informal dinner parties and asked to picnics. Soon it became habit to spend Sunday mornings in Rockville.

Around 1973 the two organizations supervising and certifying the training of internists determined that residents in many programs were not getting enough exposure to undifferentiated patients for whom they made the initial diagnosis and wrote the orders for diagnosis and treatment. Instead, they were only carrying out the instructions of specialists instead of having the responsibility for independently making the diagnosis and initiating management. To counteract this, residency programs were mandated to minimize specialty ward experiences for training and expand both inpatient and outpatient general internal medicine exposure.

During my last year in the Army, I began to get calls from friends from our days together as residents asking if I would be interested in looking at a job as a general internist at the medical school or teaching hospital where they were now on the faculty.

The first invitation came from my former attending in general medicine at the University of Chicago, John Thompson, who was now head of general medicine at the University of Iowa and wanted me to help create a new division. I turned him down, but was flattered.

Alan Robinson, with whom I had shared space in Andy Frantz's lab, had moved to the University of Pittsburgh where the chairman, Jim Leonard, was looking for someone who could teach students and residents on the new general medicine wards and take care of private patients. Alan pitched the attractions of Pittsburg to me and asked me to take a look. I accepted.

Bob and T Gongaware, who were now in Savannah, Georgia, where T taught medicine and Bob practiced surgery with T's father, wanted us to join them in Savannah. Bob and T had been good friends when we were all training at Columbia and I accepted that invitation too.

The most critical invitation came through Bill MacLean. Bill had called me the summer before he and I were supposed to start practicing with Dr. Southworth to tell me that he had decided to stay in Alabama when he finished his cardiology fellowship. He had chaffed under the pressures of his mother and father when he was growing up in New York City; after living in Alabama for a few years with his wife Ann and several children, he had decided that he didn't want to return to New York City after all. Instead, he suggested that I join him at the University of Alabama in Birmingham. A few months later, the chairman of medicine at UAB called to invite me to Birmingham.

The calls coming to me were a direct reflection of the difficulty that department chairs were having in finding enough young faculty members who were comfortable practicing and teaching general internal medicine. Graduates of the Columbia residencies were in demand to lead or start divisions of general internal medicine—my former chief resident Dick Byyny was recruited to lead the general medicine division, first at the University of Chicago and later at the University of Colorado. A resident who was a few years ahead of me was recruited from the Columbia teaching services at Bellevue and Harlem to start a general medicine division at Beth Israel in Boston. Now I was being recruited.

Although my heart was set on returning to Columbia, I visited Savannah, Birmingham, and Pittsburgh in the fall of 1974. None of the opportunities were attractive enough for me to even briefly consider not returning to Columbia, although Dr. James, Dr. Leonard, and the Gongawares would all ring me up on the phone to make a second try a few years later.

Len Wartofsky and Jerry Earle asked me to consider staying in the Army at Walter Reed. Jerry, Len, Dick Diamond and several of our fellows who stayed on as staff were planning on a twenty-year Army career. One of the major stresses for Army doctors who wanted stable schools for their children and long-term friendships was that the Army could at any moment swoop in and send them someplace else where they were needed. For career-oriented physicians at Walter Reed the choice wasn't staying at Walter Reed or returning to a university job, it was trying to stay in Washington and avoiding being sent to other Army teaching hospitals.

My goals and plans were different in several ways. Staying in the Army was never a consideration—my time at Walter Reed was a holding action between leaving Columbia and returning to Columbia. Len and most of the other endocrinologists were serious scientists for whom the Army provided the substantial benefit of funding for research without going through the challenging process of obtaining NIH funding in competition with all of the rest of the scientists in the United States. Since Len had grown up in DC and was now a full colonel, this was his equivalent of a medical school career. For me Walter Reed lacked almost all of the fascinating aspects of Columbia—in particular teaching the residents and students who were in the same clerkships and residencies that I had trained in and practicing side by side with surgeons, pediatricians, obstetricians, psychiatrists, neurologists, neurosurgeons, and orthopedic surgeons—doctors I had admired as a student and resident, who were providing lifetime care for the patients in their practices and for patients referred from around the United States for rare or complicated problems.

To my surprise, in our last months I began to feel regretful that we would be leaving Washington. Beyond the friendships with some of my colleagues at Walter Reed, we now had friendships to which Margaret and I contributed equally. Margaret and I liked living in Maryland, close to the museums, theaters and concert halls of Washington, DC. We found it less intense than New York City, and considerably less crowded.

We had been living with my acceptance of the offer to return to Columbia literally from the moment we arrived in Washington, DC. Beyond looking at the several jobs that my friends suggested to me, I was blinkered—I didn't want to stay in the Army, and there was nothing about the three medical schools in Washington, DC—Georgetown, Howard, and George Washington—that tempted me to even contact them. As had happened with my decision to leave the University of Chicago and return to Columbia to continue my residency, it was my desire to practice and teach at Columbia and live in New York City that was driving our departure. Margaret was willing to return to New York City again, if that was what I wanted to do, although she would happily have stayed in Maryland.

In the spring of 1975, just a few months before returning to New York City, we attended a concert of the National Symphony Orchestra, led by Mistislav Rostropovich, who played and conducted all three of the Haydn cello concerti in one evening. For the previous five years Rostropovich had been banned from performing outside of the Soviet Union because of his support of the dissenting author Alexander Solzhenitsyn. In 1974, the

Soviet leader Leonid Brezhnev exiled him and banned any mention of his name. Recordings and reviews of his concerts were expunged. When exiled he landed in the West where he gave historic performances, the first of which we heard. When the orchestra was seated and had tuned, Rostropovich bounded onto the stage and in a single motion —cello in his left hand, bow in his right—swept the bow to give the downbeat, sat, and began playing. His performances were frenetic, all without the scores in front of him. After each concerto the audience went crazy.

In spite of the humiliating defeat in Vietnam, the tragedy of thousands of South Vietnamese who were unable to escape, the forced resignation of President Nixon, and the unhealed wounds of the anti-war and civil rights conflicts, there was excitement in Washington in those years. The cold war was at its peak, with the western nations pushing back hard against Chinese and Russian expansionism, and artists, writers and musicians were fiercely in the heart of the battle to take down autocratic governments.

My three years had been unexpectedly happy and productive. I wrapped up my final weeks with a sense of great optimism and anticipation about returning to Columbia and New York City.

Our house sold easily. In early August our furniture was moved to Englewood, New Jersey, where we would be living. I spent a week with Margaret unpacking and arranging furniture, and then I returned to finish out my final few weeks in the Army while Margaret drove north with the girls for a vacation with her parents in Newburyport.

I spent a week sleeping in Dick Dimond's guest room and another week sleeping in the Wartofsky home while they were on vacation.

On my last night I stayed with an endocrinologist who had joined us the previous year, John MacIndoe, and his wife Maddy. As a sort of three-person celebration of my Army discharge, John offered me some marijuana that he was growing in his attic under lights. I had never tried marijuana and thought, "Why not?"

He showed me to their basement recreation room that was outfitted with a slide projector, a big screen, a Wi-Fi sound system, and a waterbed.

He flipped on a slide show with psychedelic images and music and said goodnight. After I turned off the lights, their huge St. Bernard wandered downstairs, and, as appeared to be his habit, jumped onto the waterbed with me. For three hours the show, the heaving waterbed, and the pot did an unpleasant number on me. The weed experience was weird and I never smoked or ate it again.

I drove up to Englewood the next day, now feeling euphoric, with my "real career" about to start. My plan had been to spend a night there, and then to drive up to Newburyport to join Margaret. Instead, I found that the house had been broken into and a small TV removed.

Welcome back to New York City and the career of my dreams.

Clearing trees from the back yard in Maryland and splitting the logs into firewood, just before being inducted into the Army Medical Corps. With Katharine, 1972

As an Army Medical Corps Major, Official Army photo, Fort Sam Houston, Texas, August 1972

Bedtime stories in Rockville MD with Katharine and Margaret Lea, 1973

Photos

Easter in Rockville, 1974

Learning the Art of Medicine: Two Promises

1975 - 1978

CHAPTER 25

Starting Private Practice at Columbia

About a month before returning to New York City I dreamed that I was beginning my first day in practice at the Atchley Pavilion. In the dream, my announcements had gone out a month earlier and the Department of Medicine had given my name to patients looking for a doctor at Presbyterian Hospital. In the morning of my first day of practice, I walked into my office wearing a new, very stiff long white coat, my best grey-striped flannel suit pants—a little warm for September—a new Oxford cloth white shirt with button down collar and a new bow tie. My Oxford shoes were newly shined.

I asked my secretary if I had any appointments. "One," she said, "At 2:30." That would be a long wait, so I walked into the waiting room used for the two dozen other practices on our floor—it was jammed with patients, overflowing with patients. I looked for any patient that might be mine but there weren't any.

No one called all day to make a new appointment. None of the surgeons or neurologists called to ask me to consult on one of their hospitalized patients.

In the dream, on that first day I saw one patient. The second was worse—no patients. I walked down the hall from office to office knocking on doors to see if my announcements had been received. No one knew. No one recognized me, no one smiled.

And so it went for days and days. I tried desperately to attract patients, going so far as standing on the corner of Broadway and 168th Street where people coming out of the subway could see me, with a signboard, front and back saying "Gordon Noel MD announces the opening of his office," but still no one came.

I had this dream almost every night right up until my first actual day in practice—and I continued to have it off and on for years: the doctor with sixteen years of medical education and experience who no one wanted to see.

In the early spring of 1975 Presbyterian Hospital had started my credentialing process. It was a "closed hospital"—that is, only physicians with an appointment by the medical board of the Presbyterian Hospital and a faculty position at the College of Physicians and Surgeons could have a practice at the medical center and admit patients who needed hospitalization.

There were dozens of community hospitals scattered around New York City's five boroughs, each dependent on local practitioners admitting their patients to stay in business. The physicians only had to have a medical license and provide proof of being trained to do whatever procedures they admitted their patients for.

The academic medical centers limited their private practice staff to those physicians who they felt were appropriate to teach their residents and students and who offered unique skills. At Columbia, in each department—medicine, pediatrics, surgery, obstetrics and gynecology, dermatology— there was a private practice group hand-selected to practice in the Atchley Pavilion and to admit their patients to the private service in Harkness Pavilion. Physicians who spent the majority of their time doing research did not have private practices, although along with the private practitioners, they were the attending physicians supervising the residents on the teaching wards of Presbyterian Hospital and in the

Vanderbilt Clinic where patients who did not have insurance were cared for.

Most of those who received admitting privileges were graduates of Presbyterian Hospital residencies, although occasionally a physician who had a skill needed to provide comprehensive, up-to-date care at the Medical Center would be recruited from another teaching hospital.

For credentialing I sent the medical board my curriculum vitae, and made copies of my college, medical school, and fellowship training diplomas, obtained letters of recommendation from several of the physicians who practiced at Columbia, filled out forms detailing whether I had ever been sued or denied hospital privileges or had my medical license suspended or used drugs or had committed felonies.

Once the Presbyterian Hospital Medical Board had granted me privileges in internal medicine and endocrinology, Dr. Southworth advised me to have letterhead stationery and business cards printed. He suggested that I mail printed notes to the entire clinical faculty to notify them that I was beginning a practice. They looked like this:

GORDON L. NOEL M.D.
Announces the opening of his office for the
Practice of Internal Medicine and Endocrinology
Atchley Pavilion 220
Columbia-Presbyterian Medical Center

When the boxes of stationery and business cards and announcements arrived in Maryland, I was excited that after four years of college and four years of medical school and three years of residency and two years of fellowship and three years of military service I was finally crossing the threshold into both a professional career and a stable home and family life. After six moves, three apartments, and two houses, I expected our third house to be where we would spend the rest of our lives.

As the letters went off to the venerable department of medicine faculty members, many of whom I had revered as a student and resident, I became apprehensive and started to have the nightmares that no one would want to be my patient. Many of the private physicians were among the most famous surgeons and internists and gynecologists and ophthalmologists and orthopedic surgeons in New York City, some nationally or internationally renowned. They had done first-ever operations, invented procedures, discovered new treatments, performed the first catheterizations of the human heart, and some of the first open heart surgeries. They sat on education and licensing boards, testified at the U.S. Congress, took care of presidents and sheiks and movie stars and famous actors and musicians. I had twinges of apprehension that I didn't belong in their league.

On my real first day of practice, Wednesday, 3 September, 1975, I had morning office hours and an afternoon Endocrinology clinic. I was dressed more or less the way I had been in my dream: suit, button-down white shirt, bowtie, and Oxford shoes, my rendition of the East Coast uniform of propriety and expertise.

Dr. Southworth had secured for Tom Jacobs and me the consultation and examination rooms directly across the hall from where he and his very seasoned secretary, Mrs. Brooks, had their offices. Dr Southworth's office had windows; ours, on the inside of the building, did not, but it was otherwise fully equipped for us to start our practice.

Mrs. Brooks, unaware of my nightmares, greeted me warmly: "Good morning Dr. Noel. I like your bow tie. You have your first patient waiting."

"Ah! I have a patient! How did they find me?"

"She called the hospital and got your name. Tell me when you are ready to have me bring her to your office."

"Would it be okay if I went to the waiting room and got her myself?"

"Of course, that would be fine."

"I rather like meeting a new patient on neutral ground, and I can learn a certain amount just seeing them sitting and then walking in with me."

"Sure. Here's her chart."

Miss Brooks handed me a manila folder with a single sheet of the hospital's progress notepaper inside. "Julie Wolfson" was written on the tab.

I walked into the examination room to see what supplies were in each drawer and to figure out how to raise and lower the table and attach the stirrups for a pelvic exam. I found where the gloves and the materials for drawing bloods and getting urine samples were. There was a blood pressure cuff attached to the wall, and beside that an ophthalmoscope for examining eyes and otoscope for examining ears. A cart beside the examination table held a jar of tongue depressors and a jar of long-handled cotton swabs on top and several drawers with vaginal speculums, examination gloves, Vaseline, glass slides, and tissues.

Our consultation room was attached to the examination room and was barren except for a desk, an office chair, and two chairs for patients. I was a little embarrassed to be so proud of this stark, plain little office.

I took a deep breath, looked at myself in the mirror to be sure my bowtie wasn't cockeyed, and walked down the hall to the waiting room.

Among the dozen or so waiting patients, it wasn't obvious who Miss or Mrs. Wolfson was.

"Julie Wolfson."

A slender woman about my age and a few inches shorter stood up. She had straight brown hair and was wearing a navy polka dot blouse with a bow at the neck and buttons at the cuff, a grey pencil skirt, and low black heels.

"I'm Julie Wolfson."

I reached out to shake her hand. She seemed surprised but took mine, and I motioned her to walk ahead of me back down the hall. I showed her into the office, told her to take either chair, and walked around behind the desk.

I opened her chart and took my fountain pen out of my white coat's breast pocket.

"May I ask why you've come in?"

"Sure, I want a checkup to be sure I'm in good health."

"Okay. And will you want me to do a pelvic exam and pap smear."

"Especially that."

"So, I would like to ask some questions about your health and family, and then I'll examine you. Is that what you expected?"

"Yes."

"And do you have any particular concerns."

"Yes I do. I actually think I am in good health, and I don't have any complaints. I've been married for 14 years, right out of college, and I've had two kids, both of whom are doing fine — ordinary kids, nothing special, but doing fine. My husband still works in the same office that I met him in when I was hired to be their receptionist, an insurance office in Leona. Mike's a nice guy. He's always been kind and he does a good job with the kids, and he's fine too."

"About three years ago, when Kiki, my little one, was in the seventh grade, I decided to go back to work, but I wanted to be more than a receptionist. So I found a job in a corporation near Columbus Circle and started as a secretary. I've moved up a few times because I'm really good at what I do."

"But, I've decided that I want more in life. I'm bored. Mike is nice, but he is incredibly uninteresting." She paused for a moment as if considering what to say next. "So, here's why I am here. I want to know that I am in good health and not about to be sick with anything, and then I want to move to higher secretarial jobs in my company. I want to have fun and I intend to sleep with whoever I need to and do whatever it will take to get me there."

I was stunned, as I frequently was in practice. My impression of her when I met her was that she was rather mousey, neither especially attractive nor well dressed. That she rolled out this story to a prim-looking, bespectacled young bow-tie wearing physician changed my mind about what "mousey" predicted. I had already grown used to patients telling me, a perfect stranger, intimate and sometimes alarming details of their life just because I was wearing doctor clothes and carried that title.

I did my usual complete examination. I always asked women if they wanted me to get a chaperone for their breast and pelvic exams; most declined a chaperone, as she did.

Back in my office, I told her she seemed healthy and that I would call her in a few days with the results of the routine screening tests we had agreed on.

"So, there is no physical reason for me not to change my life?"

"None whatsoever. How do you think this will work with your family?"

"I doubt that my husband will even notice, and my kids are wrapped up in their own lives and aren't paying attention. If I'm going to have a rewarding life, I'll have to do it on my own. And if it blows up, well, the kids are almost out of the house already."

She thanked me, and asked, "Can I come back if anything medical comes up?"

"Of course."

"Mrs. Brooks told me that you had just returned from the Army and that today was your first day in practice. I'm happy that I am your first patient."

By the time Tom Jacobs joined me in the Atchley office in mid-September, my office hours were about half full and I was eager to start our practice together. Tom was as relaxed and straightforward now as he had been in residency: warm, funny, with a dry sense of humor, unassuming, unpretentious, grateful for what he had. After serving in Vietnam he spent one more year in a stateside post, and then went to the University of Washington to finish his residency and become a fellow in one of the most famous endocrinology programs in the country.

When Bill Maclean decided not to come back to New York City to practice with me, Dr. Southworth asked if I had any suggestions about who might replace Bill. I mentioned Tom and told Dr. Southworth what Tom's many strengths were and that I would love practicing with him. With Dr. Southworth's approval, I called Tom and asked if he would be interested.

Tom was thrilled and it was agreed that when he finished in Seattle, he would return to Columbia.

Our plan was that I would see patients in our office on three mornings a week; Tom would take the other two mornings in the office and also see patients there one afternoon. Our practices would be identical—internal medicine and endocrinology, with three months of inpatient ward attending during which we would not schedule patients between 10 and 12 in the mornings and a weekly general internal medicine clinic and a weekly endocrinology clinic. We would each be the attending for endocrinology consultation rounds once or twice a year. We were offered identical salaries of $37,500 a year, which could be increased by 70% of anything we earned after our startup debt, salary, parking, the departmental 20% cut, and office overhead were paid. We were told that most of the new physicians in the past few years started to receive something above their base salary in about two years. Columbia also paid us $3000 a year for our attending round months and our two afternoons a week of seeing uninsured patients in the clinic. Those arrangements seemed fine to both of us.

I suggested to Tom that we hang our credentials on the office wall: college and medical school diplomas, certificates from our training programs, board certifications, and licenses.

He called those things "patient fodder" and declined to put up anything other than his license and his board certification documents, a level of unpretentiousness that didn't surprise me. On the other hand, I framed and hung up everything, including my Harvard and Columbia diplomas and residency certificates. We agreed to keep several medicine textbooks in the office for references. Otherwise, we didn't spend anything on furniture or decoration.

Another task was to establish ourselves with insurance companies, primarily Blue Shield. Two practitioners who had begun a few years before us advised us to set our fees high, because once Blue Shield paid us at the rate we chose they wouldn't pay us more.

"What should we charge?"

"Well, most of us charge $75 for a new patient workup that takes an hour, and $25 for a half hour follow up visit. Same for a new patient workup in the hospital, and then $25 for seeing the patient every day."

"And if we see a patient several times a day?"

"Still, just $25 a day, no matter how much time you spend."

It was hard to find out what the Blue Shield rates were—they didn't publish them for physicians to see, because they feared that everyone would simply charge the maximum. However, I managed to get ahold of the Blue Shield codes. For internal medicine there was a half page: new and continuing hospital and office visits, and then a few fees for procedures: rigid sigmoidoscopy, rigid esophagoscopy, ECG interpretation, pulmonary function tests, spinal tap, liver biopsy, thoracentesis, paracentesis, joint aspiration, cardioversion. General internists did a few of those procedures, but for the most part only specialists did them. Cardiologists had several procedures beside interpreting ECGs: exercise tests, the infrequent cardiac catheterizations for valvular disease, and conversion of irregular heart rates. General internists and endocrinologists were paid at the same rate, so that the fellowships that Tom and I had done didn't result in higher incomes.

I flipped through the code book: for orthopedics the codes went on for pages, and the same was true for surgeons and gynecologists, and urologists: every procedure had a code, and every variant of that procedure another code, and most operations were broken down into a half dozen parts, from preoperative prepping through incision and various maneuvers during the operation and closing.

During our first months Tom and I learned the ins and outs of fee-based practice. We had been warned that we wouldn't see our first reimbursement for six months. Since Columbia was paying us a regular salary, our debt for the salary they gave us and paying for our overhead grew steadily. After six months of seeing office patients three half days a week and up to ten inpatients every day, insurance companies had reimbursed me the lordly sum of $7000. It wasn't until February of 1976 that our incoming reimbursements from insurance companies began to approach our monthly salary, which was less than half of the department's support of our salary, overhead, and the 20% tax collected by the Department of Medicine.

Initially we had no expense for our secretarial support—Dr. Southworth contributed Mrs. Brooks' time to book our patients, paste in the lab and radiology reports, and file our notes. I regarded her with awe: she was working for the most elegant and famous physician (as far as I knew) in New York City, and certainly at Columbia-Presbyterian. She was calm, a bit sarcastic, helpful, and protective. If she thought patients calling in to see one of us might be difficult, she deferred them "until there is an opening." She asked every patient if they had seen other doctors at the Medical Center and if she found that a patient had shopped around for doctors or for the advice they wanted, or failed to pay their bills, she also put them on her waiting list, which, curiously never had an opening. There weren't many of these patients and after a while, we simply trusted her to make the decisions about which patients she thought we had best not take on.

When our practices got busier and we had insurance payments coming in, Mrs. Brooks asked if we wanted her to look around for our own secretary. We did, and within a few weeks she found Marcy Nolan, who, with Dr. Southworth and Mrs. Brooks, taught us how to practice.

Marcy had grown up in a prosperous family in Alpine, an affluent suburb of New Jersey north of Englewood. She had gone to private schools and college, but hadn't planned on a definite career. When an obstetrician who was a family friend offered her a job in his Atchley Pavilion office, she went to work for him. Mrs. Brooks knew all the other secretaries and when Marcy's boss retired she nabbed her before other doctors could hire her.

Marcy later told me that she took our job rather than working for one of the crusty old doctors who tried to recruit her because Tom and I, though entirely hopeless, were sweet. Marcy was as efficient and sassy as Mrs. Brooks and therefore a perfect roommate to share her office. Marcy reorganized our files, took over all the billing, screened patients calling for appointments, and made dozens of suggestions about what we needed to do: "When you see a patient in the office at the request of another physician, you always write them a letter," she told me, "both thanking them and summarizing your findings and recommendations." She handed me her revision of a letter to an ophthalmologist who referred a patient in which I simply gave a summary of my findings and recommendations. Marcy's version now started: "Thank you for referring your delightful patient, Mrs. Ferguson, for her troubling complaint of intractable and socially embarrassing gassiness." From there the letter went on to explain the chewing, swallowing, and dietary changes I had recommended, and concluded with thanking him again and telling him that I would be ready to fit Mrs. Ferguson into my schedule anytime she needed further clinical evaluation.

Marcy said that I should say this even though Mrs. Ferguson was confused, had brought in a long list of problems that she complained no doctor had ever adequately addressed, and promptly argued with everything I recommended.

Marcy then sent me home with a sheaf of letters that Mrs. Brooks culled from Dr. Southworth's files with his stately prose, detailed findings, and invariably a reference to something he had in common with both the referring doctor and the patient, both of whom often shared his New York City or Yale College or Johns Hopkins backgrounds.

In return I got back similar letters from physicians to whom I referred patients that I knew to be constitutionally unable to answer any question without starting ten years back in time, thanking me for sending them such a charming, interesting person.

Marcy once said to Tom, "What would you think about getting newer shoes than the Hushpuppies you wore as a resident?" She told us that doctors always had rundown shoes that they were reluctant to discard because they were comfortable. Tom declined her fashion tips.

Marcy could wangle an appointment for our patients with other Medical Center specialists whose practices were "full"; she could find spots on the radiology schedule for a speedier study; and she could cajole our cranky and chronically put-out floor nurse to help us with minor procedures and pelvic examinations when a chaperone was needed, even though we hadn't booked it ahead of time.

After a few months Marcy was essentially our third practitioner, gentle and understanding on the phone when patients called with billing problems or a need to talk to one of us urgently or needing advice about who they could see at the Medical Center for this or that.

Both Tom and I saw many patients whose insurance for private care was marginal, often requiring them to pay a substantial portion of their bill: we would send a bill for $75 for a first visit; three or four months later their insurance would pay $25 or $30 and the patient would receive a second bill from the Medical Center for the unpaid balance. Usually the patient could pay the balance, but sometimes Marcy got calls from patients saying they couldn't pay all or any of it. Marcy could sort those with the capacity to pay from those who couldn't, and she would ask us if we wanted to send a second bill or send the bill through the Medical Center billing office for "collection." For those patients who we felt were genuinely unable to pay, we said, "Don't try to collect it and do what you can to assure the patient that we want to continue to see them. Say that we will always send a bill for the full amount the first time, but after that, if they can't pay the balance, we won't rebill them." Physicians had been doing this for years, although in time New York State regarded it as unfair to expect the full amount from some patients, but not others—especially once Medicare and Medicaid, already in their tenth year when we started, became aware of the practice of forgiving payments a few years later and deemed it illegal.

We hadn't learned any of this in medical school or residency or fellowships: we knew nothing about insurance or billing until we started practice. Marcy had learned it during her years working for her obstetrician.

I left for the hospital around 7:00 in the morning, allowing me a few minutes with the girls when they woke up. The commute from Englewood on New Jersey Highway 4 and then across the George Washington Bridge was about 20 minutes on a good day, twice that on a day when a traffic accident closed lanes. The Medical Center parking garage was two blocks from the Atchley Pavilion. The doctors shared the garage with patients and those of the staff who drove to work, although most of the employees arrived by city bus and subway. We also shared the sidewalk with the innumerable leashed mutts who deposited yesterday's dog chow in large piles, making the walk to work like crossing a minefield.

By 7:30 I was usually in the office and had about an hour to check on my sickest patients in the hospital before starting office hours at 8:30. On the afternoons I wasn't in clinic, I spent the day seeing new inpatient consults and dictating letters to patients with the results of their last visit, or writing letters of referral or thanks to other specialists.

My goal was to always be home to have dinner with the girls and Margaret, as I had been able to do when I was in the Army and during most evenings when I was a fellow. The evening commute back to Englewood was more spread out than the morning rush and rarely took more than a half hour. By 7:00 or 7:30 we could sit down for dinner, and after that one of us would clean up while the other helped Katharine and Margaret Lea get ready for bed. On most nights I read to them in my study sitting in a large wingback chair, one girl tucked on each side, my sweetest memory from those years.

After the girls were in bed I reviewed the notes I had written on patients that day to make sure that they were complete, I did some medical reading, and then I proofed the letters I had dictated so that Marcy could mail them out the next day. By 10:30 or 11:00 we were in bed.

That is how our weeks went: I was in the hospital at 8 AM six days a week. Every other week Tom covered for me Saturday afternoon and Sunday, and the next week I covered for him: we each took a Saturday afternoon and all of Sunday off twice a month.

If one of our patients called our office number at night or on the weekend, the hospital operator would call us with their message. Generally, we could take care of our patients over the phone, but when we thought that they were sick enough to require admission, we would send them to the emergency room and then come in to see them. Tom lived ten minutes further away from the Medical Center than I did, but at night the trip was quick. On the rare occasions that one of our patients needed to be directly admitted from home, we would call the resident covering the private service in Harkness Pavilion to plan what the patient needed to have done immediately, and then we would come in to work them up, write orders, and get treatment started.

If we came back to the hospital once—or occasionally twice—we might be in the hospital as much as 30 hours with only a few hours of sleep. But it didn't happen often—perhaps every three or four weeks. We were providing the nearly continuous availability to our patients that we had planned for. And for the first year or so the excitement of practice and teaching was all that I had hoped it would be.

CHAPTER 26

Family Life

During my final year in the Army, when it was clear that I would be returning to Columbia-Presbyterian to practice and teach, I thought that New York City was going to be our permanent home, where the girls would grow up, where I would spend my entire career, where we would build new friendships, find a Unitarian congregation like the one at the Unitarian Church in Rockville, and take advantage of the theaters, classical music, and restaurants of mid-town Manhattan.

In January, on a trip to New York City to work on a research paper I was writing with Andy Frantz, I talked with several faculty members who lived in the New Jersey suburbs close to the Medical Center—Englewood, Tenafly, Cloister, and Alpine—to begin planning where we would live. Don Holub, the senior clinical endocrinologist, lived in Englewood and invited Margaret and me to call on him when we started looking for houses. He recommended his neighbor Mrs. Hanson as a good real estate agent.

In the early spring we spent a weekend looking at houses with Mrs. Hanson. The Englewood and Tenafly neighborhoods she showed us were filled with lovely houses, many built in the 19th Century, with expansive front lawns laid out along quiet streets that were canopied by ancient hardwood trees. In the hilly areas the streets curved in a pattern that suggested that two centuries ago the properties had once been part of large estates or farms with meadows.

I have had house lust from the sixth grade, when I began to check out architecture magazines and photo books from the library and designed my notions of dreamy modern houses with more windows than walls and rambling wings around interior courtyards.

When I moved to Boston for college I saw houses from the Sixteenth and Seventeenth Centuries and my tastes changed: the old houses I saw in Boston and Newburyport and Salem had multiple floors and crazy numbers of bedrooms, formal dining rooms and formal parlors, screened porches and ancient yards. As I fell in love with Margaret I fell in love with old New England houses.

We had no reason to rush making a decision about which town and which house we would choose because we didn't need to move until the end of July; we also had to sell our Maryland house in order to know what we could afford. We expected to make several trips to find the right place.

The last house Mrs. Hanson showed us was next to hers on Linden Avenue, three doors away from Don Holub and his concert-pianist wife. Like many of the houses we had seen, it had dark-brown stained shingles. It sat on nearly an acre of land, with a few old fruit trees from which swings could be hung, and a porte cochere through which carriages had once passed so that in rainy weather guests and family could stay under cover transferring from carriage to the long, covered porch. There was a circular drive in front that looked out on Dwight Place and rows of huge trees along Linden Avenue.

Inside there was a study with a marble fireplace on the left of the central hall, a formal parlor with a carved Italian marble fireplace and a bow window on the right. A door in the parlor led into an even larger formal dining room that had a third fireplace and floor to ceiling windows overlooking the backyard.

On the second floor there were four bedrooms and two baths, and on the third two more bedrooms and a bath. The basement had stone walls and a large den with a fireplace. The master bedroom had a fireplace, and another fireplace in the kitchen had been turned into a grill.

The owner was the divorced wife of Dr. Melcher, one of the attending physicians at the Medical Center. Living alone she found the house too hard to maintain by herself and far bigger than her needs. She planned to move to a condominium apartment as soon as possible and she was in a hurry to sell. She was asking $92,500, a little less than twice what our Rockville house had cost.

We decided to buy it on the spot.

The girls started school in September at the public school a few blocks from our house, Katharine in kindergarten and Margaret Lea in pre-kindergarten. Margaret was a full-time mother while the girls were getting settled, taking on almost all of the duties of caring for the girls and the house while I spent most of my waking hours at the Medical Center. During my scarce weekend time I gradually put in a large vegetable garden and flowerbeds, rebuilt a patio, and tended to the ancient neglected trees.

The house was in good condition and there was very little that needed to be done, but the inside wall paint and wallpaper didn't appeal to us. By the middle of that first year we found a wonderful wallpaper guy, Ray Jenson, whose claim to celebrity was wallpapering every surface in the famous pop pianist Liberace's Manhattan home, including his piano, every key, the windowpanes, and the toilet paper dispenser. Our house had a lot of corners, sloping ceilings, and woodwork. Ray was a meticulous craftsman, cutting the paper so that when it turned corners the seams were invisible. We chose historic 18th and 19th Century wallpaper patterns and in four or five months Ray had practically created a museum in the fifteen rooms and halls and stairways.

Built in 1860, the house was solid and handsome, with high ceilings, lovely woodwork, and windows looking out on trees and gardens in every direction. Even the original cobble stone gutters along the street went back to the origins of the town in the 1700's, known as the "English Town" in largely Dutch-speaking New Netherland on the Hudson's west shores. In time English Town became Englewood and New Netherland became New Jersey.

The house had hidden rooms under the eaves, a meat locker in the cellar with ceiling hooks for curing sides of meat, and a reputation as part of the underground railway, about which we sometimes told visitors who probably faked being impressed.

We had gone to Flathead Lake the summer before Katharine was born. After Margaret Lea was born we returned to visit Mom in Missoula and spend a week at my father's cabin on King's Point. When Dad died in 1974 his widow and third wife, Alix, who was already sick with advanced breast cancer and rarely used the cabin, made it available to us whenever we could fit it into our summer plans.

The Kings Point vacations were total relaxation. We cooked simple meals—it was hard to buy more than basic groceries in the little town of Polson—and other than simple housekeeping and washing our clothes and hanging them to dry on a long line attached to a giant ponderosa pine 50 feet from the house, we had nothing to do but lie on the dock, swim, play in the water, and go fishing.

There were abundant Kokanee salmon. If we were using Dad's speedboat, we could go to deeper parts of the lake, where we slowed down as much as we could by dragging a bucket, or we used the little aluminum outboard boat, trolling in leisurely circles just one or two hundred feet off the shore of several islands that we could get to in 10 or 15 minutes.

Most of the days were hot and we basked on the dock, in and out of the water two or three times in an hour. During "mountain lows," when clouds rolled in for two or three days, filling the valleys and obscuring the dramatically jagged Mission Mountains, it was chilly. The cabin had a wood burning stove and a large store of dry, pitchy pine. With the fire crackling we would bundle up and stay inside reading. We took books out from the Polson library, fifteen or twenty at a time. When it got too stuffy in the cabin we would run outside and jump off the dock and then race back to the house to warm ourselves before the fire.

Most summers we also drove up to Newburyport. The trip was very familiar, five hours of heavy, weekend traffic around New York City and on the toll roads in Connecticut. Arriving in Newburyport was always exciting, like arriving in the previous century. High Street, where Margaret grew up, meanders along a ridge above where the Merrimack River flows into the Atlantic Ocean around a sand spit that creates a long harbor. We loved the first smell of the salt marshes and the masses of hundred-foot oaks and maples and elms along the ancient lawns and gardens of the houses, and the nearly perfectly preserved collection of 19th and 18th Century houses that once were owned by ships' captains and wealthy merchants.

The kids were excited as we passed each landmark on High Street. The minute we stopped they were out of the car, running around their favorite haunts in the backyard, then through the central hallway and broad stairs leading to the upper bedrooms. To them it was like a palace, and it was to me too—its spacious rooms filled with antiques and paintings and middle-eastern carpets. Margaret's mother, also Margaret, was a storybook grandmother who always laid in double supplies of our favorite foods and, most importantly, let Katharine and Margaret Lea rummage through the chests of beautifully preserved dolls and toys left behind by Margaret and her brother and sister.

We spent much of our time together in the kitchen, the most ordinary but also the most used of all the rooms. Meals were served mostly in the kitchen, with Peggy hovering to be sure everyone's plate was full, and RW, as he asked me to call him, telling stories and asking the girls about their interests and lives. Their unreserved embrace of our visits had replaced whatever reservations RW and Peggy had once had about Margaret marrying me.

Our walks on the Newburyport beaches and our time in Montana were most of what we experienced of the outdoors beyond our own backyard in those years. We tried sampling the nearby hiking at Harriman State Park, about an hour from Englewood. On one sunny outing on Bear Mountain we found ourselves in an endless queue of people shuffling along narrow trails with nothing like Montana's solitude or lofty mountain views or cliffs from which we could dangle our feet and contemplate vast stretches of primeval wilderness.

Chalking up our first crowded hike as a bad choice of days, I was determined that the girls should have the experiences of hiking and camping that I had had growing up. I assembled the necessary equipment—a small tent that would hold Margaret and the girls, sleeping bags, pots and pans for cooking, sets of plates and bowls and utensils of light aluminum.

We set out to camp for two nights, again in Harriman, thinking that if we arrived by early afternoon and only hiked for an hour or two we would be at a campsite well before it would get full. There were a dozen or so other campers when we arrived, but there was a decent spot for us to set up the tent and cook dinner over a little gas fire. As it became dark the girls disappeared inside the tent and I bedded down on the ground outside the tent. A few hours later the rumbling of thunder and flashes of lightning woke me. Soon it began to sprinkle; I stuck it out, but in minutes it was pouring. I hadn't set up the girls' tent with trenches so that the rain could drain away from it and soon its floor was a puddle. I told them that they should grab their sleeping bags and try to squeeze into the little hut that many other campers had retreated to. I moved my sleeping bag to a woodshed where I was kept company by rats running over me all night.

We were a dreary mess at dawn. As soon as we could pull our wet gear together we hiked out to our car and found a country diner for breakfast. We were home by noon.

At Christmas, the Englewood house, with its lovely fireplaces and countless windows was a wonderful place to decorate. We had room for a big tree in the living room bow window. In the front windows on each floor, we put electric "candles" that were visible from Linden Avenue. We wound ribbons and evergreen branches on the columns and rails of the front porch and decorated the mantles with more evergreen branches and candles.

Mom came to see us every few years at Christmas. The first time she came I decided we should take up a tradition I had read about in English novels. We were living in an 1860 house that had once been heated by its fireplaces, we had an old meat locker in the cellar where, after hunting, geese and ducks and deer might have been hung. With 1860 England in mind, I decided that we should see what it was like to have a roast goose rather than roast turkey or roast beef. After some scouting around we found a goose in a butcher shop in the Bowery. We clearly did not know how to prepare a goose: it came out of the oven looking appealing but was so greasy that we couldn't eat it. Still hungry that evening, I found an open Italian deli and we ate Fettuccini Alfredo.

CHAPTER 27

Settling into Practice

By the end of our first year our office practice was almost fully booked and Tom and I expanded our office hours by each adding a half-day. We regularly saw patients sent to us by Columbia surgeons, neurologists, or psychiatrists who felt that a patient they were caring for needed to have a Columbia internist manage their medical issues.

At the same time, we both were taking care of about 10 hospitalized patients, half of them on the surgery or neurology or psychiatry services, and half our own patients.

Some of our admissions came directly from our office, but we also regularly received telephone calls from the senior medicine resident in the emergency room asking us to admit a patient to the private service. These calls could occur at any time, night or day:

"Dr. Noel, can I talk to you about an elderly gentleman who came into the ER today with a week of coughing and two days of fever and chills. He has pneumonia and really nasty looking sputum . . . looks too sick to send home. He has Medicare, is retired, used to be a high school teacher . . . really nice guy, not much medical history."

"How much of a workup have you done?"

"Chest X-ray and blood count: he has a high white count... electrolytes and kidneys are normal, chest x-ray looks awful, pneumonia in both lungs. . . and he is pretty dehydrated."

"Did you check to see if there were any Harkness beds?"

"There are some in the Harkness Annex and he doesn't mind a roommate."

There were no rules for how we should respond to these calls. Presbyterian Hospital rarely turned away a patient without insurance—the medicine teaching wards seemed endlessly expandable and there were no caps on resident admissions. The first priority of the private practice in the Harkness Pavilion was to take care of the patients who already had a private doctor. The more senior practitioners had long-since given up admitting patients new to them from the emergency room and rarely agreed if called. As a result, the calls came to Tom or me and just a few other young internists still building their practices. Tom and I usually said yes. It meant adding unexpected hours to our day, and if the call came in the evening, we would drive back into Manhattan to meet the patient and take a complete history, do a physical exam and write orders.

If the patient arrived in the middle of the night, the ER resident would generally offer to admit the patient to the overnight ward and start care, so that we could wait until the next morning to meet the patient and assume care. When that happened I left home at 6 AM in order to get the workup done and the patient settled before I started my hospital visits and office hours.

There were no procedures for patients to rate their physicians at that time. The main feedback we got from our patients other than their occasional thank you notes was their referrals. Both Tom and I were gentle, kind and interested, and rarely would one of the patients we were caring for abandon us and go searching for another doctor. Many of our patients referred their family members and friends to us, which we took as evidence that they were satisfied. At first it was rewarding to know that a patient liked me enough to refer people that they cared about. Most of the patients they referred turned out to be enjoyable to care for, but a side effect of spending a lot of time listening and supporting those patients who came with a long list of complaints—the causes of which had been undiagnosable by a string of previous doctors—was that they sent their friends who similarly felt that no doctor had ever taken them seriously or given them enough time and information.

My heart sank when a new patient said something like, "I heard that you are a miracle worker. I am so glad to finally meet a doctor who won't brush me off." These patients would often offer me an annotated list of their problems and some had a grocery bag full of pill bottles. With these patients, invariably I went over the hour Marcy had scheduled, and even as they were going out the door they would be telling me about other things that worried them and asking if I could see a brother or sister or friend, "who has even more problems than I do." Meanwhile, my next few patients were stacking up. I hated to keep patients waiting and I almost always ended these days with a pounding, sick headache.

Marcy suggested that I see these never-quite-satisfied patients at the end of the day, so that if I did run late at least no one else would be affected.

That was one of the downsides of being endlessly available and wanting to meet the needs of even the most talkative patients. When my practice grew to the point that I had few openings, Marcy took to checking with any new person calling for an appointment to see who had suggested me to them; if it was one of my patients who found ways to talk and ask questions beyond the hour we had scheduled for a new patient, or the half hour for follow-up, and whose friends or family members they had sent to us were invariably similar to them, Marcy would gently suggest that they try the office of that year's new internist who was just starting a practice.

Since I had no previous experience with insurance companies, I didn't anticipate that some of my patients who had insurance would still not be able to pay my bill. The first was an artist who a friend sent to me; he had a serious medical problem but little income and an insurance policy that he bought through an artists' association. He arrived in paint-streaked jeans, a blue work shirt, and a pair of spattered sneakers through which his great toes poked out. After I had taken his history and examined him, we sat in my office while I outlined what would be needed to manage his problem. He told me what he could afford: his insurance would pay for the office visit and the few tests he needed, but not much beyond that. I told him that he should not pay me and use what money he earned to pay for the medications he needed. "If at some point in the future you sell some paintings to a museum or a rich widow, you can pay me," I told him.

He laughed. "Doc, there's a long line of people ahead of you hoping the same dang thing."

After that a physician in the Yale student health service asked if I would see a young African American woman with galactorrhea, a condition in which she spontaneously lactated, who had just graduated from the Yale Drama School. He had read the *New England Journal* article that Andy Frantz and I had written about galactorrhea and called Columbia to get my phone number. He had already ordered all of the tests I would need to start caring for her because Yale would pay for them, but, he told me, once she left Yale she would have no money and no insurance to pay a doctor's bill. She was understudying the role of the Lady in Brown in the Broadway play *For Colored Girls Who Have Considered Suicide When the Rainbow is Enuf*. It was a hit and tickets were hard to come by. At the end of our first visit I said that I would not send her a bill. After thinking about it for a minute, I asked if she occasionally got tickets that she could give to friends and family: if she did, I would love to see the play on a night when she was performing. In a few weeks she called Marcy and told her that she would leave two tickets in the box office for a performance. On the night of the play I showed up at the box office to pick up our tickets: the ticket seller asked, "Cash or credit card?" I was expecting free tickets, but I gulped, pulled out my credit card and meekly paid the $40.00.

The play was terrific, the more so because I knew her.

I remembered that in the years before Medicare, my friend Roland's father, Doctor Trenouth, often got paid in eggs, chickens, bacon, carrots, and hunting rights. She had paid me by moving us to front of the line to buy tickets that otherwise would have been months in the future.

Both Tom and I had decided not to limit our practices to endocrinology and while we saw many patients with diabetes and thyroid disease and pituitary and adrenal problems, more than half of our patients had inflammatory bowel disease or ulcers or chronic lung disease, heart failure or degenerative neurological diseases, rheumatoid arthritis or gout or kidney failure or obesity.... the list went on and on.

A pediatric psychiatrist who specialized in eating disorders asked me to take care of the medical problems of her patients who had begun to go through puberty and no longer would be seen by a pediatrician. The first of these was a fourteen-year-old girl who was a student at the New York City Ballet School. She and her mother had moved from Omaha, where her father had a successful car dealership, to an apartment near Carnegie Hall. She had been dancing since she was four and was regarded as having potential for a professional career. Her days were spent in hard physical activity. She ate a vegetable diet and had bulimia—self-induced vomiting after eating—and she used laxatives in order to meet the weight expectations of her teachers. The psychiatrist was trying to get her to stop binging on sweets and then purging. The referral to me was triggered by her recent development of severe ankle pain.

When I saw her, it was clear that she had arrested puberty. At 5 feet 4 inches she weighed 92 pounds, had virtually no breast development, no pubic or leg hair, and no butt. She almost certainly was calcium and protein deficient, with inadequate bone formation and cartilage repair to deal with her linear growth and the stress of constant high-level weight bearing from jumping and dancing *en pointe*.

The situation was strained. If I talked directly to the daughter, her mother took over.

"First," I said, "You are going to need to have more calcium in your diet, and given that you don't drink milk and aren't getting vitamin D, and aren't making estrogen, you are almost certainly going to have continuing foot and ankle problems."

"What can we do about her period, then," her mother asked, before the girl could speak.

"Well, she is unlikely to menstruate until she gains weight."

"She absolutely can't gain weight. She will be dismissed from the school."

"We can start her on a small dose of estrogen."

"You have to promise that she will not—will not!—gain weight."

"She needs an adequate diet, with more protein, with calcium, and without vomiting. Her exercise is at such a high level that she will stay slim, but she almost certainly will have some breast development and some deposition of waist and buttock fat."

The conversation went back and forth, with the daughter sitting sullenly not looking at either of us. We reached an uneasy compromise. This mother was devoted to—perhaps fanatical—about her daughter becoming a professional ballet dancer, having for two years left her husband and the rest of her family behind in Omaha so that she could manage her daughter's training and keep her safe in New York City. She made me promise that if we induced puberty with estrogens she would not gain weight, and I told her that I couldn't guarantee that, but that continuing her physical stress without the capacity for her body to normally develop was putting her at risk of fractures and inadequate muscle development which would end her career before it even began.

In something of a staredown, the mother agreed, with a, "I have my eyes on you" squint. Two months later she called to tell me that she was stopping the estrogens: her daughter had gained three pounds. I never saw her again.

Over several years I saw a string of girls referred by the psychiatrist who had functional anorexia due to high physical activity like dance or running or gymnastics, often complicated by purging and vomiting; in almost every case we struggled with the difficult decision about whether to leave the prepubescent level of hormone secretion alone and not intervene with hormone replacement, or take the risk of the bodily changes that puberty, artificial or natural, would probably entail. For the runners it was occasionally less a problem than for the gymnasts and dancers, for whom body appearance constantly outweighed healthy body physiology.

Tom and I also frequently cared for teen aged girls who thought that they were too tall or too hairy, and boys who were short or not hairy at all. There are a variety of reasons why those conditions develop, and lacking the external constraints of career management by coaches and teachers, these patients were easier to help once we had made a diagnosis, which included genetic abnormalities and gland failure or cellular resistance to testosterone or estrogen.

Much stranger was my unexpected and unprepared entry into the world of sex therapy. One of my friends from residency who now lived in California called me to ask if I would see his college roommate, who was suffering from continuous abdominal pain suggestive of peptic ulcer disease. I said I would and a few weeks later I met him.

Tony was 36 and the owner of a successful furniture business in Montclair New Jersey that he inherited from his father. He had never wanted to be in his father's business or to live in Montclair, but he realized a few years out of college that his mother and younger brothers and sisters needed the income from the business, the former to keep her house and club memberships, the latter to pay for their college expenses, marriages, and getting started in their own businesses. Tony gave up his dream of a life in California and returned to New Jersey, where he struck up a relationship with his former high school girlfriend and soon had children of his own. Until recently he had been healthy, but for the past year and a half he had been having frequent, and then almost continuous abdominal pain, often made worse by eating. Gradually he had lost weight, and was now down to his high school graduation weight.

My histories were always long: I started with his complete social and family history, review of past medical history, the over-the-counter remedies he was using to treat his abdominal pain, and then a review of symptoms by system—pulmonary, cardiovascular, neurological, skin, endocrine, and so on.

Nothing much turned up that was helpful until I started to ask about his psychological history and current status. That always included questions about sexual function and satisfaction.

"Aside from your abdominal pain, how are things going?"

"Fine, fine. Just the usual stuff you have when you have kids and brothers and sisters and a lot of family obligations"

"How is your wife's health?"

"She's fine Doc. Oh, she's got her complaints, but they're not medical. The kids get on her nerves."

"Are you sexually active?"

"You might say that."

"With your wife?"

"Sometimes."

"And do you find that is satisfactory?"

I had not yet learned that men's answer to the question was rarely "yes."

"Not really."

"Would you like to talk about it?"

He paused, frowned and adjusted his position in his chair. "It's like this Doc," he said. "We have three kids. She—Shirley—lost interest along the way, and then I lost interest in her, or at least I lost interest in having sex with her. It wasn't any fun."

"And so, do you have any other partners?"

Usually when I asked if someone was sexually active, if they said yes, I followed up with "with men, women, or both?" I felt very enlightened, although I rarely encountered someone who revealed promiscuity or a same-sex partner.

His answer floored me: "I have sex with my secretary every day in the showroom."

"In the showroom?" I asked, incredulous.

"Doc, a furniture store is full of beds and couches. We 'try them all out'"—here he made quotation marks with his fingers— "so that we can

Settling into Practice

give useful information to our customers.'" He gave me a devilish grin. Now that he had surprised me he was having fun.

"When do you do this?"

"Before the store opens, or after it closes." I go in a little early or stay a little late, usually both."

"And do you enjoy the sex?" I was pretty sure that he enjoyed it.

"Yes. It's great sex. The best is when we do it on one of the beds or a couch or a chair in the showroom window. Sometimes on a dining room table."

"Can't people see you?"

"Well, we do it in the window after dark, and the shop is on a triangle where two busy roads intersect. There are windows on both sides, but very few people walk by. The lights make it psychedelic. It feels risky and exciting."

"And you have been doing this for a year and a half?"

"Yes."

"And when did the stomach pain begin?"

"About then."

"And do you think the two things might be related?"

"Ed sure thinks so." Ed was the mutual friend who referred him. "Ed says, 'Tony, no piece of tail is worth what you are going through.' I told him that he is a smart guy, but in this instance he doesn't know what the hell he is talking about."

"So how do you feel about this ... this ... what do you call it?"

"I don't have a name for it. It feels more like a marriage than my marriage does."

"Does your wife suspect anything?"

"I don't think so."

"Have you thought about what you could do so that you weren't getting ulcer pain from the stress?"

"Of course. I think I would have the pain if I ended it, and I will have the pain if I don't."

"And you are sure that it is worth it?"

He looked at me with slack-jawed mock irony: "Would I still be doing it if it weren't worth it?"

"Could you get divorced?"

"I'm Catholic, Doc, born and baptized. I have three kids. I have brothers and sisters and my mom, devout Catholics. Probably half my customers are Catholic, practicing Catholics. It would be a mess. Everybody would lose."

Eventually we got around to my telling him what I could and could not do for him: I could prescribe more aggressive medication, but I couldn't fix his marital situation and the stress it was causing him.

I asked, "Would you be willing to talk with a psychiatrist to see if you could untangle this and decide whether you could make your marriage work better, or could leave it?"

"I don't like shrinks."

I persuaded him to give it a try, and even ran the idea of couples' therapy by him. I suggested a psychiatrist who I thought would be a good match and arranged the referral.

Tony came back a month later. He told me that the stomach pain was better and thanked me.

"Ah," I said. "So, seeing the psychiatrist worked!"

He shook his head. "Doc, I am not nuts. Do I sound nuts to you? I am definitely not nuts! I don't think my mother had anything to do with this, and I already know that what I am doing is causing the ulcer pain. But the guy you sent me to is weird, a real spook. I stopped after the second appointment. Doc, I feel comfortable talking with you. Can't I just continue to come here and have you help me with this?"

This happened a lot. There was a stigma attached to seeing a psychiatrist that outweighed the risk of having an affair. Women more often would see a psychiatrist, but men mostly ended up not trying or quitting. While the idea of sex therapy was often of interest to women, men did not want to talk about their sexual behavior and feelings with a stranger.

I had read Masters and Johnson's book, *Human Sexual Response*, and from time to time I made suggestions to a couple about a few things they could try, not that I knew very much—but I was in no position to do couples' therapy. Everything I suggested to Tony about trying to have enjoyable sex with his wife so that he didn't need to have an affair he threw back to me:

"Doc, don't take this personally, but do you think I haven't tried? Candles and wine and music aren't going to make being in bed with Shirley exciting. When I get to the store in the morning I am humming. I have this warm, sexy woman who one way or another will find time to have sex with me and I know I am not making her do something she doesn't really want to do. She wants it as much as I do."

"Does she want to continue this way? Where does she think this is going?"

"She knows I am not leaving my wife and kids, she loves her work, she gets paid well, and she has no other plans—at least not right now. She doesn't want kids, and she doesn't want me to leave my family. We've got the best part of marriage and none of the hassles."

It was not my job to argue with him. The medications I had prescribed for his ulcer pain made him feel better and he had gained back some of the weight he had lost. He came to see me every few months and said that he was better and grateful. I didn't bring up his life arrangements again, and neither did he.

A few months later my friend Ed called to thank me for taking care of Tony. We chatted a bit about each other's family, and then he asked if I would see a young woman who was his laboratory technician; she was moving to New York City and needed a doctor to manage her hyperthyroidism.

When she came for her first appointment, I did my usual history, asking about symptoms, her medical history, her social life, education, current work, and plans. When I asked if she was sexually active, she said, "I am, although not at the moment."

"With men or women or both?"

"Only men—or rather, just with one man for the past few years, and before that for a while in college, also with a guy."

"Do you take birth control pills, or what do you use for contraception?"

"I've never used anything. In college my boyfriend used a condom."

"And recently?"

"I didn't have to use anything. He had had a vasectomy."

I asked if she expected that relationship to continue, and she told me that the partner was someone at the University who was married; she had come to New York City to end the relationship.

From that and other details it was clear that her partner was Ed. I didn't mention that to her, and of course I never brought it up with Ed either. I suspected that Ed knew that I would make the connection and didn't mind.

My naïveté had always made the world seem less complicated than it actually is.

Over the years I had gotten to know most of the senior nurses on the private floors of the Medical Center. Every few months a nurse would ask me if I was still taking patients and even though the practice was ostensibly closed, Marcy was always able to make room for them and their families. Most of the nurses had ongoing but not serious problems, or they wanted a checkup. It was much more complicated when a nurse wanted me to write a prescription for a medication to help them sleep or for anxiety or weight loss. When I said I would have to see them in my office, they would agree, but when I said that I didn't prescribe medications without doing a complete history and physical and some basic laboratory tests, they looked disappointed and then awkwardly said that they would think about it. If I ran into them later, some said they had gotten a prescription from a resident.

Some of the patients other doctors asked me to take care of were quite colorful. Carmen Vicale was a well-known neurologist with a large international practice of patients who flew in once a year for a checkup.

The first patient he asked me to see was a Saudi prince, "Not a major prince," he said, "Just one of the hundred minor princes."

Dr. Vicale's secretary called Marcy to be sure that on the day that Dr. Vicale admitted him I would leave the entire morning open in case something came up that needed immediate attention.

I was to see him at 9:00 AM; following that he was scheduled to have a hernia repair. When I arrived at Harkness's most expensive room, two very large men in pantaloons and gold tunics wearing keffiyeh stood arms crossed in front of the prince's door, each carrying a large sword. A hospital orderly carrying a tray covered with an operating room towel was a few steps ahead of me. The guards crossed their swords in front of the door and signaled the orderly to lift the towel. Beneath it was a bowl of hot water, a basin of liquid soap, and a large straight razor.

Apparently there had been no communication between the prince's staff and the surgeon: certainly no orderly was going to get anywhere near the prince and his groin with a straight razor. If the surgeon wanted him shaved for the operation, the surgeon would have to do it—with the guard standing behind him with sword drawn to prevent any mishaps.

The orderly exited quickly and I entered and introduced myself. With the prince's physician standing next to me, I asked the long list of questions needed for me to write a history. His physician answered, and the prince watched television, indifferent to the whole process. I was told which parts of him I could examine, and once again it was made clear that his nether regions were not considered public domain and would be taken care of by the surgeon later that morning.

While I was writing my note Dr. Vicale paged me.

"Gordon? This is Carmen Vicale. Did you find anything in the history or examination that I should know about?"

"Nothing, other than that the prince has an aversion to someone coming close to the crown jewels with a straight razor."

"Yes, yes, I heard. Well, please let me know when the lab data are back. And, may I ask what you are going to charge him? He'll be paying cash."

I told him that my usual charge for a new patient in the hospital was $125. Actually, for people with the usual insurance policies, it was $75, but I was embarrassed to tell Dr. Vicale that.

"No, no, no. You can't do that. He won't think that he has gotten the best care. You must charge him at least $500. I'll be charging him ten times that."

A few weeks later I mentioned to a more senior physician that I had taken care of a Saudi prince that I discovered he had seen about ten years ago when I reviewed the prince's hospital record.

"Yes," he responded, "every few years he comes here and always wants a new doctor to make sure nothing is missed. Next year he'll go to the Cleveland Clinic. And a few years after that, to the Mayo Clinic. In between he will go to Geneva, London, Paris. They shop around."

Dr. Vicale often took care of people who were very wealthy, most of whom didn't have neurological problems. He was a kind of traffic controller who arranged each visit ahead of time. He was alleged to have a better wine cellar than the Four Seasons restaurant. I ran into him in the hall one day and he told me that he had opened a case of 1961 Chateau Margaux Margaux and uncorked two bottles for guests who were coming for dinner later that day. He tasted them, determined both were not yet ready, and poured them down the drain. I thought, "I could probably have figured out a way to hold my nose and choke them down."

Two weeks later one of the prince's attaches came to the office in a white caftan and red-checked keffiyeh, carrying a black velvet pillow on which perched a large silver bowl full of crushed ice; nested in the ice was a crystal old fashioned glass full of caviar and a silver spoon which he gave to us with great ceremony, and then departed. At the end of the day we had a small party.

In the autumn of 1977 Marcy got a call from one of the surgeons about a former patient who was complaining of nausea, right-sided abdominal pain, and fatigue. The man's surgery was years earlier and appeared to have nothing to do with his current problem. He asked Marcy if I could squeeze his patient in that afternoon. I told Marcy to go ahead and schedule him at the end of the day, and after our office hours were over, I met him in the waiting room and escorted him into my office. James was a tall, slender, elegantly dressed Black man with a faint British accent. When I shook his hand and introduced myself, I could see that he had jaundice, hard to detect in his hands, but easy to spot in his eyes. His symptoms were typical of hepatitis. He had a swollen, tender liver but no signs of an acutely inflamed gallbladder.

In those days we typically hospitalized people with jaundice, and I asked if he was okay with that. I called the Harkness admitting office and arranged for him to be admitted to one of the private isolation rooms. I wanted to get his laboratory tests done and so without further questioning him to find out how he had gotten hepatitis, I sent him to the laboratory and told him after that to walk across the street where he would be taken to his room, telling him that I would see him again later that evening.

By the time I finished rounding on my other inpatients James was installed in a bed and picking at a dinner on a tray that straddled his bed. His tests confirmed that he had moderately severe hepatitis. At that time we had no tests to separate serum hepatitis—contracted from blood transfusions or sharing needles or syringes—from infectious hepatitis, contracted from fecally contaminated food or water or shellfish. When I took a history, I learned that he had grown up in Jamaica, graduated from an Ivy League university, done a fellowship at a British University, and had gone to law school at Columbia before becoming an attorney for the ABC television network. This wasn't the usual profile of a drug injector, and he had never had a transfusion. I reviewed his recent contacts, which proved difficult, since he was in constant contact with many different people and frequently went out for meals with his coworkers or friends, none of whom he was aware of having hepatitis.

He got rapidly better and after ten days returned home; I reminded him about what he needed to do to not infect anyone and a week after that he returned to work.

The day after he went back to ABC he called to tell me that some of his friends were worried that they may have been exposed to him and would like to see me. I had noticed that a constant string of men visited him in the hospital, many of them Black, but others who were Asian or Caucasian, all well dressed.

I saw several of them and checked the liver tests that would be abnormal in hepatitis, all of which were negative.

As planned, James came to the office to see me ten days after discharge. He was doing fine, with no further symptoms. I told him that a half dozen of his friends had come in to be checked.

I was puzzled. "I have taken care of a number of people with hepatitis like yours, but I have never had them send their friends to see me—and I think more of them are scheduled to see me next week."

He looked at me for a long moment then frowned and began to speak quietly.

"Doctor, I am going to tell you something and it's really important that it remain private. I don't want you writing this in my record."

He paused. "I have sex with men, with all the men you have seen and those who are coming to see you. We have sex with many of the same people. So, everyone is worried that they may get hepatitis or spread it."

"Are some of your partners also at ABC?"

I was trying to seem matter-of-fact, as though I knew about his sexuality all along and that it was no big deal.

"No, no, no! No one at ABC knows anything about me, about this part of my life. I am already an oddity there. It would be the end of my job if anyone knew. These are people I meet before work, after work, at lunch. Most days I have sex with three or four different men. I spend almost all of my free time having sex or looking for the next person I am going to have sex with."

"How do you do that and still show up at work on time."

"I know where to go, Doctor Noel, which bars, which coffee shops, which bath houses, which parties. I'm always cruising, we're all always cruising. At lunch I grab something to eat and in ten minutes I'm in the bathroom with another guy, maybe two other guys."

I asked him how many partners he thought he had had in the past year, not that it was something I needed to know at this point.

"At least a couple of hundred. It could be twice that."

"Good grief, are they all going to make appointments?"

He smiled. "I don't know the names of most of them, and they don't know me. The ones you are seeing are my friends, the people who know I was in the hospital with hepatitis."

In time I would read about the explosion of gay sex starting in the late Sixties, about San Francisco bathhouses, about the rising incidence of venereal disease. When I met James I didn't know any of this and hadn't quickly caught on when the small army of his friends began coming in to see me.

James must have told his friends that I knew they were gay, and, now comfortable with being open, their stories flowed out of them like water under pressure.

As far as I know James was the first gay man I had cared for. When I took a history, I asked everyone, "Do you have sex with women or men or both?" Among the priests, artists, musicians, teachers, chefs, athletes, students and others I was taking care of there must have been more, but none had acknowledged it.

A month later I saw the last of James' friends. He had the same history as the others I had seen.

When we were done talking, I showed him into the examination room, asked him to undress except for his underpants, and gave him a sheet to wrap himself in.

In a few minutes I walked in. He was lying flat on the examination table with an impressive erection, masturbating. The hair went up on the back of my neck. I grabbed the sheet that he had dropped on a chair, tossed it to him and told him to cover himself up. I was in and out of the room in 7 seconds.

I gave him time to dis-erect. When I went back into the examination room the hair on the back of my neck was still standing up. I performed a thorough exam but couldn't bring myself to do a genital or rectal exam.

"You aren't going to do a rectal exam, Doc?"

"No, sorry."

I told him what I thought he needed to know about hepatitis and its transmission. Usually, I did that in my office after patients had dressed, but I was so uncomfortable with him that I sent him straight to the laboratory and back out into the world. "You don't have any evidence of current hepatitis. I'll let you know the laboratory results in a few days."

CHAPTER 28

Dollars and Sense

My learning curve as a full-time practicing physician at an academic medical center was very steep. Although after residency I had two years of fellowship in which I spent a substantial amount of time teaching and caring for patients on the Presbyterian Hospital side of Fort Washington Avenue, private practice across the street had dimensions that I wasn't prepared for: the art of writing letters to referring doctors and patients outlining the results of my consultation; taking care of the medical issues of patients admitted to the private practices of psychiatrists, neurologists, and surgeons; writing letters to patients; resisting the pressure to narrow my practice to endocrinology when my preference was to take care of all of the medical problems of my patients, not just their thyroid or diabetic or adrenal problems.

I was surprised that a large part of my practice was seeing the patients admitted by physicians in other specialties. Some of the physicians asked me to see all of the patients they admitted to the hospital for evaluation or surgery. While I was flattered at first, gradually I had to fire some of them because of the way they took care of patients and the way they were exploiting me. One was a neurologist with a large practice on the Upper East Side who only came to the Neurological Institute to see his patients in the evening. I saw them on the day of admission and soon discovered that he was trading on my complete history and physical examination instead of writing one of his own, limiting his notes to just the patients' neurological problems. I found his progress notes to be sketchy and often his patients asked me to tell them how they were doing and what Dr. W's plans were because he communicated very little to them. A series of his patients refused to pay my bill because Dr. W had neither explained my role nor confirmed that they were able to pay for my evaluation as part of their admission. When I told him about the unpaid bills, he said that he would call those patients to tell them that they needed to pay, but they never did. After more than a dozen of these experiences, I told Marcy that when his secretary called she should inform her that I would not see any additional inpatients for him. He called me, first angry that I was refusing to take care of his patients, which he said was unethical, and then whining that he didn't know how he could take care of his patients without me. In time I discovered that a number of previous internists at Atchley had similar experiences and had also stopped accepting his consultation requests.

The billing issue came up with other physicians, as well. It had happened with Dr. Neer, a famous shoulder orthopedist whose patients came from all over the world. His secretary called Marcy and made sure that the admission date was convenient for me; she sent over the complete office notes so that I would know the patients' past operative history; and she told me that any time I had a question or needed to discuss a patient, she would put Dr. Neer on the phone with me immediately. Dr. Neer's patients often required fairly extensive preoperative studies and if I felt that they were not ready for surgery, he would discharge them and either their local physician or I would try to get them in shape for surgery. Dr. Neer wasn't a great talker. He often rounded at 6 AM when patients were barely awake and in the days after surgery they would ask me questions about physical therapy, when their bandages or cast would be removed, or when they would be able to go home, questions that only Dr. Neer could answer. However, aside from that, he was exemplary: when several of his patients refused to pay my bill because "all Dr. Noel did was come in and talk to me twice a day," Dr. Neer sent them a letter commanding them to pay my bill, which they did. His secretary always followed up to be sure. Marcy loved her.

Once we were fully busy, Dr. Southworth raised another issue. He knew that both Tom and I took patients with marginal insurance. While he had said that he wanted us to take over his practice when he retired, at the age of 70 he was showing no signs of slowing down, although he didn't want to expand his already busy practice and he steered some new appointment requests he received to Tom and me.

Quietly, with patrician sensitivity to avoid any hint of discrimination, he advised me to be more selective in the patients I accepted so that there would be room for me to take care of the kind of patients that had filled his practice—people at the top: shipping company owners, publishers, bankers, Wall Street executives, prominent lawyers and politicians, University professors, other physicians.

I thanked him for his concern and didn't argue, but this was not welcome advice. After pondering my conflicted feelings for weeks, I labeled myself a "prairie democrat." I constructed an entirely personal mythology of Montana and the high-plains states as places in which, where you came from, who your parents were, what your family lineage was associated with, where you had "prepped" and where you had "summered", and which prominent people were counted as your friends did not matter. A high percentage of non-Native-American families in Montana had emigrated from Europe in the past few generations, most had scraped through the Dust Bowl and Great Depression, many had been in the armed services during one of the World Wars, and most were in one way or another hard working and self-made. In my mythical view of Montana, what was important was what kind of person you were, not how much money you had earned or how much power you had achieved or the provenance of your surname.

While I did see a small but steady stream of prosperous and well-insured patients and enjoyed taking care of them, I also enjoyed taking care of the families of the nurses, students, and doctors I worked with, many of whom came from less affluent backgrounds.

Eileen Toohey had been the nurse on my neurology rotation when I was a second-year resident. She was a wonderful caregiver and manager, and she had become a workplace friend. From time to time she asked if I would see one of the nurses she worked with or call me to ask questions about a medical issue she wanted to understand.

One day she left a message with Marcy and when I finished office hours I called her back.

"Would you be willing to see my father, Michael Toohey," she asked. "He retired a year ago and I am worried about him. He worked all his life on the New Jersey docks, hard, hard work—and I thought when he retired, he and my Mom would travel and enjoy themselves, something they never were able to do when I was growing up. But it's been a year and he hasn't struck up any new friendships or found any hobbies. He sits on the front porch or in the living room waiting for the mailman and the evening newspaper, and after he has read the paper, he watches a little television and waits until it's time for the TV news so that he can have his evening drink. He seems listless, and he has lost weight. I am worried about him."

Eileen was a nurse esteemed by everyone who came in contact with her. Any internist in the Medical Center would gladly have taken care of Michael Toohey. Having her ask me to take care of one of the two most important people in her life meant more to me than seeing a dozen Wall Street stockbrokers.

In time I ended up taking care of Eileen's mother, Mary, and Eileen herself.

In one sense, Dr. Southworth was correct: it wasn't just that the kinds of patients that Dr. Southworth hoped I would be seeing were prominent in business or academia or politics, they also were better insured, and after nearly two years of practice, I still was not generating enough income to pay back Columbia for what they had invested in my practice. Some of my patients could not pull together enough money to cover what their insurance didn't pay for, and if I were to raise my fees it would become even harder.

In the autumn of my third year a butcher from Queens created a crisis for me. Myles Behrens was an ophthalmologist who regularly referred patients to my office. His specialty was eye muscle surgery. Some of his patients had Grave's disease, a rare condition in which a patient has hyperthyroidism and inflammation of the tissues around and behind the eyes. As their Grave's disease progressed, inflammation and swelling in the tissues behind the eyes pushed their eyeballs forward and they were unable to move their eyes up and down or sideways. A Grave's patient seems to be staring because the forward movement of the globe makes it difficult for the eyelids to fully close, often with resulting damage to the cornea. Myles could operate to remove some of the inflamed tissues, allowing the eyeball to move back into the eye socket, but the surgery sometimes caused a dangerous worsening of their hyperthyroidism, which could result in death.

Myles asked me to see the patients he was going to operate on before they were admitted to be sure that their thyroid disease was well controlled and so that I would know them in case the surgery caused sudden worsening of their hyperthyroidism.

One of these patients was named Mario Lombardi. Mario had inherited his father's butcher shop that he ran with an apprentice who helped with the routine work; his wife managed the books. The shop didn't make Mario wealthy, but it paid the bills and he had hopes that his kids would do well enough in school that they might be able to go to college if they could get some help from scholarships. As a kid, Mario's main attachments to his dad were working in the butcher shop and working on his dad's coin collection. Every few days they sifted through all the change that crossed the counter, looking for the occasional rare coin, something that he now did with his own kids. The coin collection, he said, was going to be the down payment on his oldest daughter's college tuition in a few years.

Mario had well-controlled hyperthyroidism for several years, but then he developed Graves disease and he couldn't safely use knives because his eyes no longer moved together, resulting in double vision and loss of depth of field. He had already cut off the tips of two of his fingers. His physician referred him to Myles to see if surgery was feasible. Mario had to hire another butcher to do the meat cutting. While he could still do a lot of the chores of the shop, like ordering and wrapping and moving meat out of his lockers, with the additional salary added to his costs he was now losing money. In addition to his four kids he had a mortgage and he was worried about being able to keep the house. His wife had begun to work part time as a bookkeeper in another business, but Mario felt the two youngest kids needed a full-time mother and he was ashamed of no longer being able to support his family without her help.

Mario was a lovely guy—thoughtful, interested in world affairs and Renaissance art, very involved with his children.

I saw Mario in my Atchley Pavilion office before the surgery. His hyperthyroidism was stable and he had no other health issues to prevent Myles from performing the surgery, since it was the best hope for Mario to resume meat cutting. During the admission I saw him several times to assure that his thyroid was behaving. He had a handful of other medical issues, none severe, but the question of more definitive treatment of his hyperthyroidism needed to be dealt with—he had been on a medicine which lowered his thyroid's output of hormone for a number of years, but it was clear that his hyperthyroidism wasn't going to go into remission without either radioactive iodine treatment or surgical removal of part of his thyroid gland.

Mario hadn't seen anyone for his thyroid for more than a year when I began to care for him. His eye surgery went without a hitch, and when I saw him a few weeks after his surgery he asked me if I would take over his care. I asked if it wouldn't be better to find an endocrinologist closer to his home in Queens, but he said he was impressed with the care he had gotten at Columbia Presbyterian.

I liked Mario a lot and was glad that he was willing to put up with the long commute to the medical center when he needed to see me.

A few weeks later Marcy said that Mario had cancelled his appointment because he couldn't afford our bill. As with many patients with Blue Shield-Blue Cross he had limited coverage: his hospital surgery bill had been covered, but not my several hospital visits or follow-up office visits with me. He apologized to Marcy and asked her to thank me for him.

I told Marcy to please call him and tell him that he didn't need to pay for the visits to me, and that we wouldn't send the bill to collection. I wanted him to come back even if he couldn't pay now or ever.

Two weeks later Marcy caught me between patients: she seemed agitated. "Mario Lombardi just came in and paid his bill."

I was shocked. "What? Why did he do that?"

"He wouldn't accept our cancelling the bill. He said, 'I have always paid my debts, and I'm not going to stop doing that now.' He sold his coin collection to cover your bill and other expenses related to his eye surgery. He wouldn't let me talk him out of it."

"Did he write a check? Can we just not deposit it?"

"He paid in cash."

I was distraught about this, and knowing how he treasured the coin collection and hoped to use it to send his kids to college made his paying my bill even more painful. I stewed over it for a week. Finally, I called him on a Sunday afternoon when I thought I would catch him at home. Try as I might to get him to take the money back, he said the coin collection was gone, and that he felt good that he could pay me for taking care of him.

"You are a good doctor. You cared about me and you deserved to be paid. That stuff happens, Doc. It's done now, can't be undone."

I never heard from him again. Myles told me a year later that the operation had relieved the threat of corneal erosion, but his double vision had not gone away and Mario still couldn't cut meat. He said that Mario was planning to sell the Lombardi and Son Butcher Shop and find another line of work.

In the early fall of 1976, one of my new patients was Jennifer Scaffoli. She was about 40, five years older than I was. She had come to my office because she was feeling tired. Her history and examination were not unusual: recent fatigue keeping house and taking care of her large, active family; mild depression; recently reduced menses; some mild abdominal discomfort. She was pale and she had a few bruises on her legs. Her pulse was a little fast, her blood pressure a little low. My examination of her was otherwise normal.

I spent an hour with her taking her history, examining her, talking with her about the most probable causes of her symptoms, and explaining the laboratory tests I recommended she have done before she returned home.

At the end of the day I always went through the laboratory results that had returned from patients I had seen earlier in the day. This could be fun, learning whether I had made a correct diagnosis or discovered something interesting or had totally missed the boat. Most of my office patients had relatively benign problems that could be cured or managed without much difficulty and the lab results either confirmed a diagnosis or indicated whether my management was effective.

I got to Mrs. Scaffoli's results at the bottom of that day's pile: nearly every test was abnormal. She had an extraordinarily high number of white blood cells, most of them abnormal; she was profoundly anemic; her platelets (essential in normal clotting) were very low. I had expected nothing more than, perhaps, anemia, or hypothyroidism. She had acute leukemia.

I stared at the page, only slowly comprehending what I was looking at. She was not scheduled to see me for a few weeks, so I would have to call her tonight. What did I tell a woman with five children at home, who I had known for one hour, about the life-ending disease revealed by the numbers on the paper I held in my hand?

A few days later Mrs. Scaffoli saw the hematologist I recommended, Dr. Gross. She agreed to be admitted for chemotherapy. During that first admission I saw her twice a day, as did Dr. Gross. I managed her hospital care and he ordered the chemotherapy, adjusting doses each morning based on the previous afternoon's blood tests. In her room I met her husband, a harried and tired-looking man who owned a dry-cleaning shop, and I met her children, several of them wrapped in the self-absorption of teenagers, the others still in elementary or middle school, all uncomfortable visiting their drained-looking mother who was in bed attached to a dripping IV delivering blood or chemotherapy.

The plan was for one week of chemotherapy, and then three weeks at home while her bone marrow recovered. When she came to our office building for laboratory tests a week before her second scheduled admission, she asked to speak with me.

"We received our bills and a statement from Blue Shield. They paid all of your bill, but only for Dr. Gross's first visit. We found out that our insurance will only pay for one physician during a hospitalization, and for one consultant's visit. His bill was sent in later than yours, so only the first day was covered. The rest was very expensive. I don't know where the money will come from to continue being treated."

I was dismayed, but had a solution. "I will have Dr. Gross admit you, and his will be the only bill. I will come by to see you every day, but I won't write your orders and I won't send you a bill. That way all of his future bills will be covered."

During her second admission Dr. Gross was in charge and I came by once or twice a day for "social visits" during her stay. From time to time I suggested minor change to her medications to Dr. Gross, but I didn't write progress notes or orders.

After her discharge she told me that she did not care much for Dr. Gross.

"I am sure that Dr. Gross is a very smart and competent man. But he barely pokes his head into the room every morning and evening to tell me the lab results and his plans. He is not warm or communicative. He's gone before he gets here—he has never really talked to me or my husband beyond asking me medical questions and telling me what his plan was."

She asked me to resume being her attending doctor as long as the chemotherapy was going on. After the second hospitalization I admitted her, wrote the history and daily progress notes, wrote the orders other than chemotherapy, and saw her twice a day. I never sent her a bill after that first month. That would be illegal now, but the rules were more flexible then.

As the season progressed toward winter we admitted her each month. Dr. Gross continued to manage her chemotherapy, and I wrote the admission and progress notes, took care of her inflamed mouth and diet adjustments and skin care and ordered transfusions. There really wasn't a lot more for me to do. During our evening visits I sat with her for about a half hour talking about our children or the major league play offs or the current state of politics. She didn't care much for Gerald Ford, but was glad to have Nixon gone. She bet against the hated Yankees in the World Series and was for Cincinnati and cheered up a bit when the Reds won. She worried about finances and how her husband was coping with five children. She wanted me to tell her stories about growing up in Montana. Saying that she was only five years older than I, she asked me not to call her Mrs. Scaffoli, which made her feel old, but to call her Jennifer, or, even better, what everyone called her, Jenny.

By the fifth round of chemotherapy, Jenny had grown thinner and even weaker. Her chemotherapy was providing little benefit. In late January I admitted her for a transfusion and her next round of chemotherapy. I had called her every few days, so I knew that she had been having a fever, that she could not keep food down, and that she was short of breath walking to her bathroom and now needed her oldest daughter to help her bathe.

It was already dark outside when I arrived at her room to see her. She was standing in the middle of the room in a long white flannel nightgown with faded pink and blue flowers. She looked wrung out, tired, gaunt, sad. Where I could see her skin, she was very pale and slightly yellow and bruised. Her hair, hanging down to her mid-back, was dull and lightly streaked with gray.

She greeted me calmly, warmly: "Thank you for coming."

"Of course."

"This is my last admission. I'm . . . I'm not going to make it to spring. I want to stop chemotherapy. No more transfusions." After a long pause, at first watching me and then dropping her gaze, she said, "I'm sorry that I haven't been a better patient."

My mouth went dry. Her youngest child was just a few years older than my daughters. I had talked with her when she was at home several times a week for months and had spent hours sitting beside her bed listening to her stories, telling her mine. I didn't know what to say. We were both still standing, just a few feet apart.

"I want you to promise me something. I want you to be with me as you have been, every morning and evening. I need to know that you are not going to give up on me."

"What do you want me to do?"

"Just be there, talk to me, talk to my family. When I can't talk, just hold my hand. I'll know that you are there." There was a pause, and then she said, "You can start now. Will you hold me?"

I had never held a patient before. I had a vague sense that touching a patient in this way was improper. She was very thin. I could feel all of her bones. She was quietly sobbing, and her arms were shaking. I could feel her chest against my chest, her breath on my neck. I never had held someone in my arms who was dying, who would very soon be dead. She held on to me for a long time.

She did die, four nights later, quietly in her sleep, her husband also asleep in a chair beside her.

That evening I had visited her just before I left the hospital to go home to my own family. I sat with her for a while holding her hand, as I had been doing every day. As I stood up and let go of her hand, she gave my fingers a weak squeeze. Her final words, the only words she had spoken to me in a day, were "thank you," nothing more than that.

Jenny taught me how to care for her when there was nothing more to be done. She seemed to know instinctively that what she needed was to have me present—to be beside her on the brink as she left. Over time I learned that being asked by someone to care for them when they are sick or suffering or dying—not just to be a gentle and humane technician that monitors and prescribes, but also to be with them as a friend—has been the greatest reward of being a physician.

Taking care of Jenny also had the effect of abruptly changing my focus, from the total preoccupation with day-to-day practice, to beginning to think about the unknowable future.

We sometimes went out with the girls to a fancy restaurant called La Petite Auberge a few towns to the north in Cresskill, NJ. At 6 and 7 they wore long dresses and brought along coloring books and crayons and stories and sat through three-course dinners like little princesses. I loved being with the girls with this tinge of elegance, so different from my childhood in Montana where the only restaurant Mom could afford was the Golden Pheasant and I grew to hate chop suey.

We had gone to La Petite Auberge a few weeks before Christmas and I had the idea that it might be nice to take the girls in their long dresses to make rounds on Christmas afternoon. The girls moved with me from floor to floor. I parked them in the doctors' charting area in the nursing stations, where the nurses made a fuss over them. In half the rooms, when I told the patients that my girls were with me they asked to see them and I brought the girls in for a few minutes. Jenny Scaffoli happened to be in the hospital receiving chemotherapy and when I went in to see her, I left the girls in the chart room. I was hesitant to even mention that the girls were with me because her circumstances were so wretched and mine were so happy, but Jenny had gotten wind that the girls were with me, and asked if I could bring them in. We were there for just a few minutes while Jenny asked about their presents and admired their dresses.

I was overwhelmed by my sense of what she was missing by not being with her family on Christmas, what she was about to lose. As we walked out I could see tears in her eyes, and she could see that I was choking back tears of my own.

Although being on the Columbia faculty teaching students and residents and fellows and in private practice were beyond my dreams when

I was a student and resident, I began to think about the unpredictability of who and when diseases struck, began to imagine my daughters becoming ill. I began to think that if I died young our family would have missed the opportunity for camping and hiking and fishing and living in a more relaxed, less crowded place than New York City.

That winter I pushed myself to find what I could do to make life in New York City fuller and richer. One February morning a heavy snowfall closed New York City down. With two feet of snow on the streets, there was no moving traffic. The George Washington Bridge was closed. The on-call resident in Harkness told me that he could round on my patients and call me if there were any problems. I asked him just to see anyone that the nurses felt had an urgent issue and I would try to come in.

The Montanan in me that I had tried to hide for years suddenly wanted to break free and declare himself. I put on my cross-country skis and a parka and skied a mile to the deserted NJ Route 4, then skied down the middle of the George Washington Bridge, and then down the middle of Broadway from 178th Street to 168th Street. Suddenly I felt like a westerner, inhaling large breathes of frosty air, breaking fresh tracks where no one had skied before me. I rounded in my wool stocking cap, Nordic ski sweater, and wool pants. I felt refreshed and physically vigorous in a way I hadn't for years. That afternoon I skied home and built a fire in my study fireplace. I dug out a copy of the *Country Journal*, which I jokingly referred to as "the journal of the midlife crisis," and began wondering what it would be like to spend the rest of the girls' childhood years some place other than New York City.

CHAPTER 29

A Life Out of Balance

By the summer of 1977, a little less than two years after returning, I was ambivalent about both my medical career at Columbia and about whether New York City was where I wanted Katharine and Margaret Lea to grow up, where Margaret and I should spend the rest of our lives. The joy with which I had begun practice had gradually subsided into the satisfaction of doing a good job taking care of my private patients and those of the doctors for whom I was consulting. Many of my patients wrote notes of gratitude and referred others in their family and their friends. I loved making attending rounds three months a year on the teaching services and enjoyed being asked by medical students to advise them about residency.

I was caught between reimbursements that remained below what the department was paying and my already long hours. I was unwilling to charge patients more for my office and hospital care, because of my determination not to price myself over what patients like Mario Lombardi and Jennifer Scafolli and Michael and Mary Toohey could afford.

I wanted to spend more time teaching, but the medical school's model was to ask faculty members to pay their salaries from their research grants or private practices, and to volunteer their time for teaching. When I inquired, I found out that there was no money for managing residency or student clinical education: the external accrediting bodies had not yet begun to require that teaching hospitals hire clerkship and residency program directors who would be reimbursed to spend time managing education and supporting learners.

During our three years in Maryland, with my life no longer completely commandeered by learning, practicing, and teaching medicine and doing research, I had time for the affairs of the rest of the world to seep into my daily consciousness. Commuting home from Walter Reed every day listening to National Public Radio's *All Things Considered* had revealed to me that democracy and opportunity were only partially true, the rest lying someplace between nurtured myth and propaganda. At the Unitarian Church we weren't receiving lessons from an ancient document ill-suited to sorting out contemporary problems, or hearing ministerial mandates about how we should lead our lives and raise our children: we were hearing minister and congregation alike struggling with the contradictions of what people were told that they should believe and the stark realities of the genocide and continuing betrayal of the Native Americans and the deeply embedded racism affecting not only Blacks, but also Hispanics and Asians, Jews and Muslims. America's support of the lingering colonialism in Southeast Asia, Africa, and the Middle East was becoming clear to me.

In Maryland, for the first time in our marriage most of our friendships developed outside of work with people with whom Margaret had as much connection as I did. The Rockville church had frequent events that brought us together socially and, for the first time since high school, I had begun to sing in the choir. Every Sunday at Rockville Unitarian Church our kids had spent time with other children in what was called religious education that, as far as I could tell, was a very soft approach to comparative cultural anthropology: what did people from other parts of the world believe in, and why?

Our efforts to find a similar church and friendships in the New Jersey suburbs completely failed. The Congregational church we visited a few times was too churchy, although they had a very cool annual antiques sale.

The several Unitarian churches we visited seemed inbred, righteous about their liberal values, and unwelcoming.

In February of 1977, Ellen Nelson, the youth minister at the Rockville Unitarian Church, called Margaret asking her if she could spend a week at the end of July to work in the children's program of a conference on an island off the coast of New Hampshire, where Ellen and many UCR members went every year. Margaret had been a frequent teacher in the children's programs at UCR and liked Ellen very much.

I was still skeptical of any kind of organized religion, even Unitarianism, and did not jump for joy when the call came. Ellen told Margaret that the week was so popular that it was almost impossible for new people to get in because every one of the 200 people who attended the conference each year wanted to come back; working in the children's program was the only way to get in. Since we usually spent a week with Margaret's family in Newburyport each summer and Star Island was only an hour away, Margaret accepted the invitation. We figured out how to fit in a separate trip to Montana, and our summer was suddenly very full.

In mid-July we drove up to Newburyport on a Thursday afternoon and left on Saturday morning for Portsmouth, New Hampshire. Peggy, like Margaret, was born a Unitarian and so knew about Star Island and its legends, but her idea of our vacation was that we should spend it entirely with them in Newburyport. I felt like we were jumping into something we might not like and sided with Peggy, although I didn't tell Margaret that.

We drove the 90 minutes north to Portsmouth. We had been warned to come a little early for the 2 PM departure, since the parking lot where we caught the ferry that would shuttle us to Star Island would fill up and time was needed to load the boat with our luggage. Just before the Piscataqua River we turned east and followed the river a short distance to the dock, which I at first passed by because it was surrounded by a mountain of rusty scrap metal on one side and by a mountain of highway salt and sand on the other, with a long line of cars waiting to enter. We had been told about the heavenly beauty of Star Island, not about a departure dock that looked like the gateway to an industrial suburb of Hell.

It took a half-hour to creep into the parking area and discharge our baggage in a mob full of happy kids, parents, and elderly people. Everyone knew everyone else: they were all meeting after a year apart but seemed to know each other like college roommates would, with a degree of intimacy and affection I had never seen before in a group of two hundred people.

Ellen and the few people we knew from UCR had gone to the island the night before to prepare for the conference's arrival. On the boat the four Noels looked and felt like aliens who had landed in the midst of a reunion. Clustered in excited groups focused on each other, for about half the trip not one of them paid us any attention. In unfamiliar company I become an introvert and I concentrated on watching the shores of the river pass by as the ferry picked up speed and took on the moderate waves of the open Atlantic. I was strongly wishing that we had stayed in Newburyport. Finally, a few people took notice of us, introduced themselves, found out how we learned about the conference, and, more to the point, how on earth we had managed to get in: there was a waiting list of one hundred.

Gradually, like Brigadoon emerging from the Scottish mists, the 19th Century hotel and the 18th Century fishing village on the island took shape and as we got closer, we could see that the dock was crowded with people waiting for us to land and then, suddenly, there was a chant from the people onboard announcing, "We did come back, we did come back," echoed back to us by the people waiting on the dock, "You did come back, you did come back."

The word "overwhelm" means to turn over, to cover over completely, to overthrow. Star Island did all of that. For a week we lost track of the mainland, of the reunification of Vietnam by Ho Chi Minh, of the political conventions getting underway that would nominate Gerald Ford and Jimmy Carter, of the lethal infections in Philadelphia that would be known as Legionnaires Disease. We ate our meals family style at tables of twelve, served by college kids, called pelicans, who, when they were children, had attended one of the island's twelve summer conferences every year and had fallen in love with the place.

We adults attended morning talks about truth and lying in international affairs, delivered by speakers invited from the State Department, newspapers, universities, or overseas businesses. The hundred children and teenagers were grouped by age in programs of their own. We swam in 60-degree water at 7 AM, did workshops in the afternoon, got mildly loosened up at a happy hour, and spent the evenings in more talks. We became friends with the Star Island staff members, spent long hours on the rocks watching the Atlantic roll by, ate lobster caught only hours earlier in the primevally clear waters around the islands, and stayed up late singing the folk songs of the sixties and early seventies.

On the last night the pelicans put on a talent show, some acts excellent, others laughably bad, all delivered with irreverent good humor. We cheered, went off to a final candlelight service, and woke the next morning sad, on the verge of tears, which, as we trooped down the front walk and boarded the ship, swept like a wave over kids and adults alike. Farewells in the parking lot went on and on, promises were given to return next year.

When we arrived we didn't know anyone other than Ellen and a few people from the Rockville Unitarian Church. In a week we had made more friends than we had in New York City in the previous two years.

Driving back to Newburyport our exhausted, tearful kids were silent. Margaret and I didn't talk. When we stumbled into the Wilkins house we couldn't explain why we were so silent and put-offish, couldn't explain what we had just passed through that made everything around us seem too loud, too phony, and too preoccupied with all the wrong things.

Margaret would stay on with her folks for a few more days, but I had arranged with Tom to cover his practice the next week while he went on vacation. At 6:00 PM Margaret dropped me at the Eastern Airlines shuttle gate in Boston. I arrived at Newark Airport about 8:00 PM as dusk was settling in. Tom was waiting for me in his ancient Volvo. If the car ever had air-conditioning it had died. The night was hot and humid; the airport and its exit roads smelled of jet fuel, car exhaust and hot asphalt. The drive took an hour. The car windows were down and as freight trucks and taxis and buses and an endless torrent of cars roared by us on the New Jersey Turnpike, Tom told me about patients of mine that he had admitted or seen in the office or talked with on the phone, and then he went through the list of his patients that I would round on the next morning and for the next ten days.

He dropped me at the Englewood house. I gave him a cheery farewell and told him not to worry about a thing, opened the hot and stuffy house, dropped my bag in the kitchen, and went out the back door with a beer. I sat on the back porch steps for a half hour. Not more than a minute or two passed between the sounds of a distant police car or fire engine or ambulance siren, a roaring truck on Highway 4 a mile away, an airplane thundering overhead.

Twelve hours before I had been on a pristine Atlantic island surrounded by people that I had quickly become friends with. The only sounds there were of the waves washing in on the rocks, sea gulls, and children laughing. There were no radios on Star Island, no hair dryers, no sirens. Showers were 5 minutes twice in a week. There were no TV's, no newspapers, no presence of the world's sorrow.

As summer simmered around me, I had a single persistent thought: why were we living in New York City?

During the month of August Tom and I covered Dr. Southworth's practice as well as our own while he spent the month at a very old family summer house in the town of Quogue, so exclusive that there were no road signs on the Long Island Expressway indicating its existence. The previous summer Tom, Jan, and their family had spent a weekend there, and this summer Margaret, the girls and I were invited. We were installed in small upper floor bedrooms in bright rooms with many windows, faded wallpaper, and simple furnishings, not unlike Star Island. The walls were thin, the house unheated, the windows perpetually open to catch the breezes off the Atlantic. Dr. Southworth and his wife Katharine were there to greet us. One of his daughters and her children had been drafted to share in the obligations of hosting us.

The first afternoon we caravanned to a private tennis and beach club where the kids got happily sunburned and I tried to mask my growing alarm that we had not managed to intuit the upscale dress code of this ancient and refined summer community or to have acquired the easy grace with which they met and conversed with each other.

Katharine Southworth had sent word through Marcy that we would be going to the home of the editor of the financial pages of the *Wall Street Journal* for a cocktail party and made clear what the dress expectations would be: she suggested that I wear a summer casual suit with a tie, and that Margaret wear a cocktail dress. For this, at least, Margaret and I were forewarned and came up with a passable seersucker suit and summer dress.

While the kids were taken over by their daughter Kate and her children, the Southworths drove us over to the party in an elegant, sprawling house in which all the first-floor rooms opened onto flagstone terraces. Butlers took drink orders and the maids toted silver platters with finger food. The chatter was animated, people catching up with each other's past year and family events. Many were journalists or bankers, and there were writers and actors and a sprinkling of full-time Quogue residents.

The Southworths kept an eye on us, thoughtfully introducing us to people with whom we might have something in common—a few doctors and their families, a couple whose wife I had taken care of, a few people from Harvard with whom we had nothing in common other than having lived in Cambridge for four years. With each introduction there was a friendly, interested conversation, superficial but welcoming. In a few there were discrete searches of who we were, not as people—cocktail parties aren't really designed for that purpose—but who were our families, who were we connected to, what was our importance? I felt like a pound-puppy being sniffed out at a fire hydrant by purebreds.

On Sunday afternoon we went with the Southworths to a lawn party at a massive estate in the Hamptons owned by a Greek shipping line owner, a large white mansion with layered terraces stair-stepping down a long lawn to docks where a few yachts were tied up. There was a small orchestra playing in a summer house, kids running around the lawns with various entertainments set up for them, a large pool where a few guests with their children had changed and were swimming. We mostly stayed with the girls, watching as one might a major league baseball team from the cheap seats in the deep outfield.

Over the course of the summer we had spent a week in Montana, ten days in Newburyport and Star Island, and a long weekend in Quogue. The distances between those three places were huge, both in miles and in culture. Of course, Montana came naturally for our family, and, although Star Island was totally unfamiliar to us, it and the people we met also came naturally. I found it hard to imagine ever wanting to spend time again with the summering residents of Quogue, although I think that Dr. Southworth was hoping that I would get the idea of how I might change my practice to attract more people like the ones we met.

At the beginning of our third year after returning to Columbia, with the girls now at the Elisabeth Morrow School and Margaret there teaching science to fifth and sixth graders, our lives had settled into a pattern. Katharine was now seven and Margaret Lea six. They were happy at school, they had friends with whom they swapped homes for play dates, and they loved the Englewood house with its great spaces for playing in the third-floor attics and in the basement den. Although I was at the hospital thirteen out of fourteen days, I was home nearly every evening for dinner and to help put them to bed. We had created a large vegetable and flower garden in the spacious backyard, and there was a rose garden along a curving sidewalk between the back door and the garage. I gradually sank back into feeling grateful for our New York Life.

After a summer that had opened my eyes to how narrow life had become with almost all of my waking hours spent at the hospital, I decided with Margaret to try to make better use of New York City. The arts section of the *Sunday New York Times* on the first weekend after Labor Day was always overwhelming, jammed with season-summarizing articles and advertisements for the hundreds of concerts, ballets, operas, plays,

A Life Out of Balance

lectures, and movies that would be available during the fall and early winter: there were simply too many appealing choices and it was tempting to just give up. But I knew that unless we bought tickets at the beginning of the season, we would never get around to it.

We managed to find enough babysitters to have a subscription to eight concerts of the Chamber Music Society of Lincoln Center on Sunday afternoons. Although our friend Judy Blegen sang regularly at the Metropolitan Opera and we had gone to the Met once or twice a year, we preferred the more experimental and unusual repertory of the City Center Opera Company for which we bought a subscription. We attended a ballet or two and occasionally went to the theater.

Even then it was expensive and complicated to take a night out. During the Sunday afternoon chamber music concerts parking was easy, but for the evening performances of the opera and ballet, every auditorium was full to the chandeliers and in order to get parking that was not a long walk away, we went into Manhattan early, parked at Lincoln Center, and then went out to dinner—restaurants like Coq au Vin, now gone, and Cafe des Artistes, still in business now at princely prices, but then a bit down at the heels and affordable.

New York City was a fabulous place at Christmas. Katharine and Margaret Lea were just old enough to see Judy Blegen as Gretel in the Met Christmas production of *Hansel and Gretel* and to go out for ice cream sundaes with her and her niece at the legendary Rumpelmayer's on Central Park West. Judy said, "Now, in spite of the cold, you simply have to have ice cream sundaes with hand whipped cream and the best chocolate in the world." The girls did not object.

In the summer she had invited us to have a picnic and listen to the New York Philharmonic with her and her niece and our kids on the Great Lawn in Central Park. When we arrived at her apartment overlooking Central Park West, we were in jeans. Judy was in a pink and white sundress with pearls and high heels, not exactly my idea of picnic clothes.

I asked her, "Judy, don't you have jeans?" She was, after all, a girl who had grown up three blocks away from me in Missoula Montana.

She answered, "Judith Blegen doesn't own jeans."

It took me a few seconds to digest and understand this. Judy was a highly regarded opera star and was therefore always a celebrity in public and always on stage. For her, maintaining the image that she had worked hard to create and needed to perpetuate was integrated into every action and had become who she was. She wasn't so famous that she needed to disguise herself in order to have privacy when in public: being recognized was important and gratifying to her.

A few months later she invited us to a party in the home of Tatiana Troyanos, a world-famous mezzo-soprano, in a new apartment tower overlooking Columbus Circle. We arrived around 8 PM as the party was just getting underway. Judy introduced us to Michael Tilson Thomas, one of the Met conductors, and then to Tatiana and other singers and musicians, but soon we were on our own as she went off on a tour of the rooms.

We joined a circle already in conversation, trying to look interested and intelligent. None introduced themselves or asked who we were. Because they were famous (or we assumed they were), we didn't ask their names because if we knew anything about opera we would obviously know.

The party was glitzy and noisy and everyone except us sparkled. They were not so much on stage as very connected with each other, with no way of connecting with us and no need to do so. Except for the few people there whom Judy had referred to me who were now my patients, we were Judith Blegen's friends and not people who it would have been thrilling for them to know.

Of course, the reverse would have been true had I invited some of the less luminary Met musicians and singers to a party of doctors who all knew each other, I suppose.

In September Dr. Bradley's successor as the Bard Professor of Medicine, Dan Kimberg, asked if I would be willing to design a new curriculum for finishing second year students. The most formative experience in the third year was the three-month clerkship in internal medicine, where students learned to perform and record in-depth histories and physical examinations, write daily progress notes, perform procedures, present patients, and use the vast array of literature and text resources to understand their patients' multiple clinical problems. A quarter of the students could begin the third year in the medicine clerkship, but all the others started elsewhere. The other departments—in particular surgery, obstetrics and gynecology, and neurology—recognized that students who had medicine before those clerkships did much better than those who arrived without yet having had three months of medicine. However, all the students couldn't do medicine first, and some would not do it until the last quarter.

Dan wanted me to create a four-week "pre-clerkship" at the end of the second year in which all the students could build decent history taking, physical examination, and presentation skills. He had secured the support of the other chairs and the dean to make room in the second-year curriculum and wanted me to create it. In a month I wrote the curriculum content and the structure of the blocks and figured out in which locations to teach it and who the teachers would be.

In October I presented the proposal to the medical school curriculum committee, which approved it to start in the spring of 1978.

The faculty members of the department of medicine were central to the course, along with pediatricians and neurologists, whose clinical methods and skills were similar. Dan asked me to present the proposal, now essentially a done deal, to the department of medicine monthly meeting. I created slides and handouts and did the presentation.

There was stony silence at the end and no excitement whatsoever. The department of medicine already had what it most cherished, three months to shape the students as clinicians. Creating another four-week course in which they would teach because the surgeons and other departments did not want to or could not teach those skills to their beginning students was just one more drain of time for faculty members who far and away spent more time in student education than those in any other department.

After a minute of silence, Dan asked if there were any questions.

John Loeb, who many of us saw destined to be as great or greater than his father—the former chair Robert Loeb—put up his hand:

"But Gordon, why do we need to do this? The curriculum is perfect as it is. It doesn't need to be changed. We're Columbia!"

I had no answer for that. I walked to the blackboard and was about to challenge John's presumption by writing something that the poet Alexander Pope had written that had horrified me at the time I first read it: "Whatever is, is right."

For a change, I controlled myself.

Pope had meant this as a defense for the authority of the church and aristocracy to make all of the rules, and as an optimistic assurance that even if injustice and evil existed, God wanted it that way.

I was crestfallen, not because I loved the idea of the pre-clerkship, but because I recognized the benefit to the students. But even more, I was disappointed in the self-satisfied belief that nothing needed to be changed because Columbia was already perfect.

Despite the department members' antipathy, the pre-clerkship was put in place the following May and I added managing the course to my workload.

A few weeks later I met with Dr. Kimberg to sort through my growing feelings of discontent.

I began:

"I appreciate the opportunity you gave me to put the pre-clerkship together. I'm happy that you asked me to get it started this spring. Were you surprised by the department's faculty members' lack of enthusiasm?"

Dan replied, "Well, there really isn't anything in it for the department or for them. We already do what the other departments want—teach all of the students the basics of clinicianship—it's just that we can't do it for everyone before they start other clerkships when medicine isn't their first."

I moved on to my main reason for talking with him. "I'd like to see if there is a way for me to spend more time with the student education programs?"

"What do you have in mind?"

"As you know, after two years my practice hours are close to full. I have about ten patients in the hospital at any time, half mine, and half patients I am seeing for surgeons or neurologists.

"Even so, collections have fallen short of my salary and the overhead and I have started seeing patients for two of the ophthalmologists in the evening before some of their patients' surgeries—they mostly don't have medical issues, but the ophthalmologists want to be sure the patients are okay to go through surgery. That means that I finish rounding on my own patients around 6:30 and then stay another hour or so just to try to generate enough income to cover what you pay me.

"All of the time I spent meeting with faculty to create the new pre-clerkship was rewarding, but it was entirely uncompensated. You have asked me to manage the course, and I would be doing a lot of the teaching, both of which would mean cutting my office hours for a month. But as far as I know that also isn't compensated. I attend on the inpatient service three months a year and I don't want to cut that either—it is the most enjoyable of my teaching activities."

Dan was listening thoughtfully, saying little. He asked me to tell him who I was seeing in my office practice. I reviewed how new patients got to me and what other doctors referred patients to me. I told him about the new patients that Dr. Southworth was referring to Tom and me, and Dr. Southworth's recommendation that I leave time in my schedule to see "important" patients—bankers, lawyers, corporate leaders, and of course their families.

"Here's the thing," I said. "I see a lot of patients that don't have great insurance. We usually don't know that for several months, not until we get the insurance payment, or until the patient tells us. These are people I want to care for—teachers, sometimes ministers or artists or musicians, sometimes the parents of our students or nurses. I don't try to collect—

which would force them to give up seeing me—and I don't want to stop seeing them."

Dan pursed his lips, nodded and tapped a pencil on his desk for a few seconds. "We know what you are doing, and we don't want you to stop. But we can't increase your salary until your collections exceed your expenses—that's the way the contract applies to everyone, and in the past most of the new physicians started getting bonuses by the end of the second year."

I thought about that for a moment, and then asked, "Is there any way I can keep doing what I am doing but just take a flat salary so that I don't have to do the eye surgery clearances?"

"We don't have any one in the department on a flat salary. Everyone's salary is based on their grants and their clinical income. Many of the research faculty actually earn less than you do, but in almost every case they are independently wealthy or single and don't need more than what we pay them."

"Are there any jobs in the department that you pay for—the clerkship director for example?"

"No, all of that is uncompensated, an add-on to other duties that are compensated."

He paused for a moment, frowned a bit, and then went on: "The student health job is going to be open. Al Lamb is retiring this spring. That would be about a half time job."

I had the feeling that people who took jobs in the student health or employee clinic were no longer in the mainstream of teaching and practicing. It wasn't that I wanted to do less private practice and ward attending. I just wanted to do more teaching and curriculum development, and I wanted to spend more time coaching and supporting students and residents who could use some guidance and encouragement. Columbia hadn't allocated money for any of those things.

I told Dan that the student health job wasn't really a solution since the salary wouldn't allow me to spend more time teaching.

I was very reticent to ask the more senior physicians for advice. I knew that the physicians who had private offices on Park Avenue or in other affluent neighborhoods on the East Side must have been charging their patients more. Outside of my single conversation with Dr. Vicale, who wanted me to raise my fees for the cash-only care of his Saudi Prince, I never talked with anyone about fees once Tom and I started. I could have asked Don Holub, the senior endocrinologist, for his advice, but again my reticence to talk about money kept me from doing it. I had the feeling that a preoccupation with income was a violation of the highest traditions of caring for people. I myself had written a piece for the *P & S Class of '67 Yearbook*, "The History of Bellevue Hospital", that a famous Columbia physician, Austin Flint, had declared (to his wife): "My only concern is with the care of my patients. The good lord will take care of my pocket book." How his wife felt about that has been lost to history, but I had at least partially embraced that attitude.

Although every first-year orthopedic resident seemed to know exactly what fees each of the attendings charged for their operations, in internal medicine one didn't talk about money—or at least I wasn't present if the subject came up. With our practices filling, it certainly would have been reasonable to raise our fees, but we had been told (without my ever digging deeper to confirm it) that once we set our fees Blue Shield, the major insurer of our less wealthy patients, would not reimburse the increment in the fee and our patients would be stuck with the unpaid portion.

I never knew whether Tom had financial resources from his family, but since he had many siblings, I supposed not. The one time that I broached the subject of money with him by asking what he thought two former residents who had gone into practice a few years before us were charging, he more or less dismissed them, implying that I wouldn't be happy practicing as they did.

Even more baffling, I don't remember ever talking with Tom about whether he had broken even and was now getting a collection-based bonus.

Although Tom and I had very similar ideas about our near-total commitment to our practices, he seemed to have come back to Columbia with a fuller sense of how to put his career together beyond practice and teaching. Tom spent his military service as a general medical officer, and then had a two-year fellowship in endocrinology at the University of Washington. When he returned to Columbia, he arranged to continue doing clinical research with a prominent bone researcher, although at the time I never knew exactly what he was contributing to the research projects in that lab. And I didn't know if he was reimbursed for his time.

Andy Frantz had wanted me to come back as a full-time researcher, and I turned him down. The research was pleasant, but I had no drive to make discoveries, write papers, get grant funding, or attend scientific conferences. I had no notion of how promotion worked for physicians in the clinical practice track, although I knew that it was slow. But Tom seemed both to want to do research and to understand that it would speed promotion along.

I could have looked for someone to talk with, a mentor to help me navigate my way to a better balance at Columbia, but I was reticent to ask Dan Kimberg for more of his time, I was in too much awe of Dr. Southworth to reveal my uncertainty and dissatisfaction, and I was uncertain that Andy Frantz would know enough about private practice at Columbia to be able to help me.

When I was still in the Army, Tom James had offered me a position at the University of Alabama as an alternative to returning to Columbia. I visited Birmingham without Margaret, partially as a courtesy to Bill Maclean, who was originally going to be my partner at Columbia. I was impressed with the size and quality of everything I was shown in Birmingham, but at that time it was beyond my ability to imagine that living there would be better than returning to Columbia to the dream I had been offered of practicing and teaching in an institution that I revered.

One evening in the late fall, as I was finishing up after my last patient, Marcy told me that a Dr. James was calling from Alabama.

"Hello. This is Tom James. I thought I would call and see how you are doing."

"Really? What a surprise!"

In a soft southern drawl he asked, "How are you enjoying your position at Columbia? Is New York City agreeing with you?"

I wasn't about to admit to the complexity of my feelings. I told him that things were going very well. "Happy as a clam," I said.

There was a drawn-out silence while he waited for me to say more. I was so surprised that all I could think of was to repeat, "I'm surprised to have you call."

"Well, I have learned over a long career that when someone we are interested in joining us has gotten settled in a new position it is worth checking in with them again to see how it is working out. We haven't seen anyone else that we would like to have here as much as you, and Bill Maclean keeps urging us to give you another try."

I was flattered. I wasn't expecting to ever hear from Alabama again once I decided to return to Columbia. After all, almost no one given admitting privileges ever left Columbia and until this past summer I hadn't been considering leaving.

Dr. James wanted me to create a new division of general internists at Alabama. Like most university hospitals, the department of medicine was made up of specialty divisions—cardiology, gastroenterology, oncology and so on—but there was intense pressure from the American Board of Internal Medicine and the Residency Review Committee in Internal Medicine to ensure that internists' pre-specialty training should prepare them first of all to be good generalists. Bill Maclean insisted that I was a person who could do that. And they wanted me to bring Margaret along on the visit, because they knew that a recruitment effort would never succeed unless she could be convinced to move to Alabama.

I told him that I would give it some consideration and let him know.

When he signed off, he said: "I'm a patient man. A good person is worth waiting for. I hope you and your wife will come down and take a second look."

Bill Maclean called a few days later to tell me how much he enjoyed living in Alabama and practicing at the University.

When I asked Margaret whether she would want to take a look at Alabama, she was noncommittal. Margaret had loved Chicago and Washington DC far more than New York City, but she had steadfastly said that she wanted me to be happy and would go where I thought that was most likely to happen.

With both skepticism and secrecy, we went to Birmingham. When we got there Dr. James pledged the resources to recruit a half dozen well-trained general internists to join me to practice and teach general medicine. He and the senior faculty he had me meet went out of their way to convince me that someone from Montana and the East Coast could be happy in the deepest of the deep south. Dr. James threw a big party for us: all of the guests had grown up or trained in the north. We met New Yorkers, Bostonians, Chicagoans, and a few people from Hopkins. There was nothing subtle about what they were trying to do and I noticed that my resistance was beginning to soften. The responsibilities, opportunities, and resources they were offering were impressive, far beyond anything I would be likely to be offered at Columbia.

Their efforts to convince us that Birmingham would be a good place for our daughters to grow up imploded the next day. The real estate agent who the university had asked to take us around apparently hadn't been given the battle plan. First she showed us a few lovely neighborhoods in the city of Birmingham, talking about the private schools that were nearby, having learned that Katharine and Margaret Lea went to a private grade school in New Jersey. Then she took us to Mountain Brook, where many of the faculty members lived. Mountain Brook was a neighborhood that had successfully fought for years to block annexation into Birmingham, which would have forced a merger of their school system with the Birmingham schools. It had been the focus of efforts to force integration of all public schools in the center city and the suburbs. The Mountain Brook streets were lovely, the houses were lovely, there were old trees and gorgeous parks. The agent assured us with pride that the town took no state or federal money for its schools, so that they weren't subject to any federal regulations. In effect, the citizens taxed themselves to support the school system so that it could not be forced to integrate through bussing. Margaret and I didn't say a word to each other the rest of the morning. She went on with the agent to look at shopping areas and cultural buildings, and I went back to the university to meet with Dr. James. He asked my thoughts, I told him that I was impressed with the university and what he was offering. I asked how soon he would like me to make a decision. He said he would call in two weeks.

On the flight back to New York City I asked Margaret if she thought she would like to live in Birmingham. She said she didn't think so. It was quite clear to me that if Margaret and I had been brown or black and not white, we would not have been shown houses in Mountain Brook. We also noted that in a city with a huge black population, we had been introduced only to white doctors and their white wives.

For the next two weeks I dreaded having to tell Dr. James that we wouldn't pursue Birmingham any further. His department had made a considerable effort to attract us and they had offered me an interesting opportunity. The University of Alabama School of Medicine was well funded—the Chairman of the House Appropriations Committee was from Alabama and buildings paid for with federal money were going up all over the campus; the university had not one but four NIH cardiology training programs.

There was no mystery about why I dreaded his call: I hated disappointing people, and I also was absolutely sure that I could not tell him that we were uncomfortable with Alabama's implacable culture of segregation.

When he called, I weaseled out: I told him that the university and the position were impressive, but that Margaret didn't feel that she could move to Alabama. I suppose this came as no surprise to him and that it had happened many times before. I entirely avoided saying that I would never be happy in a segregated city.

In November, a few months after returning from Birmingham, I got a call at home from a surgeon for whom I had been seeing patients since we were both residents. We had discovered that we lived not far apart in Englewood; I appreciated him as a quiet, dignified, and highly competent surgeon who took good care of his patients, but other than that I didn't know anything about him outside of the hospital.

"I got your home number from the page operator," Paul said. "I hope that you don't mind my calling. Am I interrupting anything?"

"Nothing other than doing the dishes. This is a good time to talk."

"I want to talk to you about considering joining the Englewood Field Club. I know that your girls go to Elisabeth Morrow and already are friends with a number of our members' children. Shall I go on?"

"Sure."

Paul explained that the origin of the club had been to provide families with a place to play tennis, swim, and ice skate.

"As their children grow up," he said, "Some of our older members move into the City or into another town and we have vacancies. Your daughters are just the age for them to want to be with their school friends to swim and skate. You can play squash and tennis there too, if you're interested in that."

I asked a few more questions about the costs and the procedures for becoming a member. He said that he would propose us and that he was sure that some of the other faculty members at Columbia who were members would be glad to sponsor us.

Without any idea why, I asked him to tell me something about the members.

He went in an unexpected direction with his answer, perhaps wishing to reassure me: "We screen members carefully; the bylaws don't allow Jews or Negroes."

A Life Out of Balance

I thanked him for thinking of me and told him I would talk it over with Margaret. I never tried to calculate it, but I guessed that half the faculty at CPMC were Jewish and a few were Black. Some of my patients were Black and quite a few were Jewish.

We had hoped to have Katharine and Margaret Lea in integrated public education when we rushed into buying a house in Englewood that we loved, but hadn't understood that the majority of Jewish children went to one of the two local Yeshivas and that most of the other white children went to private schools, so that there were only a few white children in their classrooms. Now the girls were in a private school, which was not formally segregated, but was too expensive for most non-whites. Although the idea of the girls having a place to socialize and do sports was appealing, we could not join a club that would have excluded many of our friends and the patients I took care of.

Early in 1978, Tony D'Amato, a grateful patient of mine called me from Maine and asked if I knew what to do with twelve lobsters. I said that I did. He told me his pilot would be flying the lobsters down to New York and that one of his men would bring them to my office.

I had suspected that Tony might be connected with one of the mobs, and when I saw the spooky man who delivered the icy, dripping green-black lobsters to my office, I was pretty sure that there must be some story behind the lobsters and the fact that Tony, who had no visible means of income, could fly lobsters around the country in his private plane.

What do you do with twelve live lobsters? You eat them right away. I called Margaret and asked her if I could invite a few friends over for a lobster feed at our house at 8 PM. Margaret loved lobsters and agreed. One of the people I called was Jack Morris, the doctor who had cared for me when I had hepatitis as a second-year resident. He was the first cardiologist I called when I wanted to refer a patient, and he had continued to be my doctor. He still practiced with the dedication that I had admired when I was a resident. Jack asked me a question that has haunted me ever since: "I was planning to go to the laundromat tonight. Would you mind if I brought my laundry over and did it at your house while we are eating?"

I had heard that he and his wife Betty had separated. I never asked Jack about it, but I speculated that Betty had grown tired of waiting for him to come home night after night and that she had decided to move on. I imagined that it might be even more complicated than that. She kept their daughters and the house.

Jack was the best doctor I ever knew, and he was living alone in an apartment, doing his laundry in a laundromat.

The dinner was pretty lively. Our house had a big parlor and an even bigger dining room with a large butler's pantry; it was a great place for our infrequent parties. When I got home we boiled the lobsters and melted a half-pound of butter. I chilled bottles of good French Chablis, started a fire in the dining room fireplace, covered the table in newspapers and served the lobster on our best china. We cracked the lobsters apart with our bare hands, laughing at the mess we were making. Jack ate two lobsters and a part of someone else's. I was disappointed that there would not be so much as a claw left for tomorrow's dinner.

When the other guests had gone and I had tucked Katharine and Margaret Lea into their beds upstairs, I went looking for Jack down in the basement where he was folding his laundry. The upstairs rooms were grand, but the basement ceiling was low, the walls were stone, and it was impossible to keep the walls and rafters free of cobwebs or scrub away their dank smell. Jack had to stoop a bit to avoid hitting his head on the light above the dryer, his big hands methodically folding underwear and towels on an old ironing board already piled with balled up socks. His reach was wide and high enough that he was able to fold his sheets in half, then in quarters in a single move without the bottom dragging on the basement floor. It was impressive to watch.

It was late and I was tired, but as usual Jack did not seem to be in a hurry. We chatted awhile about a few patients and I told him the story of Tony's man delivering the lobsters. When he had stacked his folded laundry in a basket I walked out to his car with him. I stood on the curb and watched his brake lights brighten as he slowed where the street bent to the right—and then he disappeared around a corner, headed back to his empty apartment with his clean laundry.

I had set myself up to practice like Jack, but I was gradually coming to realize that my view of Jack, Hamilton Southworth, and many of the other great physicians I had admired in medical school and residency had been two-dimensional. It had taken the nearly three years in which I was practicing like them for me to understand the third dimension—the impact that a life devoted to caring for patients can have on a doctor's family and friendships. Like Jack, I had very little time to do anything else.

Although I attempted to suppress the feeling that perhaps New York City wasn't the best place for the girls to grow up or the best place for me to be able to spend more time with them, my discontent wasn't getting any better.

A few weeks later Margaret invited a friend who was in New Jersey for a reunion of his Drew University Theological School classmates to have dinner with us. I had met Steve once or twice but didn't know him well. He had grown up in Texas and had a bit of swagger and a drawl that I hadn't run into in a Methodist minister before. He was serving a congregation in Baltimore. After dinner we moved to the living room. He told me about his church and then he asked how I was doing.

There was something about Steve that invited openness and I began to tell him about my practice and teaching at Columbia and some of my dissatisfactions, both with the amount of time I was spending at the hospital, and with my sense that I hadn't had much luck with establishing friendships or finding the time to do more with Margaret and the girls.

Steve began gently to ask me questions:

"Sounds to me like you work most of the time—even much of the weekend. I thought we ministers had a monopoly on that!" He chuckled at his own joke.

"So, you are always giving your time and your attention and your support to other people. After giving away so much of yourself, how do you restore yourself? How often do you see friends? Who do you go out to lunch with? I can't remember, do you play golf or tennis with anyone?"

"Good heavens no! There isn't time for any of that—but the idea of going out to lunch sounds appealing. I don't think I have ever gone out to lunch with anyone, except when I was dating Margaret. But I have no idea how I would block out the time. I have an hour for lunch in the doctors' dining room and I use it to check in with other doctors whose patients I am seeing, or who are seeing mine."

"Can't you go out to a restaurant for lunch with your friends at the hospital?"

"My time is tightly programmed. My office hours are full, and when I am not in the office seeing patients I am seeing them in the hospital, or in one of the clinics. I already have trouble getting home in time for dinner. And the doctors I am friends with are just as busy as I am."

"Well, do you ever ask your favorite patients to come to your office to visit with you?"

The idea seemed so preposterous that I laughed. "Good grief, Steve! I charge patients. I can't send them a bill for coming in to perk me up!"

"I see. Well, now, can you go out to dinner with them?"

"No. I can't do that. Patients are patients, not friends—I mean, I really like some of them and probably would enjoy them socially, but it just isn't something I would do—they're patients. The tradition is that we don't cross those lines by making friends with people we are caring for, and we don't care for our friends. And anyway, if I went out to dinner, I wouldn't be with the girls more than a few minutes in the morning for two days."

Steve pondered this for a long minute, nursing the scotch and soda I had made for him. If we had been talking outdoors in Texas, I'm pretty sure he would have scraped some dirt into a mound with his boot and spit on it.

"Do you have any friends outside of the hospital that you could spend time with?"

"That's the problem. I don't. We meet people that I like occasionally, but there just doesn't seem to be time."

Steve began to tell me about his life:

"I may be way out of my league—it seems like I don't know how doctors organize their work and their lives. It doesn't sound like you are having much fun and I wonder if it has to be that way for you to be a good doctor. You know, I take care of three or four hundred people. There isn't any insurance program that pays for ministers, which means that I have four hundred bosses, all of whom think that I work for them because they put two dollars in the plate every week—that's in a good week, and not every week is a good week—and they believe that they are entitled to my attention. Some of the parishioners are tough and draining—they're in truly miserable situations, or they're just people who are having trouble getting through life.

"I can spend many hours in a week with a wife grieving the loss of her husband of sixty years, or with a young family mourning the loss of a child, or a distraught family whose kid is in jail or failing out of school, or whose daughter is pregnant, with the Lord only knows whose baby, and she isn't telling.

"It can be exhausting . . . it's more exhausting than I ever imagined in seminary. Some mornings I look at my list of appointments and visits and I don't see a soul who is going to make me laugh or to honestly feel that I am helping anyone. On those days I might call up our treasurer or one of the committee chairs and ask, 'If you are coming into the church, could you stop by my office for a chat." They'll ask me what's on my mind, and I can tell them, 'It would just be good for me to see you, we haven't talked in a while.'"

"If I am making a few house visits in a neighborhood, I might call somebody I enjoy, tell 'em, 'Mildred, I'm going to be at the O'Conner house this afternoon, you going to be in?' I can be pretty sure that there will be a cup of tea and some fresh cookies when I arrive.

"If I have this right, you are giving your attention to other people all day, some of them very sick, and you don't have a lot of options for restoring yourself. In my job I can fill myself back up again, renew my energy and my sense that I am helping people and that they care about me.

And the fact is, for these folks I like to see, I am probably restoring them while they are restoring me. It's the way we take care of each other."

After Steve went back to his reunion I sat for a while in my study pondering what he said. I was tempted to write off his suggestions as naïve and out of touch with what a doctor's life is like. But I couldn't deny that after nearly three years of practice I had neither friends nor family with whom I could sit down in my kitchen or theirs and have a cup of coffee, go out for a beer, or take a long run.

The second attempt of Alabama to recruit me wasn't the last inquiry I got. I hadn't let anyone know that I was thinking of leaving, and yet there were more phone calls.

There had been the call from Dr. Thompson who had been my attending physician for a month when I was an intern at the University of Chicago. He had moved to the University of Iowa and was looking for someone to help him start a general internal medicine division there. I wasn't far enough along in thinking about leaving Columbia to want to visit Iowa, but I was intrigued that another highly subspecialized department of medicine was trying to find broadly trained internists comfortable with taking care of complicated patients to serve as role models for their residents and students.

Early in the winter I got a third call, this time from two people who wanted me to return to Washington DC. When I was still in the Army, Alan Robinson had tried to get me interested in coming to the University of Pittsburg to be a general internist there. I had liked the chair of medicine, Jim Leonard, but had trouble grasping what the job would be and was head over heels in love with the glamour of returning to Columbia. After my visit to Pittsburgh I didn't pursue his invitation.

Now Dr. Leonard was moving to become the chair at the new Uniformed Services University in Bethesda, Maryland, the medical school that Congress had authorized to assure a supply of doctors for the armed services because there was no longer a doctors' draft to force doctors to enlist. Dr. Leonard remembered me from my visit to Pittsburgh.

A Life Out of Balance

The first call was from Jerry Earll, who had had been my chief of endocrinology at Walter Reed, telling me that Dr. Leonard, Jay Sanford—who had been recruited to be Dean—and the physicians in the Walter Reed endocrinology unit wanted to recruit me to create the student internal medicine teaching programs at USUHS—a brand new curriculum in a brand new medical school.

I had left the Army with booster rockets attached to my heels, eager to return to the tradition and sophistication of Columbia to join the beyond-my-wildest-dreams practice with Dr. Southworth and Tom Jacobs. A few years earlier when I first heard about a "military medical school", I thought it was a bad idea. Had I been in Congress, I might have voted against it, thinking that it would be better to have more students go to the existing medical schools on scholarships that required military service after residency. But the country was woefully short of doctors and needed to double the number of medical students: medical schools were being subsidized to expand their class sizes, and the government was underwriting the creation of new medical schools around the country. Starting a military medical school that prepared students specifically for careers in the armed services turned out to be a good decision.

I asked Jerry if I had to rejoin the Army and put on the uniform.

He responded, "The services realize that they don't have all the physicians and scientists they need to start a medical school. There is a substantial budget to bring in physician scientists, most of whom will be civilians. Most of the department chairs will be the military service chiefs at the teaching hospitals. Medicine is an exception. Jim Leonard will be a civilian, and the dean, Jay Sanford, will be coming from Texas Southwestern and will also be a civilian. You could do it either way: if you want to come in uniform, we would promote you to Lieutenant Colonel, or you can come as a civilian."

A few days later I got a call from Dr. Sanford, one of the most famous infectious disease experts in the world and the head of the Division of Infectious Diseases at Texas Southwestern. He had found out a little about me and surprised me by knowing that I grew up in Montana, had been an

English major at Harvard, and fought forest fires during the summer. He knew about my residency and fellowships at Columbia. He told me that he had also served in the Army at Walter Reed, during the Korean War and felt that it was an honor to be the school's first dean.

There it was: I had a choice about whether to stay at Columbia or do what seemed impossible— break away from Columbia. Slightly less than three years after I returned to Columbia, without my lifting a finger I was being offered full-time jobs in which I would have the opportunity to set up new clinical and teaching programs on a full-time salary.

I couldn't decide whether it was cosmic irony or a death wish that I was tempted to return to a military institution that I had tried to resist, to which I had gone with reluctance, and which I had left as though fleeing the plague.

Just before midnight on a frigid January night I got a call from Howard Kiernan, an orthopedic surgeon who frequently asked me to provide pre- and post-op care to the elderly patients with hip fractures that he took from the emergency room.

"Gordon, it's Howard. I am in the ER with an 82-year-old woman with a hip fracture, whose family brought her in from her home. She fell this morning and couldn't get up to tell anyone. When she didn't answer her phone this evening her daughter went over to her apartment and found her on the floor. She was a little dehydrated, but she seems alright otherwise. She has insurance and I have a 3 AM slot in the operating room if she is okay to go to surgery. Would you be able to come in to see her?"

Howard was only a few years into his practice and still open to taking patients from the emergency room. Like all the orthopedic surgeons he didn't feel competent to determine if his patients were medically safe to operate on, so his ability to operate was based entirely on one of the internists making that decision.

The practice among orthopedic surgeons at the time was to operate on elderly patients as soon as possible. If they were medically fit there was no advantage to waiting: lying in bed they rapidly lost muscle mass and calcium from their bones and, with the pain medication they got for the fracture, they became constipated; in very little time they had bed sores or clots in their legs and would be too frail to ever be operated on.

I had grown weary of Howard's calls. Initially I had been pleased that he wanted me to see his patients, but the reality was that he needed some internist to see his patients in order to be able to operate and make a living, and I felt more used than appreciated. Once I had served his needs, he never talked to me about the patients, although I continued to see them until they were discharged; he never told me how well they had recovered after returning home, and he never struck up a conversation about our mutual practices, although his office was two doors down the hall. A combination of fulfilling the role of "good physician" by accepting patients like this who really did need the care of a good internist, and my sense that I needed to generate more income, led me once again to say yes.

It was 11:30. The phone was by our bed and Margaret had been lying awake listening to the conversation.

"You going in?"

"Unfortunately, yes."

This wasn't quite being fetched to a wood cabin in a prairie blizzard to deliver a woman with a difficult labor where it was life or death for both her and her baby, but on a cold night driving back to the hospital it felt close. The temperature was in the teens; as I drove across the George Washington Bridge, howling winds whipped dry snow across my windshield that the freezing wipers turned into ice. There was no traffic and in twenty minutes I was at the parking lot and in ten more I had gone to my office, gotten my white coat and black bag, and had trekked to Mrs. Dougherty's semiprivate room. I spent an hour taking a history from her, her daughter, and her son-in-law. She had been mobile and able to take care of herself before the fall; her health problems were mild enough that she should be able to make it off the table. Blood tests were okay and her ECG normal except for infrequent irregular beats. I called Howard and told him she was okay for surgery.

I was home in bed by 2:30.

At 4:30 I got a call from the surgery recovery room: Mrs. Dougherty had gotten her hip pinned without difficulty, but as she awoke from anesthesia the nurses noted a fast pulse and a falling blood pressure. There were no surgery ICU's at that time and surgical residents did not diagnose or treat heart problems. By 5:30 AM I was back in the hospital; I ran a bedside ECG that showed that she had atrial fibrillation, a fast heart rate that can cause the heart to be inefficient. Our treatment at the time if the patient was reasonably stable was to give them digitalis to slow the heart rate; usually when the shock of surgery and pain went away, the patient would return to a normal rhythm. Her ECG did not show damage to the heart. I stayed with her while the nurses gave her the first dose of digitalis and then I increased her pain medication. She wasn't in heart failure and her blood pressure was sufficient to keep her brain and kidneys happy.

I got home about 7, showered, ate breakfast, kissed the girls, and returned to the hospital, stopping by the recovery room to check on her again. During the rest of the day, between patients I made two more trips to see her. By dinner time her heart rate had slowed and she was doing fine.

The previous night and through the day I had spent about five hours with her, separate from the two extra trips to and from the hospital. Because my initial visit occurred on the same day as my return visit my total bill for caring for her would only be the $75 initial fee.

Howard Kiernan was with her for three hours and his residents did most of the postoperative care. His fee was $750.00.

I spent the remainder of the week seeing her twice a day and sorting out her narcotic-induced constipation and post-operative delirium. The notes from Howard and his residents were a few lines each day, dealing with wound healing, mobilization, and physical therapy plans. The calls from her daughter and her scattered family asking how she was doing came to me.

Patients like Mrs. Dougherty came my way every few weeks. The general surgeons were far more self-sufficient and involved in the pre- and post-operative care of their patients and they were always apologetic when they had to ask for help, but the eye surgeons and orthopedic surgeons and neurosurgeons were dependent on the internists to care for their patients. Without us they couldn't perform these operations, and the hospital couldn't generate their operating room, bed, imaging and laboratory fees. The compensation was out of whack—not the surgeons' fault, but a burden that the internists carried nonetheless.

By February I was deeply ambivalent about both my medical career at Columbia and about living in New York City. My greatest pleasures were making attending rounds and taking care of the parents and grandparents, artists and musicians, teachers, writers, pastors and working-class family members of our hospital staff like Michael Toohey. I stubbornly refused to raise my rates and shut them out.

I had fought fiercely to avoid going into the Army in order to stay at Columbia, but the time away in Washington DC exposed me to a much wider view of the opportunities for both career and personal satisfaction. The quality of the physicians I had met in the Army was similar to those I knew from Columbia and the University of Chicago; they had trained all over the United States in well-respected residency programs and fellowships, most had become specialists, and they were excellent clinicians and teachers. Many of them had become friends in a way that my current Columbia colleagues had not: the Walter Reed friends had lived no more than a few miles of easy driving from each other, while my Columbia colleagues were spread out around a congested metropolis. In Washington I had time for conversations both at work and with non-medical friends on evenings and weekends, and the conversations were authentic and intimate.

The week at Star Island had put us back together with a few of our best friends from the Rockville Unitarian Church and I could see that the paucity of friendships in New York City was partially because I was busy practicing and teaching. The doctors my age who I liked didn't have any more time for friendship than I did. And we were not meeting people outside of my world of medicine who, like us, were raising families and trying to balance work and family while also paying attention to the problems of the rest of the world.

The conversation with Steve Anderson had unsettled my thinking by widening my horizons—perhaps there were places I could practice and teach and have opportunities for creative change in medical education and also have a rewarding family life.

Over the next month I scheduled a round of visits to Andy Frantz, Don Holub, and Tom Jacobs, all of whom were surprised that I was thinking about leaving. Andy was beyond surprised—he was shocked—he couldn't imagine anyone ever leaving Columbia and New York City, where he had spent all but a few college, Navy, and fellowship years.

"Gordon," he told me, "You are made for New York City—all of your interests can be met here better than anywhere else in the world, you have a perfect practice with Tom and with Hamilton Southworth, you are loved as a teacher. I think it would be a terrible mistake for you to leave. Stick it out a little longer."

The general tenor was that no one who was privileged to be at Columbia would ever leave, that I would be ruining my career, especially if I went to a military medical school; that I would miss the wonderful residents and students at Columbia, miss the interesting cases, miss the cutting-edge clinical innovations and basic research.

I had a telephone conversation with a Columbia graduate a decade older than I who had left the previous year, the only physician anyone knew of who had been given admitting privileges and had chosen to leave. Wendell Hatfield, who grew up in Colorado, had decided that New York City was not for him and had returned to Colorado. He didn't encourage me to leave, but he didn't think I was making a mistake. He broadened the scope and inevitability of my dissatisfaction by pondering that for both of us, having come from the West simply gave us a different sense of what was possible and what we were missing than most of our Columbia colleagues, who had grown up on the east coast, many of them in New York City.

A Life Out of Balance

This made me crazy. How could I walk away from a career at Columbia that was beyond my dreams when I was a medical student? If I wasn't happy with Andy's "perfect fit," would I ever be happy? Was there something wrong with me—were my college years of floating in and out of existential crises and the blue funk that went with them not behind me? Would I end up dragging Margaret and the girls around the country from one place that didn't satisfy me to another?

For the previous few years, Donald Kornfeld, a psychiatrist, had been making psychiatry rounds on the medical and surgical floors, providing both consultation about the care of existing and new psychiatric issues of our patients and also meeting with physicians to help them reflect on and deal with some of their reactions to the death or suffering of their patients. Don was low-key and non-judgmental; when I first started thinking about leaving I asked if he would be able to meet with me to talk about my distress. Instead, because we were colleagues, he recommended that I see a psychoanalytically trained senior psychiatrist who practiced a few floors above me in the Atchley Pavilion.

I arranged a 7:10 AM appointment with Dr. Weiss and for two months I saw him every Thursday. We spent a few sessions exploring my background and experiences and goals and then narrowed the focus: why wasn't I satisfied? would I ever be satisfied? what was I looking for? what were the barriers that kept me from leaving? what were the things I had control over if I stayed that might make me more satisfied?

Without a conscious effort I can be encyclopedic about things for which I feel a passion. Over the years I had retained the names of many of the first chair violinists, cellists, and French horn players of the world's orchestras, the names of most of Paris's three-star restaurants, and a list of many of the French new wave and Swedish movies. It was no surprise to me that my lists of reasons for staying and leaving were similarly extensive. Every week I ran down the list, restating the good, the bad, and the reasons why I was unable to decide what to do.

I stretched out on a long couch looking at my toes and Dr Weiss—tall, thin, bent, and grey—slumped in a chair behind me and listened without saying a word. I couldn't see him, but I could hear him. After a few weeks of this I noticed that he was snoring softly by 7:20 as I droned on and on. At 7:40 I gently raised my voice in order to wake him up. We agreed to meet the next week, I went back to my practice, and nothing changed.

My story was simple and repetitive: I had started out in medical school as a just-acceptable, run of the mill English major with an adequate but not strong aptitude for science and an appalling lack of worldliness by New York City standards. As medical school progressed, I became a good, and then a very good clinical student, but not good enough to be taken as a resident at Columbia or the most competitive of the residencies that invited me to interview. After the year at Chicago I came back to Columbia and surprised everyone, including myself, by becoming a very good clinician and teacher and then being asked to join the faculty when I finished my stint in the Army. When I came back to Columbia we bought a house that we had redecorated and remodeled expecting to be there for the rest of our lifetimes. I had put in a large garden that I had been designing in my head for years, started a dream practice, had gotten to know music and theater performers—and with all that, which should have satisfied me, should have thrilled me, I was dissatisfied.

I was thinking about leaving, meaning uprooting the girls from their private school, finding a new home, and beginning over in another medical school. Everyone told me I was crazy to leave, and even crazier to be considering the places that had invited me. The Uniformed Services University? Really? Iowa? You can't be serious! I got credit for turning down Alabama, which in the minds of the congenital New Yorkers who comprised much of our faculty was a no-brainer.

The psychiatrist had nothing to offer in the way of a solution. He didn't tell me that I was crazy. He also didn't tell me that I wasn't.

The notion of leaving felt hugely risky—and beyond not being sure that I would ever be happy anywhere, I also was afraid that whether I left or stayed I might be risking Margaret's and the girls' happiness.

A Life Out of Balance

In March I got a comprehensive offer from the Uniformed Service University: My salary would be $50,000, rather than the $37,500 I was getting at Columbia, with a better retirement program. I would be hired as an associate professor. How I used my time was entirely up to me, with as much practice as I wanted and as much inpatient teaching as I wanted. My first job would be to create the internal medicine clerkship for third year students, two blocks of six weeks of medicine at the three military teaching hospitals with large residency programs—the National Naval Medical Center in Bethesda, Maryland, Walter Reed Army Medical Center in Washington DC, and the Wilford Hall Air Force Medical Center in San Antonio, Texas. The Washington DC clerkships would include third year students from Georgetown and George Washington Medical Schools who were already doing six weeks of clerkships at Walter Reed or Bethesda. Once that was underway, I would create advanced experiences in general and specialty internal medicine for the fourth-year students. I would have two additional faculty positions I could fill to help run those programs.

My only weekend responsibilities would be during my three months of inpatient attending, when I would make rounds on Saturday and Sunday mornings. When my own patients needed to be hospitalized they would be admitted to the teaching services and covered by residents.

I called the dean of students at USUHS to ask what kind of students would apply for admission to a military medical school. He said that they were mostly students whose families couldn't afford to pay for medical school. The students came from all over the United States, often from small towns in rural states. Some already had been in one of the military services, or had gone to West Point or the Navy or Air Force academies. Since the school would pay not only the tuition but also their salary as a junior officer and provide medical insurance, many of the students who were attracted had families. In exchange for having an income and not going into debt for medical school, the students would do residencies in military hospitals and then would owe seven years of service in military postings.

I liked the idea of being able to help students who otherwise couldn't afford to become doctors, and I loved the idea of starting a new medical school curriculum from scratch with an all-full-time faculty whose teaching time was paid for.

I kept thinking about my conversation with Steve Anderson and the friendships I had made in just a few years during my time at Walter Reed, both with the medical staff I would be rejoining and our friends at the Rockville Unitarian Church—and how warmly welcomed we had felt in Washington and at Star Island.

Would I miss Judy Blegen's opera parties, our occasional brushes with celebrities and high achievers, and our monthly Sunday afternoons listening to chamber music at Lincoln Center?

Could I really disappoint all the people who had invited me back and then helped me get started?

The crux was—did I need to be at Columbia University College of Physicians and Surgeons any longer to know who I was and to feel good about it?

CHAPTER 30

Leaving

Nearly every day I had to make calls to one or the other of the internists whose patients I was seeing, or who were seeing my patients. Some had been on the faculty when I was a student ten years ago. Like me, in addition to their private practice they each spent two half days a week in Vanderbilt Clinic where they saw uninsured patients and taught residents, fellows, and students. On any given day I knew where I could find them—what days they were in their private offices or in the cardiology or gastroenterology or pulmonary clinics—I knew what time they would arrive and leave, I knew their clinic phone numbers, I knew on what days I would likely encounter them in the doctors' dining room. They had each been doing the same schedule for as long as I had known them, and I realized that if I stayed at Columbia I too would be doing the same thing every week for five or fifteen or forty years.

Columbia had an amazing tradition that gave it great predictability and stability and guaranteed that students and residents who graduated would be trained to care for patients to a high standard that made them desirable as residents, fellows, and faculty. The downside of Columbia's consistency was that it had proved to be very hard to change the structure of the curriculum or to create for myself a way of having more time to teach and to support and advise students and residents.

After two months of inducing my psychiatrist's morning naps, I quit psychotherapy, realizing he had no answers to which was the better idea, leaving or staying. He said nothing about missing me, or anything useful or encouraging. I felt that I had done him a favor to quit, imagining that it must have been profoundly boring to listen to me, although he had solved that problem by falling asleep.

In early May Margaret and I had long conversations. She was willing to give up our beautiful home and leave New York City. I made the choice to build something new in a place that had substantial resources, where we had friends and where I would have more time to spend with my family and those friends.

I began to visit the faculty members to whom I felt indebted to tell them of my decision. I felt as though I had I had just been diagnosed with a terminal disease that I had given myself. They were surprised in a way that suggested that I was betraying our mutual religion, our cause, the beauty and virtue of Columbia Medicine with its long history of discovery, innovation and excellence in care.

For some inside the Columbia-Presbyterian paradigm there was never a doubt that we taught and cared for patients better than the Harvard hospitals and Johns Hopkins and the University of Pennsylvania. Those at least could be mentioned in the same breath as Columbia, while many other prestigious academic medical centers like the University of California in San Francisco, Washington University, Yale, Pittsburgh, and Cornell did not belong in the same conversation, and the Uniformed Services University did not even belong in existence.

We made a trip to Maryland to look for a new house in the two best school districts, Bethesda and Potomac, with the help of Len Wartofsky's wife, who had become a successful realtor. We had hoped to find an old house but most of those were further away from Walter Reed and Bethesda or in less good school districts. Within two days we had chosen a house just north of the Beltway, two miles from Potomac Village where we could buy groceries and get our cars serviced, a quarter mile from the Potomac River, 20 minutes from the Kennedy Center and the downtown restaurants, and 20 minutes from Walter Reed on a good day. The house was a brick reproduction colonial with four bedrooms and, most important two and a half acres of land, most of it horse pasture.

The Englewood house was within walking distance of two Orthodox Jewish synagogues and was therefore attractive to people who were already members of those congregations. The house sold in a few days. Tom Jacobs and Hamilton Southworth took the news of my departure matter-of-factly. Within a few weeks Tom told me that a graduating endocrinology fellow had agreed to join him and take over my patients. I was shocked—I of course knew that my patients would be in better hands remaining within the Southworth-Jacobs practice under Marcy's watchful eye, but discovering that I could be so easily replaced felt like a knife in the back.

Don Holub's wife was a classically trained pianist who had given up a solo career to raise a family. In late May she gave a Sunday afternoon recital with one of her students at two Steinway grand pianos side by side in their living room. There were twenty or thirty of us in attendance, mostly from the medical center. After the party I invited John Loeb and Andy Frantz and a few others to come to our house just a half-block away for a small party of wine, cheese and crackers. Andy and John had never seen our house—they both lived in elegant old apartment buildings on Manhattan's Upper East Side. Our moving preparations had not begun and the newly redecorated house with its beautiful old furniture from Newburyport felt like a well-curated museum. I walked John around the house and then out into the garden.

As he was leaving he shook his head: "I just don't understand how you can leave all of this."

In April, month earlier, I had been in Boston for a meeting of the American College of Physicians. Between morning and afternoon sessions I wandered out into the square around the Old South Church and the

Boston Public Library to get some fresh air, but found the streets jammed and police cars blocking off intersections. People were lining both sides of Boylston Avenue and as I scouted out a break in the crowd to see what was going on, I asked a stranger why everyone was there.

"Boston Marathon," he said. I had no idea.

"Can I stand here?"

"Sure, be my guest."

"When will the winners come in?"

"Won't be long," and he lifted his head to point with the visor of his cap at the helicopters circling over Kenmore Square.

He had a little portable radio pressed against his ear. I asked him who was leading.

"Boston Billy," he said.

"Who's that?"

I settled in and looked around at the crowd of happy, jostling fans and friends and family and sightseers. To my left I saw a police motorcycle round the corner from Hereford Street to Boylston Street and over the heads of those in front of me tried to spot the runner, but there was none. Then I looked down, not at shoulder level but closer to the road, and there a man with no legs was barreling toward the finish line with incredible speed in a wheelchair. Ninety seconds behind him another wheelchair competitor tore past me. It took my breath away—I had no idea that someone could power a wheelchair over twenty-six miles of hills and finish ahead of the runners.

When Bill Rodgers—called by the locals "Boston Billy" because he lived there and had won Boston several times—came in sight I was surprised by how tiny he was. He was smaller than I am, with pale skin and pale hair, wearing white painter's gloves and a skimpy singlet and shorts. He didn't even look tired. And then a struggle of other leaders passed by, all equally small, and then dozens and then hundreds, the crowd's roaring drowning out the helicopters overhead and the distant sirens of ambulances.

Leaving

My practice wound down slowly and by late May my office hours were half-empty. Now I had time to run, mostly on the local roads in Englewood, but once a week I drove south to a park along a branch of the Hackensack River in Leonia. The park was a previous land-fill garbage dump that had obliterated the wetlands adjacent to the river, the garbage now sculpted into low hills with newly planted willows and meadow grass, the occasional tin can or beer bottle poking up through the grass and dirt. There was a figure-8 loop of about 1.8 miles with a good asphalt path. As the time of leaving New York approached, I dealt with my mild depression and anxiety by adding a loop a week, with a goal of getting to ten loops or eighteen miles. Until Boston, I hadn't really thought of running a marathon, but my growing weekly mileage certainly was inspired by wondering if I could continue to run even while working fulltime in Maryland, and the achievement of growing mileage served as a counterbalance to the grief I felt for my dying Columbia dream.

I ran eighteen miles on my last weekend.

In the final weeks a few of the doctors I met at lunch or in the doctors' offices in Harkness Pavilion wished me luck and told me that they were sorry I was leaving. No one said, "Good for you. I wish I could have done the same thing." Still embarrassed that I was leaving Columbia in exchange for the Uniformed Services University, I tried to dodge a few of the younger physicians with whom I had trained.

Making rounds one day in the Neurological Institute, I saw a former chief resident who had gone into practice the year before standing with his black bag waiting for the elevator. On a hunch I asked him whose patient he was seeing.

He told me that he had been asked to see a new admission by Dr. W, the neurologist from whom I had stopped accepting consultation requests the previous year. Dr. W had evidently just moved on to the newest fresh recruit. I didn't say a thing.

A few days before I left, Dan Kimberg staged a little party for Margaret and me. Before the party, Margaret and I sat in his office and I thanked him for his support and expressed my disappointment in not having been able to craft at Columbia a different kind of career.

He said, "I've enjoyed working with you for the past two years. Every time you have come to my office you have had an idea for a project and volunteered to do it. That happens very rarely. Most of the people who knock on my door want one of three things: more space, more money, or more power. Very few people come here wanting to give something."

I gave him a very good bottle of wine and said that I would try to remember what I learned from him when I was dealing with battles in my new position.

His answer surprised me: "Try not to have battles."

The party had been at two. Margaret left for home, and I went back to see my last few patients.

At 5 PM Marcy came to the door and said that my last patient had just checked in. She handed me her chart, labeled "Julie Wolfson". I remembered the name and thought it ironic that my very first patient in practice would also be my last. I walked to the waiting room, but it was empty except for an elderly gentleman with a walker and a fashionably dressed woman in her late thirties with long, dark brown hair. That wasn't Julie Wolfson, and without saying anything I began to walk back to the office. The woman stood up and called out, "Doctor Noel, do you remember me?"

I turned around. "Have I seen you before? You don't look familiar."

"I have. I was your very first patient, Julie Wolfson. When I got your letter saying that you were closing your practice and transferring your patients to Dr. McConnell, I called Marcy and asked if I could be your last patient. I want a checkup—I know you're leaving, but I haven't seen a doctor since my appointment with you three years ago."

We both sat down. It took me a few moments to recover my astonishment. I asked her questions about any symptoms or questions she might have. There were none other than that she felt she needed to have her blood pressure checked, a breast exam, and a pap smear.

I commented that she was quite transformed from when I first met her.

"After I saw you and knew that I was in good health, I began to transform myself. My kids were doing well in school; between my husband and me we had enough income that I hired someone to do the housework; and I took management classes in a night school. Gradually I worked my way up in the company, as a secretary to several managers and now as the executive assistant to the vice president. I have gone out with quite a number of people from the office and I have had a series of short affairs with some of the men I worked for. I have had a wonderful time and enjoy what I do. I get to travel a certain amount, and I earn a great salary, more than my husband."

I absorbed this astounding account silently.

After reviewing her history, I ushered her into the examination room, asked her to change into a gown, and asked if she wanted me to have Mrs. Kelly join us as a chaperone.

"Heaven's no. Absolutely not. That's not necessary."

I spent a few minutes finishing writing her history, then knocked and walked through the door into the examination room.

Mrs. Wolfson was sitting on the table naked except for black lace bikini panties. The gown was folded neatly on the counter next to the sink.

"You know that I am on birth control pills," she said, looking into my eyes steadily. "I have looked forward to this since I knew I would be seeing you today."

I was surprised at how calm I was, as though this happened every day. Trying not to seem prudish I said that I was glad to see her too. I fetched the gown and handed it to her: "I think I will be more comfortable if you are wearing this."

As she was leaving, we shook hands. She said, "You are the kindest, most decent man I know. I wish you were staying. Good luck. Remember me. Julie Wolfson, your first patient and your last patient."

That evening I walked away from the Atchley Pavilion with a box full of my diplomas and cards and letters from Marcy's "Somebody Loves Me" file.

My heart was in my throat. I felt an immense sadness.

A few days later the Newburyport moving company that had been moving us since our furniture first came to New York unloaded the last of the furniture into our Potomac house. Margaret and the girls were unpacking boxes into their bureaus. It would take a day or two for the kitchen to be functional, and we planned to go out to dinner.

I hadn't run in almost a week. I asked Margaret if I could and run around our new neighborhood, and she let me go. I headed out Horseshoe Lane and crossed Brickyard Road. I had heard that there was some kind of path about a quarter-mile away along the Potomac River, but I had no idea how to find it. Our house on Horseshoe Lane was at the top of a hill above the river. I turned right, to where it ended at Brickyard Road, turned left and descended until I came to MacArthur Boulevard. Directly across the road there was a break in the dense thicket of hardwood trees that separated the road from the river. I ran along a path that cut between the trees and found myself on a bridge over a canal. I had heard that there was a barge canal beside the Potomac River that a century earlier had been used to carry coal and other goods 184 miles between the Allegheny Mountains and Washington, DC. The barges were pulled by mules along a towpath that ran beside the canal.

I turned west on the clay towpath and ran mile after mile, the roar of the Potomac River on my left, the placid canal on my right . . . home to ducks and herons and a hundred other kinds of waterbirds that barely noticed me. There was not a soul in sight. I ran for an hour, thrilled that I had gone from running in a landfill dump on the polluted Hackensack River to something close to a runner's paradise just a few minutes from my doorstep.

Leaving

Forty-two years have passed since then. Until I began to write this story, I never looked back. Now I can't stop thinking about what our lives would have been like if we had stayed.

OUR HOUSE ON LINDEN AVENUE IN ENGLEWOOD, NJ, 1975

Learning the Art of Medicine—a Memoir

THE PORTE COCHERE

Leaving

THE LINDEN AVENUE HOUSE, TABLE SET FOR THANKSGIVING

CHRISTMAS 1976

Leaving

MARBLE FIREPLACE IN MY STUDY. MARGARET SPENT DAYS REMOVING LAYERS OF PAINT

KATHARINE (BACK ROW CENTER, WITH A BOW IN HER HAIR), FIRST GRADE AT THE ELIZABETH MORROW SCHOOL WITH MISS MCGAVIN (FAR LEFT), 1977

MARGARET LEA AT THE ELIZABETH MORROW SCHOOL (BACK ROW ON FAR RIGHT) FIRST GRADE WITH MISS MCGAVIN, 1978

Leaving

MARGARET (FRONT ROW, 4TH FROM RIGHT) WHEN SHE WAS TEACHING SIXTH GRADE SCIENCE AT THE ELIZABETH MORROW SCHOOL, 1978

THE OCEANIC HOTEL ON STAR ISLAND, 1978

GOSPORT HARBOR, STAR ISLAND

EARLY MORNING, FOGGY DAY, FRONT PORCH, STAR ISLAND

Leaving

CEDAR ISLAND AND LOBSTER BOAT, AS SEEN FROM
THE FRONT PORCH OF THE OCEANIC HOTEL

THE LAST OUTING IN NEW JERSEY BEFORE MOVING TO MARYLAND, 1978. PHOTO TAKEN BY
TOM JACOBS

Learning the Art of Medicine—a Memoir

TOM AND JAN JACOBS WITH TWO OF THEIR CHILDREN

Postscript

We moved to Potomac, Maryland in June, 1978. The weather there was still lovely—warm, without the humidity that builds as the summer progresses. In spite of the disruption of moving out of our beloved Englewood home, we were all in good spirits.

Margaret and I have lived in four apartments and six houses. It is a great pleasure to see how a set of empty rooms transforms when filled with familiar furniture and rugs and lamps, when the kitchen goes from empty cabinets and bare counters to an efficient working space. The girls were quick to explore the large backyard and the horse meadow and woods behind it, romping with Ruffles, our sweet old Golden Retriever that had belonged to my dad.

Even before all the boxes were emptied into dressers and closets and cabinets, I began to chop at the hard clay earth in what had been a horse paddock, hoping to plant a small vegetable garden before the season was too far advanced. The back yard was full of dogwood trees along its edges that became a cloud of white blossoms in the spring; that autumn I filled in the grassy areas between them with daffodils, tulips, and crocuses. By the next spring I had put in a large vegetable garden, fruit trees, and beds of annuals. The meadow was too big to mow by hand and I bought a riding mower.

From the beginning our life at home was entirely different than it had been in Englewood. While I quickly developed a small practice at Walter Reed and attended on the teaching wards, I no longer had nighttime and weekend call coverage thirteen out of fourteen days except when I was on service. I was home most nights by 6 PM and I was with Margaret and the girls every weekend.

The first clinical rotations for the third year USUHS students would be starting in the fall and there were numerous meetings that had the one-time-only excitement and optimism of a new enterprise with the doctors charged with creating the surgery, pediatrics, family medicine, and Ob-Gyn clerkships.

Margaret's family had sailed on the Parker River near Newburyport and I had learned to sail on Long Island Sound when I was a fellow. We bought a sailboat with space for four to sleep that we docked at a marina on the Magothy River where it empties into Chesapeake Bay, near Annapolis. We were there most spring, summer, and autumn weekends.

We resumed active participation in the services and events of the Rockville Unitarian Church; I joined the choir and Margaret returned to teaching in the children's program. After a few years I was invited to be on the church board.

The several Washington repertory theaters and classical music series were excellent and accessible—and just 20 minutes from our Potomac home, with easy parking. We developed a taste for Blue Grass music and went out with friends to clubs with greasy food and good acoustics. Within a few years both Margaret and I became long distance runners.

One Saturday morning in the autumn of 1979 I was putting in a new brick sidewalk in our front yard when Margaret suddenly skidded into the driveway from Horseshoe Lane and screeched to a stop on the front lawn. She skipped down the loose bricks while I yelled at her that the sidewalk wasn't ready. She was singing and laughing.

"What on earth has gotten into you?"

"I'm pregnant!!!

Postscript

"You can't be pregnant. You've got an IUD!"

"Not anymore!"

"What??"

"The obstetrician I went to took it out. He said maybe I would miscarry, but told me usually that didn't happen."

In April of 1980 Jennifer Noel was born. She was ten years younger than Katharine, nine years younger than Margaret Lea—and the apple of everybody's eye.

We divided our summer vacation time between Flathead Lake in Montana and Star Island, where Margaret became a regular in the children's program. We added a second week in a different conference during which I was the Island doctor, and within a few years both Margaret and I were invited to be on the International Affairs steering committee, and each of us ultimately became the committee chair. The girls made friends on Star Island that they are still in touch with decades later.

Margaret had a lot on her hands as the primary caretaker for first two, and then three daughters. However, shortly after we returned, she began part-time work producing educational programs for Montgomery Country Public Schools. She went back to school at Montgomery College to study videography, which included several internships and some work for private corporations.

Tom Jacobs continued in the practice we started together until his death in 2019. After I moved to the West Coast in 1992, my daughter Margaret Lea was living in Brooklyn, where I frequently came to visit her. I saw Tom on several of those trips and we reminisced about our days together as residents and partners. His practice had filled with faculty members and their families—including some who I had cared for who he took over when I left. Tom won many awards for teaching and for humanism. Around the time of his death, one of his patients endowed a professorship in Tom's name. Tom had reached the level of institutional respect that Dr. Southworth had when we joined him in practice.

At the time of my last visit with Tom I had begun writing this memoir; the visit with Tom briefly left me feeling regretful as I pondered his exemplary career and what I had given up.

Dr. Southworth retired in 1987, nine years after I left and not nearly as soon as I had imagined when I accepted his offer to practice with him. He had begun the practice 50 years earlier in 1937, after graduating from residency at Columbia. He had functioned at a very high level in the administration at the medical center and with the American Board of Internal medicine, and had a long-term involvement in medical ethics. After retirement he joined the board of Choice in Dying, which publicized living wills. At the time of his retirement Columbia created an endowed chair in his name. He died in 1994 at the age of 84.

Andy Frantz was an active investigator until near the end of his life in 2010. Shortly after I left, he became the associate dean for admissions, a position that he relished, meeting medical school applicants and having the pleasure of watching them develop as students and often as residents and faculty. He was a dedicated alumnus of Columbia, serving as the long-time president of the medical alumni association. I briefly saw Andy during a couple of visits to P & S reunions but once I left Columbia we otherwise didn't keep in touch.

Andy had been the most important of my several mentors as a resident and fellow. His overflowing enthusiasm for science was hard to match, but he was equally knowledgeable about literature, history, sociology, theater, and music. It was my loss that I didn't seek his guidance when I returned to Columbia after the Army. Once I decided not to pursue a career similar to his focused on research, I felt that I had disappointed him. Rather than talking about this and asking for his guidance about things I knew little or nothing about—like academic promotion and combining scholarship with teaching and patient care—I left him out of my struggle to balance my clinical life with my home life.

In truth, other than the more or less useless psychiatrist I put to sleep for several months, I left everyone at Columbia out of my deliberations until I was already exploring the offers that I was receiving from other medical schools.

At times of transition for the rest of my career I tried not to make unilateral decisions, seeking out friends and more senior faculty members to test my mounting desire to begin something new.

After returning to Maryland and beginning to teach and care for patients at the Uniformed Services University of the Health Sciences (USUHS), I rarely thought about Columbia or New York City. All my grieving had been done in the year that I was thinking about leaving. My new responsibilities at USUHS consumed my intellectual energies totally: only once in the life of a medical school is a curriculum totally negotiable—and I was given free rein to adapt the best of the Columbia curriculum and to create nuances that would have been hard to accomplish at Columbia. Like Columbia, the core experience in internal medicine was three months long, divided into two six-week blocks. As a fulltime faculty member with freedom to spend my time as I chose, I focused on developing faculty skills that hadn't previously been taught. While all three of the teaching hospitals taught students from the local medical schools, the curriculum and standards were informal, the grading was uncalibrated, and feedback to the residents, faculty, and students random. Students came, spent six weeks with resident teams, and then received a grade that usually was A or B but with no definition of what constituted an A or B performance, and no process for recognizing and helping the occasional students who were floundering.

I started monthly grading sessions in which I met with the interns, residents, and attendings to discuss each student and review a structured grading sheet. In response to my questions, far more information was elicited than had previously been recorded. Within a few months all of the attendings and residents had a sense of what we were looking for and what their responsibilities were in helping the students achieve strong skills. I also met with all the students every month to give them feedback from the resident and faculty evaluations.

For the first six years I conducted the faculty and resident feedback sessions every month at Walter Reed and Bethesda Navy Hospital. I also flew to San Antonio Texas twice a year to meet with the Wilford Hall Air Force Hospital faculty and to conduct grading sessions to train their faculty to run them when I wasn't there.

Around 1984 I was able to recruit a wonderful clinician and teacher who had been an endocrinology fellow at Walter Reed, Louis Pangaro, to take over managing the clerkship, and a rheumatologist, Joan Harvey, to manage the fourth-year programs. I became vice-chair for medical education and started a fellowship program for general internists to become teachers with preparation in health policy, clinical epidemiology, ethics, critical appraisal, and teaching.

I also became active in two academic organizations, both founded within a year of our arrival in DC—the Society of General Internal Medicine and the Association of Residency Program Directors in Internal Medicine. I developed educational programs for their annual meetings and in time I was elected to the councils of both.

The difficult decision I made to leave Columbia and New York City paid off. I had much more time with my family and I was compensated for the teaching and management I was doing. I was just at the front edge of the wave of medical schools and residency programs being required to provide salary for faculty members who managed training programs. At the same time divisions of general internal medicine were being formed with support for faculty members who became the primary teachers of residents and medical students.

Satisfied with its strong traditions, it was many years before the department of medicine at Columbia joined in the national organizations that were growing up to support student and resident education in internal medicine, while Johns Hopkins, the Harvard teaching hospitals, the University of Pennsylvania and the major West Coast teaching hospitals in California, Oregon, and Washington joined early.

The irony is that it was my three years of military service—which I had at first resisted—that gave me an opportunity to see what life might be like when I had more time for my family and could manage my professional activities without having to worry about whether my billing covered my salary, overhead, and the department's twenty percent "tax". If I had managed to wiggle out of military service, I would never have had a chance to experience life in a city less hectic and more accessible than New York City was at that time. I would not have met and made friends with a very large group of people with whom I shared values and an interest in family life, would never have known about Star Island, certainly the pivotal experience in our decision to leave New York City, and would probably never have had the time for my many activities in the national organizations dedicated to medical student and resident education and developing careers in academic general internal medicine.

At the time I left Columbia I had chosen a path that I was discouraged from taking, but it has led to a wonderfully rewarding life. It wasn't our last move. After the older girls graduated from high school, we left Maryland to move to Dartmouth Medical School, where I was the director of primary care. A few years after that I was recruited to be the chief of medicine at the Portland VA Medical Center and professor of medicine at the Oregon health and Sciences University.

We have been in Oregon now for twenty-eight years. After Jenny left for college in 1998, we bought back my grandparents' home and orchard at Flathead Lake in Montana where I had spent my childhood summers as a place for our family's summer vacations.

Learning the Art of Medicine—a Memoir

I wouldn't have anticipated any of this in 1963 when I arrived on a plane, fresh from a forest fire in Yellowstone Park, to begin my long, sometimes rocky, and profoundly fulfilling life in medicine.

WINTER 1979

WINTER, 1979

Photos

MARGARET, 1979

SPRING IN OUR BACK YARD 1979

SAILING IN CHESAPEAKE BAY, 1979

Photos

HIKING WITH ALL THREE GIRLS IN 1981

OUR ONE ATTEMPT AT A FORMAL FAMILY PORTRAIT. JENNY, 9 MONTHS OLD. POTOMAC, MD, 1979.

CHRISTMAS IN POTOMAC, 1982

Photos

IN MY STUDY IN THE EVENING AFTER THE GIRLS WERE IN BED, 1979

ASSOCIATE PROFESSOR OF MEDICINE AND VICE-CHAIR FOR EDUCATION, 1982

Acknowledgements

Why does one write a memoir? Perhaps there are great stories to tell. Perhaps it is to share a history with one's colleagues who have lived through the same epoch, or an opportunity to celebrate and thank the individuals who were friends and mentors along the way.

Who did I have in mind during the two years I have been writing this memoir? First, this is a partial origin story for our family: our daughters, their husbands, and our grandchildren —Simon, Solomon, Aya, Clem, Levi, Nate, and Abe—and the great grandchildren who will never have known Margaret and me beyond faded photographs and a handful of recollections.

But always present in my thoughts were the hundreds—probably thousands— of medical students and residents and young faculty members I have had the privilege of working with. For forty years I met them when I was the attending physician for their inpatient team or during my chief of service rounds. Since I stepped down from being chief of medicine I have spent much of my time advising medical students. Some are referred by their friends or faculty members, but most of the students I meet in the narrative medicine sessions I facilitate. When I finish a session with 8 or 10 or 12 students, I invite any who are interested to meet for a cup of coffee; one or two say yes, and often a professional friendship begins. I suspect that I get more out of these relationships than the students do—the students inspire me and give me hope during difficult times like those of the past few years—political turmoil, a pandemic, economic collapse, massive inequities, climate change fast moving in—that the future will be alright for them and for all of our evolving planet's children and critters and plants.

My special thanks to my daughter, the novelist Katharine Noel, for her insightful suggestions after reading an early draft of the memoir, and to my dear friends Barbara Cooney, Rachel Gribby and Christine Hunter for their close reading of a late draft: their comments, encouragement and proofreading were invaluable.

I am grateful for my many years of personal and professional friendships with Tom Cooney, Larry Strausbaugh, Sarah Dunham, Jim Reuler, Kelly Redfield, Louis Pangaro, Sahana Misra, David Kagen, Heather Parks-Huitron, Brett Swift, Nicole Ahrenholz, Kate Luenprakansit, Erin Fennern, Alanna Mozena, Thu Pham, Lily Zhong, and Natalie Wu; and my Montana childhood friends with whom I have been swapping memories for seventy plus years—Roland Trenouth, Dick Ainsworth, Jerry Agen and the Missoula County High School '59 Tuesday Morning Coffee Club.

www.ingramcontent.com/pod-product-compliance
Lightning Source LLC
Chambersburg PA
CBHW030429010526
44118CB00011B/554